MW00578444

"John Bergsma has written a rich bi[…]
that distills the teaching of both the [...]
strong exegetically owing to the auth[...]
its content is accessible to lay readers. Bergsma writes from a Catholic perspective, integrating Church teaching and patristic learning with his biblical exegesis. This book will enlighten, inspire, and challenge those who aspire to live God's plan for marriage."

—Peter S. Williamson, Sacred Heart Major Seminary

Praise for the Catholic Biblical Theology of the Sacraments Series

"Sacraments are at the heart of Catholic spirituality and liturgical life. They are celebrated in the context of the proclamation of God's Word. This excellent series will help Catholics appreciate more and more both the relationship between Word and Sacrament and how the sacraments are grounded in the riches of Scripture."

—Thomas D. Stegman†, SJ, Boston College School of Theology and Ministry

"This series shows tremendous promise and ambition in laying out the multiple living connections between the Scriptures and the sacramental life of the Church. Taken together, these books could accomplish what Jean Daniélou's *The Bible and the Liturgy* accomplished for a previous generation of biblical and theological scholarship. And like that work, this series gives to students of the Bible a deeply enriched view of the mesh of relationships within and between biblical texts that are brought to light by the liturgy of the sacraments."

—Jennifer Grillo, University of Notre Dame

"In recent years, theological exegesis—biblical commentary by theologians— has made a significant contribution. This series turns the tables: explicitly theological reflection by biblical scholars. The result is a breakthrough. Theologically trained, exegetically astute biblical scholars here explore the foundations of Catholic sacramental theology, along paths that will change the theological conversation. This series points the way to the theological and exegetical future."

—Matthew Levering, Mundelein Seminary

"The sacraments come to us clothed in images that carry their mystery and propose it to our hearts. These images come from Scripture and are inspired by the Holy Spirit, who wills to transfigure us each into the full measure of Christ. The books in this series, by situating the sacraments within the scriptural imagery proper to each, will over time surely prove themselves to be agents in this work of the Spirit."

—John C. Cavadini, McGrath Institute for Church Life, University of Notre Dame

A CATHOLIC BIBLICAL THEOLOGY
OF THE SACRAMENTS

SERIES EDITORS

Timothy C. Gray

John Sehorn

ALSO IN THE SERIES

The Bible and Baptism: The Fountain of Salvation
   Isaac Augustine Morales, OP

*The Bible and the Priesthood: Priestly Participation
in the One Sacrifice for Sins*
   Anthony Giambrone, OP

*The Bible and Reconciliation: Confession, Repentance,
and Restoration*
   James B. Prothro

THE BIBLE
and MARRIAGE

The Two Shall Become One Flesh

JOHN S. BERGSMA

B
Baker Academic
a division of Baker Publishing Group
Grand Rapids, Michigan

Published by Baker Academic
a division of Baker Publishing Group
Grand Rapids, Michigan
BakerAcademic.com

Printed in the United States of America

Library of Congress Cataloging-in-Publication Data
Names: Bergsma, John Sietze, author.
Title: The Bible and marriage : the two shall become one flesh / John S. Bergsma.
Description: Grand Rapids, Michigan : Baker Academic, a division of Baker Publishing Group, [2024] | Series: A Catholic biblical theology of the sacraments | Includes bibliographical references and index.
Identifiers: LCCN 2023059365 | ISBN 9781540961846 (paperback) | ISBN 9781540965530 (casebound) | ISBN 9781493436439 (ebook) | ISBN 9781493436446 (pdf)
Subjects: LCSH: Marriage—Religious aspects—Catholic Church. | Marriage—Biblical teaching.
Classification: LCC BX2250 .B475 2024 | DDC 265/.5—dc23/eng/20240126
LC record available at https://lccn.loc.gov/2023059365

Nihil obstat:
Rev. James M. Dunfee, M.A., S.T.L.
Censor Librorum
February 12, 2024

Imprimatur:
Bishop Paul J. Bradley
Apostolic Administrator of the Diocese of Steubenville
February 12, 2024

Cover design by Thinkpen Design
Cover art of Isaac and Rebecca's wedding feast used with permission, Superstock/DeAgostini

Baker Publishing Group publications use paper produced from sustainable forestry practices and postconsumer waste whenever possible.

24   25   26   27   28   29   30   7   6   5   4   3   2   1

To my wife, Dawn

לֹא־ט֖וֹב הֱי֣וֹת הָֽאָדָ֣ם לְבַדּ֑וֹ אֶֽעֱשֶׂה־לּ֥וֹ עֵ֖זֶר כְּנֶגְדּֽוֹ

Contents

12. Conclusion: *The Symphonic Witness of Scripture to the Dignity of Matrimony*   242

Sidebars

Series Preface

But one of the soldiers pierced his side with a spear, and at once
there came out blood and water.

—John 19:34 (ESV)

The arresting image of Jesus's pierced side has fed the spiritual imagination of
countless believers over the centuries. The evangelist tells us that it "took place
that the Scripture might be fulfilled" (John 19:36 ESV). Extending this line of
thought, St. Thomas Aquinas goes so far as to compare the opened heart of
Christ to the Scriptures as a whole, for the passion reveals the secret depths
of God's trinitarian love latent in the Word, both written and incarnate. The
Fathers of the Church—Latin, Greek, and Syriac alike—also saw in the flow
of blood and water a symbol of the sacraments of Christian worship. From
the side of Christ, dead on the cross, divine life has been dispensed to humanity. The side of Christ is the fount of the divine life that believers receive, by
God's grace, through the humble, human signs of both Word and Sacrament.

Recognition of the life-giving symbiosis between Scripture and sacrament,
so richly attested in the teaching of the Fathers of the Church, has proved
difficult to maintain in the modern world. However much the Church has
insisted upon the unity of Word and Sacrament, "the faithful are not always
conscious of this connection," and so "there is great need for a deeper investigation of the relationship between word and sacrament in the Church's
pastoral activity and in theological reflection" (Benedict XVI, *Verbum Domini*

53). This series seeks to contribute to that "deeper investigation" by offering a biblical theology of each of the seven sacraments.

One classic definition of theology is "faith seeking understanding." Catholic theology operates with the conviction that the deposit of faith—that which theology seeks to understand—has been brought to completion in Jesus Christ, is reliably transmitted in Scripture and Tradition, and is authentically interpreted by the Church's teaching office (see *Dei Verbum* 7–10). Accordingly, the teaching of the Catholic Church is the *initium fidei* or starting point of faith for theological reflection. The series does not aim primarily to demonstrate the truth of Catholic sacramental doctrine but to understand it more deeply. The purpose of the series, in short, is to foster a deeper appreciation of God's gifts and call in the sacraments through a renewed encounter with his Word in Scripture.

The volumes in the series therefore explore the sacraments' deep roots in the revelation of the Old and New Testaments. Since the study of Scripture should *always* be "the soul of sacred theology" (*Dei Verbum* 24), the expression "biblical theology" is used to indicate that the series engages in a theological reading of the Bible in order to enliven our understanding of the sacraments. The guidelines for such theological interpretation of Scripture are specified in *Catechism of the Catholic Church* 112–14 (cf. *Dei Verbum* 12): attention (1) to the entire content and unity of Scripture, (2) to the living Tradition of the whole Church, and (3) to the analogy of faith. A few words on each of these criteria are in order.

In keeping with the series' character as "biblical theology," the content and unity of Scripture is the criterion that largely governs the structure of each volume. The *Catechism* provides a helpful summary of the series' approach to this criterion. Following "the divine pedagogy of salvation," the volumes attempt to illuminate how the meaning of the seven sacraments, like that of all liturgical signs and symbols, "is rooted in the work of creation and in human culture, specified by the events of the Old Covenant and fully revealed in the person and work of Christ" (CCC 1145). Each volume explores (a) the Old Testament threads (including but not limited to discrete types of the sacraments) that (b) culminate in the ministry and above all in the paschal mystery of the incarnate Christ.

The series' acceptance of the Church's sacramental teaching ensures that the Church's Tradition plays an integral role in the volumes' engagement with the Bible. More directly, sidebars offer specific illustrations selected from the teaching and practice of the postbiblical Church, showing the sometimes surprising ways in which Tradition embodies the Church's ongoing reception of the biblical Word.

In the case of the sacraments, attention to the analogy of faith means, among other things, keeping always in mind their origin and end in the eternal life of the Blessed Trinity, their relationship to the missions of the Son and the Spirit, their ecclesial context, their doxological character, their soteriological purpose, their vocational entailments, and their eschatological horizon.

The series' intended readership is broad. While the primary audience is Catholics of the Roman Rite, it is hoped that Catholics of the non-Roman rites as well as Eastern Christians who are not in full communion with the Bishop of Rome, whose sacramental theory and practice are very close, will find much to appreciate. Protestant Christians, of course, vary widely in their views of sacramental worship, and their reception of the series is likely to vary similarly. It is our hope that, at the very least, the series helps Protestant believers better understand how Catholic sacramental teaching is born of Scripture and animated by it.

We pray that all those who read these volumes will together delight in the rich food of God's Word (cf. Isa. 55:2), seeking the unity in faith and charity to which we are called by our common baptism into the life of the Blessed Trinity. To him be the glory.

Timothy C. Gray
John Sehorn

Acknowledgments

I would like to thank Tim Gray and John Sehorn for the privilege of being invited to contribute to this wonderful series on the biblical theology of the sacraments. Gratitude is also due to Fr. James L. Dunfee, Censor Librorum of the Diocese of Steubenville, for reading the whole manuscript and providing valuable feedback, and to Mr. Gregory Downs of Catholics United for the Faith and Fr. Bradley Greer, JCL, Chancellor of the Diocese of Steubenville, for consulting on issues of canon law.

Abbreviations

//	parallels
§(§)	section(s)
1 En.	*1 Enoch*
AB	Anchor Bible
ACCS:OT	Ancient Christian Commentary on Scripture: Old Testament
ACT	Ancient Christian Texts
ACW	Ancient Christian Writers
ANET	*Ancient Near Eastern Texts Relating to the Old Testament*. Edited by James B. Pritchard. 3rd ed. Princeton: Princeton University Press, 1969.
ANF	*Ante-Nicene Fathers*
Ant.	Josephus, *Jewish Antiquities*
AT	author's translation
Bar.	Baruch
BDB	Brown, Francis, S. R. Driver, and Charles A. Briggs, *A Hebrew and English Lexicon of the Old Testament*
BECNT	Baker Exegetical Commentary on the New Testament
b. Pesaḥim	Babylonian Talmud tractate *Pesaḥim*
BTCB	Brazos Theological Commentary on the Bible
BZABR	Beihefte zur Zeitschrift für altorientalische und biblische Rechtsgeschichte
ca.	*circa*, around
CBQ	*Catholic Biblical Quarterly*
CCC	*Catechism of the Catholic Church*
CCSS	Catholic Commentary on Sacred Scripture
CD	Cairo Genizah copy of the Damascus Document
cf.	*confer*, compare
chap(s).	chapter(s)
CIC	*Codex Iuris Canonici*
ClQ	*Classical Quarterly*
Douay	Douay-Rheims Bible
e.g.	*exempli gratia*, for example
esp.	especially
ESV	English Standard Version
ESVCE	English Standard Version, Catholic Edition
ET	English translation
ExpT	*Expository Times*
FC	Fathers of the Church
GKC	*Gesenius' Hebrew Grammar*. Edited by Emil Kautzsch. Translated by Arthur E. Cowley. 2nd ed. Oxford: Clarendon, 1910.
ICC	International Critical Commentary
i.e.	*id est*, that is
JATS	*Journal of the Adventist Theological Society*

JBL	*Journal of Biblical Literature*		J.-P. Migne. 217 vols. Paris: Migne, 1844–55.
JETS	*Journal of the Evangelical Theological Society*	*RB*	*Revue biblique*
JNES	*Journal of Near Eastern Studies*	RSV	Revised Standard Version
		RSV2CE	Revised Standard Version, Second Catholic Edition
JPS	Jewish Publication Society Tanakh	*RTR*	*Reformed Theological Review*
JSJSup	Journal for the Study of Judaism Supplements	SBLSP	Society of Biblical Literature Seminar Papers
JSOT	*Journal for the Study of the Old Testament*	SNTSMS	Society for New Testament Studies Monograph Series
JSOTSup	Journal for the Study of the Old Testament Supplement Series	StBibLit	Studies in Biblical Literature
		STDJ	Studies on the Texts of the Desert of Judah
Jub.	*Jubilees*	*TDNT*	*Theological Dictionary of the New Testament.* Edited
KJV	King James Version		by Gerhard Kittel and Ger-
Life	Josephus, *The Life*		hard Friedrich. Translated
lit.	literally		by Geoffrey W. Bromiley. 10
LSJ	Liddell, Henry George, Robert Scott, and Henry Stuart Jones. *A Greek-English Lexicon.* 9th ed. with revised supplement. Oxford: Clarendon, 1996.		vols. Grand Rapids: Eerdmans, 1964–76.
		TDOT	*Theological Dictionary of the Old Testament.* Edited by G. Johannes Botterweck and Helmer Ringgren. Translated by John T. Willis et al. 17 vols. Grand Rapids: Eerdmans, 1974–2021.
LXX	Septuagint		
m. Giṭṭin	Mishnah tractate *Giṭṭin*		
m. Middot	Mishnah tractate *Middot*		
MT	Masoretic Text		
m. Yoma	Mishnah tractate *Yoma*	trans.	translation
n(n).	note(s)	*TS*	*Theological Studies*
NABRE	New American Bible, Revised Edition	*TynBul*	*Tyndale Bulletin*
		v(v).	verse(s)
NICOT	New International Commentary on the Old Testament	*VT*	*Vetus Testamentum*
		VTSup	Supplements to Vetus Testamentum
NPNF¹	*Nicene and Post-Nicene Fathers*, Series 1	Vulg.	Latin Vulgate
		War	Josephus, *Jewish War*
NPNF²	*Nicene and Post-Nicene Fathers*, Series 2	WBC	Word Biblical Commentary
		WTJ	*Westminster Theological Journal*
NSBT	New Studies in Biblical Theology		
p(p).	page(s)	*ZAW*	*Zeitschrift für die alttestamentliche Wissenschaft*
PL	Patrologia Latina [= *Patrologiae Cursus Completus. Series Latina*]. Edited by	ZECNT	Zondervan Exegetical Commentary on the New Testament

1

Introduction

Prologue

This is a book about the biblical theology of the sacrament of matrimony.

That there should even be such a book is provocative and controversial, since the status of matrimony as a sacrament is disputed by many baptized Christians. John Calvin is famously dismissive toward matrimony in his *Institutes*, saying virtually nothing about this fundamental cell of Christian society and culture except to dispute its status as a sacrament: "The last of all is marriage, which, while all admit it to be an institution of God, no man ever saw to be a sacrament, until the time of Gregory. And would it ever have occurred to the mind of any sober man? It is a good and holy ordinance of God. And agriculture, architecture, shoemaking, and shaving are lawful ordinances of God; but they are not sacraments."[1]

As I hope to show in the course of this book, Calvin's comment is misguided in light of the centrality of marriage to the plot and message of Sacred Scripture, which tells the story of God's salvation of humanity, beginning with the marriage of Adam and Eve (Gen. 2:18–25), ending with the marriage feast of the Lamb and his bride (Rev. 21–22), and resting in the marriage of Solomon and his beloved at the midpoint (Song of Songs). Matrimony is central to God's purposes in creation and redemption in a way wholly incommensurate with "agriculture, architecture, shoemaking, and shaving." None of these latter items could serve adequately as a central organizing theme for

---

1. John Calvin, *Institutes of the Christian Religion*, trans. Henry Beveridge, 2 vols. (Grand Rapids: Eerdmans, 1989), 2:647.

the presentation of the divine economy or "salvation history," but arguably marriage can, because it is one of the two primary forms of covenant (the other being adoption), and covenant is the central theme of Scripture.

Whether the Bible has a central theme and, if so, what it might be are, of course, matters highly debated among theologians and Bible scholars. As just suggested, though, the position taken here is that there *is* a theme around which all of biblical revelation can be organized, that that theme is covenant, and that the divine economy can suitably be summarized with the pleasing phrase from the Fourth Eucharistic Prayer, "*time and again you offered them covenants.*"[2] It is crucial, however, that *covenant* be properly defined, not as "contract," "law," or "obligation," as some have proposed, but as the extension of kinship by oath—in other words, as a means of making a stranger into a family member by a sworn commitment. All human societies have covenantal relationships, known by various names, and the two primary ones are marriage (through which an unrelated man and woman form a family) and adoption (through which an unrelated child is brought into a family). Covenant, then, is a means of family formation.[3] It is not an end in itself, but the kinship bond formed is the end; or better, the intimate interpersonal communion made possible by the bond is the end.

The telos of reality is interpersonal communion. The ground of reality, the trinitarian Godhead, is himself a circle of interpersonal communion, which may be described as the Father giving himself wholly to the Son, the Son in return giving himself wholly to the Father, and the Self exchanged, consisting in the Spirit. For a human being, the closest natural analogy to this mystery of divine interpersonal communion as mutual self-giving is the reality we call marriage. There are various ways of understanding the marital unit as an analogy of the Trinity. In marriage, two persons give themselves wholly, exclusively, and permanently to one another in a bond of love, and that love bond becomes incarnate in a third person, the child. This resembles the mutual self-giving of the First and Second Persons, which is personified in the Third. Other scholars point out that, in the creation of the first husband and wife, Adam the son proceeded from God the Father, yet Eve proceeded from both God the Father

2. On the definition of *covenant* and its role in biblical literature, see John S. Bergsma and Scott W. Hahn, "Covenant," in *The Oxford Encyclopedia of the Bible and Theology*, ed. Samuel Balentine, 2 vols. (Oxford: Oxford University Press, 2015), 1:151–66.

3. For an extensive exploration of this theme, see Scott W. Hahn, *Kinship by Covenant: A Canonical Approach to the Fulfillment of God's Saving Promises* (New Haven: Yale University Press, 2009).

and Adam the son, and thus the creation of the first groom and bride resembles the processions of the Second and Third Persons from the First.[4]

No marital analogy of the Trinity is without disanalogies, of course—not least because no person in the Trinity is named "Bride" or "Mother." There is Father and Son—familial terms—but there is no Mother and Bride to correspond. Yet even this absence of a feminine name among the persons of the Trinity is a profound mystery that speaks to the nuptial dimension of reality. God reveals himself to us consistently as masculine, not because masculinity is self-sufficient and absolute but because masculinity is always ordered to communion with femininity. And the femininity toward which the masculine Godhead reveals himself as being open is found in the person of his people: that body of humanity that corresponds to his offer of love and accepts his invitation to enter into his circle of self-giving love. The people of God become the bride and mother corresponding to the masculine names of the trinitarian persons,[5] and in a singular and extraordinary way, the Blessed Mother, Mary, who instantiates, represents, and embodies the entire people of God, fulfills this role. This mystery is great: the eternal Godhead, who lacks nothing in himself and exists with perfect beatitude within himself, nonetheless creates creatures in his own image and reveals himself to them as being open to the most intimate of relationships with them. He reveals himself as masculine to their femininity and invites them to share in his nature (2 Pet. 1:4), so that they may commune with him on the basis of equality of nature—a communion whose icon and foretaste is human marriage. Other religions, both ancient and modern, have not dared to suggest that such intimacy with God is possible, and even Christian theologians sometimes shrink from acknowledging the outrageous offer of love and communion that Jesus Christ extends to humanity.

All this is by way of saying that marriage lies at the heart of the meaning of all reality and, in particular, of God's plan of salvation for the human race. Matrimony is justifiably called a sacrament—if a sacrament is understood as a sign, instituted by God, that participates in the reality that it signifies. For even in the state of nature, the natural love of husband and wife that becomes personified in the child is a sign of the mutual self-giving of the First and

4. "The Fathers compared the procession of the Holy Spirit . . . with the 'procession' of Eve from Adam." Deborah Belonick, "Father, Son, and Spirit—So What's in a Name?," in *The Politics of Prayer: Feminist Language and the Worship of God*, ed. Helen Hull Hitchcock (San Francisco: Ignatius, 1992), 305.
5. See C. S. Lewis, "Priestesses in the Church?," in *God in the Dock: Essays in Theology and Ethics* (Grand Rapids: Eerdmans, 2014), 255–63.

Second Persons that constitutes the Third. Yet when husband and wife are themselves infused with the Third Person through baptism, it becomes necessarily the case that their mutual self-giving, which *signifies* the self-giving of the Godhead, now also becomes a *participation* in that mutual self-giving, since they each have already become "participators in the divine nature" (2 Pet. 1:4 AT) through the Spirit, who brings with him the Father and the Son as well.

And yet the purpose of this book is not to explore or articulate the mystery of nuptiality or the truths about the divine nature that it reveals. Other books have addressed those topics.[6] Here, our task is more limited: to demonstrate how the *reality* of marriage—notice we do not say *metaphor*—forms a central theme in all of Scripture, from Genesis to Revelation, such that there is a complex reciprocal relationship between God's covenant bond with his people and the practice of marriage among the people of God. On the one hand, the reality of marriage is taken up by the sacred authors under the inspiration of the Holy Spirit and employed to communicate truths about divine and human nature and the relationship between the two. On the other hand, this very use of marriage to communicate truth about God, humanity, and the relationship between God and his people informs the celebration and practice of marriage among God's people as a society. In the end, the *fittingness* of the Church's recognition of matrimony as a sacrament will hopefully be evident to all, and many implications for the Church's ongoing catechesis, celebration, practice, and discipline of this sacrament will become apparent.

A Brief Overview of Catholic Teaching on the Sacrament of Matrimony[7]

Marriage is unique among the sacraments in that it exists both as a natural institution and as a sacrament.[8] The Church recognizes the legitimacy of

6. See, e.g., Angelo Cardinal Scola, *The Nuptial Mystery*, trans. Michael K. Borras, Ressourcement: Retrieval and Renewal in Catholic Thought (Grand Rapids: Eerdmans, 2005); John Paul II, *Man and Woman He Created Them: A Theology of the Body*, trans. Michael Waldstein (Boston: Pauline Books & Media, 2006); Edward Schillebeeckx, *Marriage: Human Reality and Saving Mystery*, trans. N. D. Smith (London: Sheed & Ward, 1965).

7. The treatment here is necessarily cursory. See, further, John Hugo, *St. Augustine on Nature, Sex, and Marriage* (Princeton: Scepter, 1969); Charles T. Wilcox et al., trans., *St. Augustine: Treatises on Marriage and Other Subjects*, FC 27 (Washington, DC: Catholic University of America Press, 1955); Thomas Aquinas, *Summa Theologiae*, Supplement, qq. 41–68; Pius XII, *Casti connubii*; Paul VI, *Humanae vitae*; CCC 1601–66.

8. On marriage as a natural institution, see Sherif Girgis, Ryan T. Anderson, and Robert P. George, *What Is Marriage? Man and Woman: A Defense* (New York: Encounter Books, 2012).

marriages contracted between unbaptized persons—these are sometimes called "natural marriages"—but marriage only becomes a sacrament, a means of grace, when both parties are baptized. Thus, "adhering to the teaching of the Holy Scriptures, to the apostolic traditions, and to the consensus . . . of the Fathers," the Catholic Church professes matrimony to be among the seven "sacraments of the new law" that "were . . . all instituted by Jesus Christ our Lord" (CCC 1114). Unlike the other sacraments, however, Christ did not institute a new form or ritual for the liturgical celebration of this sacrament. The Church, under the guidance of the Holy Spirit, has developed liturgical rites for the celebration of matrimony that express its dignity, communicate and teach its nature, and ensure the valid formation of the marital bond. In both the Western (Latin) and Eastern (Oriental) traditions, the licit celebration of matrimony normally requires *the public expression of consent* to the sacrament by both husband and wife in the presence of two witnesses and a bishop, priest, or deacon who confers a blessing upon the couple.[9] However, there is a difference between the two traditions concerning the minister of the sacrament and the act by which the sacrament is established (CCC 1623). The Western tradition holds that the expressed consent of the parties forms the sacramental bond, and thus the groom and bride are themselves the ministers of the sacrament (CCC 1626). The Eastern tradition holds that the blessing of the priest or bishop establishes the sacramental bond, and thus the cleric is the minister of the sacrament. In this book it will be assumed that the Western understanding is correct, in which case matrimony is the only sacrament ordinarily ministered by the laity.

Although not necessary for liceity or validity, it is highly appropriate and customary practice that matrimony between two Catholics be celebrated within the context of the eucharistic liturgy (CCC 1621). In this way, the nuptial significance of Christ's self-donation to his bride, the Church, through the giving up of his body on the cross is clearly connected to the sacramental relationship into which bride and groom are entering, and it is shown that the new couple is inducted into a particularization of the relationship between Christ and the Church, such that each spouse will be the mediator of Christ's love and self-gift to the other spouse. Indeed, the connections

---

9. However, the presence of the cleric and the bestowal of the blessing are not necessary in all circumstances—e.g., in danger of death or when a cleric is unavailable for a month or more. See, e.g., *CIC* 1108 §1; 1112 §1; 1116 §§1–2.

between the Eucharist and matrimony are profound, as these are the only two sacraments that involve not only the spiritual but also the bodily union of the parties in a covenant. But these connections will be enumerated and explicated later.

Since matrimony is a public institution with social, legal, financial, liturgical, and other consequences, it is necessary that the consent between the parties be expressed publicly, and thus the Church currently mandates that, in addition to one in Holy Orders, others must witness the wedding (CCC 1631). Ordinarily, a large group of family and friends of the bride and groom is present for the ceremony, and this should be encouraged, because the creation of a marriage changes the state of the couple within the Church as a society and has a cascade of implications for everyone connected to them and ultimately even to the Church and society as a whole.

Other sacraments (i.e., baptism, confirmation, and Holy Orders) induce a permanent ontological change in the recipient, described as a "seal" or "character," and thus they cannot be repeated. Matrimony does not create a new character in the husband and wife, but the analogy to the permanent character in these other sacraments is the *indissoluble marital bond* created by the sacrament (CCC 1638–40). As these other sacraments cannot be repeated, so a valid and consummated marriage is indissoluble, and no other marriage can be contracted as long as both spouses live.[10] Death dissolves the marital bond, which does not continue in the life to come (Matt. 22:30), although the extraordinary bond of love in Christ between those who had been spouses will surely remain.

Faithful to the Lord's teaching that "whoever divorces his wife and marries another commits adultery against her, and if she divorces her husband and marries another, she commits adultery" (Mark 10:11–12 ESV), the Catholic Church does not recognize divorce and remarriage. However, there are cases in which a man and a woman do not contract a valid and sacramental marriage, even though they appear to do so. The consent that forms the marital bond must be given by parties free to do so, and thus the consent must be completely uncoerced, and the parties must not be forbidden by any "natural or ecclesiastical law" to contract marriage (CCC 1625). Competent ecclesiastical authority may judge that, due to impaired consent or the impediment of law, a valid marriage never existed; in such a case, the

10. For apparent exceptions to this principle—e.g., decrees of nullity or nonconsummation, Petrine privilege—see *CIC* 1141–50.

apparent marriage is null and void (CCC 1629). This "declaration of nullity" is essentially different from the concept of divorce. A divorce purports to break a marital bond that was once in existence. A declaration of nullity by the Church constitutes a recognition that a valid marriage was never formed by the respective parties.

In the course of the Church's centuries-long reflection on the reality of matrimony, two overlapping traditions have arisen in the attempt to describe its nature and purpose. One tradition, having its roots in patristic discussion and summarized by St. Augustine,[11] is to speak about the *goods* of marriage (*bona*)—that is, what the desirable features of marriage are, such that virtuous human beings would wish to enter into the married state. Augustine enumerated these goods as three: the good of children (*bonum prolis*), the good of fidelity (*bonum fidei*), and the good of the sacrament (*bonum sacramenti*). By "the good of fidelity," Augustine referred to the total, exclusive, and mutual love of the spouses, by which they give themselves completely to one another, such that they subsequently "belong" to each other in a way that supersedes the claims of all other persons and interests. When he spoke of "the good of the sacrament," he did not employ the term *sacramentum* in the same technical sense that it later acquired. Rather, the *sacramentum* of marriage, for Augustine, was its permanent and indissoluble nature, an unbreakable bond. Thus, Augustine's answer to the question, What is marriage? would be: a union of a man and a woman characterized by procreation (*proles*), mutual faithfulness (*fides*), and indissoluble permanence (*sacramentum*). This Augustinian formulation is still recognizable in, for example, the *Catechism*'s summary of the goods of conjugal love (CCC 1643).

In the late nineteenth century, when the Church had to respond to secular challenges to the institution of marriage raised by thinkers and movements rooted ultimately in the Enlightenment, theologians and magisterial documents began to use the terminology of the *ends* of marriage, using the term *end* in its philosophical sense of "purpose" or "goal."[12] The development of this terminology was complicated, and different magisterial documents stated the ends of marriage in slightly different ways. But in the course of time, it

11. Augustine, *On the Good of Marriage* (*De bono coniugali*), esp. 1–7 and 32.
12. See Robert Fastiggi, "The Ends of Marriage according to the 1917 and the 1983 Codes of Canon Law in Light of Vatican II," *Antiphon* 18, no. 1 (2014): 32–47; Peter J. Elliott, *What God Has Joined: The Sacramentality of Marriage* (New York: Alba House, 1990), 108–14.

has become customary to speak of two ends (purposes) of marriage: the procreation and education of children, on the one hand, and the good of the spouses, on the other.[13] Of these two ends, the procreation and education of children is primary in the sense that it is definitional of the nature of marriage itself.[14] Other institutions or relationships can foster the love and mutual support of two persons, but only marriage is oriented to the rearing of children. Moreover, that goal of children—or more broadly, family life—characterizes the nature of the love and relationship of the spouses, such that their bond of love is uniquely *nuptial* and *conjugal*, in distinction from other kinds of love that exist. Nonetheless, the good of the spouses should not be thought of as "secondary," as if it were a less important or noble goal of the marriage relationship. To the contrary, matrimony is a sacrament, and the end of every sacrament is the *sanctification* of the one who receives it; therefore, in a certain sense, the *sanctification of the spouses* is the highest end of matrimony.[15]

The two ends of marriage can be distinguished but cannot be separated from one another without doing damage to the sacrament.[16] Without the *unitive* end, marriage becomes depersonalized and instrumentalized as a means of producing children. Without the *procreative* end, marriage loses its very essence—what makes it unique among human institutions and relationships— and it becomes confused with nonmarital forms of union or friendship. The inseparability of the *procreative* and the *unitive* ends of marriage finds expression in Catholic sexual ethics, particularly in the refusal of the Church to condone *contraception*, which is an attempt to remove the procreative aspect of the marital act and retain only its unitive dimension. Yet "what therefore God has joined together, let not man separate" (Matt. 19:6 ESV). When the procreative aspect of sexuality is removed, the unitive begins to dissipate as well, such that the sexual acts become reduced in meaning to mutual physical pleasuring rather than a true conjugal union of two persons in spirit, mind, and body, open to the life that God ordained as the blessing and goal of such a union.

13. Already latent in Augustine, *On the Good of Marriage* 3.

14. For this and what follows, see the discussion in Girgis, Anderson, and George, *What Is Marriage?*, 23–37.

15. See the discussion in Thomas Aquinas, *Summa Theologiae*, Supplement, q. 49, art. 3.

16. On this and what follows, see Paul VI, *Humanae vitae*, esp. §12; John Paul II, *Gratissimam sane*, esp. §12; and Pontifical Council for the Family, "The Truth and Meaning of Human Sexuality: Guidelines for Education within the Family," Holy See, December 8, 1995, https://www.vatican.va/roman_curia/pontifical_councils/family/documents/rc_pc_family_doc_08121995_human-sexuality_en.html#, §32.

The Plan of This Book

The purpose of this book is to explore the Scriptures for the light they shed on the meaning, celebration, and living out of the sacrament of matrimony. Whereas the passages of Scripture relevant to some other sacraments may be rather limited, in the case of matrimony we are faced with the opposite problem: marriage forms such a pervasive concern and theme throughout the Scriptures that all the major genre divisions of the Christian canon—law, history, poetry (i.e., Wisdom), prophecy, Gospels, Epistles, and apocalyptic— have important contributions to make to our understanding of what marriage is, how it functions in God's plan of salvation, and how it should be practiced by the people of God.

Accordingly, the structure of this book will follow the order of the canon, which also more or less follows the flow of the divine economy or salvation history. We will begin with the creation narratives (Gen. 1–2) and devote considerable space to exploring these texts in chapter 2, since their importance for biblical theology generally and the theology of matrimony in particular is completely disproportionate to their actual length. Genesis 1–2 reveals in a singular way the purpose and intention of marriage in God's original plan for humankind in the state of nature, and it serves as a constant reference point for scriptural and ecclesial teaching on matrimony.

Next, in chapter 3, we treat the significance and practice of marriage in the period directly after the fall (Gen. 3–11), where we observe sin distorting the husband-wife relationship during the development and degeneration of human culture.

In chapter 4, we will see that the patriarchs (Gen. 12–50) are not un- affected by the distortions of marriage introduced by human sin; nonethe- less, their marriages are crucial to the history of salvation. In fact, their mar- riages are *the means by which* salvation history advances. God's aboriginal blessing to Abraham of a great nation, a great name, and universal blessing to humanity (Gen. 12:2–3) could only be realized through Abraham's mar- riage to Sarah, as well as the subsequent marriages of their children and heirs.

The arrival of Moses introduces a new epoch in the story of God's people— one that we will explore in chapter 5—and the career of Moses (Exod. 1–Deut. 34) leaves an indelible mark on the understanding and practice of marriage until the coming of the Christ (cf. Matt. 19:8–9). The law of Moses, in its treatment of marriage and other issues, includes concessions to the hardness of Israel's heart. But it also includes intimations of a higher understanding of this institution and a latent promise of a new era when it would be purified and restored.

The Historical Books (e.g., Judges, 2 Maccabees, discussed in chap. 6) usually do not teach didactically about marriage, but they do include an abundance of instructive stories about marriages, some exemplary (Ruth 1–4; Tob. 6–11) and others tragic (Judg. 19–21; 2 Sam. 11). Moreover, the relationship of Israel to her sacred kings—David and his heirs—is described in spousal terms (2 Sam. 5:1–5; 17:3). Here we observe, to a lesser degree, the same principle so evident in the patriarchal narratives: the fortunes of the people of God pass by way of their marriages.

In the prophetic literature (i.e., Isaiah–Malachi, analyzed in chap. 7), Israel's covenant with God continues to be portrayed as a spousal relationship, and the Minor Prophets begin (Hosea 1–3) and end (Mal. 2:10–16) with reflections on both the nuptial union of the Lord with Israel and the various ways it can be reflected in the marriages of Israelites themselves.

The Wisdom books (i.e., Job–Sirach, featured in chap. 8) do not ignore this central institution, even if not all of these books treat it equally. In the didactic books (Proverbs, Sirach), marital fidelity becomes a primary symbol and expression of fidelity to the covenant with God, and this truth is explored in a more mystical and poetic way in other Wisdom books (Song of Songs, Wisdom of Solomon) that describe the relationship between God and Israel (or God and the believer) as a nuptial union.

All the nuptial themes of the various Old Testament divisions converge and culminate in the person and ministry of Jesus, as presented to us in the New Testament. There are two aspects of New Testament nuptiality: first, the portrayal of Christ as eschatological bridegroom of the people of God (which receives treatment in chap. 9). The synoptic Gospels already contain hints of the nuptial dimension of Christ's ministry, but it is especially in John that the redemptive mission of Christ is portrayed as a nuptial act, prefigured at Cana and consummated on the cross. This Johannine emphasis on Christ as bridegroom continues in the Apocalypse of John, which portrays the consummation of salvation history as the wedding feast of the Lamb.

The second aspect of New Testament nuptiality comprises the explicit teaching on matrimony in the Gospels and, more extensively, the Epistles (addressed in chaps. 10 and 11, respectively). Thus, we conclude this book with a close reading especially of 1 Corinthians 5:1–7:40 and Ephesians 5:21–33, rightly recognized as Paul's most mature reflection on the nature of marriage within the economy of salvation. A concluding chapter (chap. 12) gathers together thematically the exegetical fruit of this study.

2

"Male and Female He Created Them"

Marriage in Eden

The creation narratives (Gen. 1–2) have always enjoyed a special place of authority in establishing the doctrine of marriage for the people of God, since they precede the account of the fall into sin (Gen. 3) and therefore represent God's original and perfect intention for marriage within the cosmic economy.

Two Complementary Narratives

As is well known, there are two creation accounts (Gen. 1:1–2:3 and 2:4–25) that may be distinguished but not separated from one another, as the sacred author has joined them in a complementary relationship. The second account (2:4–25) does not attempt to replicate all that is done in the first (1:1–2:3)—saying nothing, for example, about the creation of the heavenly bodies, the sea and the sky, and so on—but it does expand greatly on the events of the "sixth day" (1:24–31), recounting these events in such a way as to clarify the relationship between animals, man, and woman within the divine plan for the cosmos. Some orientation to the structure and general message of these creation narratives would be helpful before focusing at higher resolution on those passages that most concern the origin and purpose of man and woman and their mutual relationship.

Cosmic Temple-Building: An Overview of Genesis 1:1–2:3

Genesis 1:1–2:3 is widely recognized as a temple-building narrative, analogous to other ancient Near Eastern cosmogonies that understand the cosmos as a temple built by one or more of the gods as a sanctuary for the worship of the divinity (or divinities).[1] The initial statement, "In the beginning God created the heavens and the earth," can be understood as God's aboriginal calling into being of an inchoate creation, which is subsequently described in Hebrew as *tōhû wābōhû*, "without form and void"—that is, lacking in both form and content. God addresses these twin privations in the subsequent days, first *forming* the creation in three days with the principal forms of time (light and darkness), space (sea and sky), and habitat (dry land and vegetation). This formed but empty creation God then *fills* in the next three days, populating time with the heavenly bodies (sun, moon, and stars), space with the fish and birds, and the habitat with man and animals. The creation of human beings (both male and female) is a highpoint of the narrative, since they constitute a priesthood in this temple-creation that God is constructing—but more on this momentarily. The culmination of the account, however, is the sanctification of the seventh day, the sabbath, which would have been known to the readers as the day of rest and corporate worship (cf. Lev. 23:3). Thus, the temple-creation as a sanctified space is capped by the sabbath, a sanctified time, because the telos of the creative process has been to establish the conditions for *worship*, which should be understood as the restful *communion* of persons—specifically the communion of the personal God with the persons made in his image, who are the mediators (priests) of God's communion with the nonpersonal cosmos (the natural world).

The Creation of Humanity in Genesis 1:26–28

Let us look more closely at the account of the creation of man (Hebrew *'ādām*), which manifests several peculiar and significant features. After the creation of the animals on the sixth day, we read: "Then God said, 'Let us make man in our image, after our likeness'" (Gen. 1:26). We observe two unique features: for the first time, God *gives a command to himself*. Up to this point in the narrative, God has commanded the waters and the earth to produce and has simply spoken things into existence, but now he makes a cohortative

1. See G. K. Beale, *The Temple and the Church's Mission: A Biblical Theology of the Dwelling Place of God*, NSBT 17 (Downers Grove, IL: IVP Academic, 2004), 29–121.

statement: "Let *us* make man." This indicates God's unique and extraordinary involvement in the creation of humanity; in no other case does God *exhort himself* to action. Second, God is referred to for the first time in the plural. Although the Hebrew word for God, *'ĕlōhîm*, is grammatically plural, the noun is complemented with singular verbs and singular pronouns in verses 1–25. Then, we are surprised in verse 26 with the curious and provocative self-reference to God in the plural. We note how the text juxtaposes, without apparent discomfort, both plural and singular references to the divinity:

> Then God said, "Let *us* make man in *our* image . . ." (v. 26)[2]
> So God created man in *his* own image . . . (v. 27)

Only one other creature in the whole of creation displays this grammatically awkward combination of singular and plural: *'ādām*, the creature in God's image. So the text goes on to say:

> So God created man in his own image,
>   in the image of God he created *him* [singular];
>   male and female he created *them* [plural]. (Gen. 1:27 ESV)

Presumably, this characteristic of paradoxical unity and plurality is part of the image and likeness of God that *'ādām* bears. God is a multipersonal unity, ultimately revealed as the Trinity, but humankind is also a multipersonal unity, a truth particularly manifested in the original couple, who together were singular *'ādām* yet also male and female persons. The mystery of maleness and femaleness is a nontrivial and indispensable dimension of being in the image and likeness of God. The fact that *'ādām* exists as two complementary persons whose union produces a third is central to the way that humanity resembles and manifests the divine nature, which is trinitarian. Although marriage per se is not yet mentioned in the text, this truth has profound implications for understanding the nature of marriage in the divine economy, since marriage is the only institution in which the male and female may be licitly united in openness to a third person, and thus it is in the *married couple* rather than in a single male or female person that the *imago Dei* is most fully expressed.

---

2. Italics in biblical quotations have been added for emphasis throughout.

Later in the narrative, the sacred author further illuminates the meaning of "image" and "likeness." In Genesis 5:3, Adam fathers a son, Seth, who is "in his own likeness, after his image." This informs us that "image" and "likeness" are words of filiation: the way a son resembles his father. Taking this information back to Genesis 1:26, 28, we can recognize that Adam's created status is that of a *son of God* (cf. Luke 3:38). This in turn has a covenantal sense. A covenant is nothing other than the extension of kinship by oath,[3] a means of family formation. Males in antiquity could be sons through birth or through adoption by covenant. Which is Adam? In the next chapter, he is not presented as birthed from God, but as created from the ground like other animals (cf. Gen. 1:24; 2:7), yet given the unique privilege of inhaling the breath of God directly from God's lips, as it were (2:7). This suggests adoptive sonship: not made of the divine nature itself but of the stuff of the earth, he nonetheless is given the privilege of *participating* in the divine nature (cf. 2 Pet. 1:4). This implies that a covenant exists already between God and Adam at creation.[4] Thus, the sabbath—elsewhere considered the sign of God's covenant (Exod. 31:16–17)—is given here, immediately after the creation of man.[5] As we will see, this covenant relationship between God and 'ādām-humanity will in turn be reflected in a covenant between the male and female persons of 'ādām. The fundamental, metaphysical relationship between these two covenants is reflected throughout biblical literature and forms the basis for the sacramental nature of matrimony.

Immediately after their creation, God gives male-and-female 'ādām a set of *blessings* and *mandates*—that is, injunctions that both *impose* a moral obligation to do something and also *confer* the divine favor that facilitates the achievement of the indicated outcome:

And God blessed them. And God said to them, "Be fruitful and multiply and fill the earth and subdue it, and rule over the fish of the sea and over the birds of the heavens and over every living thing that moves on the earth." (Gen. 1:28 AT)

3. See John S. Bergsma and Scott W. Hahn, "Covenant," in *The Oxford Encyclopedia of the Bible and Theology*, ed. Samuel Balentine, 2 vols. (Oxford: Oxford University Press, 2015), 1:151–66, here 151.
4. Bergsma and Hahn, "Covenant," 155.
5. Joseph Cardinal Ratzinger (Benedict XVI), *"In the Beginning . . .": A Catholic Understanding of the Story of Creation and the Fall*, trans. Boniface Ramsey, Ressourcement: Retrieval and Renewal in Catholic Thought (Grand Rapids: Eerdmans, 1995), 29–32.

The first three blessing-mandates are roughly synonymous: "Be fruitful and multiply and fill the earth." We note that these injunctions can only take place by the union of the 'ādām-male with the 'ādām-female. Paradoxically, when the two become one—when "they" become "him" again through conjugal union—it will result in the one becoming many: being fruitful and multiplying and filling. Thus, sexual differentiation (the existence of both male and female) and sexual union (marriage) are absolutely essential features of humanity necessary to fulfill the first three blessing-mandates given by God. The fourth and fifth blessing-mandates are also roughly synonymous: "subdue it, and rule . . ." Here the sacred author employs terms with royal or imperial connotations—Hebrew *kābaš* and *rādāh*—later used to describe the dominion of David and Solomon over the nations surrounding Israel.[6] The human couple is royalty, representing the authority of the divine king on earth.

The narrative of Genesis 1:1–2:3 concludes with the sabbath, the day on which God rests in communion with all his creation. Later, it will become explicit that man is also to rest on this day, which is a kind of imitation and participation in the divine nature (Exod. 20:8–11). The sabbath, as a day of rest and worship, is the privileged time of communion between God and man, between divine and human persons. By placing the sabbath as the end and climax of the creation narrative, the sacred author implies that the interpersonal communion facilitated by the sabbath is the goal of creation. Thus, there is an eschatological dimension to matrimony as well: the intimate interpersonal communion of the married state is an image and foretaste of the goal of all creation.

The Creation of Humanity in Genesis 2:4–25

After the panoramic overview of creation provided by 1:1–2:3, Genesis 2:4–25 focuses specifically on the creation of man and woman, culminating in the first marriage and the establishment of the institution of matrimony.

We have observed that Genesis 1:1–2:3 should be understood as a temple-building narrative in which the cosmos forms a macrotemple for the worship of God and humans serve as the natural priests of this cosmic temple.[7] Temple

---

6. See *kābaš* in 2 Sam. 8:11; 1 Chron. 22:18; see *rādāh* in 1 Kings 4:24; 2 Chron. 8:10; Pss. 72:8; 110:2.

7. Jeff Morrow, "Creation as Temple-Building and Work as Liturgy in Genesis 1–3," *Journal of the Orthodox Center for the Advancement of Biblical Studies* 2 (2009): 1–13.

themes are also strongly present in Genesis 2:4–25, though it is focused on Eden, which is a garden-sanctuary within the larger "temple of creation."[8] In the account of the creation of the man's body and his placement in the garden (vv. 4–17), the sacred author suggests that Adam is created as priest and image of the deity to inhabit the garden-sanctuary and to celebrate the liturgy that should take place there.[9] Then begins the account of the origin of the woman:

> Then the LORD God said, "It is not good that the man should be alone; I will make him a helper complementary to him." (Gen. 2:18 AT)

For the first time in the combined creation narratives, something is declared "not good." Reading in light of Christian faith, we may understand that solitude is not good because it does not adequately image God, who is not a solitary individual but a tripersonal communion. Nor does solitude correspond with the telos for which man was created—namely, interpersonal communion. To rectify this solitude, God declares his intention to make the man a "helper" (Hebrew *'ēzer*). This noun, which can be translated "helper" or simply "help," is typically used in the Hebrew Bible either in reference to God (e.g., Ps. 124:8) or with respect to military assistance sent by a king (e.g., Josh. 10:33; 2 Sam. 8:5). Strikingly, it is *never* used of the help or service given by servants, retainers, or other subordinates. Thus, the term in no way conveys a sense of inferiority or subservience of the woman; rather, the frequent use of the term with respect to divine aid (e.g., Exod. 18:4; Deut. 33:7, 26, 29; Ps. 20:2) suggests that the woman is the *means* by which God will help the man. Already the structure of matrimony is coming into view; it is a sacrament in which the spouses offer themselves as mediators of God's grace (i.e., favor, strength, assistance) to one another.

However, the woman will be no generic helper, but one "complementary to him" (Hebrew *kənegdô*). This rare Hebrew word—really a concatenation of prepositions with a pronominal suffix—is striking and occurs only here in

8. See Beale, *Temple and the Church's Mission*, 66–80.

9. Beale, *Temple and the Church's Mission*, 81–121; John S. Bergsma, "The Creation Narratives and the Original Unity of Work and Worship in the Human Vocation," in *Work: Theological Foundations and Practical Implications*, ed. R. Keith Loftin and Trey Dimsdale (London: SCM, 2018), 11–29; Catherine L. McDowell, *The Image of God in the Garden of Eden: The Creation of Humankind in Genesis 2:5–3:24 in Light of the* mīs pî pīt pî *and* wpt-r *Rituals of Mesopotamia and Ancient Egypt*, Siphrut 15 (Winona Lake, IN: Eisenbrauns, 2015), 140–41.

Genesis 2. It would have been easier for the sacred author to have said, "I will make a helper *like him* [Hebrew *kəmô*]" or "a helper *for him* [Hebrew *lô*]." "Like" (Hebrew *k-*) would have implied similarity without difference: a clone. "For" (Hebrew *l-*) would have implied that the helper's purpose of existence was found solely in helping the man; she exists *for* him. In distinction from either of these options, the sacred author employs a rare phrase composed of Hebrew *k-*, "like," combined with Hebrew *neged*, "in front of, opposite, facing," a term particularly used for a position that faces someone or something else (e.g., 1 Kings 8:22; 21:10; Ps. 16:8; Ezek. 42:1). The unique combination implies both *likeness* and *difference*: the woman will be "like" the man but not *simply* "like" him—also "facing" him or "opposite" to him. This has the sense of a mirror image; there is a kind of equality here, yet not one of identity but of reciprocity: *complementary* or *corresponding* to him.

In response to the need for a "complementary helper," God brings the various animals to Adam "to see what he would call them" (Gen. 2:19). Nonetheless, none of the animals is found to be the "complementary helper" (v. 20). Read in light of faith, this entire exercise is not a trial and error on the part of the deity, who knows what he will do from the beginning, but rather a *pedagogy for Adam*, (1) to delay the satisfaction of discovering his true partner and thus heighten the delight and appreciation of the final discovery and (2) to teach Adam through counterexamples about his true needs and what sort of partner would satisfy them. Thus, the naming of the animals becomes a journey of self-discovery for Adam, as he learns about himself and his own needs, and it also builds anticipation for and the capacity to appreciate the woman when she is finally revealed.

"So the Lord God caused a deep sleep [Hebrew *tardēmāh*] to fall upon the man, and while he slept took one of his ribs and closed up its place with flesh" (Gen. 2:21). The rare term *tardēmāh* usually refers to sleep with a numinous quality, either sent by God or associated with prophetic dreams.[10] Abraham likewise falls into a *tardēmāh* when God forms the divine covenant with him for the first time (15:12). Both Adam and Abraham fall into this mystic sleep and then awaken to a covenant-making ritual that will profoundly alter salvation history.

The creation of the woman, together with Adam's participation in it, is entirely unique from that of the other animals. Adam was passive in the

10. It occurs seven times in the MT: Gen. 2:21; 15:12; 1 Sam. 26:12; Job 4:13; 33:15; Prov. 19:15; Isa. 29:10. Only in Prov. 19:15 does *tardēmāh* lack a numinous dimension.

St. Methodius of Olympus on Marriage

Some early Fathers used the creation narratives, with their positive view of marriage and procreation, to combat rigorist heresies that regarded marriage as at best a concession to weakness, if not evil in itself. So St. Methodius of Olympus:

> But now it is necessary that human beings cooperate in producing the image of God, since the universe continues to exist and to be created. "Increase and multiply," Scripture says [Gen. 1:28]. We must not recoil from the commandment of the Creator, from whom we too have received our existence. . . . This perhaps is what was signified by that ecstasy which fell upon the first man in his sleep [2:21]; it prefigured the enchantment that man would find in love, when thirsting for children he falls into ecstasy and is lulled to sleep by the pleasures of procreation, so that once more another person might be created from the bit that was torn from his bone and from his flesh [2:23]. . . . For this reason, it is well said that a man will leave his father and mother [2:24], because a man forgets everything else when he is joined to a woman in tender embraces, overwhelmed with a desire for children. He offers his rib to the divine Creator to be removed [2:21–22], so that he the father might reappear again in his son.[a]

a. Methodius of Olympus, *The Symposium: A Treatise on Chastity*, trans. Herbert Musurillo, ACW 27 (New York: Newman, 1958), 16.

creation of the animals, but in the case of the woman he must experience a kind of death, a cutting—one might say a sacrifice—of his own flesh, and the *donation* of his own body in order for his future bride to come forth. The death, sacrifice, and self-donation involved in Eve's genesis—like the long ordeal of naming the animals—seems designed to increase Adam's appreciation, gratitude, and ultimately love for Eve, as that which is gained by great sacrifice is much more valued than that which is acquired without effort. Needless to say, the Fathers saw clearly that this death, sacrifice, and self-donation of Adam prefigured and typified the passion of the New Adam, Jesus Christ.[11] Specific connection can be made to John 19:34, the flow of blood and water from the side of Christ, which the Fathers understood as birth imagery: just

11. *St. Augustine on Genesis*, trans. Roland J. Teske, FC 84 (Washington, DC: Catholic University of America Press, 1991), 133.

St. Augustine on the Creation of Eve

St. Augustine articulates a widespread patristic tradition concerning the typological relationship between the creation of Eve from Adam's side and the piercing of Christ's side on the cross (John 19:34):

> For this reason the first woman was made from the side of a sleeping man, and she was called the life and the mother of the living. For indeed it signified a great good, before the great evil of collusive transgression. Here the second Adam, his head bowed, slept on the cross in order that from there might be found for him a wife—that one who flowed from the side of the One sleeping.[a]

a. *St. Augustine: Tractates on the Gospel of John 112–24; Tractates on the First Epistle of John*, trans. John W. Rettig, FC 92 (Washington, DC: Catholic University of America Press, 1995), 51 (tractate 120, §2).

as Eve is born from the side of Adam, so the Church is born from the side of Christ.[12] Indeed, the evangelist likely intended such an allusion, because—as we will see later in this book—the Gospel of John presents Jesus as a messianic bridegroom through the deployment of nuptial imagery at strategic points in the narrative.

Eve is also the only creature in whose creation Adam participates. St. Methodius of Olympus saw here a trinitarian image: as the Son proceeds from the Father, but the Spirit from both the Father and the Son, so Adam proceeds from God, but Eve from both God and Adam.[13] The procession of Eve, in this analogy, is parallel to the procession of the Spirit, and other theologians have explored the "bridal maternity" of the Spirit and its relationship to the New Eve, Mary.[14]

"And the rib that the LORD God had taken from the man he built [Hebrew *bānāh*] into a woman and brought her to the man" (Gen. 2:22 ESV, modified).

12. E.g., Augustine, *On John*, Tractate 120, §2.
13. Scott Hahn, *First Comes Love: Finding Your Family in the Church and the Trinity* (New York: Image, 2002), 169–70, 208–9.
14. H. M. Manteau-Bonamy, *Immaculate Conception and the Holy Spirit: The Marian Teachings of St. Maximilian Kolbe* (San Francisco: Ignatius, 1998), 40, 45–46, 91; Hahn, *First Comes Love*, 154–55, 199.

God does not simply "make" (*ʿāśāh*) the woman but "builds" (*bānāh*) her, an architectural term probably deployed because the woman is understood as a temple.[15] Thus, throughout Scripture, temple and bride are associated (cf. Rev. 21:2–3). This reading is supported by the fact that all but one (2 Sam. 16:13) of the thirty-eight occurrences of the word for "rib" or "side" (Hebrew *ṣēlāʿ*) in the Masoretic Text outside of Genesis 2:21–22 are found in the tabernacle-building account in Exodus 25–40, the temple-building account in 1 Kings 6–8, and the description of the eschatological temple in Ezekiel 41. The woman's temple nature may be intended as a complement to Adam's priest nature, implied by Genesis 2:15. God then "brings" her (*hiphil* of *bôʾ*, "to cause to come") to Adam, acting as a divine wedding attendant—in Judaism, the *šôšbîn*—who ushers the bride into the presence of the groom (cf. Ps. 45:14–15; Song 1:4).[16]

> Then the man said,
> "This one, at last, is bone of my bones
> and flesh of my flesh!
> She shall be called Woman [*ʾiššāh*],
> because she was taken out of Man [*ʾîš*]." (Gen. 2:23 AT)

Let us observe with what literary flourish the sacred author marks the revelation of the bride and the introduction of the first couple to each other: this is the first recorded speech of Adam—indeed, of any human being in history. Commentators recognize it as a cry of delight or ecstasy.[17] One might consider it also the first lyric poetry in the Bible or human history. "This one, at last!" Adam exclaims (Hebrew *zōʾt happaʿam*), indicating an end to the frustration of searching the animals and the delight and relief upon finally discovering the object of his desires and needs. His declaration, "This one . . . is bone of my bones and flesh of my flesh!" should not be understood merely as a statement of recognition, but as a *performative utterance*: Adam is *declaring* Eve to be his "bone and flesh"—that is, his kin or family. This expression is used in covenant-making contexts (cf. 2 Sam. 5:1–3), and indeed, this episode in the

---

15. The highest concentration of the use of the verb *bānāh* is in 1 Kings 6–8, the account of the building of Solomon's temple.

16. See André Villeneuve, *Divine Marriage from Eden to the End of Days: Communion with God as Nuptial Mystery in the Story of Salvation* (Eugene, OR: Wipf & Stock, 2021), 14; Nahum M. Sarna, *Genesis*, JPS Torah Commentary (Philadelphia: Jewish Publication Society, 1989), 23.

17. E.g., Sarna, *Genesis*, 23.

garden should be understood as the formation of the first marital covenant.[18] Adam authoritatively declares Eve to be his kin, his "flesh and blood," thus receiving her as his own, and then bestows on her a name—another feature of covenant-making rituals (cf. Gen. 17:5; 35:9–15; 2 Sam. 7:9; Isa. 56:4–5). The giving of the name is an authoritative gesture on Adam's part, indicating he is the leader or initiator of this covenantal relationship, but all that was said earlier in this book about the connotations of the phrase "complementary helper" should be borne in mind, and Adam's authority should be understood within the context of an intimate kinship relationship between two persons sharing a common nature, complementary and reciprocal to one another, achieved at the cost of death, sacrifice, and self-gift.

"She shall be called Woman," Adam says, "because she was taken out of Man" (Gen. 2:23 AT). Much as in English and other languages, the word for "woman" in Hebrew (*'iššāh*) appears to be a variant of the word for "man" (*'îš*). Indeed, since the ending *-āh* in Hebrew can be a third feminine possessive suffix (i.e., "her"), the form *'iššāh* could be read as "her man." The names of the man and the woman, then, express the mystery of both identity and difference. The sacred author has expressed this mystery in several ways so far, each time conveying the idea that male and female are the same and yet distinct.

The sacred author goes on to ascribe the origin of the institution of matrimony from this original covenantal bond between the first man and woman: "Therefore, a man shall abandon his father and his mother and hold fast to his wife, and they shall become one flesh" (Gen. 2:24 AT). This is the first time the origin of an element or aspect of human culture is ascribed to a feature of the creation narrative. In fact, the importance of marriage to human culture and to salvation history is indicated by the fact that it is the *only* human institution *explicitly* grounded in the acts of creation. Granted, ideas of liturgy, priesthood, kingship, prophethood, and possibly other cultural institutions have been implied, but none is explicitly marked in the way matrimony is.

The sacred author employs vigorous language with covenantal connotations. "A man shall *abandon* [*'āzab*] his father and mother and *hold fast* [*dābaq*] to his wife" (Gen. 2:24 AT). The Hebrew term *'āzab* is forceful, usually meaning "abandon" or "forsake." Likewise, the term "hold fast"— Hebrew *dābaq*—is robust, indicating a strong adhesion between two things, as if stuck together and difficult to remove (2 Sam. 23:10). Combined, these

---

18. Walter Brueggemann, "Of the Same Flesh and Bone (Gn 2,23a)," *CBQ* 32, no. 4 (1970): 532–42, esp. 540.

two words indicate a more or less complete break in the relationship between a man and his parents and the assumption of a new and very strong bond between the man and his wife. Elsewhere in the Hebrew Bible, ʿāzab is employed for covenant breaking (Deut. 29:25) and dābaq for covenant fidelity (Deut. 10:20; 11:22; 13:4; 30:20; Josh. 22:5), further supporting the covenantal nature of marriage in the Old Testament. Within the context of ancient Israel, the point of Genesis 2:24 is that the solemn words uttered or ritualized in the marriage rite—in the present instance, Adam's performative utterance declaring Eve to be his "bone and flesh," his own kin—do in fact form a legal kinship bond (that is, a covenant) superior to and taking precedence over other kinship bonds, even that between a man and his own parents.[19]

Monogamy is implied at least three times in the text. First, a man leaves "his father and his mother" (both singular), not his fathers and his mothers (plural). This envisions a stable, monogamous parental couple: they inhabit a social and material "place" that can be "abandoned" or "forsaken." It does not envision a female-headed society in which fathers participate in conception but not the rearing of children. In that case, the sacred author would have simply said, "a man will abandon his mother." Rather, the sacred author envisions a stable parental couple that is still in existence when the man reaches majority, such that he can leave the original familial nucleus and form the nucleus of a new family.

Second, the man leaves and cleaves to his *wife* (*ʾištô*), not his *wives* (*nāšāyw*). The sacred author does not envision multiple spouses. There is a balance between the *father* and *mother* who are abandoned and the *man* and his *wife* who are established: one parental unit succeeds another. Harems and other forms of polygamy disturb the creational pattern.

Third, the man and wife become *one flesh* (*bāśār ʾeḥād*), not several "fleshes." The sacred author does not envision multiple unions, and further, such would not be in keeping with the frequent interplay of duality and singularity that have characterized the narrative so far, such as "in the image of God he created *him*; male and female he created *them*" (Gen. 1:27).

The "one flesh" that the man and wife become may be understood in different ways. First, the marital embrace unites their bodies in, as it were, a unity joined in the act of procreation. This is only possible because the woman is not simply the same as the man (Hebrew *kəmô*, "like him") but

19. See Gordon P. Hugenberger, *Marriage as a Covenant: Biblical Law and Ethics as Developed from Malachi* (Grand Rapids: Baker, 1998), 156–60.

Tertullian on the Oneness of Marriage

Although monogamy is not taught explicitly in the Scriptures, the Fathers were convinced that many passages presume it as the divine ideal. A good example is Tertullian's exegesis of Genesis 2:18–24:

> The very origin of the human race supports the law that prescribes a single marriage. It attests that what God established in the beginning ought to be observed by future generations. For when he had formed the man and foreseen that he would need a companion, he took one of the man's ribs and made one woman from it. Both the Craftsman and the matter were capable of creating more. Adam had several ribs, and God's hands were tireless, and yet God created no more wives. Therefore, the man of God, Adam, and the woman of God, Eve, by observing a single marriage, established a rule for the people of God based on the authority of their own origin and on the primordial will of God. In short, he said: *They will be two in one flesh* [Gen. 2:24], not three, not four.[a]

a. Tertullian, *An Exhortation to Chastity* 5, in *Marriage in the Early Church*, trans. and ed. David G. Hunter (Eugene, OR: Wipf & Stock, 2001), 39.

complementary to him (Hebrew *kənegdô*). Ironically, complementary things may join together in a unity, but identical things typically cannot.

Second, the child that results from the marital embrace is a personified union of the bodies of his father and mother: they have become "one flesh" in the person of their child. Thus, the union of man and wife actualizes a kind of return to the original state of creation, restoring the original unity of *'ādām*. The accounts of Genesis 1 and 2 each portray *'ādām* as first a unity and then a duality, first "Adam" and then "male and female" or "man and woman." This unity is restored in matrimony, especially in the act of procreation.

Third, "flesh" could be a metaphor for "kin" or "family" in Hebrew; thus, "one flesh" means "belonging to the same family or kin group." In other words, the man and his wife now form a new family—or at least the nucleus of one—which is expected to grow. This relates to the covenantal understanding of marriage presumed by the text.

Genesis 2:25 could be rendered literally: "The two of them were naked [*'ărûmmîm*], the man and his wife, but they were not ashamed [*yitbōšāšû*] in front of each other" (AT). The verb for "were ashamed," *yitbōšāšû*, is in the Hebrew *hithpael* stem, which has an iterative and reflexive sense, often used to describe back-and-forth action, like pacing or hovering. Here the verb conveys the sense of the exchange of glances between the face-to-face couple.

The nakedness of the man and wife represents transparency; everything about each one is visible to the other, and yet there is no "shame," because nothing needs to be hidden. Their innocent, even naive covenantal relationship has yet to be marred by manipulation, domination, or struggle for control. Nakedness also clearly suggests sexual potential, yet the facts that marriage and, by implication, the "one flesh" acts of procreation are introduced in Genesis 2:24–25 prior to the fall into sin and do not result in "shame" indicate that they are pure in themselves. Thus, Genesis is at odds with other religions and philosophies throughout history that have regarded marriage as base and marital relations as inherently evil or at least low. Finally, nakedness represents vulnerability. This nakedness (Hebrew *ʿārôm*) of the human couple—emblematic of the innocent, transparent, potentially sexual and fertile, yet vulnerable nature of their marital relationship—will serve as the linking motif between the end of this narrative (Gen. 2:4–25) and the beginning of the next (3:1–24).

Summary of Matrimony in the Creation Narratives

In this chapter, we have performed a close reading of the complementary creation narratives comprising Genesis 1:1–2:3 and 2:4–25. Temple motifs characterize both narratives, though in different ways, and man is cast in the role of royal priest within the divine sanctuary. Human sexual differentiation and marriage play a very significant role in both of these narratives. In 1:26–28, the paradoxical unity and plurality of God is recapitulated in *ʾādām*, who is also paradoxically both singular and plural, both "him" and "them." The union of the two—marriage—will be the necessary means of fulfilling the divine blessing-mandates of fruitfulness, multiplication, filling, subduing, and ruling (1:28). Humanity cannot fulfill these original, divinely given mandates *except* through matrimony, the origins of which are given in the second account (2:4–25).

Turning to that account, it is remarkable how much of it is devoted to explaining the origins of matrimony. Depending on how one conceives of the text and its purposes, one could argue that its *entire* narrative is one long explanation of how the institution of marriage came into existence. But even under a less maximalist reading, at least a third of the text—and the final third at that—is devoted to solving the problem of Adam's solitude, resulting in the creation of Eve and the forming of the first marital covenant. Thus, the account of the origin of matrimony does, in fact, form the lengthy conclusion and climax of the combined creation accounts comprising Genesis 1–2. This cannot be accidental, and it must show us that there is something climactic and eschatological about matrimony within God's plan for humanity. Something about matrimony must be very close to God's central purpose in creating the cosmos generally and human beings in particular. The intimate communion of persons in matrimony is a foretaste of the intimate eschatological communion of the beatific vision, which is God's intended (but not irresistible) destiny for all humanity.

We have observed that Adam's words, "bone of my bones and flesh of my flesh . . . ," should be understood as a performative utterance functioning as the oath to form a covenant with Eve,[20] constituting the couple as a kinship relationship and the nucleus of a family. Since Adam is, at this point of his existence, full of the Holy Spirit, infused in his nostrils by the Father (Gen. 2:7),[21] and since we can safely assume Eve is as well, it follows that their matrimonial bond is not merely natural but truly sacramental even by the standards of the New Covenant. Through their marriage, each is united with another person who is a partaker—and thus also a mediator—of the divine nature. This is even suggested by Eve's characterization as an ʿēzer, a "help" or "helper" typically found in contexts of divine assistance (e.g., Pss. 10:14; 20:2; 28:7; 30:10; 33:20). Thus, Adam and Eve are channels of grace toward one another prior to the fall.

20. See Hugenberger, *Marriage as a Covenant*, 216–39, esp. 238–39.
21. For "breath of life" as God's Spirit, see Job 27:3; 32:8; 33:4; 34:14.

3

"They Knew
They Were Naked"

Marriage after the Fall

In Genesis 3–11, we witness the introduction of sin into human history (chap. 3) and then its distorting effects on the nature of matrimony and the relationship between men and women generally (chaps. 4–11).

The Fall into Sin: Genesis 3

Genesis 3 begins with a disjunctive clause marking the introduction of a new narrative,[1] but a wordplay on "nakedness" joins it to the preceding narrative. "The man and his wife were naked [*'ărummîm*]" (Gen. 2:25); but "the serpent was crafty [*'ārûm*]" (3:1 AT). Hebrew "naked" (*'ārôm*) and "crafty" (*'ārûm*) have the same consonants and similar vowels. The nakedness symbolizes innocence, vulnerability, sexuality, and naivete, and it particularly describes their marital bond as yet unstained, perfectly transparent and vulnerable in the absence of the fear of that vulnerability's abuse. The crafty serpent will

1. The continuation of thought in Hebrew narrative is indicated by the conjunction *waw*, "and," attached to the beginning of a verb. When the conjunction *waw* is joined to a nonverb, it usually indicates a break in narrative flow. Genesis 3:1 begins *wəhannāḥāš*—lit., "And the serpent," but translated dynamically, "Now the serpent."

target their nakedness to dethrone them from royal priesthood and to cover them with a shame (*bōšet*) they have not yet known.

The serpent begins his temptation by casting doubt on the truth of God's Word: "Did God *actually* [*'ap*] say, 'You shall not eat . . . ?'" (Gen. 3:1 ESV). The very presence of the unclean serpent (cf. Lev. 11:42) represents a failure of Adam's priestly duty to guard (Gen. 2:15). Other Old Testament texts associate serpents with evil and chaos (Job 26:12–13; Isa. 27:1; Amos 9:3) and exclude them from the eschaton (Isa. 65:25). Adam's failed duty makes possible Eve's temptation.

Now the serpent moves from doubt to outright denial of God's Word: "You will not surely die" (Gen. 3:4 ESV). He sows distrust of God's motives: "For God knows that when you eat of it . . . , you will be like God, knowing good and evil" (v. 5). The serpent is the father of the "hermeneutic of suspicion." He suggests God is jealous of sharing his status with humans, but the irony is that God has already been immensely generous in sharing himself and his nature with them: making them in his "image" and "likeness" (1:26, 27), establishing them as his cosmic viceroys (1:28), infusing the man with the "breath of life" (2:7), and granting him divine authority to name creatures (2:19). Despite this, the serpent imputes selfish motives to God in an effort to tempt the woman to *steal* something that God had and would *share* with her and the man: participation in the divine nature (cf. 2 Pet. 1:4).

The meaning of the phrase "knowing good and evil" (Hebrew *yōd'ê ṭôb wārā'*) deserves some discussion.[2] Some take this as a reference to the awakening of moral consciousness, others as the establishment of moral autonomy (i.e., "knowing" means "determining" right and wrong), and still others as the acquisition of omniscience ("good and evil" as a merismus for "everything"). Probably the phrase is polyvalent, and all three ends are in view.

In response, Eve "saw that the tree was good for food, and that it was a delight to the eyes, and that the tree was to be desired to make one wise" (Gen. 3:6). First John 2:16 summarizes this threefold temptation as "the lust of the flesh and the lust of the eyes and the pride of life," establishing the traditional formulation of concupiscence. "She took of its fruit and ate, and she also gave some to her husband who was with her, and he ate" (Gen. 3:6 ESV). The little phrase "who was with her" (*'immāh*) emphasizes *Adam's consent* and thus the cooperative nature of the fall into sin as a joint act of

2. See Gordon J. Wenham, *Genesis 1–15*, WBC 1 (Nashville: Nelson, 1987), 63–64.

husband and *wife*. In fact, the sacred author chooses to say she "gave some to *her husband*" (*'išāh*) rather than "to Adam" or "to the man." The fall is the act of a married couple, and its repercussions directly affect both spouses: "Then the eyes of the two of them were opened, and they knew that they were naked. And they sewed fig leaves together and made themselves loincloths" (v. 7 AT). The uncommon phrase "the two of them" (*šənêhem*) was last used in 2:25 ("The two of them were naked, yet not ashamed," AT). Accordingly, the mutual nakedness revealed in 3:7 inverts the shame-free innocence of 2:25, implying that the two now *are* ashamed in each other's presence, motivating the making of *ḥăgōrōt*, "loincloths" (ESV). These are not complete "garments" (*kotnôt*; see 3:21) but coverings for the sexual organs, suggesting that the physical union unique to marriage has been profaned. Why shame in each other's presence due to an act mutually undertaken? The prohibited act of eating in Genesis 3:6 violates the covenant with God: one can define sin as covenant violation.[3] But the covenant of God and humans resonates metaphysically with the covenant between man and wife, "entangled" like two particles in physics. Throughout Scripture, we observe that violation of one inevitably entails violation of the other. If humans would violate their covenant with God, how much more likely is it that they would they do so with each other? Therefore, they can no longer be completely vulnerable and transparent ("naked") in each other's presence. Fig leaf garments—uncomfortable, ineffective, and fragile—epitomize their pitiful inability to mitigate their vulnerability and protect themselves from each other.

We see dark humor in that the serpent promises omniscience ("You will be like God, knowing good and evil," Gen. 3:5), but the only knowledge they gain is that of their nakedness (v. 7). The quest to steal divine power backfires into a revelation of humankind's own vulnerability. So the covenant breakers must hide themselves (esp. their sexual potential) not only from each other but also from God: "And they heard the sound of the LORD God walking in the garden in the cool of the day, and the man and his wife hid themselves from the presence of the LORD God among the trees of the garden" (3:8 ESV). Covenants form families to facilitate intimate interpersonal communion; now the communion between God and man, as well as man and wife, has been disrupted. But God seeks to restore communion: "Where are you? . . . Have you eaten of the tree of which I commanded you not to eat?" (vv. 9, 11 ESV).

3. Benedict XVI, *Verbum Domini* 26.

The man evades responsibility for his actions: "The woman whom you gave to be with me, she gave me fruit of the tree, and I ate" (v. 12 ESV). It's the woman's fault, and it's God's fault for giving man the woman. Everyone is at fault but Adam. God moves on to question the woman: "What is this that you have done?" (v. 13 ESV). She responds straightforwardly: "The serpent deceived me, and I ate" (v. 13 ESV).

Having ascertained the facts, God pronounces judgment on the three, beginning with the serpent, whom he curses and to whom he says:

> I will put enmity between you and the woman, and between your seed[4] and her seed; he shall crush[5] your head, and you shall crush his heel. (Gen. 3:15 AT)

The "seed" of the woman can mean the whole human race, descended from Eve. Humanity, though wounded by the serpent, will eventually deal him a fatal blow. The woman will conquer the serpent through her power of procreation, actualized by her marriage to the man. The serpent targeted the "nakedness" of the couple—the vulnerable purity of their marital bond. Yet that marital bond will produce the seed or descendants of the woman who will be the undoing of the serpent. Thus, marriage plays a central role in the process that leads to the defeat of the Evil One.

But "seed" can also mean a single descendant—the Messiah—and when Genesis 3:15 is reread in light of Christ, other nuances of this prophecy come to the fore. The "woman" (cf. John 2:4) who bears this seed is Mary, the New Eve. It was uncommon to speak of the "seed" of women in ancient times, because descent was reckoned through fathers.[6] The expression "seed of the woman" finds a singular application in Jesus Christ, the only man whose generation was exclusively from a woman (not also from a man).

God then pronounces judgment on the woman: "I will surely multiply your pain in childbearing; / in pain you shall bring forth children. / Your desire shall be contrary to [or against] your husband, / but he shall rule over you"

---

4. Often translated "offspring," the Hebrew *zera'* is literally "seed," being employed both in agricultural and genealogical senses. I retain the literal translation here because of its provocative polyvalence.

5. The Hebrew *šûp* is often rendered "bruise" in modern translations, but without clear justification. It only occurs in two other places in the MT: Job 9:17 and Ps. 139:11. In Ps. 139:11, the context seems to demand the sense "cover over, encompass," but "crush" best fits the context of Job 9:17 and Gen. 3:15.

6. Maryanne Cline Horowitz, "Aristotle and Woman," *Journal of the History of Biology* 9, no. 2 (1976): 185–87.

(3:16 ESV). The consequences of sin impact the woman in her role as wife and mother, introducing pain within her relationship with her husband and children. Although the gift of fertility will save her from the serpent's evil (v. 15), nonetheless fertility will be linked to suffering (v. 16)—not only the pain of childbirth but also that of rearing children, often more psychological and social than physical. Thus, children become a cause of pain to the wife-mother and likewise her husband; the obscure Hebrew *ʾel-ʾîšēk təšûqātēk* (lit., "toward your husband your desire") probably means "your desire(s) shall be contrary to your husband." This desire seems to be a desire for control,[7] because the next clause begins with a disjunction with the force of "but" or "nonetheless," followed by an assertion of the husband's rule. Thus, despite her desire for control, he will "reign" (*māšal*), a term associated with kingship (1 Kings 4:21).

The same struggle for power that the man and wife have introduced into their covenant with God now invades their once-peaceful marital covenant. True, a certain authority accrued to the man even before the fall, indicated by his naming of the woman (Gen. 2:23);[8] nonetheless, this authority was benign, exercised in the context of delight, love, and perfect transparency ("nakedness") between the spouses. The royal mandate to "rule" (*rādāh*) and "subdue" (*kābaš*) the creation was to be *jointly* exercised by *ʾādām*-male and *ʾādām*-female, phrased in the second-person plural: "You (two) be fruitful and multiply, fill the earth and subdue it. You (two) rule over the fish of the sea" (1:28 AT). Whereas God's intention was for *ʾādām* as a male-female unity to rule the creation, the breach of covenant results in the spouses struggling to rule over each other. Sin has spoiled the peace and integrity of the matrimonial bond.

To the man, God says: "Because you have listened to the voice of your wife / and have eaten of the tree / of which I commanded you, / 'You shall not eat of it' . . ." (Gen. 3:17 ESV). Hebrew "listen to the voice of" typically means "obey."[9] Adam's sin is a disorder of covenant priority. He has elevated the covenant with his wife above that with God, resulting in catastrophic damage to *both* covenants. The Lord teaches a proper priority of fidelity: "If any one comes to me and does not hate his own . . . wife . . . , he cannot be my disciple" (Luke 14:26). Ironically, Adam's greater loyalty to Eve than to God

7. Susan T. Foh, "What Is the Woman's Desire?," *WTJ* 37, no. 3 (1975): 376–83.
8. Cf. Wenham, *Genesis 1–15*, 64.
9. Cf. Exod. 15:26; Lev. 26:14; Judg. 2:20.

ultimately disrupts the very relationship with Eve he has ostensibly sought to preserve. "Whoever seeks to preserve his life will lose it" (Luke 17:33 ESV).

God issues the judgment:

> Cursed is the ground [*'ădāmāh*] because of you;
>   in pain you shall eat of it all the days of your life;
> thorns and thistles it shall bring forth for you;
>   and you shall eat the plants of the field.
> By the sweat of your face
>   you shall eat bread,
> till you return to the ground,
>   for out of it you were taken;
> for you are dust [*'āpār*],
>   and to dust you shall return. (Gen. 3:17b–19 ESV)

Motifs from man's creation (2:5–9) return: the man (*'ādām*) has been taken from the ground (*'ădāmāh*), molded from the dust (*'āpār*) and set to till (*'ābad*) the plants of the garden. The terms *'ābad* and *šāmar*, "work" and "guard" (2:15), have a priestly sense but also a natural one. Adam has been a priest in a garden-sanctuary, but his liturgical work has been the cultivation of its plants. Now, he will be cast from the garden into the larger creation, which will not submit to Adam's rulership any more than Adam has submitted to God's. The ground that Adam works will bring forth "thorns and thistles"— worthless and painful weeds. Adam will eat in "pain" (*'iṣṣābôn*, 3:17), the same word for Eve's pain in childbearing (v. 16). The spouses experience comparable pain, each in their respective contribution to the family: Eve in procreating, Adam in providing.

After the pronouncement of these judgments, "the man called his wife's name Eve [*ḥawwāh*], because she was the mother of all living [*ḥāy*]" (Gen. 3:20). This is now the second time Adam names his wife (cf. 2:23), and again it represents a role of authority. Yet Adam exercises his authority to honor his wife, because he gives her an exalted name, one of the most auspicious in the Bible. "Eve" (*ḥawwāh*) derives from the verb "to live" (*ḥāyāh*), possibly meaning "she gives life" or "she makes alive."[10] In verse 12, Adam blames Eve for the eating of the fruit; after the curses pronounced in verses 14–19, one would think Adam's resentment of Eve has grown, and he might have

---

10. Understood as an archaic third feminine singular *piel* perfect.

named her "covenant breaker" or "deceived one" rather than "life giver." Yet remarkably, Adam honors his wife by naming her for the mysterious and wonderful gift she possesses but he does not: the power to give life. This power is God-like, as all life so far has come from God. So we recall the divine connotations of "helper" (*ʿēzer*) applied to the woman earlier (2:18, 20). The absence of vindictiveness and the laudatory character of Eve's name indicate a reconciliation of the spouses after the fall.

Likewise, the following verse indicates a degree of reconciliation between God and the human couple. God performs a work of mercy for the man and the woman: "The LORD God made for Adam and for his wife garments of skins and clothed them" (Gen. 3:21 ESV; cf. Matt. 25:36). God replaces the flimsy and ineffective "loincloths" of fig leaves with a true garment (*kuttōnet*) made of durable leather. Skins cannot be had without killing an animal, so the first animal sacrifice is implied by this statement. The sacrifice results in an effective covering of the shame of the man and the woman, restoring to them something of their dignity.[11] This shows the kindness of God, who is unwilling that they abide in unrelieved disgrace. It also introduces the sacrificial principle into salvation history, whereby sacrifice restores the righteousness lost through sin, a process often described using the metaphor of clothing.[12]

The last act in the drama of the fall is the expulsion of Adam and Eve from the garden. "'Behold, the man has become like one of us in knowing good and evil. Now, lest he reach out his hand and take also of the tree of life and eat, and live forever—' therefore the LORD God sent him out from the garden of Eden to work the ground from which he was taken" (Gen. 3:22–23 ESV). God does not wish the man to gain immortality while in a state of rebellion against him; "knowing good and evil" in this place probably means determining good and evil for himself—that is, functioning as an autonomous moral authority. So God expels him from the garden, placing the armed cherubim to the east of the garden to prevent his return. This presumes that the garden had only a single entrance that faced east, which is typical of ancient Near Eastern temples. The married couple must now begin life anew outside the sphere of *shalom* or peaceful integrity provided by the garden, facing resistance now

---

11. Clothing is associated with dignity and honor: Exod. 28:2, 40–42; Esther 6:11; Job 40:10; Pss. 104:1; 132:9; Prov. 31:25; Isa. 61:10; Ezek. 16:8–14; Zech. 3:4–5.

12. Job 29:14; Isa. 61:10; Zech. 3:4–5; Rom. 13:14; Gal. 3:27; Eph. 4:24; Rev. 3:5, 18; 7:14; 19:13.

from nature and their own bodies in their efforts to fulfill their roles and fill the earth.

Genesis 4–11: The Degradation by Stages of Marriage and Human Culture

The Preflood Epoch

Although expelled from the garden and no longer enjoying their original intimacy with God, Adam and Eve set about fulfilling the blessing-mandate of fruitfulness, multiplication, and filling the earth. "Now Adam knew Eve his wife, and she conceived and bore Cain" (Gen. 4:1). Intriguingly, the Hebrew *yāda'*, "to know," is used to describe the marital embrace. The sense of *yāda'* here is personal, not intellectual, knowledge, like the distinction between *kennen* and *wissen* in German. There is also a less intimate expression for sexual relations: "to go/come in to" (*bô'*), as when "the sons of God *came in* to the daughters of men" (6:4). This expression emphasizes the physical act more than the relationship of the spouses. But for this first act of procreation, the sacred author chooses to use the expression that is more evocative of interpersonal communion: the spouses "know" each other.

In the birth of Cain, Eve's firstborn, we find another example of the association of Eve's life-giving power with God's. The remainder of the verse reads: "She bore Cain [*qayin*], for she said, 'I have acquired [*qānîtî*] a man with the LORD'" (Gen. 4:1 AT). The last prepositional phrase, "with the LORD," doubtless means "with *the help of* the LORD." Eve acknowledges the lordship of God over the power of procreation. Although the power to reproduce is within her, and even her husband acknowledges her as the "life giver," nonetheless that power remains mysterious and ultimately under the control of God. Indeed, throughout Genesis God is acknowledged as lord of the womb (20:18; 29:31; 30:2, 22; 49:25). So the woman's power of giving life is exercised in conjunction with the will of God. God has entrusted her with the power to give life, a power that is properly divine and over which he continues to exercise oversight. Recognizing this, Eve gives thanks to God for successful birth (4:1, 25).

As the biblical narrative progresses from the expulsion from the garden (Gen. 3:24) to the sending of the flood (6:13), we wish to observe a pattern of growth of aberrations and offenses against matrimony. Cain follows a

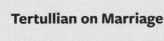

Tertullian on Marriage

Tertullian notes that it is not simply the creation of one man and one woman that suggests monogamy as the divine intention, but also that the sacred author of Genesis attributes the origin of polygamy to a despicable character in the narrative:

> The law of one marriage . . . is founded both on the creation of the human race and on the sacrament of Christ. In both cases we derive our origin from a single marriage: physically in Adam, spiritually in Christ. From these two nativities we receive the one law of monogamy. In either case, to deviate from monogamy is to degenerate. Plurality of marriage started with a man who was cursed: Lamech was the first to marry two wives, thereby making three in one flesh.[a]

a. Tertullian, *An Exhortation to Chastity* 5, in *Marriage in the Early Church*, trans. and ed. David G. Hunter (Eugene, OR: Wipf & Stock, 2001), 39.

path of sin, first killing his righteous brother, Abel, and then moving away from the presence of the Lord (4:16), indicating a choice to pursue life apart from worship and a relationship with God. Cain fathers a line of sinful descendants, none more so than his offspring of the sixth generation, Lamech, history's first recorded bigamist. In Genesis 4:19, the sacred author interrupts the genealogical pattern prevailing up to this point in order to inform us that "Lamech took two wives; the name of the one was Adah, and the name of the other Zillah." This is an innovation. Prior to Lamech, it was not necessary to mention the wives because monogamy prevailed, and thus there was only one line of descent. But now Lamech's line of descent splits according to the children of the two wives (vv. 20–22). Furthermore, Genesis 4:23–24 informs us:

Lamech said to his wives:

> "Adah and Zillah, hear my voice;
>   you wives of Lamech, listen to what I say:
> I have killed a man for wounding me,
>   a young man for striking me.
> If Cain's revenge is sevenfold,
>   then Lamech's is seventy-sevenfold." (ESV)

The sacred author portrays Lamech as a sociopath, who boasts of his killings to his wives and claims to be eleven times more violent than his murderous ancestor. Furthermore, what is the point of boasting of his violence to his wives if not to intimidate them into compliance? So Lamech is an abusive husband as well. The fact that the sacred author portrays the inventor of bigamy so negatively is surely intentional and casts the practice in an ill light: bigamy has its origins from a violent and abusive criminal. We note, too, how uncontrolled lust is associated with violence here, as elsewhere in the Scriptures. Lamech will not constrain his lust within the bounds of monogamy, nor will he restrain his violence within the bounds of proportionate retribution. These two vices seem mutually supporting and grow together.

Significantly, the description of Lamech ends the genealogy of Cain. We are meant to understand that Cain's murderous sinfulness metastasizes over the generations till we witness the arrival of a descendant more than ten times worse, who even goes so far as to break the sacred bonds of monogamy that prevailed before him. This would seem like a dismal eventuality for the human race, so at this point in the narrative the sacred author provides us with a glimmer of hope:

> And Adam knew his wife again, and she bore a son and called his name Seth [šēt], for she said, "God has appointed [šāt] for me another seed instead of Abel, for Cain killed him." To Seth also a son was born, and he called his name Enosh. At that time people began to call upon the name of the LORD. (Gen. 4:25–26 ESV, modified)

Because of sin, Adam and Eve's first attempts at procreation end disastrously: they produce two sons, one of whom kills the other and then produces a line of descendants who descend into lust and violence. But salvation is still to be found through the fruitful marital union: the seed of the woman will crush the head of evil. So in response to the evil of Cain's line, Adam and Eve have recourse to interpersonal communion once more. They "know" each other again, and Eve bears another son, and once more she gives credit to God for his cooperation with her power of procreation: "God has appointed for me another seed" (ESV). The fact that Eve calls him a "seed" (zeraʿ) instead of a "man" (ʾîš), "child" (yeled), or "son" (bēn) intentionally evokes the promised "seed" of the woman of Genesis 3:15 and also suggests the aspect of further fruitfulness (as a seed grows and produces more) in the form of a line of descent from Seth that will save humanity from the evil festering among Cain's descendants.

Noah and the Flood

What follows is the genealogy of Adam's descendants through Seth (Gen. 5:1–32), which continues for ten generations until the arrival of a savior figure, Noah, whose name derives from the word for "rest" (*nûaḥ*), a verbal form of which was employed earlier (2:15) to describe Adam being "set to rest" in the garden like an image of a deity in a temple.[13] Noah's naming is described in this way:

> [He] called his name Noah, saying, "Out of the ground that the Lord has cursed, this one shall bring us relief from our work and from the painful toil of our hands." (Gen. 5:29 ESV)

Noah is a type of Christ and an early realization of the principle that from the seed of the woman—made possible by the fruitful union of matrimony—will arise a savior to overcome the Evil One, who provoked the curse on creation.

However, while the righteous line of Seth has been proliferating, so has the wicked line of Cain, and by the time of Noah the situation has become intolerable:

> When man ['*ādām*] began to multiply on the face of the land ['*ădāmāh*] and daughters were born to them, the sons of God saw that the daughters of man ['*ādām*] were attractive [lit., "good," *ṭôb*]. And they took [*lāqaḥ*] as their wives any they chose. (Gen. 6:1–2 ESV)

"Son of God" is a covenant term in Scripture (cf. Pss. 2:7; 89:20, 26–28), so following Augustine (see the sidebar "St. Augustine on the 'Sons of God'"), the "sons of God" here may be understood as the line of Seth that attempted to stay in covenant relationship with God, whereas the "daughters of man"—a term suggesting the absence of a relationship with God—may refer to the descendants of Cain, who intentionally "went away from the presence of the Lord" (Gen. 4:16). The men of the righteous line of Seth give in to the lust

13. Catherine L. McDowell, *The Image of God in the Garden of Eden: The Creation of Humankind in Genesis 2:5–3:24 in Light of* mīs pî pīt pî *and* wpt-r *Rituals of Mesopotamia and Ancient Egypt*, Siphrut 15 (Winona Lake, IN: Eisenbrauns, 2015), 157–58.

St. Augustine on the "Sons of God"

The Septuagint renders "sons of God" in Genesis 6:2 as "*angels* of God." None-theless, Augustine argues they are human men in the line of Seth:

> For by the Spirit of God they had been made angels of God [LXX] and sons of God [MT]; but declining towards lower things, they are called men [Gen. 6:3 LXX], a name of nature, not of grace; and they are called flesh [v. 3], as deserters of the Spirit, and by their desertion deserted [by Him]. . . . There is therefore no doubt that . . . there were many giants [Greek *gigantes*, v. 4 LXX] before the deluge, and that these were citizens of the earthly society of men, and that the sons of God, who were according to the flesh the sons of Seth, sunk into this community when they forsook righteousness.[a]

a. Augustine, *City of God* 15.23 (*NPNF¹* 2:304–5).

of the flesh. Just like Eve "sees" (*rā'āh*) that the tree is "good" (*ṭôb*) for food and "takes" (*lāqaḥ*) of its fruit (3:6), so they "see" (*rā'āh*) that the daughters of man are "good" (*ṭôb*) and "take" (*lāqaḥ*) any they choose (6:2). They engage in polygamy to satisfy lust. The end of Genesis 6:2 reads literally: "They took for themselves wives from all that they chose" (AT)—in other words, *as many as they wanted*.

Earlier, in the person of Lamech, we saw that lust and violence grew together, and now this truth is demonstrated on a wider scale:

> The LORD saw that the wickedness of man was great in the earth, and that every intention of the thoughts of his heart was only evil continually. . . . Now the earth was corrupt in God's sight, and the earth was filled with violence [*ḥāmās*]. . . . And God said to Noah, "I have determined to make an end of all flesh, for the earth is filled with violence [*ḥāmās*] through them." (Gen. 6:5, 11, 13 ESV)

The lust-induced breakdown of the monogamous union of man and woman—the basis of human society and the full expression of the image and likeness of God—results in the absolute degradation of society into a morass of evil and violence. There are spiritual reasons for this, as well as natural reasons;

for example, polygamous fathers produce too many sons to father properly, and these poorly fathered sons grow up to vent their interior pain on society.

A notable exception to the prevailing polygamy among the "sons of God" is Noah himself, who has but one wife (Gen. 6:18; 7:7). Monogamy is a practice he taught to his sons as well, each of whom has but one wife (7:13). In fact, in contrast to the polygamy and violence of the surrounding earth, every living thing that enters the ark is monogamous: "two and two, male and female, went into the ark with Noah" (7:9 ESV). The ark, likewise, is nonviolent, as there is no killing and eating among the diverse animals that enter. Most modern commentators miss the significance of the contrast between the polygamy of the sons of God and the strict monogamy of every living thing saved in the ark, but the point was not lost on the Essenes of Qumran, who employed the example of Noah and the animals (7:9) as a prooftext for their understanding of lifelong monogamy over against the views of the Pharisees and Sadducees.[14]

Not only does the flood cleanse the earth of lust and violence, but it also constitutes a re-creation: the earth once more is plunged under the waters of the abyss (cf. Gen. 1:2), and once more the Spirit (*rûaḥ*) of God (8:1; cf. 1:2) blows over the face of the waters, and the dry ground reemerges (8:13–14; cf. 1:9–10). The ark is a floating sacred garden that comes to rest on a mountain, Ararat, where Noah and his sons and their wives receive a blessing and covenant (9:1–17) in language heavy with references to Genesis 1:1–2:3. God reestablishes with Noah the covenant that Adam enjoyed prior to the fall (9:9),[15] even if the effects of sin have damaged the relationship of humanity to the rest of creation (9:2–6).

The reestablishment of the covenant with Noah gives momentary hope that a new and blessed epoch has dawned for humanity, but those hopes are quickly dashed by Noah's own actions. Getting drunk from the fruit of his own vineyard, he lies uncovered in his tent, where he becomes the victim of some deed perpetrated by his son Ham (Gen. 9:20–22). When he awakes from his drunkenness, he places a curse on some of Ham's descendants (9:25).

14. The Damascus Document reads: "The Shoddy-Wall Builders [i.e., Pharisees] . . . are caught in . . . fornication, by taking two wives in their lifetimes, even though the principle of creation is 'male and female he created them' (Gen. 1:27) and those who went into the ark 'went into the ark two by two' (Gen. 7:9)" (CD 4:20–5:1 AT).

15. The language employed for the making of the covenant with Noah in Gen. 9:9 is not the usual terminology for covenant initiation (Hebrew *kārat bərît*, lit., "to cut a covenant") but arguably the language of covenant restoration or reestablishment (*hēqîm bərît*, lit., "to cause a covenant to stand"). See William J. Dumbrell, "The Covenant with Noah," *RTR* 38, no. 1 (1979): 1–9.

This dense and suggestive text hides many secrets,[16] but it suffices for present purposes to observe here the same basic pattern of the sin of Adam and Eve: (1) the illicit consumption of fruit, which results in (2) nakedness, (3) shame, and (4) curse. Thus, Genesis 9:20–27 constitutes what might be called the "fall of Noah." The gravity of Noah's actions comes into greater relief when Noah's priestly role (8:20) and the fact that priests were never to get drunk (Lev. 10:9) or expose their nakedness (Exod. 20:26; 28:42) are recognized.

Moreover, there is the strong suggestion in Genesis 9:20–27 of some sexual offense. It is said that Ham "saw the nakedness of his father" (v. 22), which sounds like mere voyeurism, except that "seeing the nakedness of" is a Hebrew idiom for sexual relations (Lev. 20:17), and "the nakedness of the father" can refer to the nakedness of the father's *wife* (18:6–8). I have discussed the possible implications of this language elsewhere,[17] but here it is enough to recognize that this text more than merely suggests some offense involving the misuse of the act proper only to marriage. In hindsight, the fall of Adam and Eve, while apparently not involving a sexual act per se, is also described in language evocative of illicit sexuality: the eating results in seeing each other's nakedness, experiencing shame in the presence of each other and God (Gen. 3:7, 10), desperately attempting to cover the nakedness, and a curse falling on the woman's "desire" for her husband and the bearing of children (3:16). This is a pattern that will continue to be observed throughout salvation history, which may be summarized in this way: every major breach of a covenant between God and humanity in salvation history also involves an offense against matrimony, the covenant between man and woman. As we have seen and will see, this is true of the covenant-breaking episodes of the Adamic (Gen. 3:1–24), Noahic (9:20–27), Abrahamic (16:1–6), Mosaic (Exod. 32:6), and Davidic (2 Sam. 11:1–27) covenants. In each case, divine covenant breaking coincides with marital covenant breaking or a related offense. This indicates a metaphysical entanglement between these two covenants, based on the reality that one is the sacrament of the other.

The Noahic "fall" in Genesis 9:20–27 manifests the reintroduction of serious sin into the development of human society, which once again metastasizes down through the generations of Noah's sons (10:1–32) until the catastrophe of the tower of Babel incident (11:1–9), in which all humanity joins together

16. See John S. Bergsma and Scott W. Hahn, "Noah's Nakedness and the Curse on Canaan (Genesis 9:20–27)," *JBL* 124, no. 1 (2005): 25–40.
17. Bergsma and Hahn, "Noah's Nakedness," 26–39.

in a collective act of defiance against God. The Lord confuses their language, forcing them to disperse, but now they are alienated from each other and from God (vv. 7–9). What will the divinity do to reunite the families of the earth and restore the divine blessing to them? The answer has to do with a descendant of Noah's son Shem named Abram and will introduce a new epoch in salvation history (vv. 10–32). The primeval era of global creation and re-creation has come to an end, and we emerge into a time more firmly anchored in historical memory and record.

Summary of Marriage from the Fall to Babel

The period from the fall of Adam and Eve (Gen. 3) to the tower of Babel (Gen. 11) witnesses the degradation of matrimony in human society. The spousal relationship of Adam and Eve degenerates into one of conflict, disordered desire, and a struggle for power. Subsequent generations witness the rise of bigamy and then full-blown polygamy. The flood punishes these abuses and vindicates monogamy as practiced by Noah and his family. Noah is an early actualization of the salvific "seed of the woman" promise that, despite all to the contrary, the fecundity of marriage will one day bring forth one who is an antidote to the Evil One (3:15). Nonetheless, disordered sexuality reemerges after the flood in an episode that recapitulates, with variation, the fall in the garden (9:20–27). Over subsequent generations, humanity becomes alienated from God and from each other, requiring a new divine initiative to begin regathering the human family as the family of God.

4

"Say You Are My Sister"

The Marriages of the Patriarchs

Genesis 12 marks an important transition point in the biblical narrative, as the sacred author moves from an account of the origins of humanity (Gen. 1–11) to the origins of Israel specifically (Gen. 12–50). The rest of the book will follow the lives and fortunes of the three great patriarchs of the people of Israel—Abraham, Isaac, and Jacob—and also Jacob's favored son, Joseph. The narrative divides into three great cycles centered around the figures of Abraham (chaps. 12–25), Jacob (chaps. 26–36), and Joseph (chaps. 37–50). Isaac, the link between Abraham and Jacob, is also a significant figure, but in the literary structure of the book, the account of his life is split and embedded within the Abraham cycle (chaps. 21–25) and the Jacob cycle (26:1–28:5).

The patriarchal narratives are often avoided in discussions of biblical revelation on matrimony, because the patriarchs sometimes behave scandalously, especially when judged by the standards of the New Covenant doctrine on matrimony. They marry multiple women (Gen. 16:3), hand their wives into the custody of other men (12:10–20), and even engage in relations outside of marriage (38:12–19). We hope to show in this chapter, however, that the patriarchal narratives have an important contribution to make to the overall message of Scripture on matrimony. First, these chapters establish the Abrahamic covenant, the foundational redemptive covenant for all of

Scripture, whose fulfillment will be in the person and mission of Jesus Christ (Matt. 1:1). And yet the Abrahamic covenant concerns the "seed" (Hebrew *zera‘*) or descendants of Abraham and their role within humanity as a whole, so marriage—the means by which descendants come to be—is absolutely central to the fulfillment of this foundational covenant. Second, while it is true that the patriarchs behave badly at times, this behavior is *pejorativized* (cast in a negative light) by the sacred author, who tells the stories in such a way that the attentive reader can perceive that providence and the natural order reward monogamous marriage and censure aberrations from it.

The Foundational Character of Genesis 12–50 in the Bible

Before examining the marital theme in Genesis 12–50, we should explain the foundational role these chapters play in all subsequent biblical revelation.[1]

The theological backdrop for the patriarchal narratives is the tower of Babel debacle in Genesis 11:1–9, which results in the alienation of human beings from God and from each other. How can this twofold alienation be overcome? God will work with one man (Abram) and his family, reconciling himself with that man—and then, through his descendants, drawing in the whole human race:

> Now the LORD said to Abram, "Go from your country and your kindred and your father's house to the land that I will show you. And I will make of you a great nation, and I will bless you and make your name great, so that you will be a blessing. I will bless those who bless you, and him who dishonors you I will curse, and in you all the families of the earth shall be blessed." (Gen. 12:1–3 ESV)

Note three specific blessings: great nationhood (v. 2a), a great name (v. 2b), and great blessing to "all the families of the earth" (v. 3b). This promise of blessing to the families of the earth connects the Abraham narrative to Genesis 10–11, which first recounts all the clans and tribes of humanity (10:1–32) and then their dispersal and mutual alienation (11:1–9). Thus, Abram is the solution to the enmity between God and humans, as well as the enmity among humans themselves, introduced by the Babel debacle. Furthermore,

---

1. What follows is a summary of my longer treatment in John S. Bergsma and Brant Pitre, *The Old Testament*, vol. 1 of *A Catholic Introduction to the Bible* (San Francisco: Ignatius, 2018), 134–43, 163.

the threefold blessing of Abram in 12:2–3 is programmatic for the subsequent narrative. First, the promise of a "great nation" (12:2a) is solemnized by the covenant ritual of Genesis 15:7–21, the "covenant between the pieces." Second, the promise of a "great name" (12:2b), an ancient idiom linked to royalty (cf. 2 Sam. 7:9), is solemnized through the covenant ritual of circumcision (Gen. 17), in which God makes Abram's name greater (i.e., "Abraham," v. 5) while granting him a royal dynasty (vv. 6, 16). Third, the promise of blessing to all peoples (12:3b) is solemnized by the divine covenant oath (22:15–18) after Abraham's attempted sacrifice of Isaac (22:1–14), stating that "in your seed shall all the nations of the earth be blessed" (22:18 AT). Thus, before Abraham's death, all three promises have been confirmed by sacred oath or ritual, and immediately after Abraham's death (25:7–11), Jacob/Israel is introduced (25:19–26; later "Israel," 32:28), whose descendants will become the promised "great nation" as the pentateuchal narrative progresses.

The triple promise to Abraham and the corresponding covenant-making episodes (Gen. 15:1–21; 17:1–27; 22:1–19) anticipate the covenant progression of the divine economy. The promise of great nationhood and the covenant between the pieces anticipate the Mosaic covenant (Exod. 19–24), under which Israel will become a great nation. Similarly, the great name (i.e., royal dynasty) and circumcision (Gen. 17:1–27) anticipate the Davidic covenant (2 Sam. 7:4–17), when the "great name" will come to rest on Abraham's descendant David (7:9). Finally, the blessing to the nations and the binding of Abraham's "only-begotten" son, Isaac (Gen. 22:2, 12, 16 RSV2CE), anticipate the New Covenant, Calvary, and the outpouring of the Holy Spirit (Luke 22:20; John 3:16; 19:34; Acts 2:37–38). Thus, Abraham's life is salvation history *in nuce*. Yet at every step, marriage is essential, the only path by which the promises can be fulfilled and transmitted to future generations.

Matrimony in the Abraham Cycle (Gen. 12–25)

The first of the promises to Abram, great nationhood, cannot be accomplished without the cooperation and fertility of his wife, Sarai, herself an indispensable agent in the outworking of the divine promises. Threats to the fertility of Sarai (and other matriarchs) constitute a major theme of Genesis, and they are overcome only through divine assistance, because the patriarchs themselves are often their own worst enemies in this regard.

The Matriarch in the Court of Pharaoh

A key example of this self-defeating behavior occurs almost immediately after Abram's call (Gen. 12:1–3). Abram, while sojourning in Egypt, passes Sarai off as his sister (v. 13), with the result that Pharaoh takes her into his household, jeopardizing the marriage and the fulfillment of the covenant promises (vv. 14–16). God intervenes, sending "great plagues" on Pharaoh and his house (v. 17). Pharaoh is irate when he discovers the cause of the divine curse, and after rebuking Abram harshly (vv. 18–19), he sends him out of his realm (v. 20).

The sacred author pejorativizes Abram and exonerates Pharaoh in this narrative. God saves Abram from himself by defending Abram's matrimonial bond from defilement by adultery. The object of covenantal blessing is not just Abram but his one-flesh bond with Sarai through which blessing will come to all the earth (Gen. 12:3; 22:18).

The Covenant between the Pieces

Yet still God does not bless Abram with children through Sarai, and in Genesis 15, Abram is almost in despair over his childlessness (v. 2). Sarai's barrenness becomes the precipitating circumstance for God's first covenant with Abram (vv. 7–21), which guarantees his fruitfulness by divine oath consisting of spoken promises (vv. 13–16, 18–21) and enacted rituals (vv. 9–12, 17). The divine presence passes through the bisected animals in a covenant-ritual meaning: "May I become like these slain animals if I fail to keep the commitment(s) I am making." God condescends to participate in a human covenant ritual invoking a self-curse of death to assure Abram of the fruitfulness of his marriage in a most solemn and dramatic way.

Hagar as Concubine and Surrogate Mother

Despite this assurance, Sarai grows impatient and has recourse to a surrogate mother. She presses Abram to take Hagar, her maid, as a second wife, since by law and custom any of her children would be Sarai's.

Literary clues portray this as an ill-conceived and ill-fated plan contrary to divine intent. First, neither Sarai nor Abram seek God's will through prayer. Sarai conceives the plan, while blaming God for her barrenness: "The LORD has prevented me from bearing children" (Gen. 16:2). Second, Sarai urges

Abram to adopt bigamy, the practice wicked Lamech invented (4:19), not appropriate for a covenant-keeping "son of God" (cf. 6:2). Third, the clause "Abram listened to the voice of Sarai" (16:2 ESV) echoes Adam's guilt: "Because you have listened to the voice of your wife . . ." (3:17). "Listen to the voice of" (*šāmaʿ ləqôl*) is an idiom for "obey"; the fault is not attentiveness to one's spouse (a moral duty) but obedience to one's spouse *rather than* to God. When Hagar sees that she has conceived, she "belittles her mistress in her eyes" (16:4b AT), an expression using the Hebrew *qālal*, a synonym of *'ārôr*, "to curse," recalling the curses in Genesis 3:14–17. Just as conflict between husband and wife (cf. 3:16) results from the fall, and just as *ḥāmās* results from the polygamy of the sons of God (6:11, 13), so now conflict erupts between Abram and Sarai, who literally says, "My violence [*ḥāmās*] be upon you!" (AT; cf. 16:5a MT). As Adam blames Eve for the fall (3:12), conversely Sarai blames Abram for Hagar (16:5). Just as Adam fails to defend Eve and instead puts all responsibility for their mutual act on her (3:12), so Abram fails to defend Hagar and hands her over to Sarai's wrath: "Your maid is in your hand; do to her what is good in your eyes" (16:6 AT). "What is good in your eyes" may evoke the opening of Adam and Eve's eyes to know (i.e., determine) good and evil (3:5, 7, 22).

The parallel motifs and diction of Genesis 3:1–24 and 16:1–6 reveal the Hagar episode as the "fall of Abram." Both Adam and Abram receive a covenant with God (2:7//15:18), which they immediately break through lack of faith and disordered "obedience" to their spouses (3:6//16:3–4), by committing an act that gravely damages their marriage bond (3:16b//16:5). The Hagar episode contributes to the *implicit critique of polygamy* that runs through Genesis and other parts of the Old Testament, by which the sacred author shows polygamy's evil origins and results.

The Covenant of Circumcision

The "fall" of Genesis 16 sets up the renewal of the covenant in Genesis 17. Ishmael's birth complicates the covenant economy: Who is the heir spoken of in Genesis 15:4b ("Your own son shall be your heir")—Ishmael or a later son through Sarai? God must resolve the ambiguities by renewing and redefining the covenant with Abram.

Genesis 17 opens with a theophany and rebuke to Abram: "I am God Almighty; walk before me and be blameless" (v. 1). This implies Abram has not been blameless recently. God proceeds to confirm the covenant while introducing notable changes to its economy. First, Abram ("exalted father") becomes Abraham ("father of a multitude," v. 5). New names are common in family-forming covenant rituals. Second, God declares that "kings shall come forth from you" (v. 6)—a royal dynasty. Both the greater name (Abraham) and the royal dynasty flow from the promise of a "great name" (12:2). Third, whereas in Genesis 15 Abraham cuts animals, in Genesis 17:10 he cuts his own flesh as the covenant ritual. Circumcision is polyvalent, but it can represent a rebuke of the procreative power Abraham has misused in Genesis 16:1–6. Certainly, in later Judaism it represented the consecration of Jewish men to God and their commitment to follow the Torah, including abstention from all forms of *zǝnût* (sexual impurity; cf. Lev. 18:1–30; 20:10–21).[2] Fourth, God makes explicit that Sarai is party to this covenant, granting her also a new name, Sarah, and reiterating also to her the promises of fertility and royal ancestry. Indeed, God insists on blessing Abraham's wife *despite Abraham's objections* (Gen. 17:18), stating explicitly: "I will establish my covenant with Isaac, whom *Sarah* shall bear to you" (v. 21).

Genesis 17 makes explicit what was implicit earlier—namely, that in promising Abraham descendants, God always intended him to be united to his wife, Sarah, in the one-flesh union by which *'ādām* becomes whole. Surrogacy and polygamy have been shown as offenses against this union.

The Perversion of Sexuality in Sodom

Subsequent chapters include yet graver examples of the abuse of sexuality outside of marriage. In Genesis 18, the wickedness of Sodom and Gomorrah becomes so great it provokes a divine visitation (vv. 20–21). Ultimately, it manifests itself in the Sodomites attempting the homosexual gang rape of the angelic visitors who take refuge in Lot's house (19:5). Lot rebukes this as "wickedness" (v. 7 AT) but appallingly offers his virgin daughters to appease their lust. Not appeased, the mob grows enraged that anyone dare call their desires "wicked," so they attempt to molest Lot as well (v. 9). Capitulation to their own lusts has led to a willful denial of both natural and special revelation about the proper use of sexuality (cf. Rom. 1:18–27, esp. 26–27). God intended the one-flesh union (Gen. 2:24) to be intimate, consensual, complementary,

2. On circumcision as consecration, see Nahum M. Sarna, *Genesis*, JPS Torah Commentary (Philadelphia: Jewish Publication Society, 1989), 179.

fruitful, faithful, exclusive, and permanent. But the Sodomites intend an act violent, nonconsensual, noncomplementary, sterile, faithless, promiscuous, and temporary. Only angelic intervention defeats their efforts (19:11).

The Sodom debacle (Gen. 19) parallels the flood story (Gen. 6–9). In both, disordered sexuality and violence (6:1–7, 11–12//19:4–11) provoke destructive judgment. The ark and the house of Lot, where monogamous parents with married children withdraw and where divine power shuts the doors on danger (7:16//19:10), offer salvation. Heaven rains water for Noah (7:11–12) and fire for Lot (19:24). Then follow unedifying narratives of alcohol-fueled sexuality between father and child (9:20–27//19:30–38). Lot's daughters inebriate and seduce their father, another grotesque parody of matrimony, resulting in Moab and Ammon, perennial enemies of Israel. Thus, the drunkenness of Noah (9:20–27) and of Lot (19:30–38) are parallel etiological accounts of the origins of Israel's enemies through nonmarital, incestuous unions.[3]

Sarah in the Court of Abimelech

Yet Abraham is no paragon of virtue in contrast to Lot. In Genesis 20:1–18, once again Abraham exposes Sarah to possible sexual appropriation by a foreign king, Abimelech. Once again, God intervenes to preserve the exclusivity of the marital bond, and the foreign king appears as a model of integrity in contrast to Abraham's deception and cowardice (vv. 3–13). In response to Abraham's prayers, God opens the wombs of the women of Abimelech's household. This brief narrative affirms the Lord as defender of marital integrity and lord of the womb.

The Birth of Isaac

At long last, God also "visits" Sarah (Gen. 21:1, using the Hebrew *pāqad*, a covenant term), and the one-flesh union of Abraham and Sarah, threatened almost continually by external pressures and their own failures, becomes actualized in a son and heir. Ironically, although marriage is *naturally* ordered toward procreation, yet in the end the birth of "seed" (the son and heir) is a *divine act* unattainable by the couple in their own power. The marriage of Abraham and Sarah ultimately has a supernatural telos or end.

3. See John S. Bergsma and Scott W. Hahn, "Noah's Nakedness and the Curse on Canaan (Genesis 9:20–27)," *JBL* 124, no. 1 (2005): 25–40, esp. 36–37.

The birth of Isaac—the child of "laughter"—resurrects the disorders caused by surrogacy and concubinage: rivalry arises between him and older Ishmael (Gen. 21:9). Hagar must go, yet Abraham only consents when assured by God of divine provision and blessing for her and Ishmael (vv. 11–14). Nonetheless, the reader feels the full pathos of Hagar's initial suffering (vv. 15–16), part of the tragic result of violating the bonds of matrimony (vv. 15–21). Yes, Hagar's son, Ishmael, is blessed and grows up strong and prosperous (vv. 18, 20; 25:12–18)—but as for Hagar, what about the loss of the love and companionship of the man whose child she bore? Concubinage never attains the truly complementary relationship of man and woman intended by God (2:18, 20, 24).

The Binding of Isaac

We now reach the climax of the Abrahamic narrative: the testing of Abraham's covenant fidelity, in which God mysteriously asks to take back the long-expected and much-threatened fruit of Abraham and Sarah's union, Isaac, through sacrifice (Gen. 22:2). In Genesis 16:1–6, Abraham's faith falters, and he reaches for human means to fulfill divine promises. But now Abraham has learned the lesson of faith: God has given the child supernaturally—and can restore him supernaturally (Heb. 11:17–19).

The christological typology is clear. At Moriah and Calvary, we have two "only-begotten" sons (Gen. 22:2, 12, 16//John 3:16 RSV2CE) carrying the wood of their sacrifice up a mountain, only to be laid on the wood and offered to God out of love for their father. Both scenarios found a sanctuary and a liturgy.[4] Isaac is a "young man" by now (Hebrew *na'ar*, Gen. 22:5), and he carries the heavy load for his aged father (v. 6), who could not have overpowered him. Therefore, the ancient Jewish commentaries on this text all understand Isaac to be in the prime of manhood and a willing participant in this joint act of faith and obedience,[5] which at its conclusion merits an extraordinary divine oath:

> By myself I have sworn, says the LORD, because you have done this and have not withheld your son, your only-begotten son, I will indeed bless you, and I will multiply your seed [*zera'*] as the stars of heaven and as the sand that is on

---

4. Scott W. Hahn, *Kinship by Covenant: A Canonical Approach to the Fulfillment of God's Saving Promises* (New Haven: Yale University Press, 2009), 129.

5. Hahn, *Kinship by Covenant*, 125.

the seashore. And your seed shall possess the gate of his enemies, and in your seed shall all the nations of the earth be blessed, because you have obeyed my voice. (Gen. 22:16–18 AT)

This repeats the blessing of Genesis 12:2–3: the multiplication of the "seed" corresponds to the "great nation" (12:2a//22:17a), and the possession of the enemies' gates corresponds to the royalty implied by the "great name" (12:2b//22:17b). But now it is not "in you" (12:3) but "in your seed" (22:18) that all the nations shall be blessed. For his meritorious co-obedience, the solemn divine oath incorporates Isaac, the "seed" (*zeraʿ*) of Abraham, into the climactic third promise of the covenant: universal blessing.

Isaac is an early manifestation of the seed of the woman who will crush the head of the Evil One and restore the lost blessing to humanity. Abraham and Sarah resemble Joseph and Mary: bound in a marital union unfruitful merely by nature, they become fruitful by the grace of God. Thus, at Moriah and at Calvary we witness the supernaturally given fruit of two supernaturalized marriages being offered to God for the salvation of the world. Matrimony is always close to the heart of God's action in salvation history.

The Death of Sarah

The denouement of the Abraham cycle focuses on the burial of Sarah (Gen. 23) and the betrothal of Rebekah (Gen. 24), two stories that recount the "passing of the baton" from one matriarch to another. First, the sacred author amply demonstrates the significance of Sarah to the divine economy by the enormous attention he pays to the purchasing of her burial plot and her interment (23:1–20). The cave in the field of Ephron, in Machpelah, will serve as the resting place of Abraham and Sarah, Isaac and Rebekah, and Jacob and Leah (49:29–32), Rachel being the sole exception (35:19; 48:7). Notably, the patriarchs are "monogamous in death," each laid beside his first wife (49:28–32).

The Marriage of Isaac and Rebekah (Gen. 24–27)

The Courtship of Rebekah

The now-vacant role of matriarch needs immediate filling. Aging Abraham has one remaining task: seeing Isaac properly wed (Gen. 24:1–4). A Canaanite woman will not do (24:3; cf. Lev. 18:3); rather, Isaac's wife must worship "the LORD, the God of heaven and the God of earth" (Gen. 24:3 NABRE), like Abraham's kinfolk in Aram Naharaim (Mesopotamia). So solemn is the mission that Abraham's steward (presumably Eliezer of Damascus, Gen. 15:2) places his hand under Abraham's "thigh" (*yārēk*)—that is, his procreative member,[6] symbolizing the life and continuity of his lineage.

The choice of the right wife for Isaac, the covenant heir, is crucial and thus bathed in appeals for divine help. Abraham makes Eliezer swear by the Lord and affirms that the angel of the Lord will ensure the success of the mission (Gen. 24:3, 7). For his part, Eliezer calls on the name of the Lord in prayer for a divine sign of the success of his endeavor:

> Let the young woman to whom I shall say, "Please let down your jar that I may drink," and who shall say, "Drink, and I will water your camels"—let her be the one whom you have appointed [*hōkaḥtā*][7] for your servant Isaac. By this I shall know that you have shown covenant fidelity [*ḥesed*] to my master. (Gen. 24:14 ESV, modified)

Thus, the marriage is clearly submitted to the will of God. Jesus attributes the joining of spouses to God's will: "What therefore God has joined together, let not man separate" (Matt. 19:6 ESV). Likewise, Eliezer seeks the spouse God "appointed," *hōkaḥtā*, often a term for the verdict of the divine court (e.g., Isa. 2:4). This will demonstrate God's "covenant fidelity" or *ḥesed* to Abraham. Thus, Isaac's marriage covenant is intrinsically entwined with God's covenant with Abraham.

Eliezer invokes the divine assistance to locate the proper bride, but his chosen sign to identify her is also full of human prudence. Any young woman who would volunteer, uncompelled, to draw water for ten camels (see Gen. 24:10)—which can drink thirty gallons each—is not only generously kind but also physically strong, both good qualities for the future mother of the tribal chief! Recognizing in Rebekah the answer to his prayers, Eliezer produces valuable betrothal gifts— a nose ring and bracelets of heavy gold—and thanks God for his "mercy" and "truth" (*ḥesed* and *'ĕmet*), a word pair for "covenant fidelity" frequent in Psalms.

The sacred author marks the solemnity of the bridal negotiation for Rebekah by treating it with great detail and repetition (Gen. 24:24–39). Rebekah's

---

6. William D. Reyburn and Euan McG. Fry, *A Handbook on Genesis*, UBS Helps for Translators (New York: United Bible Societies, 1998), 521.

7. Second masculine singular perfect *hiphil* of *yākaḥ*.

mother and brother are willing, but the consent of the bride is necessary: "'Will you go with this man?' She said, 'I will go [*'ēlēk*]'" (v. 58). This bridal act of faith—anticipating Mary's *fiat*—complements that of Abraham. Both Rebekah and Abraham have to leave family and depart, sight unseen, to a promised land. Abraham was told:

> Go [*lek-ləkā*] from your country and your kindred and your father's house to the land that I will show you. (Gen. 12:1)

"To go" (*hālak*) is key: Abraham "went" (*wayyēlek 'abrām*, Gen. 12:4); Rebekah poignantly says, "I will go" (*'ēlēk*, 24:58). Rebekah's faith is complementary (*kənegdô*, 2:18, 20) to Abraham's: a fitting spouse for Isaac, who has shared his father's faith.

The narrative concludes with Isaac and Rebekah beholding each other from a distance (Gen. 24:62–66), a scene unnecessary to the plot but painted with delicate beauty and nuptial eroticism. Then the conclusion:

> Isaac brought her into the tent of Sarah his mother and took Rebekah, and she became his wife, and he loved her. So Isaac was comforted after his mother's death. (24:67 ESV)

The mother's tent was the place of betrothal and consummation (Song 3:4; 8:2). "Take" (*lāqaḥ*) here means "marry," including consummation. A single word, *wayye'ĕhābehā* ("he loved her"), summarizes the couple's happiness and contentment. Reference to "his mother's death" ties this chapter closely to the preceding: the vacant matriarchate is filled with a woman of faith.

The Late Marriage of Abraham

Strangely, after the beautiful narrative of Genesis 24, Abraham takes another wife, Keturah, who bears him six sons who give rise to Syrian and Arabic tribes, some of whom (e.g., Midian and the Midianites) become antagonists of Israel. As with Hagar and Ishmael, here also consistent monogamy could have prevented great grief for Israel.

Nonetheless, in death Abraham lays down not with fecund Keturah but with "Sarah his wife" in the cave of Machpelah (Gen. 25:9–10). As noted, the patriarchs are all monogamous in death, paired with their first wife.

The Happy Marriage of Isaac and Rebekah

Isaac's life, in contrast to that of his father and son, was relatively peaceful, and this is in large measure due to his happy, affectionate marriage to Rebekah, signaled through several deft comments. Note not only the "love" and "comfort" mentioned in Genesis 24:67 but also that Isaac publicly "fondles" or "caresses" Rebekah (26:8) and is the only patriarch recorded as praying for his wife. Faced with barrenness, Abraham and Sarah resort to surrogacy, but Isaac prays and is heard (25:21).

Rebekah in the Court of Abimelech

Unfortunately, Isaac follows his father's example by passing off his wife as his sister while sojourning in a foreign land (i.e., Gerar, Gen. 26:6–11). However, Isaac's public affection for Rebekah exposes the true relationship: "Abimelech . . . saw Isaac [*yiṣḥāq*] fondling [*məṣaḥēq*] Rebekah" (26:8), employing wordplay on the root *ṣ-ḥ-q*, "to laugh, play, sport."[8] Isaac is quite infatuated with his wife! Abimelech rebukes Isaac's deception (vv. 9–10) and decrees protection on Isaac and Rebekah (v. 11)—a stark contrast to the Sodomites in hosting strangers (19:4–11). The text valorizes Abimelech as defender of marital exclusivity. Abraham attempts this ploy twice (12:10–20; 20:1–18), Isaac once (26:6–11), Jacob never. The patriarchs learn, but slowly.

The Role of Rebekah in the Inheritance of the Covenant

The adult life of Isaac spans just one chapter (Gen. 26), and by Genesis 27:1 he is old, nearly blind, and almost helpless. Rebekah now is the force directing the family's history and inheritance—and even the divine economy itself. How wise it was of Abraham to find Isaac a wife of virtue who worshiped the same God, for now, as so often happens in marriage, one spouse becomes incapacitated, and the welfare of all rests in the hands of the healthy partner. So it is in Genesis 27, where Isaac foolishly conspires to ignore Esau's sworn sale of his birthright to Jacob (25:29–34), to overlook his bigamy with foreign women (26:34–35), and to grant him the covenantal blessing anyway (27:1–4).

---

8. Some translate *məṣaḥēq* as "laughing," but it probably means "playing [with his wife]"—that is, foreplay (cf. BDB 850a). The root *ṣ-ḥ-q* can indicate sexual contact; see Gen. 39:17; Exod. 32:6.

Rebekah conceives a counterplot to foil Isaac's plan (vv. 5–17), which entails Jacob impersonating Esau (vv. 18–29). She presses Jacob into it (vv. 6–10) despite his protestations (vv. 11–12), relying on her maternal authority: "My son, obey my word as I command you. Go . . ." (vv. 8–9). Rebekah takes on herself any curse or wrath of her husband, Isaac (v. 13), knowing that his infatuation with her will forestall any harm. She knows that the way to Isaac's heart is through the food that he "loves" (*'āhēb*), since she herself is the only other object of Isaac's "love" (*'āhēb*) mentioned in the text (cf. 24:67). The plan succeeds. Jacob receives his father's covenant blessing that was already his by purchase of the birthright from his rash and capricious brother (25:29–34). Rebekah is a better judge of the character of her sons than Isaac, who follows his physical passion for Esau's savory game (27:3–4). Again, she uses her maternal authority (vv. 42–43) to prevent bloodshed when Esau discovers the ruse, commanding Jacob to flee to her brother Laban (vv. 43–45), easily persuading Isaac himself to endorse and bless Jacob's flight (27:46–28:5).

The Marriages of Jacob/Israel (Gen. 28–36)

The Courtship of Rachel

Isaac commissions Jacob to seek a wife from the house of Bethuel in Paddan-aram (Gen. 28:1–5), echoing Abraham's commission of Eliezer (24:3) to find a wife for Isaac from his own people. At issue is not race but disparity of cult and culture. Isaac and Rebekah have failed to impress this on Esau, but they still can on Jacob. So, recapitulating Genesis 24, Jacob sets out for Paddan-aram to find a wife in Genesis 29. Common themes include meeting the prospective bride at a well (24:10–21//29:1–12), the bride's great beauty (24:16//29:17), and love at first sight from a distance (24:62–67//29:10–12). But Jacob comes with no wealth for a bride-price; he must work seven long years to earn his bride, but they seem brief because of his love for her (29:20). As Isaac has truly loved Rebekah, so now Jacob loves Rachel.

An Unexpected Marriage to Two Sisters

Finally, Jacob speaks to Laban: "Give me my wife, for my days are completed and I want to go in to her" (Gen. 29:21 AT). The request is understandable and legitimate, if crassly stated. But Laban slips his older daughter, Leah, into the bridal chamber, and Jacob takes her to be Rachel in the dark, under the influence of wedding wine. In the morning comes the shock. Jacob the great trickster is outtricked by Laban. Laban promises Rachel after another week, but only for a further seven years of service. So Jacob takes Rachel to be his wife also, and he loves her more than Leah (29:30). Laban's trickery ruins the prospects for happiness for three innocent young people. The first wife should be the only wife, and she deserves love (Deut. 24:5). Leah is the first wife, yet she is not loved by her husband. Jacob's intentions have only been monogamous and only for Rachel, yet Rachel will ever be the second wife.

The "Baby Battle" of Leah and Rachel

As consolation for Leah's loneliness, the Lord blesses her with great fertility. She bears children abundantly in the forlorn hope of winning Jacob's love: "Surely now my husband will love me" (Gen. 29:32); "Now this time my husband will be joined to me" (v. 34). The pathos is palpable. The reader cannot help but be drawn in and share her sorrow. Meanwhile, Leah consistently credits the Lord for the gift of children: "The LORD has looked upon my affliction" (v. 32); "The LORD . . . has given me this son" (v. 33); "This time I will praise the LORD" (v. 35).

Leah's fertility provokes envy and anger and disrupts the love of Rachel and Jacob. Rachel assaults Jacob: "Give me children, or I shall die!" (Gen. 30:1). And Jacob responds in anger: "Am I in the place of God, who has withheld from you the fruit of the womb?" (v. 2). Bigamy leads to disharmony. Rachel imitates Sarah by proposing surrogacy: "Here is my maid Bilhah; go in to her" (v. 3). The reader knows this is foolish based on the Hagar-Ishmael example. Rachel names her two sons by Bilhah based on the conflict with her sister, as if children were salvos in a war of envy between two mothers. Leah responds in kind, giving Jacob Zilpah, who also bears two sons. And Leah herself is not done yet: God "listens" to Leah (v. 17), and she bears two more sons, saying, "Now my husband will honor me" (v. 20). She also bears a daughter, Dinah (v. 21). Now the reader begins to sympathize with Rachel—beautiful, beloved, but barren, her fertile sister having trounced her in maternal combat. Yet God finally has compassion on the humbled Rachel: "God remembered [zākar] Rachel and . . . opened her womb" (v. 22). Hebrew zākar—literally, "remember"—means to renew fidelity with a covenant partner, as with Noah (8:1; 9:15–16) and Abraham (19:29), with whom Rachel now stands. Suffering

St. Augustine on the Patriarchs' Polygamy

The polygamy of the patriarchs was potentially scandalous to the ancient Christian community, and St. Augustine took pains to explain that it was a concession that God allowed for the times, not a failure of the patriarchs to control their passions:

> Among the ancient fathers, of course, it was permissible to take another woman, with the permission of one's wife, and to produce children that were shared in common. . . . [But] today there is not the same need of procreation that there was in the past. . . . In the past, they took many wives blamelessly. . . . The holy men in ancient times [had] intercourse with women, making use of the right of marriage not out of desire but out of duty. For sexual intercourse is to the health of the human race what food is to the health of a human being, and neither exists without some carnal pleasure (*delectatio carnalis*). In the same manner, just as the fathers in New Testament times took food because of their duty to care for others and just as they ate it while enjoying the natural pleasure of the flesh . . . , so, likewise, the fathers in Old Testament times had sexual intercourse because of their duty to care for others. The natural pleasure that they enjoyed did not give way to any sort of irrational or forbidden lust, nor should it be compared either to the wickedness of fornication or to the intemperance of married persons. Indeed, it was the same vein of charity, which once led them to produce children in a fleshly way, which now leads us to propagate in a spiritual way for the sake of our mother, Jerusalem. Only the difference of times caused the fathers to do different works.[a]

a. Augustine, *On the Good of Marriage* 17–18, in *Marriage and Sexuality in Early Christianity*, ed. David G. Hunter (Minneapolis: Fortress, 2018), 203–4.

the humiliation of barrenness, Rachel becomes more like Noah and Abraham, who suffered for the sake of God's covenant and thus came to experience God's grace.

Jacob's Return to Canaan

By the end of the Leah-Rachel baby battle in Genesis 30:24, all but one of Jacob's twelve sons are born. From Genesis 30:25 to 33:20, Jacob decides to flee from Laban but is unwittingly thrown in the path of Esau. During his flight from Laban, we observe a kind of reconciliation between the otherwise rivalrous sisters, who become united in resentment against their father, who has treated them as property (31:14–16). Rachel now channels Rebekah and, in the great family tradition of trickery, attempts to rectify the injustice she feels her father has done to her by stealing her father's household idols, called *tərāpîm*. In the common law of northwest Mesopotamia, possession of the *tərāpîm* greatly strengthened one's claim to be heir of an estate. By stealing them, Rachel intended to position Joseph as primary heir of Laban upon his decease.

Laban pursues the fleeing Jacob and searches his camp for his *tərāpîm*, but he ends up unsuccessful due to another clever ruse by Rachel—one worthy of her mother-in-law, Rebekah (Gen. 31:33–35). She sits on top of the idols while complaining of ritual uncleanliness. Empty-handed and disgraced, Laban is forced to listen to Jacob's diatribe (vv. 36–42), walk back his threats of force (v. 43), and reconcile with Jacob by means of a covenant (vv. 44–55). The concern for his daughters, the wives of Jacob, is instructive for what it reveals about the nature of marriage:

> [Laban] said, "The LORD watch between you and me. . . . If you oppress [*ʿānāh*] my daughters, or if you take wives besides my daughters, . . . God is witness between you and me." (31:49–50 ESV)

We see a humbler, more sober Laban, outtricked by his youngest daughter and berated by his son-in-law, now suddenly concerned for his daughters, unlike his previous indifference (31:14–15). Aside from mutual nonaggression (v. 52), the covenantal conditions Laban lays on Jacob all concern the treatment of the daughter-wives: First, they must not be "oppressed"—using the Hebrew verb *ʿānāh*, "humiliate, afflict, oppress," frequently through nonconsensual sexual relations (v. 50).[9] Laban's statement presumes that "oppression" of a wife contradicts the moral order enforced by the Lord. Moreover, Laban prohibits Jacob from taking "wives besides my daughters" (v. 50 ESV), clearly because additional wives would rival his daughters and their children for Jacob's affections, material support, and inheritance. Consistently applied, this principle leads to monogamy, the only marital situation without rivalry for the husband's resources. The law of Moses strictly forbids a man to marry two sisters (Lev. 18:18), doubtless a reaction to the sorry love triangle of Jacob, Leah, and Rachel.

---

9. See Gen. 34:2; Exod. 21:14; Deut. 22:24, 29; Judg. 19:24; 20:5; 2 Sam. 13:12, 14, 22, 32; Lam. 5:11; Ezek. 22:10–11.

The Rape of Dinah in Shechem

Having reconciled with Laban and Esau, Jacob arrives in safety to the city of Shechem. There, another drama unfolds that is relevant to our discussion of marriage:

> Now Dinah the daughter of Leah, whom she had borne to Jacob, went out to see the women of the land. And when Shechem the son of Hamor the Hivite, the prince of the land, saw her, he seized her and lay with her, thus humiliating [ʿānāh] her. And his soul cleaved [dābaq] to Dinah the daughter of Jacob. He loved the young woman and spoke to the heart of the young woman.[10] So Shechem spoke to his father Hamor, saying, "Get me this girl for my wife." (Gen. 34:1–4 AT)

Tragically, in many ways Shechem has the right disposition toward Dinah for marriage; for instance, his soul *cleaves* (*dābaq*) to her, evoking Genesis 2:24 and the union of man and wife. Yet though Shechem's love is sincere, his behavior is intolerably preemptive and entitled. He ruins the chance for what might have been a happy and equitable marriage with Dinah by enjoying her physically without first establishing the safe and proper structure and context for that enjoyment to take place, the covenant of matrimony. Hamor attempts to negotiate for Dinah to marry Shechem, even to the point of accepting circumcision, but Simeon and Levi massacre the men of the town in vengeance for treating their "sister like a whore" (34:31 AT), earning rebuke (34:30) and ultimately curse (49:5–7) from their father.

This text is tragic and morally complex, but it clearly stresses the gravity of the sexual abuse of a young woman. This offense is so grave to the woman and to her family that it is all but impossible to make right the disorder it introduces into society, even when genuine love and affection exist. When the proper order for forming a union between man and woman is disregarded, the consequences are liable to fly out of control. Sexual intimacy lies close to the heart of the self-conception and dignity of the human person; thus, there is no such thing as "casual" sex.

The Death of Rachel

The slaughter of the Shechemites forces Jacob to continue on his nomadic ways, journeying to Bethel for a covenant renewal (Gen. 35:1–15) and back

10. Hebrew *dibbēr ʿal-lēb*, an idiom for speaking tenderly; see BDB 181b §5.

(vv. 16–21). Tragically, Rachel dies in childbirth on the return trip, in the very process of bearing the son for whom she had prayed so earnestly, immortalizing her prayer in the name of his older brother (30:24). In the agony of her death, she names her son Ben-oni—"son of my affliction"— but Jacob renames him Benjamin, "son of my right hand," the symbol of strength, honor, and dignity (cf. Ps. 110:1). He also builds a pillar over the tomb of his deceased wife, which remains "to this day" in Bethlehem (Gen. 35:20 ESV). Thus, a sorrowful end falls on the romance of Jacob and Rachel, which begins as auspiciously as that of Isaac and Rebekah but, due to the craftiness of Laban, is derailed by the interposition of an older sister, who herself is innocent in the matter and is an equally tragic figure in many ways. Polygamy leads to tragedy.

Reuben's Illicit Relationship with Bilhah

There is a final narrative remark in the Jacob cycle: "While Israel lived in that land, Reuben went and lay with Bilhah his father's concubine. And Israel heard of it" (Gen. 35:22 ESV). In the ancient Near East, it was not uncommon for the son of a leader (chieftain, king, etc.) to marry the younger wives of his deceased father as part of the succession of leadership. Thus, the wives retained their place and rank in society, while also reinforcing the legitimacy of the son-successor. Therefore, such marriages were socially approved, *provided the father had died* (cf. 1 Chron. 2:24). For a son to take his father's wives during his lifetime was a social statement that the father was as good as dead and that the son was taking over (cf. 2 Sam. 16:21; 20:3). Reuben underestimates Jacob, and his efforts backfire, losing him the birthright (Gen. 49:4). Mosaic law later condemns a father and son sleeping with the same woman (Lev. 18:8, 15; 20:11–12), along with any other sexual union that confuses the kinship relations established by marriage.

Marriage in the Joseph Cycle (Gen. 37–50)

The Curse of Maternal Rivalry

The death of Isaac ends the Jacob cycle in Genesis 35:29, and the genealogy (*tōladôt*) of Esau (Gen. 36) transitions to the Joseph cycle (Gen. 37–50). If one could describe Genesis 12–36 as the history of the patriarchal marriages,

Genesis 37–50 details the sad results of the polygamy pressed on the last patriarch, Jacob/Israel. From rivalry of wives stems rivalry of their sons:

> Joseph, being seventeen years old, was pasturing the flock with his brothers. He
> was a boy with the sons of Bilhah and Zilpah, his father's wives. And Joseph
> brought a bad report of them to their father. Now Israel loved Joseph more
> than any other of his sons, because he was the son of his old age. And he made
> him a robe of many colors. But when his brothers saw that their father loved
> him more than all his brothers, they hated him and could not speak peacefully
> to him. (Gen. 37:2–4 ESV)

Joseph is not just Jacob's "son of his old age" but also the firstborn son of
his favorite wife. Rachel is the real reason Jacob favors Joseph and Benjamin
(see 42:38; 44:20, 27–29). History repeats itself: Isaac was once mocked by
Ishmael, the older son of the concubine Hagar (21:9). Now Joseph contends
with the older sons of his father's concubines, Bilhah and Zilpah (37:2).

Jacob's affection for Rachel skews the treatment of his sons. The many-
colored garment befits only his firstborn and heir (Gen. 37:3);[11] thus, he favors
his favorite wife's firstborn rather than his own firstborn, Reuben (contra
Deut. 21:15–17). This provokes the brothers' anger, which they direct toward
Joseph: "They hated him and could not speak peacefully to him" (Gen. 37:4
ESV). Joseph exacerbates the situation by relating dreams portraying himself
as leader of the family (vv. 5–11). Jacob rebukes him (v. 10), but his own
favoritism may be fostering Joseph's grandiose visions.

Joseph's Captivity and Triumph

The brothers' anger overflows in violence, and they sell Joseph as a slave
destined for Egypt. There, Joseph suffers a series of misadventures until a set of
providential coincidences enables him to perform divinatory service to Pharaoh
himself, resulting in his meteoric rise to the position of vizier or prime minister of Egypt. When famine strikes the whole region, Joseph's brothers find
themselves traveling to Egypt for food, and once there they are forced to deal
with Pharaoh's representative, none other than Joseph himself. With the power
dynamics now completely reversed, Joseph finds himself torn between longing
and resentment, and he toys with his brothers by contriving situations that place
one or more of the brothers under duress, to see how the others respond. When

---

11. Hebrew *kәtōnet passîm*, "robe of colors" or "robe of sleeves"—i.e., a garment of one
not required to do manual labor. See Reyburn and Fry, *Handbook on Genesis*, 848.

Rachel's second son, Benjamin, is framed for a crime, the unhappy situation appears as if it will degenerate and lead to the premature death of their father, but the tension and conflict are finally broken by the selflessness of Judah, who, though a son of Leah, sets aside the "maternal politics" and offers his life as a ransom for Rachel's Benjamin, out of love for Jacob, their common father (Gen. 44:14–34). Judah is loyal to his father even though he knows full well that his father will never love him as much as he loves Joseph and Benjamin. This act of selflessness on the part of the very brother who first proposed to sell Joseph as a slave (37:26–27) leads Joseph to lose his composure and reveal his true identity to his brothers (45:1–15). In time, the extended family is reconciled, and Jacob and all his descendants relocate to Egypt. Before his death, Jacob blesses his sons roughly in order of their mothers: first the Leah sons (49:1–15), then the sons of the maidservants (vv. 16–21), and finally Rachel's sons (vv. 22–27). Jacob disinherits his oldest three sons—Reuben for incest, and Simeon and Levi for murderous violence—leaving Judah as the oldest son not under a curse. To Judah, then, comes the promise of rulership in the family, the "scepter," and a future king (vv. 8–12). Nonetheless, Jacob's favoritism for Rachel's sons persists to the end, and upon Joseph he heaps praise and blessing and describes him as "prince" (*nāzîr*) among his brothers (49:26 NABRE). Jacob creates ambiguity by promising Judah the "scepter" (*šēbeṭ*, v. 10) but calling Joseph the "prince," complicating the issue of which brother and which tribe should assume leadership of the twelve. This foreshadows the eventual split, after the reigns of the Judeans David and Solomon, between the southern tribes (ruled by Judah) and the northern tribes (ruled by the Josephite tribe of Ephraim).

The Marriages of Jacob's Sons: Judah and Joseph

The only marital information we are given in the Joseph cycle concerns the two most prominent brothers, Judah and Joseph, from whom most of the kings of Israel will later be taken (e.g., 2 Sam. 5:1–3; 1 Kings 11:26–40; 12:20).

After all the effort to procure non-Canaanite wives for the patriarchs, Judah "saw the daughter of a certain Canaanite whose name was Shua, and he took her and went in to her" (Gen. 38:2 AT). This woman—simply called Bath-shua ("daughter of Shua") in 1 Chronicles 2:3—bears Judah three sons: Er, Onan, and Shelah.

The narrative then tells us that "Judah took a wife for Er his firstborn, and her name was Tamar" (Gen. 38:6 ESV). Tamar surely is a Canaanite (despite later Jewish traditions to the contrary); had she been related to the clan of Abraham, her genealogy would have been noted. That said, Er is wicked and God slays him, so Jacob weds his son Onan to Tamar to "raise up offspring for [his] brother" (v. 8). This is so-called levirate marriage (from the Latin *levir*, "brother-in-law"), an arrangement in which a man marries his brother's widow in order to provide his brother a successor and his sister-in-law a son to care for her in old age. Onan, however, refuses to cooperate with this socially approved relationship:

> But Onan knew that the offspring would not be his. So whenever he went in to his brother's wife he would waste the semen on the ground, so as not to give offspring to his brother. And what he did was wicked in the sight of the LORD, and he put him to death also. (Gen. 38:9–10 ESV)

The Church has understood Onan's act to be a form of contraception, the deliberate frustration of the marital act, rendering it unfruitful. Onan is denying Er a successor and Tamar a son to support her; moreover, he is debasing their physical relationship by not giving himself to Tamar, but rather enjoying her without regard for her well-being. This misuse of the one-flesh union of matrimony is very serious in the eyes of the Lord, such that he strikes Onan dead, leading to the conclusion that his sin is "mortal"—that is, one that leads to death. The Christian tradition has long understood this incident to condemn intentionally infertile forms of sexual intercourse.

With both Er and Onan dead, Tamar should go to Shelah—but he is not yet of marriageable age. But even when he is, Judah does not give Tamar to him. So Tamar poses as a cult prostitute, seduces Judah, and conceives twins by him (Gen. 38:12–19). When the pregnancy becomes public knowledge, she faces death as punishment for fornication but demonstrates the paternity of her unborn children by producing Judah's personal identification—his signet, cord, and staff (vv. 24–26). Publicly disgraced, Judah confesses: "She is more righteous than I, inasmuch as I did not give her to my son Shelah" (38:26). Judah takes Tamar back into his household and supports her for the rest of his life, but he has no relations with her. Tamar gives birth to twins, Perez and Zerah, forefathers of most of Judah's descendants.[12]

---

12. Cf. 1 Chron. 2:1–4:23. The descendants of Perez and Zerah make up all of 1 Chron. 2:1–4:20, but those of Shelah only 1 Chron. 4:21–23.

St. Jerome and St. Augustine on Onan

The Fathers understood the Onan narrative to be teaching, among other things, the gravity of the intentional separation of procreation from intercourse. Jerome muses:

> But I wonder why he [the heretic Jovinianus] set Judah and Tamar before us for an example, unless perchance even harlots give him pleasure; or Onan who was slain because he grudged his brother seed. Does he imagine that we approve of any sexual intercourse except for the procreation of children?[a]

Likewise, Augustine writes:

> Intercourse even with one's legitimate wife is unlawful and wicked where the conception of the offspring is prevented. Onan, the son of Judah, did this and the Lord killed him for it.[b]

a. Jerome, *Against Jovinian* 1.20 (*NPNF²* 6:361).
b. Augustine, *On Adulterous Marriages* (*De adulterinis coniugiis*) 2.12, quoted in Paul VI, *Humanae vitae* 14.

All this reflects very poorly on Judah. After all the effort Abraham and Isaac expended to avoid marrying their sons to Canaanites, Judah takes a Canaanite wife for himself and (apparently) also for his eldest son. Both of Judah's older sons are so wicked that they merit direct divine retribution, the second being so perverted as to defile the marital act itself. Judah himself is not above frequenting pagan prostitutes, and he unwittingly commits an act of incest later defined as a capital offense (Lev. 20:12), which ironically becomes the source of the majority of his descendants. Thus, we discover that the tribe of Judah—the largest, most powerful, and royal tribe—is half-Canaanite through its ancestral mothers Tamar and Bath-shua and mostly traces its origin to an incestuous act of fornication under the guise of pagan cult prostitution. Surely, Genesis 38 is reminiscent of at least two other episodes in Genesis: the shameful origins of the Moabites and Ammonites through the incest of Lot and his daughters (Gen. 19:30–38), and the shameful origin of the Canaanites through Ham's incest with his mother.[13] This narrative, then, would align

13. For Ham's offense as maternal incest, see Bergsma and Hahn, "Noah's Nakedness."

the Judahites, the royal tribe of Israel, with Israel's most hated enemies: the Canaanites, Moabites, and Ammonites.[14]

The only character who comes across positively in Genesis 38 is, ironically, Tamar herself. Though a Canaanitess, she is more righteous than her two wicked Israelite husbands and her Israelite father-in-law. She resembles Jacob/Israel, because she is willing to engage in manipulation (Gen. 25:29–34) or even deception (27:1–29) in order to remain within the covenant given to Abraham and his descendants. She resembles Rebekah (27:1–29), who tricks her husband in order to gain the covenant blessing for her favored son, and she also resembles Rachel (31:33–35), who deceives her father in order to gain the family inheritance for her sons. Thus, Tamar shows herself worthy of the people of Israel by exhibiting the "covenant hunger" that characterizes Jacob/Israel and the matriarchs. But everything in Genesis 38 is counternormative, an example of how *not* to go about procuring and betrothing a spouse.

The Chastity and Marriage of Joseph

It may not be accidental that the immediately following narrative shows Joseph's sexual behavior in stark contrast with Judah's. Joseph is sold in Egypt as a slave to Potiphar, a high-ranking official, and he quickly rises to the position of steward in his household. Young and handsome Joseph gains the attentions of Potiphar's wife, who attempts to seduce him. But Joseph refuses to sleep with his master's wife: "How then can I do this great wickedness and sin against God?" (Gen. 39:9 ESV). Even though Potiphar and his wife are foreigners and pagans from Joseph's perspective, to violate their marital bond through an adulterous act is still a "great wickedness" and indeed a "sin against God," here using the universal name of God (*'ĕlōhîm*) rather than the unique name for God used among the descendants of Abraham (YHWH, "the Lord"). Joseph's statement implies that God is the author or at least the defender of the marital bond, even among pagans, and thus the proposed adulterous act would not merely be a sin among human beings but a sin against God himself.

14. On the interpretation of the Tamar episode, see John S. Bergsma, "A 'Samaritan' Pentateuch? The Implications of the Pro-Northern Tendency of the Common Pentateuch," in *Paradigm Change in Pentateuchal Research*, ed. Matthias Armgardt, Benjamin Kilchör, and Markus Zehnder, BZABR 22 (Wiesbaden: Harrassowitz, 2019), 287–300, esp. 292–93; and Moshe Shamah, *Recalling the Covenant: A Contemporary Commentary on the Five Books of the Torah*, 2nd ed. (New York: Ktav, 2015), 183–86.

Paradoxically, Joseph's noble behavior—so different from that of Judah, who didn't hesitate to sleep with a roadside pagan cult prostitute—does not bring him any immediate benefit; rather, it provokes a vengeful attitude in Potiphar's wife, who frames him for seduction. Potiphar consigns him to the royal prison, but even there he rises in prominence once again. When the opportunity presents itself, he performs a service to Pharaoh by interpreting his dreams, and so he gains the office of prime minister over all of Egypt. Among the many honors that Pharaoh grants Joseph as prime minister is the hand of Asenath, the daughter of Potiphera, the priest of On, who bears him two sons, Ephraim and Manasseh. On is the Egyptian city known to the Greeks as Heliopolis, the center of the cult of the sun god Amon-Re, the chief deity of Egypt. Thus, Potiphera—and by extension, his daughter—would have enjoyed a lofty place in the social hierarchy of ancient Egypt, making Asenath a suitable bride for the new prime minister. Their union would also help establish a place for Joseph, an unknown Semite from Canaan, within the Egyptian caste structure and kinship networks as the son-in-law of the priest of Amon-Re.

It is interesting that Asenath's Egyptian ethnicity and connection to a pagan cult seems to give the sacred author no pause, even though in later Jewish literature much effort is spent developing an apologetic narrative for Joseph's pagan, Egyptian wife. But then again, the Egyptians are never despised in the Old Testament in the same way as some other ethnic groups, and inter-marriage with them did not seem to be so frowned upon (Gen. 16:1; Deut. 23:7; 1 Kings 7:8). The Old Testament also does not judge harshly those who are forced into marriages with non-Israelites for political reasons, as we shall see later in the case of Esther and others.

Summary of the Patriarchal Narratives through the Lens of Matrimony

Marriage figures prominently in the patriarchal narratives. The Abraham and Jacob cycles (Gen. 12–36) could be described as the accounts of the marriages of the patriarchs, and the Joseph cycle (Gen. 37–50) could be portrayed as the outworking of the marital rivalry in the household of Jacob. The sacred author devotes extensive attention to matters of courtship and marriage (24:1–67; 27:41–30:24), and the marriages of the patriarchs are contrasted with nonmar-ital procreation (19:30–38) and misuses of the marital act (19:1–11; 34:1–31) that characterize persons and groups outside of—or opposed to—the heirs of the covenant with Abraham. Repeatedly, the violation of the integrity of the marital union through adultery or premarital fornication are portrayed as grave sins that provoke fearsome punishment from God or other agents.[15] Particularly in the case of Abraham and Sarah, it becomes clear that, although the covenant promises are stated as if to Abraham alone (12:1–3; 15:4–6), it is actually the union of Abraham with his wife Sarah that God intends to bless (17:15–21). The spouses of the patriarchs are important agents in their own right, and particularly in the case of Rebekah, they are proactive and instrumental in directing the course of covenant inheritance (27:1–28:5). None of the patriarchs choose polygamy.[16] Abraham accepts it at the urging of Sarah (16:2), and Jacob has it pressed on him by Laban (29:22–27) and his own wives, Leah and Rachel (30:3, 9). This is in contrast to characters who leave the line of covenant inheritance, like Esau, who *chooses* three wives (36:1–3).

Throughout the narratives, there is a strong sense of divine providence over conception and birth. These are continually acknowledged as not merely natural human phenomena but gifts of God under his providential control.[17]

The ideal marriage in Genesis is Isaac and Rebekah's. First, no expense or effort is spared in the effort to find a suitable spouse (Gen. 24:1–67), one who shares the same religious commitments (vv. 31, 50–51) and demonstrates virtue (vv. 18–21). Rebekah turns out to be that suitably complementary (*kənegdô*) spouse, showing herself to be a woman of virtue, particularly of generosity (v. 19) and faith (v. 58), like Abraham (18:1–5; 15:6). There is mutual consent (24:57–58), not coercion, and monogamy, not polygamy. Isaac loves Rebekah (v. 67), prays for her (25:21), and shows her physical affection (26:8). For her part, Rebekah saves Isaac from rash deeds (27:1–28:5) and prompts him toward wise action (27:46–28:5), albeit sometimes by ethically dubious means.

On the other hand, the marriages of Abraham and Jacob illustrate what we have called the *implicit critique of polygamy*. In Genesis 1–11, monogamy is the divine intention prior to the fall, bigamy is invented by one of the wickedest men in history, polygamy provokes the flood, and everyone on the ark is monogamous. In Genesis 12–50, bigamy with Hagar causes grief for all

15. Gen. 12:17–20; 20:1–18; 34:1–31; 35:22; 39:7–9; 49:4.
16. The sacred author portrays Abraham's marriage to Keturah as taking place after Sarah's death (25:1–6).
17. Gen. 15:1–6; 16:2, 10; 17:6, 16–21; 18:13–14; 20:17–18; 21:1–2; 22:17; 25:21; 26:4, 24; 28:3, 14; 29:31–33; 30:2, 6, 17–18, 20, 22–24; 32:12; 33:5; 48:4, 9, 16; 49:25.

parties (16:1–16) and is linked to the fall (3:1–24) by verbal allusion. Jacob's marriage to Rachel promises at first to be a recapitulation of the happy union of Isaac and Rebekah (29:1–22), but the trickery of Laban forces heartbreak onto Jacob and the two daughters (vv. 23–30). The sister-wives enter into intense rivalry for reproductive prowess (29:31–30:24), exacerbated by recourse to surrogacy (30:1–13). This rivalry carries over into the relationships of their sons (37:1–44:17). Only the selflessness of Judah (44:18–45:15) finally breaks the cycle of envy and bitterness. Polygamy inevitably leads to grief. Poetically, in death each patriarch rests with his first wife alone (49:29–32).

The Joseph cycle (Gen. 37–50) looks closely only at the marriages of Joseph and Judah. Joseph's marriage is conventional. Pharaoh gives him the daughter of a high-ranking Egyptian priest (41:45), who bears him two sons (vv. 50–52), who inherit the patriarchal promises from Jacob/Israel himself (48:1–22). In contrast, the marital history of Judah (38:1–30) is scandalous for the father of the royal dynasty and leading tribe (49:10–11). Judah marries a Canaanite and fathers most of his descendants by fornicating with his Canaanite daughter-in-law under the guise of cultic prostitution (38:12–30). The narrative is probably meant to humble the powerful Judeans. Despite her deceptive and immoral actions, Tamar, the Canaanite mother of most Judeans, is portrayed as a woman of robust character who takes daring action to secure a place for herself and her descendants in the covenant of Abraham. In this, she resembles other patriarchs and matriarchs, like Jacob/Israel and Rebekah.

5

"That He May Make His Wife Happy"

Marriage in the Mosaic Covenant

The book of Exodus marks an epochal shift as we move from the era of the patriarchs to the career of Moses. The intense focus on the courtship and marriage of individual ancestors is replaced by laws governing the marriage practices of the people of Israel. These laws both reveal and obscure the ideal of matrimony. At times they seek to preserve the essential features of matrimony, while at other times they make accommodations for the recalcitrance or "hardness of heart" of Israel and humanity generally.

The books Exodus through Deuteronomy contribute to a biblical theology of marriage in at least two ways: First, the covenant relationship between Israel and God possesses a spousal dimension discernible already in the Pentateuch but expounded more clearly in later Scriptures (e.g., the Latter Prophets). Second, the marital laws of the Mosaic covenant reveal both God's ideals and human weaknesses.

The Covenant between Israel and the Lord as Nuptial Union

In the Pentateuch itself, explicit nuptial imagery is not applied to the covenant mediated by Moses at Sinai, as is done in the Prophets,[1] yet

---

1. Isa. 54:4–14; 62:1–5; Jer. 2:1–3, 20–25; 2:29–3:20; Ezek. 16:1–63; 23:1–49; Hosea 1–3.

the covenant is described in such a way as to lend itself to later nuptial reinterpretation.

The opening chapters of Exodus recount the plagues, exodus, and journey to Sinai (Exod. 1–19), where the covenant between God and Israel is formalized and solemnized (20:1–24:8). The prophets understand the exodus and wilderness journey as a courtship (Jer. 2:1–3; Hosea 2:14–15) and the ceremony at Sinai as a betrothal (Ezek. 16:8; Hosea 2:18–23). The texts lend themselves to these analogies. The proclamation of the law in Exodus 20–23 is analogous to the reading of the marriage contract, which may have formed part of the ancient wedding rite. The ceremony recorded in Exodus 24:1–8 actually forms the covenantal bond. The people, in the role of the bride, express their consent to the terms of the covenant just proclaimed: "All the words which the LORD has spoken we will do" (24:3). It is likely that ancient marriage rites also included ritual expressions of consent. Moses, with the help of some "young men of the sons of Israel" (v. 5 AT), offers sacrifices and, taking the blood of the sacrifices, sprinkles half on the altar (v. 6) and half on the people (v. 8). The altar symbolizes the presence and participation of God. The blood equally distributed on God (i.e., the altar) and the people indicates that the parties enter the covenant on the basis of mutuality, albeit not a strict equality. Blood represents kinship, the sharing of a common bloodline; a covenant forms new kinship bonds. Conversely, shed blood represents death, the punishment for breaking kinship commitments. The sprinkled blood of verse 8 indicates that Israel is now bound to the terms of the covenant on pain of death. The Sinai covenant forms a kinship bond between God and Israel analogous to a marriage. Thus, the ceremony proper is followed by a celebratory feast shared by God and the representatives of the people on Mount Sinai (vv. 9–11), a kind of "wedding feast" of God and Israel.

After a wedding, the new couple needs a home or chamber to begin their common life, and in Exodus, the nuptial chamber is the tabernacle, preparations for which commence immediately after the solemnization of the covenant (24:12–31:18). An act of "adultery" interrupts these preparations only forty days into the "honeymoon." The people press Aaron to make for them an idol, a golden calf, and the text tells us that "they rose up early . . . and offered . . . offerings; and the people sat down to eat and drink, and rose up *to play*" (32:6)—an expression employing the Hebrew ṣaḥēq, a sexual euphemism, used before of Isaac and Rebekah (Gen. 26:8). Scholars debate the prevalence of sexuality in ancient Near Eastern religion, but the Old Testament often associates paganism with illicit erotic activity. The description of idolatrous worship as committing "adultery" ($nā'ap$)[2] or "harlotry" ($zānāh$)[3] adds depth inasmuch as it literally involves nonmarital sexuality.

After the calf incident, Moses returns to the Lord on the mountain and admits, "This people has sinned a *great sin*" (Exod. 32:31 ESV), a term for adultery in Egyptian and Ugaritic literature.[4] Fittingly, when God renews the covenant at Moses's request (34:10), he reiterates its laws, beginning with the prohibition of the religion of the land's inhabitants (34:13), who "play the harlot [$zānāh$] after their gods" (v. 15) and will entrap Israel through intermarriage, such that Israel's sons will "play the harlot after their gods" (v. 16). Similarly, in Leviticus 17:7 we find a law compelling all animals to be ritually sacrificed only at the tabernacle, so that the Israelites "shall no more slay their sacrifices for satyrs [or demons], after whom they play the harlot." This imagery implies that the Sinai covenant is a marriage of God and Israel and that worship is analogous to the marital act.

After the renewal of the covenant in Exodus 34, the construction of the "nuptial chamber," the tabernacle, recommences (Exod. 35–40) until it is complete (40:33–38). This is not the end of Israel's infidelities, however. The story of Israel's covenant faithfulness during the wilderness wanderings after the year at Sinai (Num. 11–25) remains rocky and rebellious, culminating in a narrative recapitulation of the golden calf event. In Numbers 25, the men of Israel succumb to idolatry combined with sexual activity with the women of Moab at a place called Beth-peor:[5]

> While Israel dwelt in Shittim the people began to play the harlot [$zānāh$] with the daughters of Moab. These invited the people to the sacrifices of their gods, and the people ate, and bowed down to their gods. So Israel yoked himself to Baal of Peor. And the anger of the Lord was kindled against Israel. . . . And Moses said to the judges of Israel, "Every one of you slay his men who have yoked themselves to Baal of Peor."

2. Jer. 3:8–9; 13:27; Ezek. 16:32, 38; 23:37, 43, 45; Hosea 2:2; 3:1; 4:13–14.

3. E.g., Exod. 34:15–16; Lev. 17:7; Deut. 31:16.

4. See Raymond Westbrook, "Adultery in Ancient Near Eastern Law," *RB* 97, no. 4 (1990): 542–80, here 557n53.

5. Beth-peor translates as "House of [the god] Peor." The deity was called Baal Peor, meaning either "Lord Peor" or "the lord (i.e., god) of Peor." See Daniel I. Block, *The Gospel according to Moses: Theological and Ethical Reflections on the Book of Deuteronomy* (Eugene, OR: Cascade Books, 2012), 249–50.

> And behold, one of the sons of Israel came and brought a Midianite woman
> to his family, in the sight of Moses and . . . the whole congregation. . . . When
> Phinehas the son of Eleazar, son of Aaron the priest, saw it, he . . . took a spear
> in his hand and went after the man of Israel into the inner room, and pierced
> both of them, the man of Israel and the woman, through her body. Thus the
> plague was stayed from the sons of Israel. (Num. 25:1–3, 5–8 RSV2CE)

This passage is full of sexual imagery. The worship of Baal of Peor involves
sexual union with the Moabite/Midianite women. The "yoke" image can
describe conjugal union (Jer. 2:20; 2 Cor. 6:14), and Phinehas's vengeance,
with its "piercing" through the "body" (lit., the "womb"), displays obvious
sexual imagery. Israel commits "harlotry" of both spirit and body.

Parallels with the golden calf have long been noted: in both cases, Israel
engages in pagan worship mixed with sexual promiscuity, but zealous figures
put down the debauchery and so win themselves a priestly status. The two
incidents involve the first and second wilderness generations, respectively:
what the calf is to the first generation, Baal Peor is to the second.[6]

Significantly, Israel remains at this very location, in the valley opposite Beth-
peor in the plains of Moab, for the rest of the Pentateuch (Num. 25–Deut.
34). Thus, Moses delivers the entirety of Deuteronomy within sight of the
location of Israel's harlotry with the daughters of Moab/Midian (Deut. 3:29;
4:46; 34:6). Unsurprisingly, in Deuteronomy Moses adopts a zero-tolerance
policy toward idolatry and sexual promiscuity.[7]

Throughout the last book of the Pentateuch, Moses describes the covenant
with God in language facilitating nuptial interpretation. The greatest commandment, repeated frequently by Moses and his successor, Joshua,[8] is to
"love ['āhēb] the Lord your God with all your heart and all your soul and all
your might" (Deut. 6:5 AT), a love analogous to one's spousal commitment,
as this term for love ('āhēb) occurs frequently in marital contexts.[9] Likewise,
throughout Deuteronomy,[10] especially at the conclusion of the book, Moses
urges the people to "cleave" or "cling" to the Lord, using the key term *dābaq*

6. Jacob Milgrom, *Numbers*, JPS Torah Commentary (Philadelphia: Jewish Publication
Society, 1990), 211; Scott W. Hahn, *Kinship by Covenant: A Canonical Approach to the Fulfillment of God's Saving Promises* (New Haven: Yale University Press, 2009), 68–69, 84, 158–59,
174, 254, 264.
    7. Deut. 12:3–4, 29–31; 13:1–18; 16:21–17:7; 18:9–14; 22:13–30; 23:17–18.
    8. Deut. 7:9; 10:12; 11:1, 13, 22; 13:3; 19:9; 30:6, 16, 20; Josh. 22:5; 23:11.
    9. Gen. 24:67; 29:18, 30, 32; 34:3; Deut. 21:15–16.
    10. Deut. 10:20; 11:22; 13:4; 30:20; cf. Josh. 22:5; 23:8.

from Genesis 2:24 and other nuptial contexts:[11] "Choose life, that you and your descendants may live, *loving* [*'āhēb*] the LORD your God, obeying his voice, and cleaving [*dābaq*] to him" (Deut. 30:19b–20).

Conversely, infidelity to God through the worship of strange gods is *zәnût*, harlotry: "You are about to sleep with your fathers; then this people will rise and play the harlot [*zānāh*] after the strange gods of the land, . . . and they will forsake me and break my covenant" (Deut. 31:16). Harlotry provokes God to "jealousy" (Hebrew *qin'āh*): "They stirred him to jealousy with strange gods" (Deut. 32:16)[12]—a word strongly associated with a husband's desire for his wife.[13]

In sum, pentateuchal terms like "love" (*'āhēb*), "cleaving" (*dābaq*), and "jealousy" (*qin'āh*)—describing the God-Israel bond—as well as "harlotry" (*zәnût*)—describing its breach—imply a quasi-marital covenant between Israel and God made explicit by the Latter Prophets.

Marriage in the Mosaic Laws

The treatment of marriage in the law of Moses is complex, because Moses delivers at least three distinct law codes during his forty-year career:

- The Covenant Code (Exod. 21–23), delivered during the initial solemnization of the covenant at Sinai (Exod. 24:1–8)
- The Levitical Code, given to Moses at Sinai after the calf (Exod. 32–34) and the completion of the tabernacle (Exod. 35–40), comprising Leviticus 1–27 as well as many amendments or addenda in the book of Numbers
- The Deuteronomic Code (Deut. 12–26), proclaimed to Israel by Moses on the plains of Moab, days before his death and shortly before the entrance to the land under Joshua

These codes form distinct literary units: the first ends with a covenant-ratification ceremony (Exod. 24:1–8), and the other two conclude with a blessing-and-curse litany (Lev. 26; Deut. 27–28), a typical closing feature of ancient covenant documents.[14]

11. Gen. 34:3; Josh. 23:12; 1 Kings 11:2.
12. Also see Deut. 4:24; 5:9; 6:15; 29:20; 32:16, 21.
13. See Num. 5:11–31, where *qin'āh* occurs seven times.
14. J. A. Thompson, *The Ancient Near Eastern Treaties and the Old Testament* (London: Tyndale, 1963), 14.

Thus, there is a "diachronic" dimension to the Mosaic laws even from a canonical perspective. The laws change and develop as the narrative progresses, sometimes for reasons identifiable in the narrative itself.

The Ten Commandments

Of the "Ten Words" of God (Exod. 34:28), three pertain to matrimony: "Honor your father and your mother" (Exod. 20:12; Deut. 5:16 ESV); "You shall not commit adultery" (Exod. 20:14; Deut. 5:18 ESV); and "You shall not covet your neighbor's wife" (Exod. 20:17b; Deut. 5:21a ESV).

First, "Honor your father and your mother, as the LORD your God commanded you; that your days may be prolonged, and that it may go well with you, in the land which the LORD your God gives you" (Deut. 5:16; cf. Exod. 20:12). Every human being has one father and one mother, and this fact—which is not merely biological but also psychological, sociological, and theological—is reflected in the sacred text, which does not speak of "fathers" or "mothers" but of "your father" and "your mother" in the singular. The sacred author does not envision a society in which fathers and mothers are held communally, children's parentage is unknown, and children are raised corporately, as Plato envisioned in the *Republic* for his "Guardian" class.[15] Rather, it is assumed that each individual Israelite has one father and one mother whom they know and can identify and to whom they can show honor. While this does not yet necessitate that matrimony be an exclusive, lifelong union of one man and one woman, one can reason from the indisputable fact that each human being has one father and one mother, to whom he or she has a divine obligation to show honor, to show that the institution that best allows this divine command to be fulfilled is matrimony, as the Church has understood it.

We observe that the commandment comprises not two commands but one. "Honor your father" and "honor your mother" are not fourth and fifth commandments, respectively. Rather, there is one command, the masculine singular imperative "honor," with a double object: "your father and your mother." The parents are treated as a unity that is the object of the command. The situation most fitting for the fulfillment of this command is for one's father and mother to be united both socially and spatially. If father and mother are at enmity with one another—as so often happens with divorce—then

---

15. See Plato, *Republic* 3.423e–424a; 5.457–59; G. M. A. Grube, "The Marriage Laws in Plato's *Republic*," *ClQ* 21, no. 2 (1927): 95–99.

honor shown to one risks being taken as dishonor to the other, and vice versa. If father and mother are not spatially united—due to separation—then it becomes logistically difficult to honor both, given that the command to honor (*kabbēd*) in the ancient context would include not only obedience (at least until one came of age) and respect thereafter but also material support in old age. Supporting two parents in different domiciles poses practical challenges to carrying out the divine command. And while one can still honor one's father and mother in a polygamous situation, one can see the awkwardness that this poses: one seeks to honor one's father and mother, including material support in their advanced age, but there is a third person in their domicile (if not a fourth or more), with whom one's father has a relationship of equal intimacy, yet there is no defined relationship between oneself and the father's other wife, nor a divine imperative to honor her, but only an imperative to honor one's mother. So we see that the fourth commandment assumes as normative a situation in which each member of God's community is begotten and raised by one father and one mother, who are a union and who are known to their child and honored by him or her for their entire lives. Divorce and separation impede the fulfillment of this divine commandment by interposing social and logistical challenges, and polygamy confuses the situation by introducing other parties into the household, whose relationship with the child is undefined and toward whom there is no moral obligation.

Second, "You shall not commit adultery" (Deut. 5:18; Exod. 20:14 ESV). The verb is *nā'ap*, "commit adultery," a sexual act between a married woman and any man not her husband. The text emphasizes the gravity of this sin by listing it immediately after murder and before theft and assigning the death penalty for both the adulterer and the adulteress. Although adultery is called "the great sin" in both Egyptian and Ugaritic (i.e., Canaanite) literature,[16] only in Israel is marriage a sacred covenant (Prov. 2:17; Mal. 2:13–16),[17] and therefore adultery is also an offense against God, the witness and enforcer of the covenant (Mal. 2:14).[18] The seriousness of adultery follows naturally

---

16. J. J. Rabinowitz, "The 'Great Sin' in Ancient Egyptian Marriage Contracts," *JNES* 18, no. 1 (1959): 73; W. L. Moran, "The Scandal of the 'Great Sin' at Ugarit," *JNES* 18, no. 4 (1959): 280–81.

17. Gordon P. Hugenberger, *Marriage as a Covenant: Biblical Law and Ethics as Developed from Malachi* (Grand Rapids: Baker, 1998), 1–12.

18. Hugenberger, *Marriage as a Covenant*, 200–215. On p. 201, Hugenberger asserts that ancient marriage rites included "the acknowledgement of God as witness . . . with . . . the clear implication that God will take action against any perjury or infidelity."

from the integral role of matrimony in the creational order as an icon of the multipersonal union of faithful love (*ḥesed*) that is God. Adulterers, in the Hebrew Bible, are described as "covenant breakers" (*bōgədîm*; cf. Jer. 9:1 MT), whereas the most distinctive attribute of the divine character is *ḥesed* (Exod. 34:6–7)—that is, covenantal love, faithful love, or loving faithfulness. Adultery is the opposite of the divine character, just as marital fidelity is its icon.

The fact that *nā'ap* only describes acts that violate a *woman's* marital bond does not mean that other forms of extramarital intercourse were licit in Israel.[19] A sexual act between a man and a woman other than his wife was denoted by a different term, *zənût*, "fornication" or "harlotry." Many biblical texts place *nā'ap* and *zənût* in synonymous parallelism, implying moral equivalence (Isa. 57:3; Jer. 3:9; 5:7; Hosea 4:13–14). Therefore, the Church understands the sixth commandment as prohibiting all sexual relations outside of monogamous marriage, which follows logically from the theology of marriage established at creation. To effect a one-flesh union in the absence of any covenantal commitment is not an act of love (which by its nature is persevering and faithful) but only an act of desire. Furthermore, it denies the meaning of the act as intended by God, which is to symbolize and actualize the permanent union of two persons as one flesh: "What therefore God has joined together, let not man put asunder" (Matt. 19:6).

Third, "You shall not desire [*ḥāmad*] your neighbor's wife" (Deut. 5:21 AT; cf. Exod. 20:17). In Exodus 20:17, this injunction is part of a tenth commandment prohibiting the desire (*ḥāmad*) of anything that belongs to one's neighbor, whereas in Deuteronomy 5:21, this is a distinct ninth commandment prohibiting the desire (*ḥāmad*) for one's neighbor's wife (v. 21a), as opposed to the craving (*'āwāh*) for his goods (v. 21b). Nonetheless, there is no strong distinction between "desire" (*ḥāmad*) and "crave, long for" (*'āwāh*): in Genesis 3:6, the fruit is both "delightful" (*ta'āwāh*, from *'āwāh*) and "desirable" (*neḥmād*, from *ḥāmad*).

Many believe the Old Testament law governs only externals, whereas the New Testament law is internal, involving a transformation of the heart. But the ninth and tenth commandments do govern movements of the heart or soul and aim to cut off sin at its interior root (cf. Matt. 15:19). These commands imply that one's desires are governable. The human person is not simply at the mercy of uncontrolled desires but can evaluate the moral quality of different

19. Hugenberger, *Marriage as a Covenant*, 328n189.

desires, affirming the good ones and denying the evil. Furthermore, it implies that fidelity to one's marital covenant (Deut. 5:18) begins with discipline of the heart or soul.

Marriage in the Covenant Code (Exod. 21–23)

The Covenant Code (Exod. 21–23) is a brief, nonexhaustive set of civil laws given to Israel by Moses at the initial solemnization of the Sinai covenant (24:1–11). It begins with laws governing slaves (21:1–11), perhaps because the recent emancipation of the people of Israel from slavery created a sensitivity for those in this vulnerable state. These laws also govern marriage under the condition of slavery.

At first glance, Exodus 21:1–11 appears to consist of two complementary pieces of legislation, one for male slaves (vv. 1–6) and the following for female slaves (vv. 7–11). In fact, however, the two laws deal with very different situations: non-Israelite men sold as workers (vv. 1–6) and Israelite girls "sold" as brides (vv. 7–11).

Exodus 21:2 begins, "When you buy a *Hebrew* slave . . ." I have shown elsewhere that the term "Hebrew" in the Masoretic Text refers to a larger ethnic group to which Israel belonged (Gen. 14:13; 39:14; 1 Sam. 14:21), and the "Hebrew slave" envisioned here is a *non-Israelite* Hebrew, since slavery is prohibited for Israelites (Lev. 25:42–46).[20] Slavery is not part of the created order. The Mosaic law relieves Israelites from slavery (Lev. 25:42–46), and it places strict constraints on slavery imposed on a related ethnic group, the "Hebrews," limiting the term of service to six years (Exod. 21:2–6; Deut. 15:12–18). What concerns us is the slave's marital status. It is straightforward enough that if he enters service with his wife, she departs with him (Exod. 21:3). But it seems unfair to moderns that if his master provides him a wife, she and any young children remain in the master's home if the male slave goes free (v. 4). However, this was a matter of economic justice in the ancient world, given that the master paid the bride-price and the maintenance of the wife and her children up to the time of the husband-father's manumission, but in that short time (less than six years) recouped no economic benefit. Perhaps the law presumes the newly freed husband-father will work to repay the master and redeem his family. But there is another alternative: if the slave is happy with

---

20. John S. Bergsma, *The Jubilee from Leviticus to Qumran: A History of Interpretation*, VTSup 115 (Leiden: Brill, 2007), 43–47.

the situation that his master has provided for him, he can embrace it for life and become a permanent member of the household (vv. 5–6).

The situation with "maidservants" is quite different:

> When a man sells his daughter as a maidservant ['āmāh], she shall not go out as the male slaves do. If she does not please her lord [or "husband," 'ādôn], who has designated her for himself, then he shall let her be redeemed. He shall have no right to sell her outside the family, since he has broken faith with her. If he designates her for his son, he shall deal with her as with a daughter. If he takes another wife to himself, he shall not diminish her food, her clothing, or her marital rights. And if he does not do these three things for her, she shall go out for nothing, without payment of money. (Exod. 21:7–11 ESV, modified)

The term for "maidservant" here, 'āmāh, is sometimes the female equivalent of 'ebed, but in this case it is clear from the context that the 'āmāh is being sold as a bride. She is not called a "Hebrew," and the context presumes the father and daughter are Israelites, unlike 21:2–6. She does not go free at the end of six years, because manumission would be equivalent to divorce, unjustly cutting off her support. If her husband dislikes her, he must allow her to be redeemed (v. 8)—that is, bought back by a return of the mōhar ("betrothal gift" or "bride-price") by her father. Her husband is not free to sell her as a slave and profit from her, since he has "broken covenant" (bāgad) with her. Thus, separation is permitted but pejorativized: it is "covenant breaking" or "treachery" (bāgad). The Torah sometimes regulates actions it does not condone. Though the girl enters the home with the status of a maidservant, nonetheless she enjoys all the rights of a daughter if married to father or son—that is, she shares the legal status of her husband. If additional wives are taken (v. 10), her customary spousal rights may not be infringed: food (šə'ēr), clothing (kəsût), and conjugal rights ('ōnāh).[21] If he fails to fulfill these rights, she may leave "without payment of money"—in other words, without returning the mōhar.

It is too easy to judge Exodus 21:7–11 by modern sensibilities, assuming the father to be callous. On the contrary, the giving of daughters as brides for a mōhar could be an attempt to secure care and provision for one's daughter beyond one's own lifetime. The mōhar was supposed to be kept in trust for

---

21. On 'ōnāh as "conjugal rights"—a consensus of the ancient versions—see Nahum M. Sarna, Exodus, JPS Torah Commentary (Philadelphia: Jewish Publication Society, 1991), 121.

her by the father; to use it for one's own interests was shameful (Gen. 31:15). The law defended the daughter's right to be treated as wife and daughter-in-law, protected from neglect or arbitrary divorce.

The other important passage of the Covenant Code dealing with marriage is Exodus 22:16–17:

> If a man seduces [*pātāh*] a virgin who is not betrothed and lies with her, he shall give the bride-price for her and make her his wife. If her father utterly refuses to give her to him, he shall pay money equal to the bride-price [*mōhar*] for virgins. (ESV)

This is a case of consensual fornication. The Hebrew word *pātāh* can mean "deceive," "seduce," or "persuade" and usually carries a negative connotation but is sometimes morally neutral (cf. Prov. 25:15; Hosea 2:14). In the present case (Exod. 22:16–17), it indicates that the man gained the woman's consent. The woman is not betrothed, so this action does not carry the death penalty, as it does not break a covenant. However, having treated her as wife, he must now make her his wife (22:16b). The father can intervene: the Hebrew of verse 17 reads, "If, refusing, he refuses to give her . . . ," an intensive idiom meaning, "If he absolutely refuses to give her . . ." This indicates that in most situations the father would consent, since having lost her virginity, his daughter's future prospects were already severely damaged. But should the father judge the man so unworthy that marriage is unthinkable, the man must still pay the full *mōhar*, a sum of money given by a groom to a father-in-law to keep on behalf of his daughter as a kind of security for her welfare in case of some crisis.

This law presumes that the physical union of man and woman implies commitment—specifically, marital commitment. Therefore, a precipitous union should be followed immediately with the proper customs for public solemnization. The sexual act is never casual but intrinsically connected to marriage, only to be exercised within that covenantal commitment.

Biblical law is sometimes wrongly criticized for limiting the sexual activity of women but not that of men. On the contrary, men are forbidden on pain of death from sleeping with women married (Exod. 20:14) or betrothed (Deut. 22:23–27) to other men, and sleeping with an unbetrothed woman results either in marriage or forfeiture of the bride-price, often a considerable sum (Exod. 22:16–17). Prostitution is forbidden (Lev. 19:29; Deut. 23:17). Thus, the law leaves no woman of the community sexually available to a man, save his own wife (or wives).[22]

Marriage in the Levitical Code (Lev. 1–27)

A great many civil and religious matters are left unaddressed by the Covenant Code (Exod. 21–23), which was never intended as a comprehensive legal document for governing the common life of Israel. In fact, the great body of Mosaic law—much of it ceremonial—is actually given to Israel later (Exod. 34–Lev. 27), in response to the golden-calf covenant breaking, itself a reversion to Egypto-Canaanite religion.[23] What is the purpose of these ceremonial laws?

The answer is complex, but surely a major purpose is to eradicate from Israel the practices and worldviews of Egyptian and Canaanite religion: "You shall not do as they do in the land of Egypt, . . . and you shall not do as they do in the land of Canaan" (Lev. 18:3).

One feature of religious practice in Egypt and Canaan was a fixation on sex and death. In Egypt, the tombs of dead pharaohs served as temples for the worship of both the pharaohs and their patron deities. In Canaan, sexual activity was a common feature of worship and religious festivals, as many (if not most) of the gods were associated with fertility. To the contrary, in biblical law any residue of death or sexuality renders one "unclean," which in practice meant exclusion from the realm of the sacred.

The book of Leviticus, analyzed canonically, falls by topic into the following sections:

1. The Sacrificial Code (Lev. 1–7)—rules for sacrificial offering
2. The Priestly Code (Lev. 8–10)—rules for the priesthood
3. The Cleanliness Code (Lev. 11–15)—rules for distinguishing clean from unclean
4. The Day of Atonement (Lev. 16)—cleansing and sanctifying the people
5. The Holiness Code (Lev. 17–25)—rules for distinguishing the holy from the profane
6. Concluding blessings and curses (Lev. 26)
7. An appendix on religious vows (Lev. 27)

22. See Hugenberger, *Marriage as a Covenant*, 313–88.
23. The calf could be either (or both) the Egyptian god Apis or the Canaanite Baal. See Jack M. Sasson, "Bovine Symbolism in the Exodus Narrative," *VT* 18, no. 3 (1968): 380–87.

The first laws relevant to marriage we encounter in the Cleanliness Code, as many of the rules for ritual cleanliness impacted the practice of marriage for Israelites.

Thus, we encounter our first relevant text in Leviticus 12, the rules for purification after childbirth: a woman is ritually unclean for forty days after the birth of a boy (eighty days for a daughter); then she may approach the sanctuary, offer the appropriate sacrifices, and be restored to ritual cleanliness. Presumably, the flow of blood and bodily fluids in childbirth and thereafter are signs of both sexuality and death and therefore excluded from the realm of the sacred. More positively, uncleanness frees a woman from religious obligations and makes her sexually unavailable to her husband (Lev. 18:19), facilitating the rest and healing of the mother after childbirth. The ritual laws have religio-symbolic meaning but also promote the health and well-being of the Israelite worshipers, both men and women.

Similarly, in the laws of Leviticus 15:1–33, any discharge from the body renders one unclean, including sexual emission (vv. 16–18), rendering impossible sexuality within worship, as was practiced outside of Israel (Gen. 38:21–22; Deut. 23:17; Hosea 4:14).

Menstruation was so common it merited special treatment (Lev. 15:19–31). Similar to childbirth, menstruation frees women from religious and conjugal duties, precluding marital relations when such are infertile and less healthy, comfortable, and enjoyable for the wife. Return to ritual cleanliness and thus resumption of conjugal life fall one week after the cessation of menses, thus near the time of ovulation, peak fertility, and libido. Thus, these laws suit the rhythms of the female body and maximize potential for conception for most Israelite couples, a fact known already in antiquity (see 2 Sam. 11:4–5).[24]

Leviticus 18:1–30 prohibits forms of sexual union practiced in Egypt and Canaan (v. 3). No one-flesh union between close relatives (consanguineous union) is permitted (vv. 6–18): "No man shall encroach toward any flesh of his body [šə'ēr bəśārô] to expose nakedness" (v. 6 AT). The redundancy of šə'ēr bəśārô (lit., "flesh of his flesh" or "flesh of his body") functions as a superlative—not just any "kin" (bāśār) but "his very close kin" (šə'ēr bəśārô). These are defined in Leviticus 21:2–3 as "near of flesh" (liš'ērô haqqārōb 'ēlāyw): father, mother, son, daughter, brother, and sister. The two principles are (1) married persons are the same flesh, and (2) children are the flesh of

---

24. See Martin Krause, "II Sam 11:4 und das Konzeptionsoptimum," ZAW 95 (1983): 434–37.

their parents. Anyone who is the same flesh as your father, your mother, your-self, or your wife—by two steps of marriage or descent—is prohibited from having a one-flesh union with you *permanently*, not just within the lifetime of one's spouse.

Though many reasons may be imagined for the prohibition of incest, the text prohibits these unions because the two parties are *already* "one flesh," whereas marriage ought to make "one flesh" from two: "Therefore a man shall leave his father and his mother and cleave to his wife, and they shall *become* one flesh" (Gen. 2:24 AT). There are two acts: *leaving* and *cleaving*. "Father and mother" can stand for the family: one parts from one's family to establish a new one. Incest does not "leave" the father and mother—it "cleaves" to the father and mother, frustrating the second act: *becoming* one flesh. One cannot *become* one flesh when the partners *already are* one flesh. There is no transformation, no new-family formation; rather, there is family deformation. Genesis 2:24 enumerates four persons: the man (i.e., the self), the father, the mother, and the wife. The prohibited partners in Leviticus 18:6–18 are all persons who are already one flesh with any of these four, within two steps of marriage or descent: father (vv. 7–9, 11–12, 14), mother (vv. 9, 13), self (vv. 10, 15, 16), and wife (vv. 17–18).

Leviticus 18:19–23 primarily prohibits sterile forms of sexual union, which are contrary to the created order. Relations during menstruation are prohib-ited: the woman's body is not designed for union at this time, and the purpose of union (conception) is not attainable. Adultery is prohibited (18:20). Child sacrifice to the Ammonite god Molech is prohibited (v. 21): the immediate killing of the fruit of the womb is similar to sterile forms of intercourse in that it is an intentional frustration of the intrinsic end (i.e., fruitfulness) of the act. Homosexuality and bestiality, both sterile, are forbidden, being described as "abomination" (*tôʿēbāh*) and "perversion" (*tebel*; vv. 22–23). *Tôʿēbāh* desig-nates something that is not only wrong or illegal but shocking, offensive, or abhorrent. God creates by introducing separations and distinctions between things that constitute their identity (Gen. 1:4–2:3); actions that violate and confuse these distinctions are often labeled *tôʿēbāh*, "abomination," as they challenge the integrity of the whole created order by conscious defiance. That which is *tôʿēbāh* elicits revulsion not just from God but from the "land" itself—here metonymic for what we would call "nature," "the environment," or "ecosystem": "You shall . . . do none of these abominations, . . . lest *the land vomit you out* when you make it unclean, as it vomited out the nation that was before you" (Lev. 18:26, 28 ESV). The prohibited acts are all frustrations of the nature of marital union, which is ordered toward fertility and children.

Leviticus 19:20–22 states that if a man sleeps with a *šipḥāh* ("handmaid") who is promised to another man, it is not a capital offense, but the man must bring a sin offering to the sanctuary. This is a consensual act, because the text does not speak of "seizing" or "violating" (Deut. 22:25, 28, 29). It is not a capital offense (cf. Deut. 22:23–24), probably because the woman, not being freed, lacks legal standing to form a binding covenant. Thus, no covenant has been broken. In addition to offering the sin offering, however, according to Exodus 22:16 the man is also obliged either to marry the woman or pay the *mōhar* if her father does not consent.

Leviticus 19:29 insists: "Do not profane [*ḥillēl*] your daughter by making her a prostitute [*zānāh*], lest the land be a prostitute [*zānāh*] and the land become full of depravity [*zimmāh*]" (AT). The verb *zānāh*, often translated "to be or act as a harlot, whore, prostitute," generally does refer to a woman engaging in sexual acts for payment in cash or kind (Ezek. 16:33–34), but in a few examples it is used more broadly for sexual promiscuity with or without payment (Num. 25:1; Deut. 22:21).[25] This kind of activity "profanes" (*ḥillēl*) a person. No father should press his daughter into this activity, "lest the land engage in prostitution" (AT)—a vigorous expression, which probably means "lest prostitution proliferate in the land," which would result in the land filling up with *zimmāh*, variously rendered as "wickedness," "lewdness," or "depravity." The parallelism between prostitution (*zānāh*) and depravity (*zimmāh*) reveals the sacred author's opinion of sexual promiscuity, and the uncommon term *zimmāh* may have been chosen for its alliterative value with *zānāh*. The message is that *zānāh* is nothing but *zimmāh*—in other words, "prostitution is perversion."

In Leviticus 20:1–21, we are informed of the legal penalties for the prohibited sexual unions listed in Leviticus 18:6–22. Penalties for occultic activities are included (20:6), because they involve the placation or supplication of other deities, which was a religious form of *zənût*, "prostitution." Also, a penalty for the cursing of parents is included (20:9), because of its association with sexual offenses against parents that follow (vv. 11, 17, 19). From verse 10 on, the offenses in this chapter are listed by seriousness of punishment: those that carry the death penalty (adultery, v. 10; incest with a father's wife, v. 11;

---

25. It is also used extensively in a metaphorical sense for covenantal infidelity on the part of Israel, expressed by the worship of other gods, as in the very next chapter (Lev. 20:6).

incest with a daughter-in-law, v. 12; homosexual intercourse, v. 13; relations with both mother and daughter, v. 14; bestiality, both male [v. 15] and female [v. 16]); then those punished by *kārēt*, being "cut off"[26] (relations with a sister [v. 17], menstruant [v. 18], and consanguine aunt [v. 19]); finally, those punished by childlessness (relations with an uncle's wife [v. 20] or a brother's wife [v. 21]). The seriousness of the punishments imposed indicates the degree of offense to God as well as the social and religious consequences of allowing these actions to proliferate within the community. Intentional distortions of the one-flesh union that images God in humanity destroy the holiness of the community and prevent it from achieving its end, which is union with God through worship.

Leviticus 26, with its list of blessings and curses, is a formal literary feature marking the end of a covenant document. The book of Numbers adds some additional laws to this covenant, but only a few pertain to marriage. One of these is the ordeal for the suspected adulteress in Numbers 5:11–31: if a man strongly suspects his wife of infidelity, he can take her to the sanctuary, where the priest performs a ritual with the wife, and if she is guilty, she will experience a divine punishment but no legal penalty.[27] The importance of Numbers 5:11–31 is that it removes the case of the suspected adulteress from the jurisdiction of her jealous husband and even from the courts, and it puts it completely in the hands of God. The falsely accused wife is therefore safe from physical and legal abuse from her husband; she answers only to God.

Numbers 30:3–16 allows a father to revoke the vows of a dependent daughter, and it also allows a husband to revoke those of his wife. The father and the husband in these instances were legally and economically responsible for the woman in view, and the woman's vow might place significant burdens of a social, legal, economic, or other kind on the household generally and on the father or husband specifically. For example, if a woman vowed a thanksgiving sacrifice, that would have to be paid from among the flocks of her husband or father; or if a wife vowed herself to sexual abstinence for a period of time,

---

26. Being "cut off" probably indicates the divine elimination of one's entire line of descent, with the result that one's name and legacy are completely forgotten. See the discussion in Nahum M. Sarna, *Genesis*, JPS Torah Commentary (Philadelphia: Jewish Publication Society, 1989), 126; Donald J. Wold, "The Meaning of the Biblical Penalty *Kareth*" (PhD diss., University of California, Berkeley, 1978).

27. Why is there no corresponding ritual for a husband suspected of infidelity? Since husbands were obliged to support their wives materially (see Exod. 21:10–11), there was an economic motive for a man to falsely accuse his wife, whereas there was no such motive for a wife to accuse her husband; therefore, the law had to protect women from false accusation but not vice versa.

that likewise would impact her husband. The point of this law, then, was to prevent a woman from unilaterally placing the head of her household under a sacred obligation that he was unable or unwilling to fulfill. She could not oblige him without his consent.

Marriage in the Deuteronomic Code

There is a salvation-historical sea change when we move from the Levitical Code (with its addenda in Numbers) to the book of Deuteronomy, due to the rebellions that occur between the promulgation of these two bodies of law. If one counts from Moses's initial mission to Egypt to the beginning of Deuteronomy, then Israel has rebelled sixteen times over the course of her travels through the desert. If one counts from the golden calf debacle, then Israel has rebelled ten times. What is more, Moses even delivers his final laws and valedictory speeches within sight of the location of the Baal Peor debacle (Deut. 3:29; 4:3, 46; 34:6). Therefore, the backdrop of Deuteronomy is the hard-hearted recalcitrance of the people of Israel, which explains the character of many of its laws: moral standards are often compromised, yet conversely, punishments for infraction can be severe. It is a strategy to restore order among a riotous people, to stringently enforce a basic level of morality sufficient for the functioning of a civil society. It is, in a sense, a kind of martial law imposed on Israel after Moses has grown weary of their character at the end of his life.[28]

The structure of Deuteronomy includes a long introduction giving the history of Israel to that point, as well as a re-exposition of the Ten Commandments (Deut. 1–11), followed by a law code ending in blessings and curses (Deut. 12–28) and an epilogue that ties up loose ends and recounts the transition of leadership from Moses to Joshua (Deut. 29–34). Most of the laws pertinent to marriage are in the later part of the code, chapters 21–25, although the laws pertaining to the king in 17:14–20 are also relevant.

Moses places three restrictions on the king of Israel in Deuteronomy 17:16–17: he must not multiply (lō'-yarbeh) horses, wives, or money (silver and gold). However, what does it mean to "multiply"?[29] In later Jewish tradition, the Essene movement took the strictest possible interpretation: more

---

28. See the discussion in John S. Bergsma and Brant Pitre, *The Old Testament*, vol. 1 of *A Catholic Introduction to the Bible* (San Francisco: Ignatius, 2018), 275–80.

29. The Hebrew is the *hiphil* or causative stem of the verb *rābāh*, "to be large, great"—thus, "to cause or make [something] large or great."

Clement of Alexandria on Marriage

The Fathers recognized that Deuteronomy 21:10–14 was intended to restrain male desire in the wake of battle and direct it toward marriage and family formation:

> The Law wishes males to have responsible sexual relations with their marriage partners, solely for the generation of children. This is clear when a bachelor is prevented from enjoying immediate sexual relations with a woman prisoner of war. If he once falls in love with her, he must let her cut her hair short and mourn for thirty days. If even so his desire has not faded away, then he may father children by her. The fixed period of time enables the overpowering impulse to be scrutinized and to turn into a more rational appetency.[a]

> a. Clement of Alexandria, *Stromateis* 3.11.71.4, in *Exodus, Leviticus, Numbers, Deuteronomy*, ed. Joseph T. Lienhard, ACCS:OT 3 (Downers Grove, IL: InterVarsity, 2014), 309.

than one wife is "many" (*rab*, CD 4:19–5:2). God's intent for the king is that he be monogamous; and since the king's behavior sets the example for the people, the rest of the nation should practice monogamy as well. The Essene interpretation is stricter than one can defend from the wording of the law itself; yet the Essenes correctly discerned that the law recognizes the danger polygamy poses for moral character, and the only way to completely avoid this danger is by following the order of creation (*yəsôd habbərî'āh*, CD 4:21) by practicing monogamy.

In Deuteronomy 21:10–14, Moses lays out a legal procedure for marrying a woman taken captive in war. She must be allowed a full month of mourning rituals for her lost family before the marriage can be consummated (21:13). If her new husband wants to divorce her, she must be given her freedom rather than treated like a slave. Divorce is permitted but described very pejoratively: "You have humiliated her" (v. 14), using a Hebrew word (*'ānāh*) that means "oppress, humiliate, abuse," often in sexual contexts.[30] Significantly, the Mosaic legislation permits some things that are not approved: releasing the *'āmāh*

30. Gen. 34:2; Deut. 22:24, 29; Judg. 19:24; 20:5; 2 Sam. 13:12, 14, 22, 32; Lam. 5:11; Ezek. 22:10–11.

taken as a wife is "breaking faith" with her (Exod. 21:7–11); releasing the captive bride is "humiliating" her (Deut. 21:14).

This legal procedure is followed immediately by a law regulating inheritance rights in a situation of bigamy. If a man has two wives, loved unequally, still the double portion of his inheritance goes to his oldest son by age, not the oldest of the favored wife (Deut. 21:15–17). This rebukes the behavior of Jacob, who unfairly honors Joseph and appears to designate him as his heir (Gen. 37:3–4). The very need for such a law indicates that unequal affections between a man and his wives was not uncommon and that measures needed to be taken to ensure just treatment of the children (cf. 1 Sam. 1:1–8).

Several laws in Deuteronomy penalize extramarital sexual activity. In Deuteronomy 22:13–21, a rather severe law enforces premarital chastity. If a husband falsely slanders his new bride by claiming she is not a virgin, the punishment is rigorous: public humiliation by flogging, a steep fine paid to the father-in-law, and a loss of the right to divorce. If, however, the wife is not a virgin, she suffers the death penalty. It must be understood that such a situation involves not only fornication but sustained deception in a public and legal contract: the young woman has pretended to be a virgin and allowed the *mōhar* for virgins to be paid to her father, so not only has she concealed her sexual activity, she has allowed her marriage to be contracted on a false premise and committed a kind of economic fraud.

Deuteronomy 22:22 reiterates earlier applications of the death penalty to adultery, and it is followed by laws dealing with situations that are less clear-cut. Consensual relations between a man and a woman betrothed to another man also carry the death penalty: betrothal is legally binding, such that its violation constitutes adultery (22:23–24). However, if the betrothed woman was forced, only the man faces the death penalty (vv. 25–27).

The situation is different with an unbetrothed woman (Deut. 22:28–29). If a man lays hold (*tāpaś*) of her and sleeps with her, and they are discovered, the man must pay a sum of fifty shekels of silver to her father and marry her permanently, without the possibility of divorce. This is an updating of the law of Exodus 22:16–17, specifying the amount of the *mōhar*. Many translations and commentaries wrongly take this as a case of rape, translating the verb *tāpaś* as "seize" and taking it to imply force and lack of consent. However, (1) while *tāpaś* does mean "lay hold of, grasp," it is never used in the Hebrew Bible for rape, and the only other use of the term in a sexual context actually describes an attempted seduction with a *woman* as the seducer (Gen. 39:12).

The Hittite Laws on Consensual Sex

The Hittite Laws contain a close verbal parallel to Deuteronomy 22:28–29, but the context shows the scenario envisioned is consensual:

> If a man seizes a woman in the mountains, it is the man's crime and he will be killed. But if he seizes her in (her) house, it is the woman's crime and the woman shall be killed. If the husband finds them, he may kill them.[a]

The logic of the law is the same as that of Deuteronomy 22:23–24: a woman in an urban area is assumed to have consented because she could have cried out for help but did not. Thus "seize" in the second sentence means "embrace sexually" rather than "force" (cf. Gen. 39:12), as also in Deuteronomy 22:28. Note, too, that the discovery of the consensual lovers is described as "finding" them, both here and in Deuteronomy 22:28.

a. Hittite Laws §197b (*ANET* 196b).

(2) When explicitly discussing rape in Deuteronomy 22:25 (also 2 Sam. 13:14), the sacred author uses the verb *ḥāzaq* in the causative stem (the *hiphil*), "to exercise force upon, overpower." (3) The Hittite semantic equivalent of *tāpaś*, "lay hold of," is attested in the sense of "embrace erotically" or "initiate sexual activity" in a clear case of *consensual* relations in a Hittite law code.[31] (4) Furthermore, Deuteronomy 22:28b speaks of the couple "being found" or "discovered" together (using the *niphal* plural of *māṣāʾ*), which suggests mutual consent rather than the woman being forced and then fleeing. For all these reasons, it is best to understand *tāpaś* in Deuteronomy 22:28–29 as meaning "embrace erotically," describing male-initiated but nonetheless consensual relations between a man and an unbetrothed woman.

Deuteronomy 23:17–18 prohibits male and female "sacred" prostitution:

There shall not be a "holy woman" [*qədēšāh*] among the daughters of Israel, nor shall there be a "holy man" [*qādēš*] among the sons of Israel. You shall not

31. See Hittite Laws §197b (*ANET* 196b, quoted in the sidebar above) and the discussion in Hugenberger, *Marriage as a Covenant*, 251.

bring the fee of a prostitute [*zônāh*] or the wages of a dog into the house of the
Lord your God in payment for any vow, for both of these are an abomination
[*tô'ēbāh*] to the Lord your God. (AT)

The "holy woman" and "holy man" refer to male and female prostitutes who
were associated in some way with the worship of a deity or a specific sanctuary (cf. "cult prostitute," RSV, ESV; cf. Gen. 38:15, 21–22). The corollary
in Deuteronomy 23:18 prohibits the profits from prostitution from entering
the sanctuary. The parallelism of construction and the context strongly suggest that "the wages of a dog" refers to the earnings of a male prostitute.
Sacred prostitution served to support the cult and sanctuary of various Near
Eastern deities, but the God of Israel would have none of this! Nothing
that pertains to sexuality or death can contact the sanctuary or be involved
in the worship of the Lord, so here Moses imposes a legal barrier to the
kind of fusion of the sex trade with religious observance that characterized
Canaanite religion.

Deuteronomy 24:1–4 is the famous law concerning divorce:

> When a man takes a wife and marries her, if then she finds no favor in his eyes
> because he has found some indecency [*'erwat dābār*] in her, and he writes her a
> certificate of divorce and puts it in her hand and sends her out of his house, and
> she departs out of his house, and if she goes and becomes another man's wife,
> and the latter man hates her and writes her a certificate of divorce and puts it
> in her hand and sends her out of his house, or if the latter man dies, who took
> her to be his wife, then her former husband, who sent her away, may not take
> her again to be his wife, after she has been defiled,[32] for that is an abomination
> before the Lord. And you shall not bring sin upon the land that the Lord your
> God is giving you for an inheritance. (ESV)

This law is not a permission for divorce: "There has emerged a scholarly
consensus that the intent . . . is neither to authorize divorce, nor to stipu-
late its proper grounds, nor to establish its requisite procedure. Rather, its
sole concern is to prohibit the restoration of a marriage after an intervening
marriage."[33] Many interpreters, ancient and modern, have ignored the surprisingly long, complex, and specific protasis of this law (Deut. 24:1–3), but no

---

32. Hebrew *huttammā'āh*, a very rare *hothpaal* or passive-causative from *ṭāmē'*, "be unclean," meaning "she has been made unclean/defiled." See GKC §54.3h (p. 150); BDB 379b.
33. Hugenberger, *Marriage as a Covenant*, 76–77.

St. Augustine on Divorce

The Fathers recognized that Deuteronomy 24:1–4 acknowledges divorce without approving it. Augustine writes about the marriage customs of the pagans as follows:

> But who does not know that the [marriage] laws of the non-Christians are different?
>
> Among them when a divorce has been issued, both the woman and the man are free to marry whomever they wish, without any liability to human punishment.
>
> This custom is similar to something that Moses apparently permitted regarding a written notice of divorce because of the Israelites' hardness of heart (Deut. 24:1–4). In this case there appears to be more of a rebuke than an approval given to divorce.[a]

a. Augustine, *On the Good of Marriage* 8, in *Marriage and Sexuality in Early Christianity*, trans. David G. Hunter (Minneapolis: Fortress, 2018), 197.

interpretation can be considered compelling that does not attend to the very particular situation envisioned here—namely, that the woman must first be

1. divorced on the grounds of indecency, with legal documentation (v. 1); then
2. remarried to a different man (v. 2); then either
3. divorced again on the grounds of aversion (dislike or hatred), with legal documentation, or
4. widowed (v. 3).

If all of these conditions obtain, the law prohibits remarriage to the first husband (v. 4). Only Raymond Westbrook has offered a convincing explanation of why the law is so specific.[34] Based on studies of ancient Near Eastern marital law, Westbrook argues that indecency on the part of the wife

34. Raymond Westbrook, "The Prohibition on Restoration of Marriage in Deuteronomy 24:1–4," in *Studies in Bible 1986*, ed. Sara Japhet, Scripta Hierosolymitana 31 (Jerusalem: Magnes, 1986), 387–405. See also the discussion in Hugenberger, *Marriage as a Covenant*, 76–81.

(the initial situation envisioned in v. 1) justified the husband in divorcing her without financial compensation (such as a return of her dowry). However, the two means of ending a marriage in verse 3—namely, divorce merely for aversion and premature decease of the husband—both entitled the wife to a financial settlement from her husband's estate. So what Deuteronomy 24:1–4 prohibits is a husband profiting twice from the same woman: first, by keeping her dowry after divorcing her for indecency (v. 1), and second, by remarrying her in order to acquire the financial settlement she received from her subsequent husband (v. 4). Although the law tacitly acknowledges that divorce takes place and customs exist to regulate and document it, the text does not condone any of it. Indeed, verse 4 refers to her relations with her second husband as being "defiled,"[35] hardly a positive appraisal. The law of Deuteronomy 24:1–4 simply prohibits a rather egregious way of profiting from the divorce customs. The effort in later Judaism to derive the religiously legitimate grounds for divorce (m. Giṭṭin 9:10) by scrutinizing the conditions in the first verse (Deut. 24:1) is understandable but misguided, and it will be discussed in a later chapter.

There follows a law of a more cheerful spirit, pointing to the positive nature and intention of marriage:

> When a man is newly married, he shall not go out with the army or have anything assigned to him; he shall be free at home one year, to gladden his wife, whom he has married. (Deut. 24:5 AT)

This law presumes that it would be cruel for the new bride never to experience the joys of marriage, because her husband was immediately sent out to war (and possibly killed) or was too burdened with public duties (perhaps corvée) from the outset of their marriage ever to experience a satisfying common life (cf. Deut. 20:7). Instead, he is given at least one year to stay at home and "gladden his wife." This latter phrase is sometimes translated "be happy with his wife" (cf. RSV, ESV), but that is an unlikely, if not impossible, reading. The verb śimmaḥ is in the intensive stem (the piel), which often converts an intransitive meaning in the base stem (the qal, "be happy") to a transitive, and the word "his wife" ('ištô) is marked as the direct object of the verb, so

---

35. See n. 32 above. "Verses 3–4 imply that there is something adulterous about such an act" (Jeffrey H. Tigay, Deuteronomy, JPS Torah Commentary [Philadelphia: Jewish Publication Society, 1996], 220).

St. Thomas Aquinas on Marriage in the Mosaic Law

Aquinas recognized that even in the Old Law, mutual happiness of the spouses was one of the ends of marriage: "In order to foster conjugal love from the very outset, it was prescribed that no public duties should be laid on a recently married man, so that he might be free to rejoice with his wife [Deut. 24:5]."[a]

a. Aquinas, *Summa theologiae* I-II, q. 105, art. 4, quoted here from Thomas Aquinas, *Summa Theologica*, trans. Fathers of the English Dominican Province, 3 vols. (New York: Benziger Bros., 1947), 1:1104.

"cheer/gladden his wife" or "make his wife happy" would be the preferred translation (cf. NABRE, KJV, JPS).[36] The distinction is not pedantic: at issue is whether the law was established for the sake of the happiness of the husband or the wife, and grammatical analysis strongly supports the latter. One could reason that, if the first year of a man's marriage should be devoted to making his wife happy, then bringing joy to his wife is one of the purposes of marriage. The first year is devoted to practicing this art, so that thereafter he may know how to fulfill his spousal duty.

The last law of marriage in Deuteronomy concerns *levirate* marriage (from Latin *levir*, "brother-in-law"). If a man dies without a son, his brother shall marry his widow, and the firstborn son of the couple will take the name and inheritance of the deceased (Deut. 25:5–6). This was considered an act of social justice, because it preserved the name, property, and legacy of an Israelite man and provided for the material and social needs of his widow. While union with a sister-in-law was forbidden during the lifetime of her husband (see Lev. 18:16), it became obligatory if she was left behind as a widow without a son. This obligation was enforced by shame: the man who refused to support his sister-in-law in this way was made to undergo a public humiliation (see Deut. 26:7–10). Not all Mosaic laws and customs were to be enforced in the same way: some required criminal punishment (e.g., Deut. 22:13–27), others civil fines (22:28–29), still others social pressure (25:5–10).

36. In none of the other twenty-five instances of the *piel* of *śāmaḥ* in the MT does the verb have the intransitive sense "be happy." It always occurs in contexts demanding the sense of giving, causing, or making happy/happiness.

Summary of Marriage under the Mosaic Covenant

When reviewing the laws of marriage associated with the covenant of Moses, we observe that in most cases the purpose or effect of the laws is to protect the wife, the more vulnerable of the spouses (cf. CCC 1610). The purity laws of Leviticus 12 and 15 declare a woman unclean after childbirth and during menstruation, which have the effect not only of making her unavailable for sexual intercourse at times when it is undesirable or physically harmful for her, but also of freeing her from religious obligation when in physical discomfort. The prohibition of consanguineous intercourse protects women from abuse by their own male relatives (Lev. 18, 20). Daughters, likewise, are protected from being forced into prostitution (Lev. 19:29), and religiously sanctioned prostitution is outlawed (Deut. 23:17). Wives are freed from arbitrary treatment at the hands of jealous husbands (Num. 5:11–31) and released from any religious vows that would cause friction or real hardship in marriage or family life (Num. 30:3–16).

In Deuteronomy, Moses institutes legislation to protect women in particularly difficult situations. While he does not prohibit marriage with women taken as prisoners in war—in many situations, such a marriage would be to the social and material advantage of the woman, who would be given a place of support and protection in Israelite society and the opportunity to bear children, who would support her in her old age—nonetheless, he takes steps to ensure her dignified treatment and to prevent violent abuse (Deut. 21:10–14). The rights of unloved wives are protected, as well as the reputation of a wife unfairly slandered (22:13–21). Criminal sexual conduct is punished by death (22:23–27), and men who seduce women have to be prepared to marry whomever they sleep with and support her for life (22:28–29). While divorce is tacitly acknowledged, men are prevented from manipulating marital common law for financial gain (24:1–4), and a means is provided for childless widows to remain in their husband's family and have an opportunity to raise children (25:5–10).

A basic principle of Mosaic law is that a man is obliged to marry any woman with whom he has relations (Exod. 22:16; Deut. 22:28–29), unless she is already married or betrothed to another man, in which case he is subject to death. Finally, one brief law (Deut. 24:5) reveals that a husband's natural duty is to bring happiness to his bride, and this is such an important obligation that it takes precedence even over national defense (cf. 20:7)!

Nonetheless, the law of Moses does not eliminate every situation that is disadvantageous to a woman or a wife. Moses is unyielding in applying the death penalty to adulterous women. He does not outlaw polygamy and the sadness it often caused, even while taking steps to protect the rights of multiple wives.[37] He does not prohibit divorce, even though he refers to it as "betrayal" (Exod. 21:8) and "violation" (Deut. 21:14). So there is a tension in the law of Moses. It recognizes certain ideals: the command to "honor your father and mother" presumes the normativity of a monogamous couple who are the parents of the average Israelite. The "honeymoon year" law of Deuteronomy 24:5 envisions one of the sacred purposes of marriage to be the happiness of the couple, particularly that of the wife. The personal bond between man and wife is taken with outmost seriousness; the prohibited-unions legislation in Leviticus 18 and 20 exhibits almost a "sacramental realism" about the flesh of husband and wife: the flesh of one is the flesh of the other. So what we observe in the pentateuchal laws are underlying ideals and presumptions about the potential of the matrimonial union, combined with accommodations to certain social and cultural realities of the people of Israel.

37. Polygamy, despite its imperfections, may have been considered necessary or even beneficial to all parties, because the much higher mortality rate of men (associated with warfare, wild animals, and accidents) led to an inadequate societal fertility rate and a disparate sex ratio in the ancient Near East that left many women without the opportunity to raise families. St. Augustine argues that the permission for polygamy arose from the need for procreation in ancient times: "Among the ancient fathers, of course, it was permissible to take another woman, with the permission of one's wife, and to produce children that were shared in common. . . . [But] today there is not the same need of procreation that there was in the past" (*On the Good of Marriage* 15, in *Marriage and Sexuality in Early Christianity*, ed. David G. Hunter [Minneapolis: Fortress, 2018], 203).

6

"That I May Grow Old with Her"

Marriage in the Historical Books

The Historical Books of the Hebrew Bible / Old Testament are rich with nuptial themes and feature at least two romantic novellas (Ruth and Tobit) in which the hero and heroine function as theological types. The Historical Books of the Christian canon can be divided into the "primary history" and the "secondary history." The primary history consists of the books in canonical order from Joshua through 2 Kings, also called the "Deuteronomistic History" (or "DtrH" for short). This narrative is largely concerned with the people of Israel as a political body, and marriage enters into the narrative typically in two ways. First, the marital practices of the Israelites reflect their spiritual state, such that deviation from the norm of faithful, monogamous, covenantal endogamy—marriage within the group of Israelites—is characteristic of periods of religious infidelity. Second, the marriages of the kings are significant for the impact they have upon the faith, religious practice, and general welfare of the people of Israel.

Besides the books of the primary history, there are also two books of secondary or alternative history: 1–2 Chronicles, in which marriage functions similarly to the books of the primary history. Closely related to this secondary history is a collection of late eponymous biographies: Ezra, Nehemiah,

Esther, Judith, and Tobit. The challenge of intermarriage with foreigners is a dominant theme in the first four of these works, and the last, Tobit, is a romantic novella in which the marriage of the protagonists serves as the means of reconciliation and fulfillment for the tensions of the narrative, as well as a kind of icon of Israel's hope for restoration as a people in communion with their God.

Marriage before the Monarchy: Joshua, Judges, and Ruth

Joshua

In language, theme, and outlook, the book of Joshua closely resembles Deuteronomy, as it recounts the fulfillment of the instructions Moses has left to his successor Joshua, who leads the people into the promised land, conquers the Canaanites and other peoples, and renews the covenant, per Moses's instruction at Shechem, on the adjacent peaks of Ebal and Gerizim. At the end of the book, many pentateuchal themes and expectations find resolution—for example, the descendants of Abraham have taken possession of the land promised to them so long ago (Gen. 13:14–17; 15:18–21; 17:8; 24:7). At a pivotal point in the biblical narrative, Joshua gathers Israel together at Shechem to deliver his valedictory before his death (Josh. 23:1–24:28), urging them to remain faithful to the covenant through the use of nuptial language (esp. 23:6–13). Israel must "love" (*'āhēb*; Josh. 23:11; cf. Deut. 6:5) the Lord their God and "incline" their "heart" (*nāṭāh lēb*; Josh. 24:23; cf. 1 Kings 11:3) and "cleave" (*dābaq*; Josh. 23:8; cf. Gen. 2:24) to him, rather than "cleaving" (Josh. 23:12) to the inhabitants of the land they are "entering" (*bô'*; Josh. 23:7)[1] by intermarrying (*hithattēn*; Josh. 23:12) with them. In other words, Israel is married to God and therefore should not "marry" the Canaanites, either physically or religiously.

Judges

Despite Joshua's urgent final exhortation, the introduction of Judges informs us that Israel "whored [*zānāh*] after other gods" (Judg. 2:17 ESV) and actively intermarried with the nations of Canaan (3:5–6). Exogamy with the

---

1. The word *bô'*, "enter, go into," is often used in sexual contexts—e.g., Gen. 16:2; 29:21; 38:16.

Canaanites (3:6) represents religio-cultural assimilation and defection from exclusive fidelity to the Lord. After this inauspicious introduction (1:1–3:6), the book goes on to recount the careers of twelve judges (3:7–8:32; 10:1–16:31) and one short-lived king (8:33–9:57). The last and longest account of a judge is that of Samson (Judg. 13–16), for good reason: Samson, with his strengths and weaknesses, is a perfect paradigm or icon of the tragic character of Israel during this time period.

Samson

Relationships with women drive Samson's entire career. Upon reaching adulthood, he insists, against his parents' objections, on marrying a Philistine woman (Judg. 14:1–3), and that dysfunctional relationship becomes the occasion for his conflicts and victories over the Philistines (Judg. 14–15). An unnamed Philistine prostitute becomes another occasion for conflict and victory (16:1–3), but Samson's final and most famous struggle will be with another prostitute named Delilah (vv. 4–21). Samson's name means "sunny," from Hebrew *šemeš*, "sun," whereas Delilah's name is a variant of the Hebrew *laylāh*, "night." When Samson meets Delilah, it is time for his "sun" to set and "night" to reign: the loss of his eyes will plunge him into perpetual darkness.

In his relationship with Delilah, Samson exhibits almost supernatural stupidity: the reader cannot help but wonder how he could be so entranced by her physical attractions as not to realize her ill intent toward him, openly displayed in multiple attempts to destroy his divinely given strength (Judg. 16:5–17). By using this literary strategy, the author seeks to provoke the ancient Israelite reader to ask: "How can he not realize this foreign woman will be his undoing?" Then comes self-recognition: "Samson is us! Why do we not see that foreign women are our undoing?"[2]

The secret of Samson's strength is his hair, configured in seven locks—the number of oath and covenant—representing his personal Nazirite covenant with the Lord. The Israelite reader understands that our strength lies in our covenant with the Lord. Delilah represents the lure of foreign cults and gods—attractive, seductive, but ultimately heartless and cruel, leading to enslavement and oppression. Samson's relationship with Delilah is not

---

2. John S. Bergsma and Brant Pitre, *The Old Testament*, vol. 1 of *A Catholic Introduction to the Bible* (San Francisco: Ignatius, 2018), 327.

covenantal. They are not man and wife, but they live in open fornication (*zᵊnût*). Like Israel, Samson abandons his covenant with the Lord in order to fornicate with the Philistines and their gods, leading literally to darkness and death (Judg. 16:21, 30–31).

THE TRAGEDIES OF JUDGES 19–21

Judges 19–21 concludes the book with some of the worst accounts of the treatment of women in all of Scripture. A certain Levite dwelling in Ephraim takes a concubine from Bethlehem of Judah (Judg. 19:1; later David's home-town, 1 Sam. 16:1). While journeying one time through Benjamin, the Levite and his concubine stop in Gibeah (Judg. 19:15; later Saul's capital, 1 Sam. 10:26). Taken in by an old man, they enjoy his hospitality until late in the night, when, recapitulating the sin of Sodom (Gen. 19:4–11), the men of the city surround the house, demanding that the visitor be brought out for group sex (Judg. 19:22). The host and the Levite appease the mob by sending out the concubine to satisfy them (vv. 24–26). The Levite wakes to discover his concu-bine dead from the all-night abuse (vv. 27–28). He cuts her body into twelve pieces, sending them to all the tribes of Israel (v. 29). The outraged Israelites gather to wage war against Gibeah (20:1–48). All the men of Benjamin are slain in battle, save six hundred refugees (v. 47). Their anger now assuaged, the other tribes of Israel grieve over the loss of the tribe and take compassion on the survivors (21:1–4). Since all of the tribes have sworn never to give their daughters in marriage to the Benjaminites, they procure wives for the six hundred survivors by slaughtering the noncombatant men of Jabesh-gilead, taking captive all of their young women, and kidnapping additional young women from a religious festival in Shiloh (vv. 5–24). The book ends with the ominous observation: "In those days there was no king in Israel. Everyone did what was right in his own eyes" (v. 25 ESV). In other words, social and moral chaos reigned due to the lack of any effective central authority.

Through this concluding narrative, the sacred author seeks to provoke hor-ror in the reader and to justify the establishment of the monarchy by showing the chaos that ensues without it. In particular, every interaction between men and women in this narrative is disordered or destructive.

First, the Levite takes the girl of Bethlehem not as wife (*'iššāh*) but as concubine (*pîlegeš*), a category unknown to the law. Moses has established (Exod. 21:7–11) that even a purchased handmaid (*'āmāh*), once married, is a free woman, with full rights of a daughter-in-law (v. 9) or a wife (v. 10). The

Levite has already contravened God's law by contracting a kind of union it does not recognize.

Second, the Gibeahites repeat the offense of the Sodomites, demanding sexual satisfaction outside of matrimony, with multiple partners, disregarding the principles of fertility and free consent (Judg. 19:22–25). Thus, they deny the intrinsic meaning of sex, found only in the loving, faithful, exclusive, fertile, one-flesh covenant between man and woman (Gen. 2:24)—and so they merit death (Lev. 20:13).

Third, the shockingly callous behavior of host and "husband" in sacrificing the concubine to satisfy the violent lust of the mob (Judg. 19:24–26) is no less heinous than the sin of the rapists themselves, completely contravening the husband's obligation to bring joy to his wife (Deut. 24:5).

Fourth, the husband mutilates the body of his deceased wife (Judg. 19:29).

Fifth, although the war against Benjamin reveals that there is some moral conscience left among the Israelites (Judg. 20:8–13), the abduction of women for the surviving Benjaminites is nonetheless completely unlawful (21:8–24). One could only take a wife through war with Israel's *enemies*, not fellow Israelites (Deut. 21:10–14); and kidnapping carried the death penalty (24:7).

Placing this narrative at the end of Judges demonstrates that, from the heights of covenantal fidelity in Joshua 23–24, Israel has descended to a nadir of infidelity and depravity by Judges 19–21, which is now associated especially with Saul's hometown, Gibeah.

Ruth

The book of Ruth is explicitly set in the age of the judges (Ruth 1:1) but shows us that—amid the moral chaos of the era—a glimmer of light has been preserved in Bethlehem, the city of David, where the citizens still follow the letter and spirit of the law of Moses, particularly in the area of social justice and the treatment of women.[3]

Ruth is nothing if not a romance, and the romantic protagonist is Boaz, whose Hebrew name appropriately means "in him" (*bô*) "is strength" (*ʿaz*), an *ʾîš gibbôr ḥayil*, a "man mighty and valiant" (Ruth 2:1 AT).[4] The first word out of his mouth is the name of God: "He said to the reapers, 'The LORD be

3. On the contrast between Judges and Ruth in the relationship of the sexes, see Bergsma and Pitre, *Old Testament*, 343.
4. Blandly rendered "man of wealth" in the RSV.

with you!' And they answered, 'The LORD bless you'" (v. 4). In Bethlehem we find a culture that honors the Lord first in all interactions. Boaz shows immediate attention to Ruth, his cousin Naomi's Moabite daughter-in-law, who is both widow and sojourner—two categories dear to the Lord, who "executes justice for . . . the widow, and loves the sojourner, giving him food and clothing" (Deut. 10:18).[5] Boaz converses with her, urging her to stay in his fields, where she will be safe: "Have I not charged the young men not to touch [*nāgaʿ*][6] you?" (Ruth 2:9 ESV). Boaz concludes by blessing Ruth by the God of Israel, since she has "come to take refuge under his *wings* [*kənāpayim*]" (v. 12 AT). Boaz proceeds to surpass the Mosaic laws of social justice. Moses has forbidden reaping to the edge of the field or going back for forgotten sheaves, to provide gleanings for the sojourner (Lev. 19:9–10; 23:22; Deut. 24:19–21), but Boaz has his workers even intentionally pull out some sheaves to leave for Ruth. So Ruth brings an enormous load of gleanings back to Naomi, who urges Ruth to stay in Boaz's fields lest she be "assaulted" elsewhere (Ruth 2:22 ESV),[7] calling to mind the abuse of women in Judges.

Ruth 3 is the climax of the novella. At Naomi's prompting, Ruth makes herself attractive and seeks out Boaz after he has eaten and drunk freely and lain down to sleep at the harvest festival. Ruth quietly uncovers Boaz's "feet" (*margəlôt*)[8] as he is sleeping and lies down next to him (3:7). When he awakes in the night, he discovers her, and she offers herself to him: "Spread your wing [*kānāp*] over your maidservant ['*āmāh*], for you are a redeemer [*gōʾēl*]" (v. 9 AT). Ruth calls herself here the '*āmāh* of Boaz, the term used for the maidservant sold to become a bride in Exodus 21:7–11. She asks him to spread his "wing"—the corner of his cloak—over her, a betrothal ritual (cf. Ezek. 16:8), since he is a *gōʾēl*, a kinsman redeemer, a male relative eligible to marry her and raise up an heir for her deceased husband (cf. Deut. 25:5–10).[9] Thus, she signals sexual receptivity to him, hoping he will embrace her and thus be obliged to marry her according to the law (Exod. 22:16; Deut. 22:28–29).

5. Cf. Exod. 22:21–24; Deut. 14:28–29; 16:11, 14; 24:17–22; 26:12–13; 27:19.
6. Probably here a euphemism for sexual contact; see Gen. 20:6; 26:11; Prov. 6:29.
7. Hebrew *pāgaʿ* can mean "attack," as in Judg. 8:21; 15:12; 18:25; 1 Sam. 22:17–18, etc.
8. Possibly a euphemism. See Robert L. Hubbard Jr., *The Book of Ruth*, NICOT (Grand Rapids: Eerdmans, 1988), 203–4.
9. Although the law of Deuteronomy only speaks of the brother-in-law marrying his brother's widow, apparently this responsibility—in the absence of a full brother—fell to the male relatives or "redeemers" in order of proximity in kinship, as reflected in Lev. 25:25, 48–49.

However, even when half awake and feeling the effects of drinking, Boaz follows not just the letter but the spirit of the Mosaic law. Yes, the law obliges a man to marry a woman with whom he has slept (Exod. 22:16), but the law also looks upon such an action pejoratively, as it bypasses the usual rituals of gaining the consent of the woman and her family (Gen. 24:57–60), and the union could be blocked by the woman's father (Exod. 22:17). Furthermore, Boaz knows of another, closer male relative with a prior right to Ruth. So Boaz first blesses Ruth for seeking a husband according to the law, not just according to her affections: "May you be blessed by the LORD, my daughter; you have made this last kindness [ḥesed] greater than the first, in that you have not gone after young men, whether poor or rich" (Ruth 3:10). This statement implies that Boaz, while still vigorous, is significantly older than Ruth ("my daughter") and thus has not fancied himself a prospective suitor for her, but now he is delighted to discover she desires him. Then Boaz explains to Ruth the true legal situation and the proper path for them to be married (vv. 11–13)—which does not include any physical activity between them at the present moment. So they sleep separately that evening, but when morning comes, Boaz again shows concern for Ruth's reputation: he ensures that she leaves the threshing floor before daylight, so that she doesn't appear to be the sort of loose woman who would consort with menfolk at the threshing party (v. 14). He provides generously for Ruth and Naomi's immediate needs (v. 15) and then proceeds with the proper legal procedure to be established as the rightful gōʾēl for Naomi and Ruth (4:1–12). To everyone's relief, the nearer kinsman declines to redeem Ruth and the ancestral land (vv. 1–6), and Boaz is only too happy to take his place (vv. 7–12). The novella concludes with the marriage of Boaz and Ruth (v. 13) and the birth of a baby, Obed (vv. 13–17), the grandfather of David (vv. 18–22), who is mentioned for the first time in the Christian canon in verse 17.

What then does the book of Ruth teach us about marriage? The two uses of the word "wing," kānāp, are the theological key to the book. The "wings" of the Lord, under which Ruth has taken refuge, take concrete form in the "wing" of Boaz's cloak, with which he covers her in an act of betrothal.[10] For the forlorn widows, Naomi and Ruth, marriage is their salvation—the end of famine, loneliness, vulnerability, and barrenness; the return of plenty, companionship, security, and fertility. But not only the women benefit: Boaz

10. Hubbard, Book of Ruth, 71, 212–13; Bergsma and Pitre, Old Testament, 344.

is clearly delighted by his young bride and the prospect of discovering love and family life at a mature age. They are well suited for each other: Boaz is an *ʾîš gibbôr ḥayil*, a "man of might and virtue" (Ruth 2:1 AT), and Ruth is an *ʾēšet ḥayil*, a "woman of virtue" (3:11 AT)—a phrase famously used in Proverbs 31:10 of the ideal wife. So Ruth shows us that marriage is the answer for the happiness and flourishing of both men and women among the people of God.

The Mosaic law gives us an incomplete picture of the Israelite view of marriage, since law by its nature tends to focus on the *boundaries* of behavior, identifying those actions that go beyond what society can tolerate and thus must be sanctioned. Ruth, on the other hand, shows us an *ideal* of Israelite romance and marriage. In contrast to the depravity of the rest of Israel in Judges, in Ruth the spirit of God's law prevails. Everything Ruth and Boaz do follows the law of God, just as everything the actors in Judges 19–21 do offends against it. The law of God becomes, for Ruth and Boaz, the path to life, love, communion, and fertility. God shows his faithfulness especially to Ruth but also to Boaz, and God's faithfulness or *ḥesed* comes to these deserving protagonists *through each other*. Since *ḥesed* can even be rendered "grace" in some contexts, we can even say that Ruth and Boaz are instruments of God's grace toward one another. They also become types of Christ and the Church: Boaz, the loving *gōʾēl* or redeemer, becomes the image of Christ, the ultimate bridegroom-redeemer, who gathers his people under his wings (Mal. 4:2; Matt. 23:37). Ruth, the virtuous Moabite who is widowed, impoverished, and barren, resembles the Church, especially the Gentile seekers and God-fearers (Acts 10:2, 22, 35) who are attracted to Judaism but ultimately embrace Christianity: they possess some light of virtue, enough to realize their own spiritual poverty and enough to realize that salvation is to be found in the God of Israel.[11]

Ruth and Boaz become the great-grandparents of David, and David will be the great king who will lead Israel out of the darkness of the time of the judges, into a golden age characterized by a new covenant, the covenant of David. David is a righteous young man, particularly open to the Holy Spirit, such that when he is anointed by Samuel, the text tells us that the Spirit "rushed upon [him] from that day forward" (1 Sam. 16:13 ESV). But such youthful righteousness does not arise in a vacuum. It needs to be cultivated

---

11. On Boaz and Ruth as types of Christ and the Church, see Bergsma and Pitre, *Old Testament*, 348–50.

over generations, and the message of the book of Ruth is that at least in Bethlehem, this quiet town, love of the Lord and obedience to his law—which leads to charity and justice for the poor—are cultivated during the dark age of the judges, in order that—at the right time appointed by God—a savior could arise, capable of delivering the people and leading them into the worship of God. The remarkable intimacy of communion with God reflected in David's Psalms is already in gestation in the womb of Ruth through the seed of Boaz—this woman and man of *ḥayil*, virtue and valor. The future of God's people goes by way of the family and, more specifically, by way of individual marriages.

Ruth and Boaz are obedient to the covenant between God and Israel through Moses. Indeed, *both* show themselves more faithful to the covenant than strictly required: Ruth could have abandoned her mother-in-law without guilt (Ruth 1:15), but she swears a personal oath of fidelity that joins her to the people of Israel and their covenant with God (v. 16). Similarly, Boaz is only required by the law to avoid reaping the edges of his field and to not go back for lost sheaves (Lev. 19:9; 23:22; Deut. 24:19), but he intentionally has his workers pull out extra to provide for destitute Ruth and Naomi (Ruth 2:16)—without ulterior motive, since he considers himself too old to be attractive to her (3:10). By following the law, Ruth and Boaz discover love and life, illustrating the principle of Deuteronomy 30:16: "If you obey the commandments of the LORD . . . , then you shall live and multiply."[12]

To sum up, the sacred author presents the time of the Judges as an era of moral depravity, the people of Israel being similar in character to their hero Samson (full of potential but destroyed by fornication with the Gentiles) and their depravity particularly expressed in the way women are treated and in offenses against God's plan for matrimony (Judg. 19–21).[13] The story of Ruth shines like a candle in this period of darkness, giving us a window into the life of a community faithful to God and his covenant, expressed particularly in the treatment of women and the practice of matrimony. Together, these books form the backdrop for the introduction of the prophet Samuel and the establishment of the monarchy.

12. On Ruth and Boaz as models of the life of covenant fidelity, see Hubbard, *Book of Ruth*, 72–74; Laura A. Smit and Stephen E. Fowl, *Judges and Ruth*, BTCB (Grand Rapids: Brazos, 2018), 251.
13. See Smit and Fowl, *Judges and Ruth*, 20–22, 140, 217.

Marriage and the Monarchy: The Books of Samuel, Kings, and Chronicles

Marriage functions in two ways in the narrative of the Israelite monarchy: On the one hand, the natural marriages of the protagonists time and again illustrate the ill effects on family life and society of offenses against matrimony, like polygamy and extramarital relations. On the other hand, the covenant between the Davidic king and the people of Israel takes on a nuptial dimension that anticipates the nuptial union between Christ and the Church.

Polygamy recurs as a social and moral scourge throughout Samuel and Kings. In the opening chapter of the former, we are confronted with Elkanah, who has two wives: Hannah, the barren but loved, and Peninnah, the fruitful but unloved. It is the situation of Deuteronomy 21:15–16, although the loved wife has not borne an heir. There is intense rivalry between these wives, much to the pain of Hannah, but in answer to her prayers, God grants her children: first Samuel, the one destined to be a prophet (1 Sam. 1:19–20), and then others as well (2:21).

Much later in the narrative, polygamy contributes to the downfall of both David and Solomon. Already during David's youthful rise to power, there are ominous notifications of his multiple marriages and sons while in Hebron (2 Sam. 3:2–5: six sons by six wives) and Jerusalem (5:13–14: eleven more sons by unnamed wives). Thus, David violates the law of Moses: "[The king] shall not multiply wives for himself" (Deut. 17:17). Furthermore, according to 2 Samuel 5:13, David takes *pīlagšîm*, "concubines"—a form of marriage not envisioned by the Mosaic law (in which the word "concubine" never occurs)—and he marries non-Israelite women (e.g., Maacah of Geshur; 2 Sam. 3:3).[14] These multiple marriages, in the subsequent narrative, come close to destroying the house of David entirely due to rivalry between the different sons of different mothers. Amnon son of Ahinoam, Absalom son of Maacah, and Adonijah son of Haggith all posture themselves at various points as David's successors and threaten David's other children or even, in the case of Absalom, David himself. Eventually, David's loyalists have to press him to proactively establish the throne in the hands of Solomon son of Bathsheba, David's favorite wife—and this, strictly speaking, is also contrary to the law

---

14. On the ominous notification of David's polygamous marriages, see Ronald F. Youngblood, "1, 2 Samuel," in *The Expositor's Bible Commentary*, ed. Frank E. Gaebelein, 12 vols. (Grand Rapids: Eerdmans, 1992), 3:830–31, 858–60.

(Deut. 21:15–16), as David's heir should have been his eldest remaining son, regardless of David's affection for the mother. In the process, his sons Amnon, Absalom, and Adonijah all lose their lives.

Worse yet is Solomon, who, following in his father's polygamous footsteps, loved many women from all the surrounding nations (1 Kings 11:1–4). He clung (*dābaq*) to these in love (*lə'ahăbāh*) (v. 2), having seven hundred wives and three hundred concubines who "inclined his heart" (*nāṭāh lēb*; 1 Kings 11:4; cf. Josh. 24:23) away from the Lord, leading him to establish shrines for foreign gods (1 Kings 11:5–8).[15] So he commits the sin of Israel in the time of the judges (Judg. 3:6), about which the Lord had warned Moses after the golden calf (Exod. 34:11–16; summarized in 1 Kings 11:2): intermarriage and religious syncretism, which go seamlessly hand in hand. Making marital covenants with foreign women inevitably involves entering into covenants with their gods.

Several successors of David continue to "multiply wives," including foreign women,[16] a notorious example being Ahab son of Omri, of the Northern Kingdom, whose wife Jezebel, a pagan princess from Sidon, causes endless grief for Elijah and all the Israelites who kept faithful to the covenant with the Lord (1 Kings 16:29–2 Kings 9:37).

Nonetheless, it is not polygamy but adultery that stands as *the* critical turning point in the narrative arc of the books of Samuel. The fortunes of Israel and of David continually build from the first mention of David at the end of Ruth until David reaches the height of his power in 2 Samuel 10. Then David commits adultery and murder with Bathsheba and Uriah, respectively, in 2 Samuel 11, and his kingdom is thrown into continual confusion for the rest of the book, as his sons imitate his behavior, and sexual sin (2 Sam. 13:1–22; 16:20–23) and bloodshed (13:23–36; 18:9–15; 1 Kings 2:25) haunt his house.

Let us look briefly at the critical episode of 2 Samuel 11. It follows the establishment of the Davidic covenant a few chapters earlier, in which David achieves the status of son of God and is promised kingship over all the earth. But as is so often the case, the establishment of a covenant only briefly precedes the breaking of the covenant, and this is no exception. The Davidic covenant requires the king to keep the law of God—that is, the Mosaic covenant (2 Sam. 7:14; 22:22–25; 1 Kings 2:1–4; Pss. 89:30–31; 132:12)—which strictly prohibits adultery (e.g., Exod. 20:14). But in 2 Samuel 11, David has

---

15. On Solomon's errors, see Bergsma and Pitre, *Old Testament*, 392–93.
16. 1 Kings 11:19; 16:31; 20:3, 5, 7; 2 Chron. 11:18–23; 13:21; 21:14, 17; 24:3.

grown lazy and no longer leads the army into battle (v. 1). He sleeps in till late in the day and sees his neighbor's wife Bathsheba and covets her (v. 2; cf. Deut. 5:21). Then he takes her and sleeps with her (2 Sam. 11:4–5). Because she has come to the end of her monthly period of uncleanness (v. 4), she is at the point of peak fertility,[17] and she conceives immediately (v. 5). David attempts to cover up his sin by recalling Uriah and giving him an opportunity to sleep with his wife, but pious Uriah insists on maintaining the custom of continence while the army of Israel is on campaign (vv. 6–13). So David decides to have him killed (vv. 14–25), after which he marries Bathsheba (vv. 26–27).

This horrible crime casts David in a very bad light. David is already polyga-mous and could have obtained more wives for his pleasure if he so wanted, but he insists on invading and destroying the marriage of his neighbors, the pious couple Uriah and Bathsheba. Uriah is a Gentile convert to Yahwism, whereas Bathsheba is probably an Israelite woman. In any event, Bathsheba conscientiously observes the cleanliness laws of Leviticus 15 (2 Sam. 11:4), and Uriah piously observes the custom of continence while on campaign (v. 11). Moreover, they are monogamous, and Bathsheba is Uriah's one source of joy and delight (2 Sam. 12:1–7). So Uriah and Bathsheba represent an ideal of Israelite marriage, which David destroys by adultery and murder. Although David wins forgiveness of his guilt, the temporal punishment of his actions remains, and sexual immorality and bloodshed plague his household for the rest of his life, especially in the sequence of Amnon's rape of Tamar (13:14), Absalom's murder of Amnon (v. 29), Absalom's expulsion and attempted murder of David (15:14), Absalom's public bedding of his father's concubines (16:22), and Joab's murder of Absalom (18:14–15).

So in a very real sense, the downfall of the kings of Judah and Israel is due to their failure to practice matrimony according to the law and ideals of God as recorded in the Books of Moses. They practice polygamy, adultery, and intermarriage with pagan women, and these sins fatally weaken the strength of the kingdom, violate the covenant with the Lord, and merit the withdrawal of divine protection. Fidelity to one's marital covenant and fidelity to the divine covenant correlate.[18] The final epitaph on the Northern Kingdom of Israel in

17. Martin Krause, "II Sam 11:4 und das Konzeptionsoptimum," *ZAW* 95 (1983): 434–37.
18. "Throughout the Old Testament, human marriage is understood as pointing toward and being enfolded within the larger covenant of Israel with YHWH" (Smit and Fowl, *Judges and Ruth*, 29).

2 Kings 17:21–23 mentions that "Jeroboam drove Israel from following the Lord and made them commit *great sin*" (v. 21 ESV).

As we have noted already, adultery is "the great sin" in both Egyptian and Ugaritic literature.[19] If this broader ancient Near Eastern literary tradition is the context for 2 Kings 17:21, then the sacred author portrays the whole failure of the Northern Kingdom and its monarchy as a grand act of adultery against the Lord God of Israel, their proper spouse.

The Davidic King as Bridegroom of Israel

The books of Samuel and Kings also reflect a secondary nuptial theme associated with the covenant of kingship between the Davidic king and the people of Israel. In 2 Samuel 5:1, the tribes of Israel come to David in Hebron and say, "Behold, we are your bone and flesh," which should be understood as a performative utterance of the ensuing covenant ceremony (cf. v. 3). That is, the tribes of Israel are *declaring* themselves to be David's "bone and flesh"— his family—by virtue of the covenant. The first and best-known deployment of the phrase is in the marital context of Genesis 2:23: "This at last is bone of my bones and flesh of my flesh."[20] So Adam claims Eve as his "bone and flesh." Yet in 2 Samuel 5:1, the people of Israel portray themselves as Eve to David's Adam: "We are *your* bone and flesh." They are bride, David is bridegroom, and they immediately solemnize the relationship as a covenant (v. 3).

A few other texts in the Historical Books provide further hints of this quasi-marital dimension of the covenant of kingship with David.[21] Later, when Absalom usurps his father's throne and becomes king in his stead, the traitor Ahithophel asks permission to attack David immediately, promising to "bring all the people back to [Absalom] *as a bride comes home to her husband*" (2 Sam. 17:3). This analogy rests on an underlying conception of the people of Israel as wife of the son of David, the husband-king. Again, it may not be accidental that when Israel approaches Solomon's successor, Rehoboam, with a request for a lighter "yoke" (i.e., the burden of taxation

19. J. J. Rabinowitz, "The 'Great Sin' in Ancient Egyptian Marriage Contracts," *JNES* 18, no. 1 (1959): 73; W. L. Moran, "The Scandal of the 'Great Sin' at Ugarit," *JNES* 18, no. 4 (1959): 280–81.

20. On this, see Walter Brueggemann, "Of the Same Flesh and Bone (Gn 2,23a)," *CBQ* 32, no. 4 (1970): 532–42.

21. Bergsma and Pitre, *Old Testament*, 394.

and corvée), he is advised by the rash young courtiers to respond, "My little finger is thicker than my father's loins" (1 Kings 12:10). But the Hebrew is simply *qōṭen*, "little [thing]," a sexual euphemism,[22] which is especially clear in that it is compared to the father's "loins" or "thighs." The young men urge Rehoboam to make a crass boast about his virility because of the background paradigm of king-as-husband and people-as-bride. But the people are not impressed, and they metaphorically "divorce" the son of David by leaving his house and returning to their home of origin, just as disgruntled wives would abandon their husbands and return to their family home (Gen. 38:11; Judg. 19:2). "'What portion do we have in David? We have no inheritance in the son of Jesse. To your tents, O Israel! Look now to your own house, David.' So Israel went to their tents" (1 Kings 12:16 ESV).

As we will see in subsequent sections, this nuptial relationship between king and Israel will be developed further in the Song of Songs, where the bride is metaphorically Israel, and her royal "beloved one" is the Davidic king—an allegory facilitated by the fact that "my beloved" in Hebrew is the same as "my David," *do(w)dî*. It is also reflected in some prophetic texts, like Zechariah 9:9: "Rejoice greatly, O daughter of Zion! . . . Behold, your king is coming to you . . . , humble and mounted on a donkey, on a colt, the foal of a donkey" (ESV). Here, the city of Jerusalem is pictured as a royal princess, the "daughter of Zion" (cf. "virgin daughter of Zion," 2 Kings 19:21; Isa. 37:22; Jer. 14:17; Lam. 2:13), who awaits her bridegroom-king, who approaches on a donkey. This paradigm of the people as bride, waiting for the return of the son of David as bridegroom-king, lies behind the wedding imagery Jesus employs in some of his parables (e.g., Matt. 22:1–14; 25:1–13).

Marriage in the Postexilic Biographies

The early Church grouped the books Ezra, Nehemiah, Esther, Judith, and Tobit together as a collection of postexilic biographies, although critical scholarship might assign different genre classifications to them. Esther and Judith are focused on female characters, both of whom are wives; surprisingly, they have little to contribute to a biblical theology of marriage,[23] but the theology

22. Ludwig Köhler and W. Baumgartner, *Lexicon in Veteris Testamenti libros* (Leiden: Brill, 1958), 835.
23. The namesake heroine of the book of Esther becomes the wife of the Persian emperor Ahasuerus (i.e., Xerxes), and the book reflects some of the marital customs of the Persian court,

of matrimony and its proper practice do form a central topic of concern in
the books of Ezra, Nehemiah, and Tobit.

Ezra–Nehemiah

The books of Ezra and Nehemiah are considered as one book in the Masoretic Text. They share a common concern for the problem of intermarriage
or exogamy (marrying outside the clan or community), as can be seen in Ezra
9–10 and Nehemiah 10:28–31; 13:1–3, 23–37. The priest-scribe Ezra's efforts
to purge the postexilic Judean community of foreign wives and children is recorded in Ezra 9–10, especially 9:1–15, where Ezra cries out in a public prayer
of lament (vv. 6–15) over the fact that the Judeans, despite biblical warnings
(e.g., Exod. 34:11–16), have intermarried with "the Canaanites, the Hittites,
the Perizzites, the Jebusites, the Ammonites, the Moabites, the Egyptians,
and the Amorites" (Ezra 9:1 ESV). Interestingly, there is no list exactly like
this in the Old Testament. It is a variation on the traditional list of six or
seven nations found in Exodus 34:11 and Deuteronomy 7:1: "the Hittites,
the Girgashites, the Amorites, the Canaanites, the Perizzites, the Hivites,
and the Jebusites" (Deut. 7:1 ESV; Exod. 34:11 omits the Girgashites). Both
Exodus 34:11–16 and Deuteronomy 7:1–5 forbid intermarriage or making
any covenants with these groups. Interestingly, all of the ethnic groups listed
in Deuteronomy 7:1 were extinct by the time of Ezra. Ezra and Nehemiah
make a hermeneutical reapplication of the *principle* behind the Mosaic laws
to their current day, prohibiting marriages with the surrounding peoples
who do not share with the Judeans their exclusive covenant commitment to
the Lord.

It is easy to be critical of Ezra and Nehemiah from a modern perspective,
as their struggle against intermarriage outside the community of Judean repatriates offends deeply held modern ideologies about marriage and society.
However, the survival of Judean culture and religion were at stake: if Ezra
and Nehemiah had not acted, there would be no discipline of biblical studies today, since the Judean repatriates would have been assimilated into the
ecumenical paganism of the fifth-century (BC) Levant and their sacred texts
forgotten. No community can maintain its identity in the face of constant

---

but it is not clear that anything in the narrative is intended by the sacred author to be considered
normative for the practice or understanding of marriage for those who worship the God of
Israel. Likewise, Judith is an exemplary wife while her husband is alive, but the plot of Judith
focuses on her deception and assassination of Holofernes, an evil and dysfunctional admirer.

Cyprian of Carthage on Marriage

Among the Fathers, the stress on endogamy (marriage within a kin group) in Ezra-Nehemiah and Tobit is understood in terms of marrying within the community of faith—the Church. So Cyprian of Carthage supports the thesis "that marriage is not to be contracted with Gentiles" with the following citations:

> In Tobias: "Take a wife from the seed of thy parents, and take not a strange woman who is not of the tribe of thy parents" [Tob. 4:12]. . . . Also in Esdras, it was not sufficient for God when the Jews were laid waste, unless they forsook their foreign wives, with the children also whom they had begotten of them [Ezra 10:9–44; Neh. 13:23–31]. . . . Also in the second [letter of Paul] to the Corinthians: "Be not joined together with unbelievers. For what participation is there between righteousness and unrighteousness? Or what communication hath light with darkness?" [2 Cor. 6:14].[a]

a. Cyprian of Carthage, *Treatise* 12.3.62 (*Ad Quiriniam*) (*ANF* 5:550–51).

exogamy by its youth. Nehemiah recounts vividly the shocking evidence of the loss of religious and cultural identity: in Jerusalem, he saw that "half of [the] children spoke the language of Ashdod, and they could not speak the language of Judah" (Neh. 13:24).

Furthermore, it was primarily the upper castes of Judean society—"officials," "chief men," priests, and Levites (Ezra 9:1–2)—who were marrying with non-Jewish inhabitants, probably for political, social, and economic reasons, especially to assimilate upper-class Jews with the leadership castes of the surrounding peoples, creating an interrelated, elite ruling class for the entire region.[24] Those who lost out in this arrangement would be the common Jews (cf. Neh. 5:1–13), especially the poor and devout who took seriously the worship of the Lord according to the Mosaic covenant.

Whereas modern Western sensibilities regard marriage purely as a private affair based on affection, in traditional societies like ancient Judah, marriage

24. On this, see Daniel Smith-Christopher, "The Mixed Marriage Crisis in Ezra 9–10 and Nehemiah 13: A Study of the Sociology of Post-Exilic Judaean Community," in *Second Temple Studies*, vol. 2, *Temple Community in the Persian Period*, ed. Tamara C. Eskenazi and Kent H. Richards, JSOTSup 175 (Sheffield: JSOT Press, 1994), 243–65.

is a public institution with important social-justice consequences for the entire community. Ezra and Nehemiah were ministering at a time when the first generation of Judean repatriates from Babylonian exile were reaching the end of their life or had already passed away. Those still alive were witnessing, in horror, the loss of the Judean language and religion as their collective grandchildren and great-grandchildren adopted the culture of the surrounding peoples, because their mothers were not Judean. The founders of the reestablished Jerusalem community had left relative comfort and affluence in Babylon to return to their ancestral homeland. For the vast majority, it was a homeland they had never personally known, and when they arrived there, they found it a sparsely populated, economically devastated wasteland. After pouring out their entire lives in an effort to rebuild the temple, restore Judean worship and culture, and revive a dead economy, would all their efforts end with the Judean community submerged under a wave of Ashdodite-speaking young people? So we understand why Nehemiah linked intermarriage to covenant infidelity to the Lord:

> And I made them take an oath in the name of God, saying, "You shall not give your daughters to their sons, or take their daughters for your sons or for yourselves. Did not Solomon king of Israel sin on account of such women? Among the many nations there was no king like him. . . . Nevertheless, foreign women made even him to sin. Shall we then listen to you and do all this great evil and act treacherously [māʿal] against our God by cohabiting with [hôšîb][25] foreign women?" (Neh. 13:25–27 ESV, modified)

Notice that the intermarriage with foreign women is described with terms pertaining to adultery. It is a "great evil," perhaps a variant of "great sin" as a term for adultery, as noted above. Moreover, to marry foreign women is to "act treacherously," using a Hebrew term for covenant infidelity, māʿal, which functions as a synonym for adultery in the law of the unfaithful wife (Num. 5:6, 12, 27). Fidelity in the practice of marriage coincides with fidelity to the covenant with the Lord. Here, the infidelity is not formal adultery, nor fornication, but the attempted formation of forbidden unions: since the law of Moses forbids intermarriage with the surrounding peoples who do not worship the Lord, the Judean marriages with Ammonite, Moabite, Ashdodite, and other peoples are invalid because they are unlawful.

25. *Hiphil* of *yāšab*, "sit or dwell," lit., "to cause to dwell [with]," i.e., "cohabit with."

Tobit

Tobit stands with Ruth as one of the two great narrative explorations of the theme of matrimony in the Old Testament.[26] Unlike the situation with Esther and Judith, the narrative action in Tobit is definitely intended to provide a normative model: the courtship and marriage of Tobias and Sarah represents all the mature ideals of matrimony for the people of Israel at a late stage in their history, shortly before the arrival of the Messiah and the New Covenant. Different passages of the book reflect marriage-related insights drawn from the Law, the Prophets, the Historical Books, and the Wisdom literature, now all incarnated in the two virtuous youths Tobias and Sarah.[27] By the end of the book, we see how a holy marriage of two young people provides hope and healing for their parents and extended family during a dark epoch for God's people, a time marked by exile, persecution, sickness, and apparent failure of divine promises. It is a book that struggles with theodicy: Is God good, and if so, why does he permit such evil in the world? But in the end, God's goodness is richly vindicated through matrimony, causing the reader to praise the "goodness" (Hebrew *tôbît*, i.e., "Tobit") of God and confess, "The Lord is good!" (*tôbî-yāh*, cf. "Tobias").

Much like Ruth 1, Tobit 1–2 introduces protagonists whose situations rapidly deteriorate until they are close to despair and call upon God, which prompts a divine response that begins to move the plot toward a satisfying resolution. So the sacred author introduces Tobit, a faithful northern Israelite from the tribe of Napthali, taken into exile in Nineveh (Tob. 1:1–4). Although he obeys the law of Moses even in a foreign land, his righteous deeds lead not to material blessing but to persecution and misunderstanding, until a series of misfortunes leave him impoverished, blind, and estranged from his wife (vv. 5–14). He despairs of his life and cries out to God to end it (3:1–6). Meanwhile, his younger kinswoman, Sarah, is experiencing her own despair in her parents' household in far off Media. Young, beautiful, intelligent, and virtuous, Sarah is eminently eligible but has been betrothed to seven men in succession, all of whom are slain by a demon on their wedding night, before

26. "The Book of Tobit contains the most explicit and detailed Old Testament description of God's involvement in a particular marriage" (Geoffrey David Miller, *Marriage in the Book of Tobit* [Berlin: De Gruyter, 2011], 209).
27. For Tobit's synthesis of earlier OT texts, see Miller, *Marriage in the Book of Tobit*, 19–24; and Carey A. Moore, *Tobit: A New Translation with Introduction and Commentary*, AB 40 (New York: Doubleday, 1996), 8–9, 20–21.

they ever touch her (3:7–9). Being the only child of her parents, she despairs
of marriage and children and is treated contemptuously even by her own servants. She, too, cries out to the Lord for death (vv. 10–15), and in response to
the pleas of both Tobit and Sarah, the Lord sends the angel Raphael to heal
their lives and restore their hope (vv. 16–17).

Raphael poses as a kinsman of Tobit and gets himself hired to guide
Tobit's only son, Tobias, a young bachelor, out to Media to collect some
silver deposited years ago with a relative (Tob. 5:1–17). On the way, Raphael
catches a peculiar fish while crossing a river, and he instructs Tobias on the
healing properties of this unique creature, which will cure the sorrows of
Tobit and Sarah (6:2–9).

Raphael steers the young Tobias to Sarah's house, where she lives with
her elderly parents, Raguel and Edna (Tob. 7:1–9). They welcome Tobias
with open arms, and recognizing him as a near kinsman—and encouraged
by Raphael—they agree to an immediate marriage between Tobias and Sarah
(vv. 10–17). Raphael instructs Tobias to burn the heart and liver of the fish to
drive away Sarah's demon (8:1–3). The ritual is successful, and before going
to sleep, the young couple prays together movingly, offering their common
life to God and beseeching his blessings (vv. 4–9). Raguel and Edna send a
servant, who discovers the newlyweds sleeping peacefully (v. 13). Shocked
and delighted that Tobias has survived the evening, they proceed to host a
lavish, two-week wedding feast for the young couple (vv. 19–21). Raphael,
however, continues on to fetch Tobit's silver from his kinsman Gabael, but
he returns quickly with both the treasure and the kinsman (9:1–6). At the end
of the feast, Tobias takes his new bride, Sarah, back to Nineveh to the home
of his parents, Tobit and Anna (10:7–13). The older couple are overjoyed to
see Tobias back alive and married to a young kinswoman (11:5–19). Raphael
instructs Tobias to rub the gall of the fish in Tobit's eyes to cure his blindness,
and the older man's vision is restored (vv. 8–14). Much feasting and wedding
festivities ensue. In time, Raphael reveals to Tobit and Tobias that he is really
an angel, before departing from them (12:11–22). Tobit lives to a ripe age;
utters prophecies of the future for Jerusalem, Israel, and his own family;
and dies in peace (13:1–14:11). After both his parents have passed and been
buried honorably, Tobias takes Sarah and returns to her parents, Raguel and
Edna, with whom they live until they, in turn, pass on and are buried, and the
young couple, now blessed as parents of their own children, inherit Raguel's
extensive property (14:12–15).

St. John Chrysostom on Tobias's Prayer

In the early Church, Tobias's prayer before his first wedding night with Sarah was taken as a normative example for Christian spouses, as reflected in this early commentary on Matthew attributed to Chrysostom:

> Just as prayer ought to precede whenever a husband and wife are about to lie together, as the angel Raphael commanded Tobit [*sic*—Tobias], so that what is about to be conceived might be conceived in holiness, so when the only-begotten God was about to enter the virgin, the Holy Spirit preceded, so that Christ could be born in holiness according to the body, as the Divinity entered in place of the seed.[a]

a. John Chrysostom, *Opus imperfectum in Matthaeum* (*Incomplete Commentary on Matthew*), trans. James A. Kellerman, vol. 1, ACT (Downers Grove, IL: IVP Academic, 2010), 28.

Tobit's Theology of Marriage

Through both narrative and explanatory monologues, Tobit presents a fairly thorough, well-considered practical theology of marriage for the people of Israel, covering the metaphysical foundation of marriage, its purposes, practice, and rewards.

The Foundation of Marriage

Tobit grounds marriage in the creation narrative and the divine will. In his famous wedding-night prayer, Tobias appeals directly to the creation account and Genesis 2:23–24 when beseeching God for divine blessing on his union with Sarah:

> You made Adam, and you made his wife Eve to be his helper and support; and from these two the human race has come. You said, "It is not good for the man to be alone; let us make him a helper like himself." (Tob. 8:6 NABRE)

Tobias is "reminding" God, as it were, that marriage is of divine origin, as a remedy for loneliness, and therefore he, Tobias, does nothing wrong by taking Sarah to be his wife, especially since he does so with the right intention: "not out of lust [Greek *dia porneian*] . . . but according to truth [*ep' alētheias*]" (8:7 AT). The institution of marriage is founded by God himself, as revealed in Scripture, and even individual couples are intended for each other by God. Thus, Raphael encourages Tobias concerning Sarah: "She was made your portion from before eternity" (6:18).[28] And Raguel likewise confirms, "It has been decided from heaven that she be given to you" (7:11). More than older biblical books, Tobit stresses the direct involvement of God in bringing about individual marriages.[29] Jesus will likewise affirm the divine guidance and confirmation of human marital unions: "What therefore God has joined together, let not man put asunder" (Matt. 19:6).

The Purpose of Marriage

The primary purpose of marriage in Tobit is to cure the sorrow of loneliness by the establishment of familial companionship. The way that marriage cures loneliness is threefold: by establishing sibling-like companionship between husband and wife; by joining together two extended families, such that each spouse gains additional parents and siblings; and finally, by producing children who will be comforting companions for their parents.

Both Tobias and Sarah are the only children of elderly parents, and they face the prospect of being alone in the world when their parents die. In their marriage, they will find comfort and companionship in each other. So Edna praises God: "You have had mercy on two only children" (Tob. 8:17). Likewise, Tobias cites Genesis in his wedding-night prayer—"It is not good that the man should be alone" (Gen. 2:18)—and he prays that their mutual companionship may be lifelong: "Grant that she and I . . . may grow old together" (Tob. 8:6–7). The new husband and wife will be like friendly siblings toward each other: "You are her brother and she your sister" (7:11). So Tobias addresses Sarah with the term of endearment "My sister" (8:4 NABRE).

Yet through marriage, the young couple gains not only each other as brother and sister but also each other's parents as their own. So Raguel tells Tobias, "I am your father and Edna your mother, and we will be by your side and that of your sister from now on and forever" (Tob. 8:21), and he exhorts Sarah: "Go to your father-in-law and your mother-in-law, because from now

28. Unless noted otherwise, quotations of Tobit are from the ESVCE.
29. According to Joseph A. Fitzmyer, "the new element" in Tobit "is the idea that the marriage of the two young people has been foreseen by God's providence and so their joining together is heaven-blest" (*Tobit*, Commentaries on Early Jewish Literature [Berlin: De Gruyter, 2003], 48). But while more explicit in Tobit, arguably this concept is already implicitly present, for example, in the courtship of Rebecca in Gen. 24.

on they are your parents, as are the ones who gave you birth" (10:12). Edna likewise encourages Tobias: "From now on I am your mother and Sarah is your sister" (10:12; cf. 11:17). Each spouse gains an additional set of family relationships: primarily new parents but also siblings, uncles, aunts, and so on.

Finally, marriage ameliorates loneliness through children. Raphael encourages Tobias about his upcoming marriage: "I assume that you will have children by her, and they will be like brothers to you" (Tob. 6:18)—brothers that Tobias, as an only child, has never had.

FALSE PURPOSES FOR MARRIAGE

The book of Tobit not only identifies the purpose of marriage as the alleviation of solitude, but it also condemns a false but commonly embraced purpose—namely, the satisfaction of physical desire. "Beware . . . of all fornication," Tobit warns Tobias (Tob. 4:12). Here, "fornication" renders the Greek *porneia*, itself probably representing the Hebrew or Aramaic *zənût*, which in context would encompass any kind of sexual activity outside of marriage.[30] Contrary to a common misconception, there is no double standard between men and women, but chastity is expected of both (3:14; 4:12).

Furthermore, the sacred author does not adopt the position that the marriage covenant sanctifies lust between the spouses, as if selfishness and self-gratification are legitimized simply because the physical actions, in themselves, are legal. In his prayer before sharing a bed with his wife for the first time, Tobias acknowledges that some enter marriage for an unrighteous purpose, but he does not: "Not because of lust [*porneia*] do I take this sister of mine, but according to truth" (8:7 AT). The expression "according to truth," *ep' alētheias*, probably renders Hebrew *be'ĕmet*, "in truth." Hebrew *'ĕmet* is often a covenantal concept, frequently paired with *ḥesed*.[31] To act "in truth," *be'ĕmet*, means to act faithfully (cf. NABRE: "with fidelity"), in such a way as to confirm the *truth* of the promises that one has uttered when entering a covenant, to be "true to one's word."[32] Tobias's point is that his physical union with his wife is not motivated by mere physical desire but as an expression of the covenant he is forming with her. His personal marital covenant

30. William Loader, *The Pseudepigrapha on Sexuality: Attitudes towards Sexuality in Apocalypses, Testaments, Legends, Wisdom, and Related Literature* (Grand Rapids: Eerdmans, 2011), 152–53; Moore, *Tobit*, 38.
31. On *ḥesed*, see R. Bultmann, "ἔλεος," *TDNT* 2:479–80.
32. G. Quell, "ἀλήθεια," *TDNT* 1:236n12.

with her is, after all, obliged upon him by the terms of the covenant between God and Israel as mediated by Moses. Furthermore, it is strongly implied in the Greek text and made explicit in the Vulgate that, although Sarah's other suitors marry her legally, they do not approach her "in truth" but in lust—a self-interested desire to gratify physical urges—and this makes them vulnerable to the demonic attack (cf. Tob. 6:17 Vulg./Douay). So the sacred author firmly de-emphasizes the role of physical passion in marriage.

However, it is not that the author excludes love and even physical attraction from marriage—he notes, for example, that Sarah, like the matriarchs, is "very beautiful" (cf. Gen. 12:11; 24:16; 29:17) and that Tobias "loved her greatly and his heart fixed itself on her" (Tob. 6:18).[33] Rather, desire should be kept under the control of the will and not degenerate into merely physical urges. This is even clearer in the Vulgate, where Tobias and Sarah spend their first three days of marriage in prayer and continence: "For these three days we will be joined to God, and when the third night has passed, we will be conjoined ourselves" (8:4 AT; cf. 6:18).[34] In other words, our marital union will become a reflection of our union with God. By delaying gratification even when there is no moral or legal impediment to it, the young couple demonstrates the virtue of self-mastery and the proper ordering of their souls, with the physical not denied but subordinated to the spiritual. Far from denigrating marital union per se, preparing for it by three days of prayer suggests it is a holy act. Furthermore, the period of continence builds an erotic tension through anticipation and permits a couple who have only met that very day to develop some level of comfort and familiarity with each other before engaging in intimacies. Intercourse is certainly good and necessary, but always united to its procreative end (*amore filiorum*; 6:22 Vulg.). We are near to a sacramental view of matrimony.

THE PRACTICE OF MARRIAGE: THE CHOICE OF A SPOUSE

Tobit proposes several norms for the practice of marriage.[35] Foremost among those norms is the prudent choice of a spouse.[36] The sacred author assumes that the initiative will be on the part of the husband, and he should choose

33. See the discussion in Miller, *Marriage in the Book of Tobit*, 43–48.
34. "Istis tribus noctibus Deo iungimur, tertia autem transacta nocte in nostro erimus coniugio" (Tob. 8:4 Vulg.).
35. "Proper marriage is a major concern of the work" (Loader, *Pseudepigrapha on Sexuality*, 151).
36. Cf. Miller, *Marriage in the Book of Tobit*, 34–91.

"a wife from [his] father's household" (Tob. 6:16). Stern warnings are given against marrying a foreign woman (4:12) and, thus, against "disdain[ing]" to take a wife from his kinfolk (v. 13). Marrying outside the clan is considered a sign of arrogance, that the man is too proud to marry a woman of his own people. This probably reflects a period in which the survivors and exiles of Israel were socially and economically oppressed, and the successful men among them desired to marry higher-class women from other ethnic groups. Nonetheless, marriage within the Israelite community was important for the preservation of their faith, culture, language, and what little property and wealth they did accumulate. Thus, endogamy was a sign of a man's concern for his own clan and people.[37]

Divine positive law also had to be observed in the choice of a spouse. The laws of the Mosaic covenant in force at the time sometimes obliged marriage, as in the case of a brother's widow (Deut. 25:5–10). Raphael and Raguel believe Tobias has both a right and an obligation to wed Sarah, who—though still a virgin—is technically a kinswoman widow without children, despite seven previous marriages. As in the book of Ruth, the obligation of levirate marriage is assumed to follow down the line of *gō'ălîm*, kinsman redeemers. So Tobias is told, "You are nearest kin to her" (Tob. 6:12), and he is urged to "receive [his] wife, given to [him] according to the law . . . in the book of Moses" (7:12).[38]

Parental consent and blessing are held up as desirable. The sacred author makes it abundantly clear that the marriage of Tobias and Sarah has the full support of both parents. Raguel invokes blessings upon them: "May the Lord of heaven lead you both" (Tob. 7:11), and "May the God of heaven prosper your way in peace" (v. 12). So does Edna: "May the Lord of heaven grant you joy in place of your grief" (v. 17). Tobit and Anna reciprocate these sentiments when introduced to Sarah: "Welcome, my daughter! Blessed be your God for bringing you to us, daughter! Blessed are your father and your mother. Blessed be my son Tobias, and blessed be you, daughter! Welcome to your home with blessing and joy. Come in, daughter!" (11:17 NABRE).

---

37. On the importance of endogamy, see Miller, *Marriage in the Book of Tobit*, 53–81; Thomas Hieke, "Endogamy in the Book of Tobit, Genesis, and Ezra-Nehemiah," in *The Book of Tobit: Text, Tradition, Theology*, ed. Géza G. Xeravitz and József Zsengellér, JSJSup 98 (Leiden: Brill, 2005), 103–20.

38. Raguel's statements actually exceed the literal sense of the Mosaic law. See the discussion in José Lucas Brum Teixeira, *Poetics and Narrative Function of Tobit 6*, Deuterocanonical and Cognate Literature Studies 41 (Berlin: De Gruyter, 2019), 219.

Modern conceptions of marriage emphasize the consent of groom and bride, but they treat the consent of parents with indifference or contempt. However, *marriage imposes obligations on and establishes relationships with other family members besides just the spouses.* Once married, husband and wife are bound together as "brother and sister" in a union of mutual support for the rest of their lives, but each spouse also receives the other's parents as his or her own. This creates bonds of love and obligation of a most serious nature. Now Raguel and Edna are obliged to support and care for Tobias as their own son (Tob. 8:21); conversely, Tobias is obliged to care for Raguel and Edna in their old age and to bury them honorably at their death (10:13; 14:13). We might add that, if Tobias and Sarah were to suffer untimely deaths and leave behind surviving children, it would fall to one or both of their sets of parents to care for their grandchildren. So marriage creates obligations of a most serious nature, not just for the couple but for other family members, especially parents. It is an infringement on human freedom to place persons under serious obligation without their consent; therefore, the consent of parents to a marriage of their children also carries moral weight. The biblical narrative portrays pejoratively the decisions of Esau and Samson to marry without their parents' consent (Gen. 26:34–35; Judg. 14:2–3), but it presents favorably Isaac's and Jacob's respect for their parents' wishes in their choice of a spouse (Gen. 24:1–67; 28:1–5).

The book of Tobit values virtue in spouses. The sacred author presents Sarah as an ideal spouse and describes her as "sensible and courageous"— two virtues also possessed by the "valiant woman" of Proverbs 31:10–31. The author's message for readers with a choice of their marriage partner is this: Look for a wife like Sarah.[39]

Lifelong Monogamy

In the book of Tobit, marriage is characterized by lifelong monogamy. There are no handmaids or concubines. Both Tobias and Sarah are raised by parents who are monogamous till death, and they are themselves. Particularly poignant on this score is the emphasis on the married couple sharing the same grave. Tobit insists to Tobias concerning Anna, his mother, "Bury her beside me in one grave" (Tob. 4:4), and when she dies, the text tells us that "Tobias buried her with his father" (14:12). This monogamy in death is probably

39. Cf. Miller, *Marriage in the Book of Tobit*, 34–91, esp. 90–91.

inspired by the burials of the patriarchs, each united with his first wife in the grave forever: Abraham and Sarah, Isaac and Rebekah, Jacob and Leah (Gen. 49:31–33). The idealization of union for life—and even beyond this life—is reflected also in Raphael's revelation to Tobias that Sarah is "given to you from today and *forever*" (7:11). Note that the possibility of divorce never arises. Divorce does not exist in the literary world of Tobit.

THE RELATIONSHIP OF SPOUSES

While the husband takes initiative in many matters, nonetheless the book of Tobit embraces a fundamental equality between husband and wife modeled on the relationship of siblings: "You are her brother and she your sister" (Tob. 7:11). This communicates affection, loyalty, and mutual support. It is appropriate that a husband loves his wife deeply: "He loved her greatly and his heart fixed itself on her" (6:18). The husband is responsible for giving his wife happiness, provision, and protection. So Raguel tells Tobias, "You will bring gladness to my daughter's afflicted soul" (8:20; cf. Deut. 24:5), and Edna says, "I am entrusting my daughter to you for safe keeping. Do nothing to grieve her all the days of your life" (Tob. 10:12). The spouses are expected to share a common life of prayer, and Tobias and Sarah are shown prioritizing mutual prayer over their physical relationship (6:18; 8:4). Spouses become a conduit of God's blessings toward one another, and the sacred author mentions many ways in which Sarah finds blessing through Tobias and vice versa. Tobias will "deliver" Sarah (6:18) and "bring gladness" to her "afflicted soul" (8:20), recalling the obligation of a husband to "gladden" his wife (Deut. 24:5). He is trustworthy for her "safe keeping" and to see that nothing will ever "grieve her" (Tob. 10:2). Conversely, Sarah will be a "helper and support" and a "helper for him like himself" (8:6; cf. Gen. 2:18, 20), and she will give him children who will be "like brothers to you" (Tob. 6:18). Thus, the sacred author strongly emphasizes the mutual and reciprocal exchange of blessings between spouses.

Significantly, the book of Tobit portrays three marriages, each with a different relational dynamic.[40] Tobias and Sarah are quite literally a "match made in heaven," and they are so perfectly suited to each other that they scarcely need to speak to one another in the course of the narrative. Raguel and Edna also enjoy a harmonious relationship, but they communicate and cooperate

40. Miller, *Marriage in the Book of Tobit*, 179–205.

with one another much more actively toward common goals. By contrast, Tobit and Anna experience a great deal of tension and even recrimination in their marriage, but for all that, they remain deeply committed to each other. The story recognizes that individual marriages have unique dynamics and experiences. Not every couple is so fortunate as Tobias and Sarah. Spouses may encounter pain, suffering, and disagreement in their relationship, yet the sacred author still affirms the value of lifelong, exclusive, mutual fidelity, even in the face of such difficulties.

Sarah the Bride as Icon of Jerusalem

Tobit's great doxology (Tob. 13:1–18), the literary climax of the book, seems strangely out of place at first. The narrative to this point has been pre-occupied with matters of family and especially of marriage, but these themes scarcely arise in the doxology, as Tobit turns his attention to the previously unmentioned restoration of the holy city, Jerusalem (13:7–18). But upon closer reading, we observe parallels between the plight of Jerusalem and Sarah. Both are women of great beauty (6:12; 13:16–18) who have been subject to chastisement and distress (3:7–15; 13:2, 9, 12), but God brings both joy and love into their lives (6:18; 8:20; 13:10), such that everyone rejoices over them (11:16–19; 13:14). So as in Ruth, the matrimonial union of the blessed couple becomes an icon of God's restored union with his people.

Summary of the Historical Books on Marriage

Throughout the Historical Books, beginning already in Joshua, there is a constant reciprocal relationship between the faithful practice of marriage in the lives of individual Israelites and fidelity to the marriage-like covenant between Israel and the Lord. During periods of great infidelity to the Lord, we also observe grave violations of the ideals of matrimony, as in the book of Judges. But where Israel maintains fidelity to the Lord, as in Ruth, the vulnerable are cared for and young widows find a happy and secure home in a faithful marriage (cf. Ps. 113:9). In the monarchic period, the focus turns to the marriages of the kings, as the fate of the nation is bound up with the royal family. The offenses against matrimony by David and Solomon carry a large measure of responsibility for the eventual dissolution of the Davidic monarchy. The Davidic monarch is intended to be a model husband for the people of Israel, in imitation of the Lord, their true spouse. But the dissolution of the monarchy results in exile, and the people of Israel are thrust out of their land into territory surrounded by foreign ethnicities and nations. The threat of the loss of Israelite faith and identity through exogamy becomes acute in the late biographies of Ezra, Nehemiah, Esther, and Judith. Knowing that the fate of the people passes by way of marriage, the book of Tobit reflects a great flowering of the theory and practice of matrimony among devout Israelites of the late postexilic period. Already in this romantic novella, almost all of the features of the Catholic theology of the sacrament are present in at least an inchoate form, on the threshold of the coming of the Messiah and the inauguration of the New Covenant.

7

"I Hate Divorce," Says the LORD

Marriage in the Prophets

While many texts in the Pentateuch and the Historical Books imply that the covenant between the Lord and Israel has a nuptial dimension, it is really in the "Latter" or literary prophets that this imagery blossoms into full flower.[1] In this chapter, we will examine, in chronological order, the five prophets who develop the nuptial theme most extensively: Hosea, Isaiah, Jeremiah, Ezekiel, and Malachi. For these prophets, matrimony functions primarily as a paradigm for understanding Israel's covenant with the Lord. But secondarily, the divine covenant also serves as a model for the practice of marriage within Israel and, thus, as a basis for the prophets' critique of their contemporaries for sins against matrimony.

Hosea, the Historical Beginning of the Prophetic Nuptial Metaphor

Hosea is generally considered to be the second oldest of the literary or writing prophets, as his career is estimated to span from about 750 to 720 BC,

---

1. For treatments of the nuptial theme in the Prophets, see André Villeneuve, *Divine Marriage from Eden to the End of Days: Communion with God as Nuptial Mystery in the Story of Salvation* (Eugene, OR: Wipf & Stock, 2021), 75–89; Sebastian R. Smolarz, *Covenant and the Metaphor of Divine Marriage in Biblical Thought: A Study with Special Reference to the Book of Revelation* (Eugene, OR: Wipf & Stock, 2011), 61–105.

shortly after Amos's (ca. 770–760 BC).[2] He is the first of the literary prophets to describe the covenant of God and Israel in explicitly marital terminology—and does so in the most dramatic fashion.[3]

The nuptial allegory dominates Hosea 1–3, which forms a discrete opening unit of the book. He writes to northern Israel in the mid-eighth century BC, a time when the kingdom experienced great prosperity followed by decades of decline in the face of the growing threat of the Assyrian Empire, which would conquer and exile the northern Israelites by 722 BC. The temptation was strong for Israel to adopt the cultures and religions of her surrounding political powers, and Hosea likens this religio-cultural assimilation to adultery against the Lord, Israel's husband by covenant.

As a prophetic sign-act to teach the people of Israel about their relationship with God, the Lord commands Hosea to marry a woman named Gomer, a "wife of harlotry" (Hebrew *'ēšet zɘnûnîm*),[4] and to "have children of harlotry, for the land commits great harlotry by forsaking the LORD" (Hosea 1:2). In quick succession, Gomer bears Hosea a son, a daughter, and another son, each given symbolic names—Jezreel (vv. 4–5), Lo-ruhamah (lit., "No Compassion," vv. 6–7), and Lo-ammi (lit., "Not My People," vv. 8–9)—presaging God's judgment on Israel. Yet even the narrative of the birth of these ill-named children is interrupted by an oracle that looks forward to God's ultimate salvation, in which the names of the children will be reversed (1:10–2:1).

In Hosea 2, the narrative shifts from the biographical experience of Hosea and Gomer to an extended poetic allegory of God's relationship with Israel. Verses 2–13 describe Israel as an adulterous wife who has been divorced—"She is not my wife, and I am not her husband" (2:2)—who runs after her lovers because she mistakenly thinks they are the ones who provide her with bread and water, wool and flax, oil and drink (2:5), when in fact it is the Lord who provides. Israel's pursuit of her lovers proves fruitless, so like a "prodigal" wife, she vows to return to her "first husband" (2:7), with whom she had it better. Meanwhile, the Lord threatens to "strip" (2:3) or "uncover" (2:10) her—that is, to withdraw all the material blessings that Israel has wrongly

---

2. A. A. Macintosh, *A Critical and Exegetical Commentary on Hosea*, ICC (Edinburgh: T&T Clark, 1997), lxxxiii.

3. Smolarz, *Covenant and the Metaphor of Divine Marriage*, 61.

4. *Zɘnûnîm*, "immoralities," can refer to any sexual immorality, not just sex for money or professional prostitution (S. Erlandsson, "זָנָה," *TDOT* 4:99–104, esp. 100).

considered to be "[her] hire, which [her] lovers have given [her]" (2:12). Her lovers are the Baals (bəʿālîm, cf. 2:13 JPS), the foreign gods whose feast days she has celebrated (2:11, 13).

In Hosea 2:14–23, the tone turns abruptly to consolation. The Lord will woo Israel in the wilderness, and she will be responsive, as during the exodus from Egypt (2:14–15). The Lord will be Israel's "husband" (ʾîš), not "master" (baʿal), and Israel will forget the Baals (2:16–17). God will renew his nuptial relationship with Israel in a covenant like that of creation, like the renewed covenant of Noah, and he will betroth Israel to himself forever, restoring all the fertility and blessings of nature that have been removed (2:18–23).

In Hosea 3, the attention returns to the prophet's biography. The Lord tells him once again to go and love a woman who is adulterous (3:1), so Hosea goes out and buys "her"—presumably Gomer, whose profligate ways have left her destitute (3:2). He forbids her from consorting with other men but insists she live with him—albeit in continence—for many days, as a sign that Israel will be without king, priest, or temple for a long time, until they finally seek out the Lord once more, who will restore blessing to them (3:3–5).

The heart of Hosea 1–3 is the oracle of 2:14–23, the prophet's extended description of the new spousal covenant that the Lord will establish with Israel. We quote it in full here and then will discuss its implications for a biblical theology of matrimony later:

> Therefore, behold, I will allure her,[5]
>   and bring her into the wilderness,[6]
>   and speak tenderly to her.[7]
> And there I will give her her vineyards,[8]
>   and make the Valley of Achor a door of hope.
> And there she shall answer as in the days of her youth,
>   as at the time when she came out of the land of Egypt.[9]

5. Lit., "I myself will be her seducer," from the Hebrew pātāh in the piel (intensive stem), "persuade, seduce" (BDB 834b); cf. Exod. 22:15 MT.

6. An allusion to the exodus, reinterpreted as a courtship between God and Israel.

7. Lit., "I will speak unto her heart" (Hebrew wədibbartî ʿal-libbāh). Cf. BDB 181b §5.

8. Vineyards are associated with romance; cf. Judg. 21:20–21; Song 1:6, 14; 2:15; 7:12; 8:11–12; Isa. 5:1–7.

9. Alluding to Exod. 24:3: "All the people *answered* with one voice, . . . 'All the words which the LORD has spoken we will do.'"

And in that day, says the LORD, you will call me, "My husband [*ʾîšî*]," and no longer will you call me, "My Ba'al [*baʿlî*]."[10] For I will remove the names of the Ba'als[11] from her mouth, and they shall be mentioned by name no more. And I will make for you a covenant on that day with the beasts of the field, the birds of the air, and the creeping things of the ground;[12] and I will abolish the bow,[13] the sword, and war from the land; and I will make you lie down in safety.[14] And I will espouse you for ever; I will espouse you in righteousness and in justice, in steadfast love, and in mercy.[15] I will espouse you in faithfulness; and you shall know the LORD.[16]

> And in that day, says the LORD,
> I will answer the heavens
> and they shall answer the earth;
> and the earth shall answer the grain, the wine, and the oil,
> and they shall answer Jezreel;
> and I will sow him for myself in the land.
> And I will have pity on Not pitied,
> and I will say to Not my people, "You are my people";
> and he shall say "You are my God."[17] (RSV2CE)

This oracle presents a picture of how the Lord God functions as an ideal bridegroom of his people, and as such it informs the reader of the Israelite ideals of matrimony, if not its legal requirements.

So what are these ideals? First, *indissolubility*. It is striking that the oracle does not finally accept divorce as a satisfactory solution, even in the case of infidelity. The entire unit of Hosea 1–3 frequently plays on the language of divorce (1:9–10; 2:2–3, 23), but nonetheless it continually returns to reaffirm

10. A woman could call her husband either *ʾîšî*, "my man," or *baʿălî*, "my lord," but the former was more intimate. Pagan gods were called *baʿālîm*, "lords." Cf. BDB 35b, 127a–b.
11. That is, male pagan deities.
12. Alluding to the "priestly" creation narratives: Gen. 1:26, 28, 30; 2:20; 8:19; 9:2, 9–17.
13. Cf. Gen. 9:12–17, where the rainbow represents the divine war bow hung in the clouds after the flood, indicating cessation of hostilities.
14. Cf. Lev. 26:5b–6, the covenant blessings of Sinai.
15. This betrothal is characterized by six qualities: permanence ("forever," *ʿôlām*); righteousness (*ṣedeq*); justice (*mišpāṭ*); steadfast, covenantal love (*ḥesed*); mercy (*raḥămîm*, lit., "wombs"); and faithfulness (*ʾĕmûnāh*).
16. "Know" here likely has a covenantal and spousal sense: cf. Gen. 4:1 MT, ESV; Jer. 31:34.
17. This dialogue represents performative utterances or *verba solemnia* from a covenant ritual; see Gordon P. Hugenberger, *Marriage as a Covenant: Biblical Law and Ethics as Developed from Malachi* (Grand Rapids: Baker, 1998), 216–36, esp. 234–36.

the marital bond between God and Israel (1:10–2:1; 2:14–23; 3:1–3). The Lord's future covenant with Israel will be *ləʿôlām*, "for ever" (2:19a), a phrase marking the most solemn and permanent covenants.[18] Accordingly, the Lord commands Hosea to search out and redeem his unfaithful wife and take her back (3:1–5) as a sign-act of the Lord's *ḥesed*, his spousal fidelity.

Second, *generous provision*. Hosea portrays the Lord as a husband who provides generously: "She did not know that it was *I* who gave her the grain, wine, and the oil, and who lavished upon her silver and gold" (Hosea 2:8). God as husband provides not merely the legally required minimum of food, clothing, and oil (Exod. 21:10)[19] but also an abundance of jewelry (Hosea 2:8b: "silver and gold"; cf. v. 13: "ring and jewelry"). God shows his love for Bride Israel in tangible ways. In the future, the Lord will be a good husband by blessing the natural environment with peace and fruitfulness: "The earth shall answer the grain, the wine, and the oil, / and they shall answer Jezreel" (2:22)—"Jezreel" here functioning as a symbolic name for Israel. In the future restoration, the harmony of nature will be restored and God's husbandly generosity will be expressed once more through the natural environment.

Third, *attraction*. On behalf of the Lord, Hosea dares to say, "I will *seduce* [Israel]"—that is, make himself attractive to her—so she freely returns to him (Hosea 2:14 AT). The prophet uses the intensive form (the *piel*) of the verb *pātāh*, "to deceive, to persuade, to seduce," the term used in the Law to differentiate cases of voluntary intercourse from forced intercourse (Exod. 22:16–17; cf. Deut. 22:25–29). Israel feels a powerful attraction to foreign "lovers" (i.e., gods), but the Lord makes himself more attractive yet. So there is an erotic element in the marriage of the Lord and Israel.

Fourth, *affection*. The Lord says, "I will speak unto her heart" (Hosea 2:14 AT)—Hebrew *wədibbartî ʿal-libbāh*, often translated "speak tenderly," using an expression employed frequently in romantic contexts.[20]

Fifth, *freedom*. A corollary of the previous two elements—since the Lord makes himself attractive and expresses affection toward her—Bride Israel consents to the relationship by her free will: "She shall *answer* [ʿānāh, i.e.,

18. Gen. 9:16; 17:7, 13, 19; Exod. 31:16–17; Lev. 24:8; Num. 25:13; Judg. 2:1; 2 Sam. 7:16, 24–29; 22:51; 23:5; 1 Chron. 16:15, 17; 2 Chron. 13:5; Pss. 89:28; 105:8, 10; 111:5, 9; Isa. 24:5; 55:3; 61:8; Jer. 32:40; 50:5; Ezek. 16:60; 37:26.
19. Taking the disputed *ʿōnāh* in Exod. 21:10 as "oil" rather than the more common "marital rights"; see Hugenberger, *Marriage as a Covenant*, 321n161.
20. Gen. 34:3; Judg. 19:3; Ruth 2:13; Isa. 40:2.

"respond"] as in the days of her youth, / as at the time when she came out of the land of Egypt" (Hosea 2:15b). This alludes to the wholehearted assent of the people of Israel to the terms of the covenant: "All the people *answered* [*ʿānāh*] with one voice and said, 'All the words that the LORD has spoken we will do'" (Exod. 24:3 ESV).

Sixth, *mutuality*. The authority of the Lord as husband is downplayed, and the reality of mutuality or complementarity between spouses is emphasized: "In that day, . . . you will call me 'my husband,' and no longer will you call me, 'my lord [*baʿălî*]'" (Hosea 2:16 AT). The title for "husband" that emphasizes authority or possession, *baʿal*, is rejected in favor of the title *ʾîšî*, "my man"—which is perfectly complementary in a grammatical sense to that for a wife: *ʾîš* and *ʾiššāh*, man and woman, husband and wife. The relationship between spouses is mutual, reciprocal, and complementary, like the *kənegdô* concept from Genesis 2. Some authority relationship remains between the two, but it is overshadowed by their mutual love, which prevents any divergence of their wills.

Seventh, *exclusivity*. "I will remove the names of the Baʾals from her mouth, and they shall be mentioned by name no more" (Hosea 2:17). The logic of the covenant demands exclusive loyalty. If either partner were to enter into an additional covenant with a third party, it would jeopardize their ability to fulfill the all-encompassing commitments they have already taken on. Thus, exhortations to exclusive loyalty are found in many ancient Near Eastern treaties, as we have seen above: "Know only the Sun! Another lord do not know!"[21] Up to now, Israel has tried to live in covenant with the Lord but also in covenants with many divinities, but in the future covenant renewal, the Lord will ensure that Israel neither mentions nor remembers any competitors for her affection. The implication is that God will do this by the lavishness of his love. His provision for and affection toward Israel will be so overwhelming that any benefits from previous liaisons will seem so insignificant as to be unworthy of remembrance.

Eighth, *safety*. As a good husband, the Lord protects Bride Israel from all potential threats. A covenant with beasts, birds, and creeping things ensures that the natural environment will pose no danger (Hosea 2:18a), and bow, sword, and war will be abolished, so that Bride Israel can lie down in safety (v. 18b).

---

21. From the vassal treaty of Suppiluliuma. See Hugenberger, *Marriage as a Covenant*, 268.

The Great Prophets and the Development of the Nuptial Metaphor

Hosea is the first to explore so explicitly the nuptial dimension of God's covenant with his people, but not the last. The three great prophets of the Jewish tradition—Isaiah, Jeremiah, and Ezekiel—each take up this theme pioneered by Hosea and develop it in different ways.

Isaiah

In the prophet Isaiah, a subtle nuptial theme occurs occasionally through the first five chapters, in which Jerusalem appears as a harlot who once was a faithful wife. "How the *faithful* city has become a harlot, she that was full of *justice*! *Righteousness* lodged in her, but now murderers" (Isa. 1:21). "Faithfulness" (*ne'ĕmānāh*, related to *'ĕmûnāh*), "justice" (*mišpāṭ*), and "righteousness" (*ṣedeq*) are all terms of Hosea's betrothal of God to Israel (Hosea 2:19–20). An allusion to Hosea 2 is not out of the question in Isaiah 1. The prophet may be using a few key words evoking a well-known prophetic oracle against Israel in order to reapply it specifically to Jerusalem.

The bride-turned-harlot motif reappears in Isaiah 3:16–24, where Isaiah employs the "daughters of Zion" as an image, by metonymy, for the city of Jerusalem as a whole. Just as the wealthy young women of the city behave immodestly (vv. 16–17), dressing with the luxurious ostentation of high-class prostitutes (vv. 18–23), so Jerusalem has been a flirtatious, promiscuous wife who uses the wealth given her by her divine husband to indulge herself (cf. Hosea 2:8, 12–13). But this behavior will provoke the Lord's judgment, and a time will come when the young women of the city will be so eager to be rid of the suspicion of harlotry that they will desperately seek out even disadvantageous marriages, as in the case of seven wives sharing a single husband (Isa. 4:1). Then the Lord will cleanse Jerusalem, like a woman with a flow of blood ritually cleansed of her impurity (Isa. 4:4; cf. Lev. 15:19–31). Then she will be holy and glorious, like the newly constructed tabernacle in the wilderness (Isa. 4:5–6). Drawing on imagery from the Song of Songs, where the bride or her body is frequently likened to a garden or vineyard,[22] Isaiah sings "for [his] beloved a love song concerning his [beloved's] vineyard" (5:1). This vineyard is "the house of Israel, and the men of Judah" (5:7), who are both "vineyard" and "beloved one" (thus, a "love

22. Song 1:6; 4:12–5:1; 6:2, 11; 7:6–9, 12–13; 8:11–12.

St. Methodius on the Church as "Virgin Daughter Zion"

St. Methodius and other Fathers identified Isaiah's "virgin daughter Zion" as the Church, following a hermeneutical trajectory suggested by the ecclesiology of St. Paul (Eph. 5:21–33):

It is the church whose children shall come to it with all speed after the resurrection, running to it from all quarters [Isa. 60:4]. [The church] rejoices, receiving the light that never goes down and clothed with the brightness of the Word as with a robe. For with what other more precious or honorable ornament was it becoming that the queen should be adorned, to be led as a bride to the Lord, when she had received a garment of light and therefore was called by the Father? Come then, let us go forward in our discourse and look on this marvelous woman as on virgins prepared for a marriage, pure and undefiled, perfect and radiating a permanent beauty, lacking nothing of the brightness of light; and instead of a dress, clothed with light itself; and instead of precious stones, her head adorned with shining stars.[a]

a. Methodius, *Symposium or Banquet of the Ten Virgins* 8.5 (*ANF* 6:336).

song")—that is, bride. Several Gospel parables will take up one or both of these images.[23]

After Isaiah 5, the nuptial imagery for Israel and Jerusalem recedes again in Isaiah until the beginning of the second part of the book, in Isaiah 40, where Jerusalem is reintroduced as a woman, and the voice of God commands his hosts to "comfort" and "speak to the heart" (*dibbēr ʿal-lēb*) of Jerusalem, using the same expression as in Hosea 2:14 and incorporating also Hosea's imagery of the wilderness as a trysting place (cf. Hosea 2:14; Isa. 40:3–5). In several places in the following chapters, the prophet describes Jerusalem as an unfaithful and rejected wife (Isa. 50:1; 54:4; 60:15), who is now taken back (54:6–8), remarried (54:4; 62:3–5), and made fruitful (54:1). So she will decorate herself as a bride once more (49:14–18; 52:1–2; 61:10) and be surprised by children she did not remember bearing (49:19–23; 54:1–3; 60:4–7; 66:7–11).

23. Matt. 20:1–16; 21:33–46; 22:1–14; 25:1–13.

Isaiah 54:4–10 is a beautiful example of Isaiah's development of the nuptial theme:

> Fear not, for you will not be ashamed;
>> be not confounded, for you will not be put to shame;
> for you will forget the shame of your youth,
>> and the reproach of your widowhood you will
> remember no more.
> For your Maker is your husband,
>> the LORD of hosts is his name;
> and the Holy One of Israel is your Redeemer [gōʾēl],
>> the God of the whole earth he is called.
> For the LORD has called you
>> like a wife [ʾiššāh] forsaken and grieved in spirit,
> like a wife of youth when she is cast off,
>> says your God.
> For a brief moment I forsook you,
>> but with great compassion [raḥămîm] I will gather you.
> In overflowing wrath for a moment
>> I hid my face from you,
> but with everlasting love [ḥesed ʿôlām] I will have compassion [rāḥam]
>> on you,
>> says the LORD, your Redeemer [gōʾēl].
> For this is like the days of Noah to me:
>> as I swore that the waters of Noah
>> should no more go over the earth,
> so I have sworn that I will not be angry with you
>> and will not rebuke you.
> For the mountains may depart
>> and the hills be removed,
> but my steadfast love [ḥesed] shall not depart from you,
>> and my covenant of peace [bərît šālôm] shall not be removed,
>> says the LORD, who has compassion [rāḥam] on you.

So many of the themes of Hosea 2 recur here: the abandonment of the unfaithful wife, followed by her redemption and remarriage; the renewal of covenantal love and fidelity (ḥesed) and compassion (raḥămîm); the comparison with the Noahic covenant and the reestablishment of a covenant (bərît) that will establish peace (šālôm) among God, his people, and nature.

In Isaiah 62:1–5 the prophet, like Hosea, takes up the motif of symbolic renaming to denote the renewal of the covenant relationship:

> For Zion's sake I will not keep silent,
>   and for Jerusalem's sake I will not rest, . . .
> and you shall be called by a new name
>   which the mouth of the Lord will give.
> You shall be a crown of beauty in the hand of the Lord,
>   and a royal diadem in the hand of your God.
> You shall no more be termed Forsaken,
>   and your land shall no more be termed Desolate;
> but you shall be called My delight is in her,
>   and your land Married;
> for the Lord delights in you,
>   and your land shall be married.
> For as a young man marries a virgin,
>   so shall your sons [or "Builder"] marry you,
> and as the bridegroom rejoices over the bride,
>   so shall your God rejoice over you.

As in Hosea, previously given names denoting a breach of covenantal relationship ("Forsaken," "Desolate"; cf. "Not pitied" and "Not my people" in Hosea 1:6–9) are replaced by names denoting covenant renewal ("My delight is in her," "Married," cf. Hosea 1:10; 2:23). In Hebrew, the words for "your sons" and "your Builder" (*bānāyik*, v. 5) are spelled identically, so it is not clear whether Jerusalem's "sons" will marry her—that is, whether descendants of Jerusalemites will return and commit themselves to the city's welfare—or whether her "Builder" will marry her, as her "Maker" does in Isaiah 54:5. Either option has arguments in its favor, and perhaps the prophetic author intended the polyvalence.[24]

While Isaiah arguably borrows the nuptial paradigm from Hosea, he develops it in three new directions. First, in Isaiah it is typically no longer Israel as a whole, but specifically Jerusalem/Zion, who is the "bride" of the Lord. Second, in the time of Isaiah and Micah (late eighth century BC), the image of the "[virgin] daughter of Zion" begins to be employed as an icon of the

---

24. See the discussion in John N. Oswalt, *The Book of Isaiah: Chapters 40–66*, NICOT (Grand Rapids: Eerdmans, 1998), 577, 580–82; Smolarz, *Covenant and the Metaphor of Divine Marriage*, 96–97.

city generally (e.g., Isa. 1:8; 10:32; Mic. 1:13; 4:8). Zion proper is the forti-
fied spur where the palace and the dwellings of the royal family and courtiers
were originally located.[25] So the "daughter of Zion" is a highborn young
woman (see Jer. 6:2), probably of the royal house, and the term *bətûlāh*,
"virgin," is sometimes added (e.g., Isa. 37:22; Lam. 2:13), probably meaning
"marriageable"—that is, "nubile" in its classic sense. So the image of the
"[virgin] daughter of Zion" is of a royal princess at the age of peak attractiveness and eligibility. This background will inform its use by later prophets.

Third, Isaiah emphasizes the title "Redeemer" (*gōʾēl*) for God, evoking the
responsibilities of the *gōʾēl* in Israelite culture, such as marrying the kinsman's
widow (Ruth 2:20; 3:9–13; 4:1–14). So the motif of God marrying the "barren
widow," Jerusalem (Isa. 54:1, 4), fits with the theme of the Lord as Redeemer
that Isaiah never tires of mentioning.[26]

Jeremiah

In a striking reminiscence of Hosea, the book of Jeremiah likewise begins its prophetic oracles with a lengthy nuptial allegory (Jer. 2:1–3:25) that
largely follows the same shape as Hosea's. Jeremiah opens with the voice of
the Lord to Jerusalem:

> I remember the devotion of your youth,
>   your love as a bride,
> how you followed me in the wilderness,
>   in a land not sown. (Jer. 2:2)

It is the same romanticization of the exodus seen in Hosea 2:15b. But Israel
did not remain faithful: she "bowed down as a harlot" (Jer. 2:20) and ran after
other gods. In a passage also strongly reminiscent of Hosea (cf. Hosea 2:5–7,
12–13), Jeremiah portrays Israel as a "restive young camel" and a "wild ass . . .
in her heat," who *pursues* her lovers rather than merely accepting them (Jer.
2:23–24). "Who can restrain her lust?" the prophet asks, and Israel replies, "It
is hopeless, for I have loved strangers, and after them I will go" (vv. 24, 25).

Dalit Rom-Shiloni has argued that Jeremiah 2:20–25 consciously evokes
Numbers 5:11–31 (the ritual ordeal for the suspected adulteress) with the

---

25. E. Otto, "צִיּוֹן," *TDOT* 12:343–46.
26. Isa. 35:9; 41:14; 43:1, 14; 44:6, 22–24; 47:4; 48:17, 20; 49:7, 26; 51:10; 52:3, 9; 54:5, 8;
59:20; 60:16; 62:12; 63:9, 16.

prophet's rhetorical cry, "How can you say, 'I am not defiled?'" (Jer. 2:23), since the word "defiled"[27] is used heavily in Numbers 5:11–31 but is otherwise rare in the Masoretic Text.[28] The same theme of the unfaithful wife who professes innocence continues to dominate the narrative up through Jeremiah 3:20. Israel is like a bride who forgets her wedding and the commitment she has made (2:32), and so the Lord ponders divorcing her:

> If a man divorces his wife
> and she goes from him
> and becomes another man's wife,
>> will he return to her?
> Would not that land be greatly polluted?
> You have played the harlot with many lovers;
>> and would you return to me?
>>> says the LORD. (Jer. 3:1)

Here the prophet clearly alludes primarily to Deuteronomy 24:1–4, bringing up an internal contradiction already present in Hosea 1–3—namely, that if the law forbids a man to divorce a wife and then remarry her after she has been with another man, how can the Lord metaphorically "remarry" Israel after she has been "divorced" for playing the harlot with other gods? Nonetheless, amid further descriptions of northern Israel's aggressive promiscuity (Jer. 3:2–7) and her "divorce" (3:8), Jeremiah introduces—for the first time in the canon—the image of Israel and Judah as two sister-spouses of the Lord (3:7–11), an awkward analogy because bigamy with two sisters is forbidden in the law (Lev. 18:18). The prophet recounts the scandalous effect Israel's promiscuous behavior has had on her "sister," Judah (Jer. 3:7–10), but he nonetheless goes on to assert that the Lord *is* willing to receive back "divorced" Israel (3:11–20). The implication seems to be that the Lord is more faithful to his spousal-covenantal bond than even the Mosaic law "requires" him to be, as if the law could require anything of God. This sets up a tension over God's view of divorce that will be dealt with further in Malachi and ultimately by Jesus.

27. The *niphal* of *ṭāmēʾ*, used eighteen times in the MT and seven times in Num. 5:11–31. The ritual ordeal for the suspected adulteress is arguably alluded to in Jer. 2:23; Ezek. 20:30–31, 43; 23:7, 13, 30.

28. Dalit Rom-Shiloni, "'How Can You Say, "I Am Not Defiled . . ."?' (Jeremiah 2:20–25): Allusions to Priestly Legal Traditions in the Poetry of Jeremiah," *JBL* 133, no. 4 (2014): 757–75.

Jeremiah concludes his own nuptial allegory—so similar to and perhaps inspired by Hosea's—with the summative comment, "Surely, as a wife breaks covenant [*bāgad*] with her companion [i.e., husband], so you have broken covenant [*bāgad*] with me, O house of Israel" (Jer. 3:20 AT). Here, Jeremiah uses the technical term for "breach of covenant," *bāgad*, used elsewhere for faithlessness in marriage (Exod. 21:8; Hosea 5:7; Jer. 9:2; cf. 5:11).

After Jeremiah 3:20, the nuptial paradigm recedes from the forefront of Jeremiah's narrative, although it continues in the background and resurfaces with occasional allusions.[29] Of special significance are the matrimonial connotations of Jeremiah's great "new covenant" oracle, an oracle that functions as a linchpin of biblical theology:

> Behold, the days are coming, says the LORD, when I will cut[30] with the house of Israel and the house of Judah a new covenant, not like the covenant which I cut with their fathers when I seized[31] them by their hands to bring them out of the land of Egypt, my covenant which they broke, though I myself[32] was married [*bā'altî*] to them, says the LORD. But this is the covenant which I will make with the house of Israel after those days, says the LORD: I will give my law within their inward parts, and I will inscribe it upon their hearts; and I will be their God, and they shall be my people. And no longer shall each man teach his neighbor and each his brother, saying, "Know the LORD," for they shall all know me, from the least of them to the greatest, says the LORD; for I will forgive their iniquity, and I will remember their sin no more. (Jer. 31:31–34 RSV, modified)

Despite Hosea's reticence to use Hebrew *ba'al* and its derivatives to describe the Lord's marriage to Israel, Jeremiah describes Israel as breaking the matrimonial covenant with the Lord formed at Sinai with the verbal form of *ba'al* (v. 32; cf. Exod. 24:1–8). But similar to Hosea 2:14–23, Jeremiah insists that the future covenant the Lord will make with Israel will be even more intimate than the previous one. The law will not be written on tablets of stone (Exod. 24:12; 31:18) kept in the ark (Deut. 10:5; 1 Kings 8:9), but will

29. E.g., Jer. 4:30–31; 11:15; 12:7–8; 13:27; 31:3–4, 21–22.
30. In Hebrew, the initiation of a covenant is described as "cutting a covenant" (*kārat bərît*), because of the long-standing use of cutting ceremonies (Gen. 15:10; 17:9–14)—especially the bisection of animals (Jer. 34:18–20)—to solemnize covenants.
31. The Hebrew verb is more vigorous—*ḥāzaq* in the *hiphil* stem, "to cause to be strong"—than the usual translation "took."
32. The Hebrew expresses the subject emphatically: *'ānōkî*, "I, I myself."

be written "upon their hearts" and placed "within their inward parts" (Jer. 31:33). In imitation of Israelite wedding vows, God proclaims the covenant formula: "I will be their God, and they shall be my people" (v. 33). And every Israelite shall "know" the Lord (v. 34), which probably both *denotes* the recognition of one's lord by covenant and, especially considering the explicit nuptial imagery used earlier (v. 32b), *connotes* marital intimacy and union, as so often elsewhere in Scripture (esp. Hosea 2:20).[33] Thus, Jeremiah's description of the "new covenant" in 31:31–34, while incorporating developments, is nonetheless theologically and thematically very similar to Hosea 2:14–28.

Before we leave Jeremiah, it should be noted that *literal* sexual immorality and marital unfaithfulness are major issues in the prophet's critique of his contemporaries. As so often in Israel's story, a primary way the people violate their spousal covenant with the Lord is by violating their individual covenants with their spouses.

> How can I pardon you?
>> Your children have forsaken me,
>> and have sworn by those who are no gods.
> When I fed them to the full,
>> they committed adultery
>> and trooped to the houses of harlots.
> They were well-fed lusty stallions,
>> each neighing for his neighbor's wife.
> Shall I not punish them for these things?
>>> says the Lord;
>> and shall I not avenge myself
>> on a nation such as this? (Jer. 5:7–9)

Note that it is the sexual behavior of *men* that is in view here, who are "committing adultery" (*nā'ap*) in the "whorehouse" (*bêt zônāh*) (v. 7 AT). Significantly, this implies that male sexual activity with a woman other than one's spouse constitutes adultery, even if the partner is not some other man's wife but a prostitute (*zônāh*). Thus, it is against the man's *own* marital bond that he commits adultery (*nā'ap*), and this provokes the Lord to punish (*pāqad*) and avenge (*nāqam*).

---

33. Hugenberger, *Marriage as a Covenant*, 268–69, 277–78.

Ezekiel

No less than his prophetic precursors, Ezekiel takes up the marital paradigm for describing the covenant history of the Lord and his people; yet he handles it not as a running nuptial theme throughout his book but in two discrete, intense, and explicit allegorical narratives found in Ezekiel 16 and 23.

Although Ezekiel is much more detailed, explicit, and graphic in his descriptions of the rise and fall of the bride of the Lord, the plot of the allegorical narrative of Ezekiel 16 is the same in its essentials as that of Hosea 2 and Jeremiah 2–3, except that the bride is specified as the city of Jerusalem rather than Israel generally. Ezekiel's "Jerusalem" probably represents the kingdom of Judah generally, personified in its capital city, similar to the "virgin daughter of Zion" motif in other prophets. Thus, Ezekiel describes Bride Jerusalem's origin in Canaan and the humility of her infancy (Ezek. 16:1–7); her arrival at puberty and espousal to the Lord (16:8), probably representing the Sinai or Mosaic covenant; the gradual bestowal of wealth and beauty upon her by her divine husband (16:9–14), representing the rise of the Davidic-Solomonic empire; and then a long period of harlotry with Egyptians, Assyrians, Chaldeans, and others (16:15–34), representing the period of the divided monarchy and Judah's decline. A particular sin that Ezekiel alone highlights is Bride Jerusalem's taking the children she has born to the Lord and sacrificing them to her "lovers," the idols of the other nations (16:20–21, 36). Thus, the present is a time of judgment, as the husband-Lord will uncover Bride Jerusalem in the presence of her lovers and turn her over to their power (16:35–43). Her sins are even worse than those of her "sisters," Samaria and Sodom (16:44–52). But in the future, both Jerusalem and her sisters will be restored (16:53–58), and the Lord will make an "everlasting covenant" (v. 60) with Bride Jerusalem (16:59–63).

Ezekiel returns to this allegory in chapter 23, although he develops it in a slightly different way. He tells the story of two sisters, "Oholah" ("her tent"), representing Samaria and the Northern Kingdom, and "Oholibah" ("my tent is in her"), representing Jerusalem and the Southern Kingdom. Both sisters are sexually promiscuous in the land of Egypt (Ezek. 23:3), but the Lord marries them both (v. 4), only to discover that Oholah commits adultery with Assyria until she is destroyed by them (vv. 5–10), and Oholibah follows her sister's example even more brazenly, going after both the Assyrians and the Chaldeans (i.e., the Babylonians; vv. 11–21). So the Lord gives Oholibah over to her lovers, the Babylonians, and she will be destroyed by them (vv. 22–49). Unlike the allegories in Hosea 2, Jeremiah 2–3, and even Ezekiel 16, in this case there is no vision of a future remarriage or renewal of covenant between the Lord and Jerusalem.

That is not to say that Ezekiel does not foresee a future renewal of covenant or, indeed, the gift of a new covenant that will surpass the old one. His prophecies concerning this hopeful theme are largely found in Ezekiel 34–37, where the Lord promises to be Israel's God and to restore his "servant David" as "prince" when he establishes a "covenant of peace" that will bring about a restoration of nature (34:24, 25). The Lord will retrieve Israel from all the places they have been scattered and "sprinkle clean water" upon them, giving them a "new heart" and a "new spirit," a "heart of flesh" instead of a "heart of stone" (36:24–26). Indeed, the "new spirit" will be nothing other than "my spirit within you," which will bestow the power to observe the law, for "you shall be my people, and I will be your God" (36:27, 28). Thus, motifs from Hosea and Jeremiah recur: the renewal of creation and the restoration of Eden-like conditions (fruitfulness of vegetation and peace with the animals), the forgiveness of sins, the renewal of the heart of Israel, and a new level of intimacy with the Lord. While Ezekiel does not use explicitly nuptial language, the "covenant formula" he reasserts (e.g., 36:28), as we have noted before, may be based on the *verba solemnia* of Israelite weddings.

Ezekiel, like Jeremiah, roundly criticizes his contemporaries for sexual immorality and offenses against marriage, decrying the "men" who "commit lewdness in your midst," who "uncover their fathers' nakedness" and "humble women who are unclean in their impurity," defiling their "neighbor's wife," "daughter-in-law," and "sister" (Ezek. 22:9–11). But in these cases Ezekiel merely applies, rather than develops, the principles of matrimony already found in the Mosaic law (e.g., Lev. 18 and 20).

On the other hand, both Jeremiah and Ezekiel show the beginnings of the development of a theology of celibacy, which is pertinent to our interests since the theology of celibacy develops always in reciprocity and dialogue with that of marriage. Thus, the Lord commands Jeremiah:

> You shall not take a wife, nor shall you have sons or daughters in this place. For thus says the LORD concerning the sons and daughters who are born in this place, and concerning the mothers who bore them and the fathers who begot them in this land: They shall die of deadly diseases. They shall not be lamented, nor shall they be buried. (Jer. 16:2–4)

Similarly, the Lord informs Ezekiel:

> "Son of man, behold, I am about to take the delight of your eyes away from you at a stroke; yet you shall not mourn or weep nor shall your tears run down. Sigh, but not aloud; make no mourning for the dead. Bind on your turban, and put your shoes on your feet; do not cover your lips, nor eat the bread of mourners." So I spoke to the people in the morning, and at evening my wife died. And on the next morning I did as I was commanded. (Ezek. 24:16–18)

The Lord forbids Jeremiah from marrying, and he takes Ezekiel's wife from him and forbids him to mourn, for similar reasons—that is, as a sign-act to their contemporaries of the impending judgment, which will be so terrible that people will wish they had not married and raised families, and they will not even have the opportunity to mourn their deceased loved ones.

This contributes to the development of a prophetic theology and practice of celibacy. In some prophetic callings, marriage can play a role and function itself as prophetic symbolism (Isa. 8:18; Hosea 1, 3). In other prophetic vocations, though, celibacy functions as a sign of contradiction, a sign of the coming judgment and a decision to live in detachment from the things of this earth in light of their transience and imminent destruction (Jer. 16:1–13; Ezek. 24:15–24). We note that Elijah, Elisha, Daniel, and John the Baptist lived the celibate prophetic vocation.

Malachi, the Canonical Conclusion of the Prophetic Nuptial Metaphor

The marital image of God's union with his people recedes from view in most of the Minor Prophets after Hosea, but there are at least two exceptions related to the "virgin daughter of Zion" motif. Thus, Zephaniah ends with Jerusalem pictured as a young, marriageable woman about to be wed by a heroic warrior who returns triumphant from battle, the Lord God: "Sing aloud, O daughter of Zion. . . . / Rejoice and exult with all your heart, / O daughter of Jerusalem! / . . . The LORD your God . . . will rejoice over you with gladness, / he will renew you in his love; / he will exult over you with loud singing / as on a day of festival" (Zeph. 3:14, 17–18). Similar imagery occurs in Zechariah 9:9–11, where the prophet calls the "daughter of Zion" to rejoice and shout because her royal bridegroom returns triumphant from

battle, "humble and riding on an ass," a steed of peace, thus indicating that
he has defeated all foes and established "peace to the nations" in his vast dominion "from sea to sea" (vv. 9, 10). The Lord is bound to Zion by the "blood
of [his] covenant," a possible marital image, which obliges him to care for
Zion's "prisoners" (Zech. 9:11–12 ESV; cf. Exod. 4:25; 24:8). The imagery of
the renewal of peace in creation and of covenant restoration recalls similar
images recurring in several prophets going back to Hosea 2:14–23.

In the canonically last prophet, Malachi, the marital paradigm of Israel's
bond with the Lord returns powerfully and centrally, in a way that binds
together the literal practice of marriage in the Israelite community with the
community's spousal-covenantal bond with God.

The book of Malachi is structured in part as a set of six rhetorical disputes
between the postexilic Judean community and the Lord,[34] in which the Lord
takes his people to task both for their critical attitudes toward him and for
their perfunctory cultic practices.[35] The third dispute (2:10–16) raises the issue
of the infidelity of Judean men toward their Judean wives, which is construed
not only as a moral issue but also one of cultic cleanliness:

> Have we not all one father? Has not one God created us? Why then are we
> faithless [bāgad] to one another, profaning [ḥillēl] the covenant [bərît] of our
> fathers? Judah has been faithless [bāgad], and abomination [tôʿēbāh] has been
> committed in Israel and in Jerusalem; for Judah has profaned the sanctuary of
> the LORD, which he loves [ʾāhēb], and has married [bāʿal] the daughter of a
> foreign god. May the LORD cut off from the tents of Jacob, for the man who
> does this, any to witness or answer, or to bring an offering to the LORD of hosts!
> (Mal. 2:10–12)

The prophet criticizes his contemporaries for breaking covenant (bāgad) with
each other and with God. How? Personifying the people as one man, he portrays "Judah" as marrying the "daughter of a foreign god"; in other words,
the Judean men are marrying pagan women who continue to practice devotion to their ancestral deities. This religious exogamy is critiqued as a breach
of covenant (bāgad), a grotesque cultic offense (tôʿēbāh, commonly used for
taboo sexual unions), and a "profanation" (ḥillēl) of the sanctuary, worthy

---

34. Mal. 1:2–5; 1:6–2:9; 2:10–16; 2:17–3:5; 3:6–12; 3:13–15.
35. See John S. Bergsma and Brant Pitre, *The Old Testament*, vol. 1 of *A Catholic Introduction to the Bible* (San Francisco: Ignatius, 2018), 945.

of the penalty of *kārēt*, being "cut off" or dying without issue.[36] Clearly, to form a marital covenant with a woman outside the worshiping community of Israel is understood as a grave violation of the covenant, characterized by love (*'āhēb*), that exists between Israel and the Lord.

In the following verses, the prophet criticizes his contemporaries for weeping over God's rejection of their prayers and sacrifices (Mal. 2:13), while in fact the fault is their own. Addressing them directly, he contends that God is acting as "witness to the covenant between you and the wife of your youth, to whom you have been faithless, though she is your companion [*ḥāberet*][37] and your wife by covenant" (v. 14). The prophet alludes to the Genesis creation narratives (Gen. 2:7, 24) by asking rhetorically, "Did [God] not make them [man and woman] one and grant him a portion of [his] Spirit? And why one? He was seeking godly offspring" (Mal. 2:15 AT).[38] And Malachi concludes with this admonition:

> So guard yourselves in your spirit, and toward the wife of your youth let no one be faithless [*bāgad*]. "For I hate divorce, says the LORD the God of Israel, and covering one's garment with violence, says the LORD of hosts. So take heed to yourselves and do not be faithless [*bāgad*]." (Mal. 2:15–16 RSV modified)

The Hebrew grammar and syntax of verse 16 is somewhat difficult, but the RSV is most likely correct in its bold translation: "I hate divorce, says the LORD the God of Israel." Those interested in the technical issues involved in the translation of Malachi 2:16 may wish to read the following excursus. Others may wish to continue reading after the excursus.

EXCURSUS: THE TRANSLATION OF MALACHI 2:16

The translation of Malachi 2:16 is complicated by unexpected shifts in person and tense in the Hebrew verbs of the sentence. The Masoretic Text reads literally:

36. See Donald J. Wold, "The Meaning of the Biblical Penalty *Kareth*" (PhD diss., University of California, Berkeley, 1978).

37. "Companion" is a serviceable translation for *ḥāberet*, the feminine form of *ḥābēr*, "friend, companion, colleague," usually used in the Hebrew Bible to describe one with whom one has an elective or voluntary relationship and in whose company one is frequently found. Cf. BDB 288b–289a.

38. Lit., "[he was] seeking the seed of God," using the Hebrew *zeraʿ 'ĕlōhîm*, which could be "children of God" or, in an adjectival sense, "godly [i.e., holy] offspring." See Hugenberger, *Marriage as a Covenant*, 140–41.

"For he hates sending away,"[39] says the LORD God of Israel, "and violence covers over his garment,"[40] says the LORD of hosts. (AT)

There are dozens of possible ways to construe the grammar and the sense of this passage,[41] but contemporary Christian scholarship has largely followed one of two basic approaches, hinging on the identity of the subject of the first verb, *śānēʾ*, "he hates" (or "he has hated"). Either the subject is understood to be the Lord, speaking of himself in the third person, or the subject is understood to be the Israelite man who divorces his wife. The NABRE and the ESV illustrate these two approaches respectively:

> For I hate divorce,
>> says the LORD, the God of Israel,
> And the one who covers his garment with violence,
>> says the LORD of hosts. (NABRE)

> For the man who does not love his wife but divorces her,
>> says the LORD, the God of Israel,
> covers his garment with violence,
>> says the LORD of hosts. (ESV modified)

Both translational approaches resist the temptation to emend the Hebrew text as much as possible, and both are unable completely to remove all grammatical and syntactical awkwardness. Nonetheless, despite what appears to be the popularity of the second approach in recent scholarship, we defend the somewhat more traditional first option for the following linguistic reasons.

First, the spelling of *šallaḥ* ("sending away," "divorce") in Hebrew can represent only two possible grammatical forms: the infinitive construct or the second masculine singular imperative. Now, the previous Hebrew word, *śānēʾ*,

39. Or "If he hates, send away!" because the Hebrew form *šallaḥ* can be interpreted either as an infinitive construct ("to send away" or "sending away") or as a second masculine singular imperative ("[you] send away!"). The frequent use of Hebrew *šallaḥ* in legal contexts concerned with divorce, to describe the eviction of a woman from her former husband's home (see Deut. 22:19, 29; 24:1, 3; Isa. 50:1; Jer. 3:1, 8), justifies rendering the term "divorce" here, as the translations attest.

40. Or "he covers over his garment [with] violence," because the Hebrew form *ḥāmās* can be interpreted either as the subject of the verb *kissāh*, "covers," or as an "accusative of material," indicating the substance being employed to cover the garment.

41. See the extensive discussion in Hugenberger, *Marriage as a Covenant*, 48–83.

"hate," is a transitive verb—that is, it takes an expressed object.[42] Therefore, it is much more natural to take the following word, *šallaḥ*, as a verbal noun (i.e., an infinitive) and as the object of *śānēʾ* (i.e., "he hates *to divorce*" or "he hates *divorcing*") than to construe *šallaḥ* as a second-person singular imperative ("send away"), which not only denies *śānēʾ* the object it requires but also involves an awkward and confusing shift in person: "For he has hated, [you] send away!"

Second, the complex phrase "For the man who does not love his wife but divorces her" (ESV), as well as similar phrases proposed by Hugenberger and others,[43] would never naturally be expressed by a Hebrew speaker with the three words we have in the Masoretic Text: *kî-śānēʾ šallaḥ*, "for he hates divorce!" Rather, it would be expressed as follows: *kî hāʾîš ʾăšer śānēʾ ʾištô wayəšalləḥehā*.[44] The Hebrew can sustain *some* elision, but it cannot be reduced to the three words we have in the Masoretic Text and still retain this nuanced meaning. Scholars who translate this way are *virtually* emending the text, even if they do not recommend *literal* emendation. Therefore, we endorse the meaning reflected in the RSV family of translations:

> For I hate divorce,[45] says the LORD the God of Israel, and covering one's garment with violence,[46] says the LORD of hosts. So take heed to yourselves and do not be faithless [*bāgad*]. (Mal. 2:16 RSV2CE)

42. Except when used as a participle, this verb is *always* accompanied by a direct object in its over 120 occurrences in the MT.

43. Hugenberger, *Marriage as a Covenant*, 69–74.

44. Lit., "For the man who hates his wife and dismisses her."

45. This common English translation does smooth out the awkwardness of the fact that, in the Hebrew, God refers to himself in the third person: "'For he hates divorce,' says the LORD." Yet divine third-person self-references are very common in the MT (see Andrew S. Malone, "God the Illeist: Third-Person Self-References and Trinitarian Hints in the Old Testament," *JETS* 52, no. 3 [2009]: 499–518), notably in the third through fifth commandments (Exod. 20:7–12) and also later in Malachi (3:1–4). Furthermore, perhaps the consonants of *śānēʾ* in Mal. 2:16 should be repointed as the masculine singular participle *śōnēʾ*, rendering Mal. 2:16 grammatically very similar indeed to the divine statement in Isaiah 61:8: "For I the LORD . . . hate [*śōnēʾ*] robbery."

46. This clause reads literally in the Hebrew: "and [he] covers over his garment [with] violence." To smooth the English grammar, the RSV2CE translates the Hebrew perfect form, "he covers," as a participle, "covering." It is possible to repoint the third masculine singular perfect form, *kissāh*, as the masculine singular participle, *kōseh*, to appease our English (or Latinate) grammatical sensibilities, but this emendation is unnecessary. The whole clause is functioning grammatically as a second object of "he [the LORD] hates" earlier in the verse. While we would prefer a relative pronoun at the head of the clause (e.g., *ʾăšer* or *še-*) to make the grammatical relationship clearer (i.e., "and *the one who* [*wa-ʾăšer*] covers"), nonetheless the "unmarked" or "bare" relative clause is by no means unusual in biblical Hebrew; see Robert D. Holmstedt, "The

The objection has been raised that the prophetic author could scarcely have attributed hatred of divorce to the Lord God, when the Lord permits it in Deuteronomy 24:1–4.[47] But it is not clear upon close reading that those verses constitute any blanket approbation of divorce.[48] As we have seen, Deuteronomy 24:1–4 formally is a prohibition of remarriage to a former spouse under certain conditions and a tacit acknowledgment that divorce takes place. It even casts some aspersions on remarriage by describing it as "defiling" the wife (24:4). The author of Malachi could have taken the same hermeneutical approach that the Essenes and Jesus would later adopt—namely, that the doctrine of matrimony should be founded primarily on the creation narrative (the *yəsôd habbərî'āh*, or "principle of creation," CD 4:21; cf. Matt. 19:3–9) and later laws read in its light. For Malachi, the God of Israel is adamantly opposed to divorce, and the act of divorce is correlated with "covering one's garment with violence." The "garment" may be a metaphor for the spouse herself or the marital relationship (cf. Ruth 3:9; Ezek. 16:8), which suffers "tearing" via the divorce.

The literary unit Malachi 2:10–16 concludes with the solemn warning, "Do not be faithless," repeating the lemma *bāgad*, "to commit covenant infidelity, to be faithless," which has occurred four times previously in this passage (2:10, 11, 14, 15). This term is the leitmotif of the unit. Marriage is a covenant that reflects and intertwines with the covenant between Israel and the Lord. Infidelity to the marriage covenant is tantamount to infidelity to the Lord, who was called upon as a witness and guarantor of the marital covenant in the wedding ceremony itself. The men of Israel cannot disrupt their covenantal relationship with their wives without disrupting their relationship with God—in this case, resulting in the failure of their prayers and supplications (cf. 1 Pet. 3:7). Moreover, the wife constitutes the "companion" (*ḥăberet*) of her husband, using the female form of a term used several times in Scripture to describe a man's close friends or companions, his social equals who participate with him in the same endeavors and in whose company he is typically found—a term

---

Relative Clause in Biblical Hebrew: A Linguistic Analysis" (PhD diss., University of Wisconsin–Madison, 2002), 107–14.

47. Hugenberger, *Marriage as a Covenant*, 65.

48. See Hugenberger, *Marriage as a Covenant*, 76–81, and our own discussion above in chap. 5.

colloquially translated "buddy, pal."[49] To call the wife her husband's *ḥăberet* connotes companionship, equality, commonality, friendship, and the sharing of common activities and fate. It is the "companionate" view of marriage we have found also in the Wisdom literature and such books as Tobit.

Other scholars have noted that there seems to be a purpose behind the canonical ordering of the Book of the Twelve, inasmuch as we find the strongest expressions of God's fidelity to matrimony in the first and last prophets, Hosea and Malachi. Hosea affirms in no uncertain terms that God's covenant relationship with Israel is a form of marriage (Hosea 1–3), and Malachi affirms on behalf of the whole prophetic tradition, "'I hate divorce!' says the Lord God of Israel" (Mal. 2:16 AT). Despite everything and at whatever cost to himself, God will honor the covenantal bond into which he has entered with Israel, and he expects the Israelites themselves similarly to honor their covenantal bonds with him and with each other. This is the hopeful yet demanding statement of the Book of the Twelve to Israel after the exile, as she awaits the Messiah.

Summary of Marriage in the Prophets

The Prophets develop explicitly the nuptial dimension of God's covenant with Israel implicit already in the Pentateuch and Historical Books. In the eighth century, Hosea establishes a paradigmatic narrative of Israel's marital history (Hosea 1–3): the Lord courts Israel in the wilderness, weds himself to her at Sinai, and lavishes favor on her after the settlement of the land. Israel, however, runs after the gods of the nations—foreign lovers—and forsakes her marriage with the Lord. Despite all this, after a necessary period of suffering, the Lord will once more espouse Israel to himself in a new covenant relationship, a relationship more intimate and fulfilling than anything experienced previously. Although this paradigm is an allegory of God's relationship with his people, it reveals an Israelite ideal of marriage characterized by qualities including indissolubility, generosity, attraction, affection, freedom, mutuality, exclusivity, and safety. The "great prophets," Isaiah, Jeremiah, and Ezekiel, follow the paradigm established by Hosea and develop it in different directions without substantially changing it. Finally, Malachi places, as it were, a canonical seal on the prophetic narrative of God's spousal relationship with his people by emphatically affirming the Lord's rejection of divorce (Mal. 2:16) and thus his never-ending offer of forgiveness and reconciliation toward Bride Israel.

49. Ps. 45:8 MT (45:7 ET); Eccles. 4:10; Song 1:7; 8:13; Dan. 2:13, 17–18.

8

"Rejoice in the Wife of Your Youth"

Marriage in the Wisdom Literature

The Wisdom literature provides some of the most important biblical material relevant to the Christian doctrine and practice of marriage: not only Song of Songs, *the* great biblical poem on love and marriage, but also significant moral exhortations on courtship, marriage, and marital fidelity in the other Wisdom books. Throughout this literature there recurs the motif of the wise man's relationship with divine wisdom, which is construed as a form of marriage and has undeniable implications for the meaning of marriage in the economy of salvation.

Minor References to Matrimony: Job, Psalms, Ecclesiastes

Job

Matrimony is only tangentially significant in the narrative of Job. Job is, of course, married, but his wife becomes a source of temptation to him (Job 2:9), recalling Adam's temptation through Eve (Gen. 3:6, 12)—a literary strategy of portraying Job as a "new Adam," a representative figure for humanity. Unlike Adam, though, Job resists temptation coming through his spouse (Job 2:10), showing himself a worthier representative of the race.

Job's magnificent oath of innocence (Job 31) also shows great moral refinement vis-à-vis marriage and sexuality. Indeed, Job's very first affirmation of innocence is his abstinence from lust, even by sight: "I have made a covenant with my eyes; / how then could I look upon a virgin?" (Job 31:1; cf. Matt. 5:28). Nor has he allowed his "heart [to be] enticed to a woman" (Job 31:9), encompassing not only adultery per se—a "heinous crime" that "consumes unto Abaddon" (i.e., hell, vv. 11–12; cf. Matt. 5:29–30)—but the whole path of capitulation leading to it. In Job, the marriage bond, especially its sexual aspect, is holy. The slightest violation of it—even an impure glance—endangers one's "portion from God above, and [one's] heritage from the Almighty" (Job 31:2).

Psalms

There are a few notable exceptions to the general disinterest in marriage in the Psalter. Psalm 45, the "Ode for a Royal Wedding" (RSV2CE), is a sui generis composition more akin to the poetry of the Song of Songs than to any other psalm. It makes an important contribution to the motif of the Messiah as royal bridegroom, so significant in the Gospels. The historical context of the psalm appears to be a royal wedding during the reign of Solomon. A court minstrel is the speaker (v. 1), who begins by flattering the royal bridegroom with descriptions fit only for one both human and divine (vv. 2–9), even calling him "God": "Your throne, O God [*'ĕlōhîm*], stands forever" (v. 7 NABRE).[1] His robes are "all fragrant with myrrh and aloes" (v. 8), an image applied to Christ in John 19:39. The minstrel then addresses the prospective bride, telling her to forget her family of origin (Ps. 45:10), as her status will be unimaginably elevated by her imminent marriage to the king, causing foreign nations to curry her favor with lavish gifts (v. 12). He reminds her that her husband will still be her "lord" (*'ādôn*) and therefore worthy of her "worship" (*hištaḥăwāh*, v. 11 [12 MT]). After the minstrel describes the joyful wedding procession of bride and bridesmaids into the royal palace, the bride herself speaks the final verses, boasting of her power to immortalize her royal husband's legacy by her fertility: "Instead of your fathers shall be your sons; / you will make them princes in all the earth. / I will cause your name to be celebrated in all

---

1. Some take *'ĕlōhîm* here in an adjectival sense (e.g., "your divine throne"), but this seems hard to justify grammatically. See Murray J. Harris, "The Translation of *Elohim* in Psalm 45:7–8," *TynBul* 35 (1984): 65–89.

generations; / . . . the peoples will praise you for ever and ever" (vv. 16–17). The hyperbolic language makes this psalm difficult to apply to any marriage save that of Christ and the Church (cf. Eph. 5:21–33), and both Hebrews 1:9 and John 19:39 reflect such an application.

Psalm 51 also impinges on matrimony, as the context is David's adultery: "A Psalm of David . . . after he had gone in to Bathsheba" (Ps. 51:0). This psalm is *the* quintessential sacred text for the liturgical expression of contrition in both the Jewish and the Christian traditions. That the specific sin provoking this greatest penitential prayer is adultery confirms the pervasive theme in the Wisdom literature of adultery as *the* quintessential act of folly, the opposite of wisdom. The poetic expression of David's contrition in the psalm emphasizes the gravity of the sin of adultery, indirectly reaffirming the sanctity of marriage in the sight of God. David's striking affirmation, "Against you, you only, have I sinned" (v. 4 ESV), is not a denial of human victims but a hyperbolic expression meaning all sin is ultimately directed against God, especially *this* sin—the violation of matrimony.

Finally, Psalm 128 describes a man who "fears the LORD, who walks in his ways" (v. 1), whose "wife will be like a fruitful vine within your house" and whose "children will be like olive shoots around your table" (vv. 3–4). The psalm regards the realization of the procreative end of matrimony as an unmitigated good, God's blessing of those who love him. This contrasts with non-Christian construals of marriage, both ancient and modern, that downplay, ignore, or denigrate the procreative end, regarding children as an economic burden or impediment to the intimacy of the spouses.

Ecclesiastes

In Ecclesiastes 2:1–8, Qoheleth explains that he has made a test of pleasure, listing a long sequence of delights and luxuries culminating in "the greatest delight of men: many concubines" (2:8 AT). Yet Qoheleth discovers that sex, like all other pleasures, is nothing more than "vanity and a striving after wind" (3:11). Therefore, even the greatest sexual pleasures human beings can experience do not satisfy the longings of the human soul and still leave it empty and frustrated. This is an important *datum* for evaluating the role of sexuality in (1) human flourishing, (2) the economy of salvation generally, and (3) matrimony specifically. The limitations Christianity places on the sexual activity of spouses has provoked much criticism down through the centuries, frequently on the assumption that human happiness depends on continuous and unrestricted sexual experiences or the pursuit thereof. Yet Qoheleth has experienced continuous and unrestricted sexual satisfaction and still finds it ultimately empty. Based on his experience, Qoheleth declares, "Enjoy life with the wife whom you love, all the days of your vain life that he has given you under the sun, because that is your portion in life" (9:9 ESV). For Qoheleth, the companionship of a happy marriage is one of the simple goods of life—along with eating, drinking, and finding pleasure in one's work (cf. 5:18; 8:15; 9:7)—that provide some consolation amid the apparent capriciousness and meaninglessness of human existence.

Matrimony in the Central Wisdom Tradition: Proverbs, Song of Songs, Wisdom, Sirach

Proverbs

Proverbs is the oldest of the Wisdom books proper, and it is foundational for all the rest. The book consists of a prologue (chaps. 1–9) and an epilogue (31:10–31) surrounding seven discrete collections of aphorisms (10:1–22:16; 22:17–24:22; 24:23–34; 25:1–29:27; 30:1–14; 30:15–33; 31:1–9).[2] The prologue consists of an introduction that identifies the author of the book (Solomon, 1:1), its purpose (1:2–6), and its central thesis (i.e., "The fear of the LORD is the beginning of knowledge," 1:7). This is followed by a set of eleven exhortations from Solomon to his "son" (1:8–19; 2:1–22; 3:1–10, 11–20, 21–35; 4:1–9, 10–27; 5:1–23; 6:1–19, 20–35; 7:1–27), interpolated with three discourses in which Lady Wisdom speaks, one near the beginning (1:20–33) and two at the end (8:1–36; 9:1–18), forming an asymmetric frame around the main body of Solomon's exhortations (chaps. 2–7) and capped by a conclusion in which Lady Folly speaks as an inverted caricature of Lady Wisdom (9:13–18).

Remarkably, matrimony and related concerns dominate the discussion of the life of ḥokmāh, divine wisdom, in Proverbs' lengthy prologue (chaps. 1–9) and brief but elegant epilogue (31:10–31). The author employs two literary strategies. The first is direct exhortation: a large part of the prologue comprises warnings against promiscuous women (2:16–19; 5:1–14; 6:20–35; 7:1–27) and commendations of faithfulness to one's spouse (5:15–23). The

2. For discussion of the structure of Proverbs, see John S. Bergsma and Brant Pitre, *The Old Testament*, vol. 1 of *A Catholic Introduction to the Bible* (San Francisco: Ignatius, 2018), 597–99.

second is metaphor: wisdom is personified as an ideal wife ("Lady Wisdom"; 8:1–21, 32–36; 9:1–12; 31:10–31), in contrast to the promiscuous seductress ("Woman Folly"; 9:13 NABRE).

The first warning against nonmarital sexual activity in the book comes in 2:16–19, wherein Solomon exhorts his "son" (i.e., the reader; 2:1) to seek wisdom as protection from the "loose woman" (*'iššāh zārāh*) or "adventuress" (*nokrîyāh*), who "forsakes the companion of her youth" and the "covenant of her God" and therefore becomes a path to death (vv. 16–19). The *'iššāh zārāh* is literally "strange woman," "strange" meaning "not belonging to"—that is, not one's wife. The *nokrîyāh* means "foreign woman," probably also "foreign" in the sense of "not of your family" or "not belonging to you." The *'iššāh zārāh* and the *nokrîyāh* are synonymous, and verse 17 defines her not by ethnicity but behavior: she has "abandoned" or "forsaken" her first husband, her *'allûp nəʿûrêhā*, "the companion of her youth"—connoting long familiarity, affection, loyalty, equality, and friendship (see Ps. 55:14; Prov. 16:28; Jer. 3:4; NABRE)—rather than the more formal *baʿal* ("husband," "lord," "master"). Thus, the sacred author deliberately evokes a companionate vision of marriage. "Of her youth" (*nəʿûrêhā*) reflects the ancient Israelite custom of young people marrying immediately upon adulthood. This first marriage contracted in one's youth would have a sacred standing, as opposed to marriages contracted later. For Proverbs, as we will see, this *first* marriage should be the *only* marriage for the one who seeks after divine wisdom. This original marriage bond is "the covenant of her God" (*bərît 'ĕlōhêhā*, 2:17), strong textual evidence that ancient Israel understood marriage as a covenant. The unfaithful woman "forgets" (*šākaḥ*) this covenant (v. 17), a technical term for the intentional abandonment of covenant obligations (cf. Deut. 4:23, 31). As a result of "forgetting," she is a source and conduit of death (Prov. 2:18–19). The essential rhetorical features of Proverbs 2:16–19—namely, the "strange woman" is attractive (v. 16) but breaks covenant (v. 17) and therefore leads to death (vv. 18–19)—will be repeated and developed in Proverbs 5:1–14; 6:24–35; and 7:1–27.

By contrast, in Proverbs 3:13–18 we encounter the first of several passages that describe Lady Wisdom as the ideal bride. Thus, Wisdom, like a bride, is first "found" (*māṣāʾ*, Prov. 3:13; cf. 18:22; 31:10) and then makes the finder "happy" or "blessed" (*'ašrê*, Prov. 3:13; cf. 18:22; 31:11–12, 28–29; Ps. 128:1–3) because she is more valuable than precious metals or jewels (Prov. 3:14–15; cf. 31:10). Wisdom has "long life in her right hand, in her left riches and honor"

(3:16 AT)—an image of a woman weaving, with the distaff in her right hand, the spindle in her left, and the growing thread between them as a symbol of long life (cf. Prov. 31:19). Wisdom is a source of life, a "tree of life" (3:18), thus recalling not only the garden of Eden (Gen. 2:9) but also Eve, the first wife, whose name is "Life" as mother of the living (Gen. 3:20). Wisdom brings happiness to all who "hold her fast" (Prov. 3:18), a term (the *hiphil* of *ḥāzaq*) for the marital embrace (cf. Deut. 22:25; 2 Sam. 13:11). Thus, in the following chapter (Prov. 4:6–9) Solomon exhorts his "sons" not to "forsake" (*'āzab*) but to "love" (*'āhēb*) and "embrace" (*ḥābaq*) Wisdom, all terms rich in nuptial connotation. In return, she bestows a "crown" on her lover (Prov. 4:9), possibly alluding to Israelite wedding rituals (cf. Song 3:11).

Proverbs 5 opens with another warning against the "loose woman" (vv. 3–14), expanding on themes from 2:16–19, while stressing that an extramarital affair consumes a man's social, temporal, financial, and physical resources and transfers them to others (vv. 9–11). Then follows the clearest encomium of marital fidelity in Proverbs (5:15–20). Here, the "wife of your youth" (*'ēšet nə'ûrekā*) is a "well," "cistern," and "fountain" (vv. 15–18), as in the Song of Songs (4:12, 15). She is the source of "water," a symbol of life and the pleasures and powers of procreation (v. 15). This "water" should remain between the husband and his wife; it should not flow "in the streets"—that is, escape the protection and intimacy of the covenant bond (v. 16). Recalling the obligation of Deuteronomy 24:5, the husband is commanded to "rejoice" (*śāmaḥ*) in his wife (Prov. 5:18), for she is a "lovely deer, a graceful doe" (v. 19 ESV).[3] Verse 19 reads literally, "May her breasts [*dadayim*] inebriate [*rāwāh*] you at all times; may you be intoxicated [*šāgāh*] by her love continually" (AT)—employing, like the Song, the erotic imagery of breasts (*šādayim*; Song 1:13; 4:5; 7:3, 7, 8; 8:1, 8, 10) and consumption of wine (Song 1:2; 2:4;[4] 4:10; 5:2; 7:2, 9; 8:2) and granting divine affirmation of the physical and psychological attraction of spouses. The pleasure and satisfaction of the marital embrace per se are natural goods that serve to bind the spouses closer to one another, as opposed to sexual activity outside of marriage, which is literally senseless or purposeless: "Why should you be intoxicated, my son, with a 'strange' woman or embrace the bosom of a 'foreigner'?" (Prov. 5:20 AT).

---

3. Compare the cervine imagery for lovers in Song 2:7, 9, 17; 3:5; 4:5; 7:3; 8:14.
4. "Banqueting house" (ESV, RSV), lit., "house of wine," *bêt hayyāyin*; cf. MT, LXX, Douay, Vulgate.

The sacred author returns to the theme of adultery in 6:24–35: while physical attraction may be good between man and wife (Prov. 5:19), it becomes dangerous when it flares up with an "evil woman" (*'ēšet rā'*) or "foreigner" (6:24). "The price of a harlot is a round loaf of bread, but the wife of a man stalks [one's] precious life" (6:26 AT)—meaning that the consequences of adultery are graver than fornication. As a man cannot contact fire without being burned, so one cannot contact a married woman without punishment (vv. 27–29). While stealing at least makes *some* sense when one is starving (vv. 30–31), adultery is not only *immoral* but *illogical*: the adulterer "has no sense" and "destroys himself" (v. 32). He will face an enraged husband who cannot be appeased (vv. 33–35).

The entirety of Proverbs 7 is a graphic description of seduction. In the evening shadows of the back alleys of the city, a wayward wife seizes a foolish young man and entices him (vv. 6–20): "I had to offer sacrifices, / and today I have paid my vows; / so now I have come out to meet you" (vv. 14–15). This may refer to the sacrifices for purification that a woman offered at the cessation of menses, after which she was ritually clean and could engage in conjugal relations (Lev. 15). This event usually coincided with ovulation and an increase in female libido, so she intends to entice him by suggesting she is in a state of heightened receptivity.[5] Moreover, she has prepared her bed with luxuries, including "Egyptian linen," "myrrh," and "aloes" (Prov. 7:16–17), all associated with nuptial contexts (cf. Ps. 45:8; Song 4:14; John 19:39). She promises that her husband is gone for some time; that is, they are safe to indulge in lovemaking all night long (Prov. 7:18–20)—and with these "smooth lips" she persuades him (v. 21), and he follows her to his own death like an animal to slaughter (vv. 22–23).

Thus, Proverbs 7:1–24 is the last and longest exposition of the warning against promiscuity first articulated by Proverbs 2:16–19. The antidote to this lethal foolishness is to "say to wisdom, 'You are my sister,' / and call insight your intimate friend" (7:4; cf. Gen. 12:13[!]). These are spousal terms of endearment; the use of "sister" for one's wife is well attested in the Song of Songs and in Genesis.[6]

The seductress of Proverbs 7 is almost an exact foil of Lady Wisdom, who speaks in Proverbs 8. The seductress operates in secret places in the dark, but

5. See Martin Krause, "II Sam 11:4 und das Konzeptionsoptimum," *ZAW* 95 (1983): 434–37.
6. See Song 4:9–10, 12; 5:1–2; Gen. 12:13, 19; 20:2, 5, 12; 26:7, 9.

Lady Wisdom calls to the simple in public, in broad daylight (Prov. 8:1–7). Like a good wife, she

- is worth more than jewels and precious metals (8:10–11, 19//31:10);
- is full of good counsel and strength (8:14//31:25–26);
- fully reciprocates love (8:17a//5:18–19) once she has been "sought" and "found" (8:17b//31:10); and
- brings wealth to her beloved (8:18//31:11–19).

She was God's collaborator in the building of the world, and she was "daily his delight, rejoicing before him always," which suggests a quasi-nuptial relationship between God and Wisdom (cf. 8:30//Gen. 26:8). Unlike those who loiter by the doors of the loose woman (Prov. 5:8; 7:7–8), those who "lurk" by the door of Wisdom will find life (8:34) and obtain "favor from the LORD" (8:35), like the finder of a good wife (cf. 18:22).

In Proverbs 9, Wisdom once more is "calling out" to the simple from the heights of the city (8:1–3//9:1–3). "Wisdom has built her house, / she has set up her seven pillars" (9:1)—imagery of the temple, using the sacred number associated with the cult. "She has slaughtered her beasts, she has mixed her wine" (v. 2)—imagery of sacrifice and libation, in preparation for a sacred feast. "She has sent out her maids to call from the *highest places* in the town" (v. 3)—more temple imagery, the highest location in most ancient cities being set apart as the sacred precinct (compare the "acropolis," lit., "high city," of Athens). By this imagery, the sacred author suggests the proximity, even identity, of Wisdom with the divine. To the simple she cries, "Come, eat of my bread / and drink of the wine I have mixed" (v. 5)—ostensibly referring to a sacred banquet, but the eating and drinking imagery, especially that of drinking wine, can also be a euphemism for the conjugal embrace, as in Song of Songs.[7] Like a well, a tree, or one's wife, Wisdom is the source of life: "By me your days will be multiplied, / and years will be added to your life" (v. 11).

Now Woman Folly speaks (9:13–18). Like the seductress of Proverbs 7:10–13, she lacks feminine modesty and virtue: she is "noisy" (lit., "she roars"), "seductive,"[8] and "knows no shame" (v. 13).[9] She imitates Lady Wisdom by

---

7. Song 1:2, 4; 2:3–4; 4:10, 16; 5:1; 7:8–9, 13; 8:2; cf. Prov. 5:15, 19.
8. Hebrew *pətayyût*, from the root *p-t-h*; cf. v. 13 ESV.
9. Lit., "doesn't know a thing."

insinuating herself into the high places of the town and crying out, "Stolen water is sweet, / and bread eaten in secret is pleasant" (v. 17). As the meal imagery above connotes the conjugal act, so this stealthy consumption of "stolen water" and "bread eaten in secret"—parallel to the surreptitious nighttime escapades of the seductress and the young fool in Proverbs 7:7–23—connotes adultery. So Woman Folly, like the "strange" and "foreign" woman (2:16–19), is the pathway to death and the grave (9:18).

Thus, by the end of the prologue of Proverbs, it has become clear that there are two paths to life, symbolized by two women: either Lady Wisdom, whom one weds, becoming one's source of life and joy, or Woman Folly, who leads one by fleeting, illicit pleasures to death and destruction.

The aphorisms that constitute the body of Proverbs (10:1–31:9) contain some notable contributions to a biblical theology of matrimony:

> An excellent wife is the crown of her husband,
> but she who brings shame is like rottenness in his bones. (12:4 ESV)

"An excellent wife," 'ēšet-ḥayil, is literally "woman of force, valor," as in Proverbs 31:10 and Ruth 3:11. Proverbs 12:4 is the first biblical description of a wife as her husband's "crown," an image underlying other canonical descriptions of the relationship between husband and wife (see 1 Cor. 11:7). The stark contrast between an excellent wife and a shameful one follows the principle *corruptio optimi pessima*: corruption of the best is worst. A wife is so powerful that she can bring about the greatest good or worst evil, as further developed in Sirach 25–26.

Proverbs 18:22—"He who finds a wife finds a good thing [ṭôb], / and obtains favor [rāṣôn] from the LORD"—strongly resembles Proverbs 8:35, "He who finds me finds life [ḥayyîm] / and obtains favor [rāṣôn] from the LORD," establishing a bidirectional comparison of Wisdom and a good wife. Both are means of rāṣôn, "favor, grace, blessing"—Greek *charis*, "grace." Thus, the Septuagint reads:

> He who finds a good wife finds grace and receives joy from God.
> He who casts out a good wife casts out his goods. (Prov. 18:22–22a
> LXX [AT])

Here, *hilarotēs*, "joy" or "cheerfulness," joins *charis*, "grace," as the divine gifts accompanying a good wife. The one who divorces throws out (*ekballō*) not

The Venerable Bede on Proverbs 31

There is a virtual consensus among the Fathers that the allegorical sense of Proverbs 31:10–31 refers to the Church. The Venerable Bede summarizes the tradition admirably:

> Solomon . . . sings the praises of holy Church in just a few verses but with a fullness of truth. For the song in question consists of twenty-two verses, according to the sequence and number of the Hebrew letters, so that the verses each begin with a different letter. The altogether perfect sequence of this alphabet symbolically indicates the altogether complete description here given of the virtues and rewards of either the individual believing soul or the entire holy Church, which is constituted one catholic church out of all the elect souls.[a]

a. Bede, *In Proverbia Salomonis* 3.31.9, in Al Wolters, *The Song of the Valiant Woman: Studies in the Interpretation of Proverbs 31:10–31* (Carlisle, UK: Paternoster, 2001), 81–82.

only his wife but also "the goods" (*ta agatha*)—that is, "property," "wealth," or "well-being."[10]

Proverbs 19:14 ("House and wealth are inherited from fathers, / but a prudent wife is from the LORD") asserts that "house and wealth" are natural goods achievable by human means, but a good spouse is a supernatural good bestowed only by God, who deserves all thanks for it. Thus, marriage, unlike other human institutions, is *more* than purely natural or human and is somehow a participation in the divine and the result of divine action. The Septuagint reads: "Fathers distribute house and possessions to sons, but by God is a woman betrothed to a man" (19:14 AT). God, the ultimate matchmaker, directly espouses husband to wife, anticipating Christ's teaching in Matthew 19:6, based on the Eden narrative (Gen. 2:15–25), in which God is the "matchmaker" and "best man" (Hebrew *šôšbîn*) at the first wedding in human history.[11]

Proverbs knows not all marriages are blissful: "It is better to live in a corner of the housetop / than in a house shared with a quarrelsome[12] wife" (Prov.

10. For the senses of *ta agatha*, see W. Grundmann, "ἀγαθός," *TDNT* 1:11.
11. See André Villeneuve, *Divine Marriage from Eden to the End of Days: Communion with God as Nuptial Mystery in the Story of Salvation* (Eugene, OR: Wipf & Stock, 2021), 22, 27.
12. Hebrew *midyān*, "strife, contention."

25:24 ESV; similarly, 19:13; 21:9, 19; 27:15). Yet remarkably, the author never commends recourse to (1) divorce, (2) abandonment, or (3) physical force to resolve marital conflict. All a husband can do is retire to the far end of the rooftop to gain some peace. Proverbs envisions a meek husband.

The conclusion of Proverbs, the "Song of the Valiant Woman" (Prov. 31:10–31), is an acrostic poem constituting no mere appendix but rather a poetic climax or finale praising the one individual in society best embodying all the virtues of Wisdom extolled throughout the book. Strikingly, the ancient sage chooses none of the "usual suspects": the king, the priest, the prophet, or the sage. Spurning these, he chooses a woman who is wife, mother, and homemaker.

He begins his poem: "A valiant woman[13] who can find? She is worth more than jewels"[14] (Prov. 31:10 AT). This evokes Proverbs 3:15 and Lady Wisdom as "more precious than jewels" (cf. 8:11). Thus, the valiant wife embodies Lady Wisdom; conversely, Wisdom is the best "wife" a man can ever have.

The acrostic structure of the poem, each line beginning with the next letter of the Hebrew alphabet, conveys comprehensiveness: praise from "A" to "Z," omitting nothing. The woman's relationship with her husband reflects trust (Prov. 31:11), generosity (v. 12), and admiration (vv. 28–29). Her capable management of their estate frees him from domestic concerns to help direct public affairs (vv. 11, 23), winning the respect of their community for both of them (vv. 11, 31). Their relationship includes the erotic (cf. Prov. 5:19): she makes lavish coverings of purple and linen for her bed (31:22), recalling the seductress's sumptuous couch (7:16–17)—only it is *exclusively* for her husband.[15] Her virtues include industry (31:13–15, 17–19, 25, 27), prudence and foresight (vv. 21, 25), compassion and generosity (v. 20), sound judgment and business sense (vv. 16, 18, 24), leadership and delegation (v. 15), and wisdom and pedagogical skill (v. 26), thus earning admiration from her family (v. 28) and community (v. 31). The source of all her virtues is the fear of the Lord (v. 30), religious awe of the God of Israel and obedience to his commands, elsewhere called the "beginning of wisdom" (9:10; cf. 1:7).

---

13. Here I follow Al Wolters, *The Song of the Valiant Woman: Studies in the Interpretation of Proverbs 31:10–31* (Carlisle, UK: Paternoster, 2001). The phrase ʾēšet-ḥayil, "woman of valor," is quite vigorous. Hebrew ḥayil can mean "force, strength, excellence, wealth" and is frequently a military term, describing warriors (e.g., Judg. 3:29) or an army generally (e.g., Exod. 14:9). Thus, "valor" is an attempt to capture this sense.

14. Hebrew pənînîm, "jewels," traditionally often "rubies," here and in Prov. 3:15.

15. See Prov. 31:22 ESV. The word for "bed coverings" (marbaddîm) is only used once elsewhere in the MT, in Prov. 7:16, referring to the luxurious and erotic couch of the seductress.

Proverbs 31:10–31 is remarkable for the light that it sheds on biblical ideals of marriage. Matrimony does not restrict the woman's engagement with and contribution to society. She runs multiple businesses and charitable initiatives that positively impact not only her household (vv. 15b, 21)—including children (v. 28) and servants (employees, v. 15c)—but the entire community (vv. 20, 31b). She does not abandon her home to engage in these activities; rather, her home is the *base* for their operation. Far from being intellectually deficient or dependent on her husband for guidance, she is herself a source of wisdom and a teacher of the community (v. 26). Their spousal bond includes trust, generosity, mutual respect and honor, and romance or erotic love. Far from repressing or oppressing his wife, the husband leaves all his property in her hands while he seeks to guide public affairs and so gain honor for them both. Matrimony provides a structure for both spouses to exercise their personal talents or gifts and to gain much-desired human goods, such as happiness, love, and the respect of one's community.

Proverbs 31:10–31 does not deserve to be read with a hermeneutic of suspicion, as if it hides some secret ill will against the feminine. It does not imply that virtue is difficult to find among women, for the husband professes, "a *great many* women have demonstrated valor" (v. 29 AT).[16] Further, the criticism of charm and physical beauty as criteria by which to judge women in verse 30 is no disparagement of those goods per se (cf. 5:19), but who is not aware of the cross-cultural tendency to make the primary criterion for granting social honor to women physical attractiveness rather than personal virtue?[17] Finally, the point of the sacred author is not to criticize most women for falling short of an ideal, but to recognize the *absolutely indispensable* contribution of married women to human flourishing and the health of societies. He gives only one command in the entire poem: the whole community must publicly honor the valiant woman (v. 31), representative of womanhood generally. Since the woman is like Wisdom herself in *giving life* to her husband, her children, her household, and her community (cf. 3:18), she is a symbol of Wisdom, superior to figures associated with the *taking of life* (e.g., kings, priests, and warriors).

16. The Hebrew is vigorous: *rabbôt bānôt ʿāśû ḥāyil*, lit., "multitudes of daughters have done valor."

17. See Susan Milligan, "The Value of Women: Large Portions of the American Public Value Women Most for Physical Attractiveness," *U.S. News and World Report*, December 5, 2017, https://bit.ly/Value_of_Women.

We conclude our reflections on Proverbs by asking, Why does the sacred author consistently portray wisdom as a *married* woman and an ideal *wife*, and what are the implications for our understanding of matrimony? This text points to the answer:

> She opens her mouth with wisdom [*baḥokmāh*],
>   and the teaching of kindness [*tôrat-ḥesed*] is on her tongue. (Prov.
> 31:26)

"The teaching of kindness" derives from *tôrāh*, "law or instruction," and *ḥesed*, the faithful love or loving faithfulness of covenant partners. So the law or instruction concerning covenantal love is on the tongue of the valiant woman.

Hebrew poetry typically operates in two-line couplets called bicola, exhibiting "synonymous parallelism"—that is, both lines express the same idea in different ways and are mutually illuminating.[18] In Proverbs 31:26, *ḥokmāh* and *tôrat-ḥesed* are parallel to one another, giving the hermeneutical key for the book: "wisdom" is the principle of *ḥesed*, covenantal love. *Ultimately, the wise person is the one who keeps covenant love with God and other persons.* Further, since the most powerful and universal expression and experience of natural covenantal love for human persons is marriage, in Proverbs the quintessential example of wisdom is marital fidelity; conversely, the quintessential example of folly is marital unfaithfulness. Moreover, divine wisdom (*ḥokmāh*) is also a communion with the divine nature and a presence analogous to the communion of persons in marriage. From the perspective of the sacred author, trinitarian definitions will be centuries in the future, but Proverbs already moves toward the concept of multiple persons in the Godhead (e.g., 8:22–31 ESV, esp. v. 30).[19] The person of wisdom, *ḥokmāh*, who could be understood as either or both of the Second and Third Persons in Christian theology,[20] is portrayed as feminine, and the relationship with her demanded of human beings is quasi-spousal. This corresponds to the prophets' picture of the covenant bond between the Lord and Israel as a

18. See J. M. LeMon and B. A. Strawn, "Parallelism," in *Dictionary of the Old Testament: Wisdom, Poetry and Writings*, ed. Tremper Longman III and Peter Enns (Downers Grove, IL: IVP Academic, 2008), 502–15, esp. 502–3.

19. See Richard M. Davidson, "Proverbs 8 and the Place of Christ in the Trinity," *JATS* 17, no. 1 (2006): 33–54.

20. Davidson, "Proverbs 8," 35.

marriage, but it reverses gender polarity: now the believer is masculine and the divine presence feminine.[21]

It follows from this that the institution of marriage is the *primary* and *privileged* arena for most human beings to learn to express the *ḥesed* that is the heart of wisdom; furthermore, it follows that the well-lived marriage is also somehow a participation in the mystical relationship between the human being and divine wisdom, which has a marital structure. For example, the husband of Proverbs 31:10–31 clearly experiences the blessings of divine wisdom *through* his wife, who so masterfully embodies it. This is very close, then, to the idea of one's spouse as a conduit of divine grace: "He who finds a wife . . . obtains grace [*rāṣôn*] from the LORD" (Prov. 18:22 AT). In a Christian reading, we can also recognize conversely the *husband* as a conduit of divine grace for his *wife*, as emphasized, for example, in Ephesians 5:22–33.

The Song of Songs

The Song of Songs is *the* quintessential sacred description of marriage in the Jewish and the Christian traditions, which read this great poem as a spiritual allegory of the relationship of God with his people and/or with the individual believer. There is a wide range of opinions on the dating and composition of the Song.[22] Here, we take it as a collection of different love poems that have been brought together at the height of the united monarchy (the age of Solomon) and edited in such a way as to have a loose narrative development.[23] The resulting composition appears to have a chiastic structure consisting of seven panels:

A   The Opening Colloquy of the Bride, the Groom, and the Chorus (1:1–2:7)
   B   The Bridegroom's Invitation to Elope (2:8–17)
      C   The First Dream Sequence: The Bride Seeks the Groom at Night (3:1–5)
         D   Solomon and His Bride Process into Jerusalem (3:6–5:1)
      C' The Second Dream Sequence: The Bride Seeks the Groom at Night (5:2–6:10)

21. Villeneuve, *Divine Marriage*, 127.
22. Duane Garrett and Paul R. House, *Song of Songs/Lamentations*, WBC 23B (Grand Rapids: Zondervan Academic, 2004), 16–22.
23. Garrett and House, *Song of Songs*, 18–20.

> B′ The Day-Dream Sequence: The Bride and Groom Ride a Chariot
>   (6:11–8:4)
> A′ The Final Colloquy of the Bride, the Groom, and the Chorus (8:5–14)[24]

The opening colloquy (A; Song 1:1–2:7) sets the scene of excited preparations for a royal wedding (cf. 1:4). The bride addresses the chorus (1:4b, 5–6)
as well as her beloved (1:7), and the lovers praise each other's beauty and attractiveness back and forth (1:8–10; 1:12–14; 1:15; 1:16–2:1; 2:2; 2:3–7 ESV),
with occasional interjections from the chorus (1:4c–d, 11) until the dialogue
ends with this refrain from the bride:

> O that his left hand were under my head,
>   and that his right hand embraced me!
> I adjure you, O daughters of Jerusalem,
>   by the gazelles or the hinds of the field,
> that you stir not up nor awaken love
>   until it please. (Song 2:6–7)

The word for "love" here (*hāʾ ahăbāh*, lit., "the love") is feminine and can
also mean "the loved one," referring to the bride, as it clearly does in Song of
Songs 7:6 ESV (7:7 MT). This gives an alternative translation: "I adjure you,
. . . stir not up nor awaken *the loved one* until *she* please"—a refrain that
occurs three times: 2:7; 3:5; and 8:4.[25]

The second panel (B; Song 2:8–17) is a surreal vision of the lover bounding
down from the hills (v. 8) to stand outside the garden of the beloved (v. 9),
inviting her to run off with him to enjoy the spring countryside (vv. 10–15).
She speaks the formula of covenant union ("My beloved is mine, and I am
his," v. 16 ESV) and encourages him to come to her (v. 17).

The third panel (C; Song 3:1–5) is a dream of the bride seeking her beloved
at night, searching for him in the city (i.e., Jerusalem) until she finds him and
concludes with the formula: "I adjure you, . . . stir not up nor awaken the
loved one until she please" (v. 5 AT).

The central panel of the book (D; Song 3:6–5:1) envisions Solomon pro-
cessing up from the eastern desert into Jerusalem in his exquisitely crafted

---

24. See Bergsma and Pitre, *Old Testament*, 646.
25. On refrains in the Song, see Roland E. Murphy, "The Unity of the Song of Songs," *VT*
29 (1979): 436–43, esp. 436–37.

nuptial palanquin (3:9–10), borne on poles by the king's bodyguard (3:7–8). In Song of Songs 4:1–5:1, the reader enters the palanquin to hear the intimate dialogue between the royal bridegroom and his new bride, as he compliments and arouses her by flattery with exotic metaphors for her beauty and attractiveness (4:1–15), eliciting the bride's invitation for him to approach her (4:16). The bridegroom approaches for the nuptial embrace (5:1a), and the scene "goes dark" as the chorus chants an affirmation of their love (5:1b).

The fifth panel (C′; Song 5:2–6:10) repeats the plot of the first dream sequence (C; 3:1–5) but is much elaborated. The bride dreams her beloved comes to her chamber (5:2), but before she rouses to open the door, he departs (5:3–6). She goes out to search for him and calls upon her companions, the daughters of Jerusalem, to assist her (5:7–8). They ask what he looks like (5:9), and she describes him with visual imagery of the temple (5:10–16). The chorus joins the search (6:1), but she suddenly happens upon her beloved (6:2), who proceeds to describe her beauty (6:4–10) as before (cf. 4:1–15).[26]

The sixth panel (B′; Song 6:11–8:4) begins with the bride descending to the nut orchard (6:11), and she says, "Before I was aware, my fancy set me / in a chariot beside my prince" (6:12)[27]—that is, she is lost in a fantasy of riding away in a chariot with her beloved. He praises her beauty from her feet to her head (7:1–8 ESV). She restates their bond of union (7:9–10) and invites him to accompany her to the countryside (7:11), wishing he were a brother, so she could express her affection more openly and bring him into her home without shame (8:1–2). Yet suddenly, the scene ends with both her longing for his embrace (8:3) and the familiar adjuration formula not to awaken "the loved one until she please" (8:4 AT).

The concluding panel (A′; 8:5–14) of the Song of Songs is a colloquy like 1:1–2:7. The cry "Who is this, coming up from the wilderness?" (8:5 AT) is repeated, recalling Solomon arriving in his nuptial palanquin (3:6–7), though now the couple appears to be on foot. The reference to being "awakened" in 8:5 indicates we are not in a dream or daydream any longer. There are some aphoristic reflections, in the style of Proverbs, about the power of love (8:6–7)—notably, "love is as strong as death" (8:6 AT). The chorus[28] chimes

---

26. The translation of *nidgālôt* as "an army with banners" (Song 6:4, 10) may be justified, but "[female] banner bearers" is more literal. Perhaps "flag corps" is an appropriate dynamic equivalent.

27. The Hebrew is difficult; cf. ESV, RSV, JPS, NABRE.

28. Sometimes interpreted as the bride's brothers, but it seems to me more consistent to identify them as the daughters of Jerusalem, as throughout.

in about a previously unmentioned, prepubescent younger sister who awaits
the day of her betrothal (8:8). Using euphemistic language, they assert that
if she is found a virgin ("a wall"), they will heap silver jewelry on her; but
if she is found to be "a door," she will be locked up in an inner room (8:9).
After some cryptic lines about the "vineyard" of Solomon and the "vineyard"
of the bride (8:11–12), the Song ends with the bridegroom and companions
calling for the bride to respond (8:13) and the bride urging her beloved to
hurry (8:14)—possibly reflecting the nighttime approach of the groom and
groomsmen to escort the bride from her home to the wedding venue—that
is, the home of the groom's father.[29]

Thus, the literal sense of the Song expresses a sequence of dreams and
fantasies of a young woman, a bride, of her imminent wedding to her beloved
bridegroom, who is of royal status—indeed, Solomon himself. In the visions,
they approach consummation, but it has not taken place by the end of the
song, where the bride still affirms, "I am a wall" (8:10),[30] and the groom's
party approaches to take her to the wedding (8:13–14).

However, the oldest interpretive traditions have always taken the Song
of Songs allegorically. For example, Wisdom of Solomon 7–9 incorporates
imagery from the Song into the account of the romance and "marriage"
of Solomon to Lady Wisdom, reflecting an allegorical reading of the Song
in which Solomon sets the model for every wise ruler by courting and ultimately wedding the beautiful "bride," Wisdom herself. Likewise, Sirach
adorns Lady Wisdom with the erotic imagery of the Song's description of
the bride (Song 4:11–15//Sir. 24:13–20). Even the Gospel of John uses imagery
from the Song to portray Jesus as royal bridegroom (John 12:1–8//Song 1:12;
John 19:38–42//Song 4:14; John 20:1, 11–18//Song 3:1–5) and various women
disciples representing the bride (John 12:3; 20:1), which suggests a reading of
the Song already in Second Temple Judaism in which Bridegroom Solomon
is the Messiah and the bride is either the people of God or the individual
believer. So also Revelation incorporates imagery from the Song in such a

29. On the transfer of the bride in the wedding ceremony, see Edwin M. Yamauchi and Marvin R. Wilson, eds., *Dictionary of Daily Life in Biblical and Post-Biblical Antiquity* (Peabody,
MA: Hendrickson, 2017), 1066, 1078. Greek sources specify it took place at night.

30. So NABRE. The Hebrew is a nonverbal predication: "I [am] a wall." Some assume a
past-tense sense (e.g., RSV, ESV), but there is no reason in the immediate context to do so. Thus,
at the end of the Song, the bride still boasts of her physical integrity. Therefore, the central
panel (3:6–5:1b), which ends just shy of physical union, must be an anticipatory vision. The
marriage has yet to take place at the conclusion of the poem (8:13–14).

Theodoret of Cyr on the Song of Songs

The Fathers were aware of interpretations of the Song of Songs that took in merely a natural sense, but they rejected them. Theodoret of Cyr writes:

> Some commentators misrepresent the Song of Songs, believe it to be not a spiritual book [and] come up instead with some fanciful stories inferior even to babbling old wives' tales and dare to claim that Solomon the sage wrote it as a factual account of himself and the Pharaoh's daughter. . . . My view is that when they read this composition and noticed in it unguents, kisses, thighs, belly, navel, cheeks, eyes, lilies, apples, nard, ointment, myrrh, and the like, in their ignorance of the characteristics of the divine Scripture they were unwilling to get beyond the surface, penetrate the veil of the expression, gain entrance in spirit and behold the glory of the Lord with face unveiled. Rather, they gave the text a corporeal interpretation and were drawn into that awful blasphemy.[a]

a. Theodoret of Cyr, preface to Commentary on the Song of Songs, in Proverbs, Ecclesiastes, Song of Solomon, ed. J. Robert Wright, ACCS:OT 9 (Downers Grove, IL: InterVarsity, 2005), 289–90.

way as to suggest that the book was also understood by early Christians in a messianic-eschatological sense, as describing the anticipated bliss of the return of the Messiah and the Church's union with him.[31]

Certain features of the Song of Songs facilitated its messianic interpretation in Second Temple Judaism. Not only is the groom identified with Solomon, an important type of the messiah, but the woman's pet descriptor for him, "my beloved," shares the consonants of the name David (Hebrew *d-w-d*) and can be read "my David"—in other words, the messiah (cf. Ezek. 34:23–24; 37:24–25). Psalm 45 assists by portraying the bridegroom-king as dressed and anointed like Groom Solomon in the Song.

Later rabbinic tradition, following the Prophets, took the groom as the Lord God and the bride as Israel. Every verse of the Song was associated with a stage of Israel's history, including her future "history" of ultimate reconciliation

31. Cf. Rev. 12:1//Song 6:10; Rev. 22:1–5//Song 4:12–15; Rev. 22:17, 20//Song 8:13–14. See Nicholas T. Batzig, "John's Use of the Song of Songs in the Book of Revelation," *Feeding on Christ* (blog), July 1, 2013, https://feedingonchrist.org/johns-use-of-the-song-of-songs-in-the -book-of-revelation/.

and nuptial union with God, her husband.[32] The bride's beauty is so often described with geographical features of Israel[33] because she *is* Israel.[34]

The Song's implications for marriage are founded on the literal sense. In Jewish and Christian reading, the spiritual sense has always been primary, but this implies that the literal sense must be pure per se to be suitable for representing divine truth. Thus, the physical aspect of marriage described in the Song, including the beauty and attraction of the spouses and their delight in the marital embrace, is a natural good, part of the goodness of creation meant to be enjoyed. Edenic imagery of gardens, flowers, fruitful trees, and the solitude of the human couple abounds in the Song, suggesting that each courting couple mystically becomes Adam and Eve once more, recapitulating the original sexual complementarity, innocence, and one-flesh union of the first spouses.

This raises the question of the Song's attitude toward sexuality. In ancient as well as modern times, commentators have argued that the Song condones fornication.[35] It is true that, decontextualized from the rest of the Song, individual poetic units could be *interpreted* as describing lovemaking between unmarried persons. However, a contextual, canonical reading of the Song affirms chastity before and within marriage. In the central scene of the Song (3:6–5:1), the couple is explicitly married: it is Solomon's wedding day (*ḥătunnāh*, 3:11), and he calls his beloved "sister" (*'āḥôt*, i.e., "kinswoman") and "bride" (*kallāh*, 4:8, 9, 10, 11, 12; 5:1), usually in the concatenation "my sister-bride" (*'āḥôtî kallāh*, 4:9, 10, 12; 5:1). Further, he praises her virginity—the exclusive gift of her body to her husband—in metaphors not overly subtle: "A garden locked is my sister, my bride, / a garden locked, a fountain sealed" (4:12).

Then there is the statement of the chorus about what will happen to the younger sister on the day of her betrothal:

> If she is a wall,
>> we will build upon her a battlement of silver;
> but if she is a door,
>> we will enclose her with boards of cedar. (Song 8:9)

32. Villeneuve, *Divine Marriage*, 107–25.
33. Song 1:5; 2:1; 4:1, 4, 8, 11, 15; 6:4–5; 7:4–5.
34. Nina Heereman, "Behold King Solomon on the Day of His Wedding: A Symbolic-Diachronic Reading of Song 3:6–11 and 4:12–5:1" (PhD diss., École Biblique et Archéologique Française de Jérusalem / Université de Fribourg, 2017), 503–21.
35. For ancient commentators, see the comments of Theodoret of Cyr, quoted above, p. 162; for modern commentators, see Heereman, "Behold King Solomon," 51n216.

St. Methodius on Song of Songs 4:1–15

St. Methodius of Olympus understands Solomon's praise of his virgin bride (Song 4:1–15) as applying to the order of virgins in the early Church:

> Chastity is a spring flower, ever putting forth in delicate white petals the blossom of incorruptibility. Hence He is not ashamed to admit that He is indeed in love with its ripe beauty: *Thou has wounded my heart, my sister, my spouse. . . . Thy breasts are more beautiful than wine, and the smell of thy garments above all aromatical spices. . . . A garden enclosed art thou, my sister, my spouse, a fountain sealed up* (Song 4:9–12). Such are the praises that Christ sings of those who have achieved the perfection of virginity, comprising them all under the title of His spouse. For the spouse must be betrothed to the bridegroom and call herself by his name, and till then she must remain pure and undefiled, like a *sealed garden* in which all the spices of heaven's fragrance grow, that Christ alone may come and pluck them as they blossom and grow with incorporeal seed.[a]

a. Methodius of Olympus, *The Symposium: A Treatise on Chastity*, trans. Herbert Musurillo, ACW 27 (New York: Newman, 1958), 97–98.

The "battlement of silver" is the abundance of silver jewelry draped on the young woman's head, hair, and neck for her wedding. The "boards of cedar" refer to the paneling of an inner room in the house (Jer. 22:14; Hag. 1:4)—in other words, she will be confined inside to prevent the behavior that made her a "door."

Following this, the bride herself boasts of her readiness for marriage. Unlike the younger sister, her breasts are "like towers"—that is, physically mature—and she has kept herself for her husband: "I am a wall, . . . [so] I became in his eyes as one who brings peace" (Song 8:10 NABRE). Walls and towers are both defensive structures of a city, so the bride has defended herself from the entrance of strangers prior to her marriage.

The point of virginity is the exclusivity of the love relationship. The unique character of the spousal bond logically demands the gift of the spouses' bodies to one another and to no other: "I am my beloved's, and he is mine" (6:3 AT; cf. 2:16; 7:10). Complete reciprocity and mutual belonging or ownership are implied by this principle: the spouses submit the control of themselves and their bodies to each other, as St. Paul speaks of mutual rulership of the spouses' bodies (1 Cor. 7:4). Although royal polygamy is acknowledged in the Song of Songs (6:8), the logic of mutual possession ("I am my beloved's, and he is mine") requires monogamy in order to be actualized consistently; otherwise, one would have to say, "I am my beloved's, and he is mine and hers and hers and hers, etc.," which destroys complementarity, reciprocity, and romance.

Notably, the Song consistently envisions marriage as being mutually desired by both man and wife, giving happiness to both. The love is clearly reciprocal. Often bride and groom describe each other with the same or similar terms. So the groom's love is "better than wine" and like fragrant oils (Song 1:2–3), and so is the bride's (4:10). Her longing for him is amply expressed: "O that his left hand were under my head, / and that his right hand embraced me!" (2:6; 8:3); likewise, her bridegroom's "desire" is for her (7:10), and she has "ravished" his heart (4:9). He praises her beauty in detail, repeatedly (4:1–5; 6:4–7; 7:1–7), and she reciprocates (5:10–16). The love and attraction of spouses is fully mutual; foreign to the Song's perspective is the idea that only the man finds attraction and satisfaction. Marriage satisfies the legitimate longings of both man and wife. But the relationship is founded on friendship, not mere physical attraction. So the groom constantly refers to his bride as his "female companion" or "friend" (ra'yāh), often translated "my love" or "my darling" (1:9, 15; 2:2, 10, 13; 4:1, 7; 5:2; 6:4), and she once refers to him as her "male friend" or "companion" (rēʿa; 5:16). Yet her preferred term for him is "my beloved" (dôdî, which occurs forty times in the Song), a term of affection more than eroticism. At the end of the Song, she ascends from the wilderness "leaning" (mitrapeqet) upon her "beloved" (dôdāh), such that her beloved is portrayed as a source of support and sustenance in times of weariness or weakness (8:5). Like Tobit, the Song promotes a companionate view of marriage.

Earlier, we noted that the physical aspect of love in the Song is affirmed as good per se, but certain images in the Song imply more—namely, that the love and the beauty of the spouses is *holy*. Indeed, in the four detailed visual descriptions of the bodies of the lovers (4:1–7; 5:10–16; 6:4–10; 7:1–9), we discover the imagery of the sanctuary or the holy city. As Peter J. Leithart comments:

> The woman's description of her lover in Song of Songs 5:6–10 draws on terminology used to describe the temple—there's myrrh, sockets, inlays, cedars

of Lebanon. More, the sequence of the description is not only head-to-foot, but also roughly follows the pattern of the temple. Head of gold, pure gold: Holy of Holies, especially the ark. Eyes like doves . . . : Lampstands. Cheeks with herbs and spices: Incense and incense altar. Lips like lilies: The lily shape of the capitals on the two pillars, and the lily design of sea and water basins. Legs like pillars of alabaster: The structural supports of the temple. Form like Lebanon, like cedars: Cedar wood interior of the temple. . . . The lover, like his bride, is described like a temple.[36]

The bride, too, is described as the garden-temple of Eden in Song of Songs 4:12–15, where she appears as an inaccessible "garden locked" (v. 12) that contains "all choicest fruits" (v. 13), "all choice spices" (v. 14 ESV), and a "well of living water" (v. 15 ESV). She is the perfect, verdant, and supernatural garden-sanctuary of God, whose one eastern gate has been locked by the cherubim (Gen. 3:24//Song 4:12), who provides living water for the whole earth (Gen. 2:10–14//Song 4:12, 15), and who has been filled with "every tree that is pleasant to the sight and good for food" (Gen. 2:9//Song 4:13–14). Genesis itself suggests that the woman's body is a temple, since she is "built" (bānāh) out of a sacred "rib" or "beam" (ṣēlāʿ).[37] So the bride of the Song is a new Eve, a temple woman.

Solomon's wedding-day palanquin in Song of Songs 3:6–11 is also described like the Jerusalem temple.[38] The "column of smoke" (3:6a) alludes to the smoke of sacrifices ascending continually from the sanctuary, and "myrrh and frankincense" (3:6b) suggests that which emanated from the high priest's anointing oil and the altar of incense. The "wood of Lebanon" (3:9) and "silver," "gold," and "purple" (3:10) resemble the interior decorations of the sanctuary. If we are correct that the conversation of groom and bride and the movement toward consummation depicted in Song of Songs 4:1–5:1 takes place inside the curtained palanquin, then the whole unit, 3:6–5:1, symbolizes God's nuptial union with his people in the Jerusalem temple, a concept amply attested in Second Temple sources.[39] Marital union resembles the union of God with his people through temple liturgy; conversely, Israel's worship of God in the temple is nuptial communion with him.

36. Peter Leithart, "Temple Man," *Patheos*, February 16, 2010, https://www.patheos.com/blogs/leithart/2010/02/temple-man/.
37. See the discussion above, pp. 20–21.
38. Villeneuve, *Divine Marriage*, 55, 69, 111, 119, 136.
39. Villeneuve, *Divine Marriage*, 50–75.

The intrinsic connection, then, of marital love with God's love of his people is reinforced by the aphorisms in Song of Songs 8 that "Love is strong as Death" and that "its arrows are . . . flames of the divine" (v. 6b NABRE)—or that "its flashes are . . . the very flame of the LORD" (v. 6b ESV)—unable to be quenched by "waters" or "floods" (v. 7a ESV). The ancients worshiped Love and Death as gods. Death (*môt*) was portrayed as a monster with an enormous mouth that swallowed all things. Likewise, Yam, the Sea, was a divinity (cf. Neptune or Poseidon). Yet Yam cannot destroy Love (*'ahăbāh*) with his "deep waters" or "rivers" (v. 7a NABRE). In the Song, Love is a cosmic power on par with others considered divine: it is "the very flame of the LORD"—that is, a divine attribute. Thus, those who love truly participate in the action of God, anticipating 1 John 4:16: "God is love, and whoever abides in love abides in God" (ESV; cf. 1 John 4:7–8). Divine love cannot be annihilated by the strongest physical forces (Song 8:7a), nor can it be purchased with natural wealth (8:7b)—a poignant corrective in a culture in which large sums were paid upon the bride's betrothal, which could be misconstrued as "purchasing" the woman and/or her love (cf. Gen. 34:12; Exod. 22:16–17; 1 Sam. 18:25). No, for the sacred author, the love of spouses is as strong as death and the grave—implying that it lasts beyond the point of death—and it is impervious to physical forces, not subject to coercion or manipulation through human wealth. It is perfectly free and indestructible—or should we say, indissoluble?

Wisdom of Solomon

Wisdom of Solomon combines imagery and themes from Proverbs and the Song of Songs in such a way as to portray Solomon seeking out and finding Lady Wisdom as his perfect spouse. Wisdom reiterates many key concepts from Proverbs' depiction of Lady Wisdom: she is the source of all wealth (Wis. 7:8–9//Prov. 3:14–15) through her industrious labor (Wis. 8:18//Prov. 31:11–13), the fashioner of all created things (Wis. 7:22; 8:6//Prov. 8:27–30), the bestower of honor among the elders (Wis. 8:10//Prov. 31:23), the source of immortality (Wis. 8:13//Prov. 3:18), and the principle of political governance (Wis. 8:13–14//Prov. 8:15–16). Song of Songs 6:10 ("Who is this that looks forth like the dawn, / fair as the moon, bright as the sun") clearly influences Wisdom 7:29: "She is more beautiful than the sun, / and excels every constellation of the stars. / Compared with the light she is found to be superior."

Solomon's courtship of the Shulammite could be summarized by these lines: "I loved her and sought her from my youth, / and I desired to take her for my bride, /and I became enamored of her beauty" (Wis. 8:2); "I determined to take her to live with me" (8:9). Likewise, Solomon sounds like the husband of the valiant woman (Prov. 31:10–31) when he says of Wisdom: "When I enter my house, I shall find rest with her, / for companionship with her has no bitterness, / and life with her has no pain, but gladness and joy" (Wis. 8:16).

Although it stops short of simply identifying Wisdom as God, Wisdom 7:21–27 attributes to Lady Wisdom the divine attributes of creating all things (v. 22), holiness (v. 22), invulnerability (v. 22), omnipotence (v. 23), omniscience (v. 23), and omnimobility (v. 24). She is "a breath of the power of God, / and a pure emanation of the glory of the Almighty. . . . / She is a reflection of eternal light, / a spotless mirror . . . , / and an image of his goodness" (vv. 25–26)—a passage that surely influenced Colossians 1:15–16 and virtually identifies Wisdom with either the Second or the Third Person of the Trinity. Therefore, Solomon's "marriage" with Wisdom becomes a kind of spousal union with God.

The portrayal of the believer's relationship to divine truth as marriage to Lady Wisdom is profound. It implies that divine truth is personal—indeed, a Person—and that one must *love* God's truth and be *exclusively faithful* to God's truth even to the point of death. The relationship with divine truth cannot be casual, intermittent, temporary, or nonexclusive (polyamorous). Strikingly, Plato says something quite similar about philosophy in *The Republic*. The highborn and noble of society, Plato complains, have neglected truth to pursue their own pleasure, power, and profit:

> And so philosophy is left desolate, with her marriage rite incomplete: for her own have fallen away and forsaken her, and while they are leading a false and unbecoming life, other unworthy persons, seeing that she has no kinsmen to be her protectors, enter in and dishonour her; and fasten upon her the reproaches which, as you say, her reprovers utter, who affirm of her votaries that some are good for nothing, and that the greater number deserve the severest punishment.[40]

Like the biblical tradition of Wisdom, Plato recognizes that the commitment to truth must be faithful and indissoluble, like a marriage, because he who abandons truth when difficulty arises does not really love the truth and is not

40. Plato, *The Republic, and Other Works*, trans. B. Jowett (New York: Anchor Books, 1973), 186 (book 6).

her loyal companion. Plato cannot express this truth without, like the biblical author, portraying *sophia* as a person—indeed, as a spouse.

Sirach

Sirach draws together and expands upon the nuptial symbolism and nascent theology of marriage developed in earlier Wisdom books. As in Proverbs, there are two dimensions to Sirach's treatment of marriage: the symbolic-typological and the didactic.

Sirach 24, the central poem about Lady Wisdom, is Ben Sira's finest expression of the symbolic-typological role of matrimony or nuptiality in salvation history, clearly modeled on earlier Wisdom poems (e.g., Prov. 8–9). Sirach 24 forms the transition from the first half of the book (chaps. 1–23, concerning wisdom for the young man) to the second half (chaps. 24–43, concerning wisdom for the mature man). It is structurally the center of the book, a privileged location for making a synthesizing statement on the nature of Wisdom.

The narrative of Sirach 24 follows the pattern established already in Proverbs 8, describing Wisdom's aboriginal beginnings (Sir. 24:3, 9), close companionship with God (v. 11), and exercise of divine powers (vv. 3–12). But then, in verses 8–12, the author makes a connection with no previous precedent in the Wisdom literature—that is, that Wisdom is the divine presence experienced in Israel's sanctuaries, first the tabernacle and then the temple, for "in the holy tent I ministered before him, / and so I was established in Zion, / . . . in Jerusalem, my domain" (24:10–11 NABRE). Thus, tabernacle and temple, the dwelling places of God's name and presence, are the dwelling of Wisdom, enabling the conclusion that Wisdom is somehow identified with the name and presence of God and yet mysteriously distinct from him, because she "ministered before him," a priestly act (cf. Judg. 20:28; 1 Sam. 2:18; 1 Chron. 16:4). Then comes a daring passage, Sirach 24:13–21, which boldly integrates the Song of Songs' erotic imagery with Proverbs' portrayal of Lady Wisdom. Wisdom is a tall tree adorned with every exotic spice and laden with every desirable fruit, drawing on the bridal tree and vine imagery of the Song (4:13, 16; 7:6–9) as well as the garden of spices in Song 4:12–5:1. Wisdom's "tallness" (Sir. 24:13–14) indicates sexual maturity and thus desirability (cf. Song 7:6–7 and Ezek. 16:7). "Come to me, all who desire me, and be filled with my fruits" (Sir. 24:19 NABRE) echoes not only Lady Wisdom—"Come, eat of my bread / and drink of my wine" (Prov. 9:5

AT)—but also the bride: "Let my beloved come to his garden, / and eat its choicest fruits" (Song 4:16b). Thus, Sirach attests to an early reading of the Song in which the bride is simply Wisdom personified, as in Proverbs. The one who "eats" Wisdom is like Solomon, who approaches his bride to "eat" and "drink" her "choicest fruits" and "honeycomb" in the nuptial embrace (Song 4:16–5:1), just as Wisdom invites "all who desire [her]" to be "filled with [her] fruits," which are "sweeter than honey," "better . . . than the honeycomb" (Sir. 24:19–20 NABRE). Subsequently, Sirach 24:23 identifies Wisdom with the Scriptures ("the book of the covenant of the Most High") and a new Eden that flows with rivers watering the whole earth (Gen. 2:10–14//Sir. 24:25–29), combining bride-as-garden-fountain imagery (Song 4:12–14//Sir. 24:30–31) with Ezekiel's river of life flowing from the sanctuary (Ezek. 47:1–12//Sir. 24:30–33). Indeed, by identifying her with "the book of the covenant" (24:23), "Sirach thus identifies Lady Wisdom with the Torah—the ultimate source of wisdom."[41]

> Conversely, wisdom is a necessary virtue to keep the law. . . . Wisdom expresses in her song of praise the essential contents of the Torah, that is, how God created the world and man, how he chose Israel and gave her the Promised Land with the Jerusalem Temple at its center, where the liturgy to God was celebrated, and whence sprung the word of the Lord (Isa. 2:4; Mic. 4:2). In Sirach, Wisdom is the "fulfillment of the law" (Sir. 19:20), and in our present passage she is nothing less than a personal hypostasis of the Torah (cf. Bar. 3:37–4:1).[42]

Villeneuve shows that Sirach 24 is a truly remarkable synthesis of scriptural themes tied to nuptiality[43] by associating Wisdom with Eden, Sinai, the tabernacle, and the temple—four natural or architectural sanctuaries understood as places of nuptial communion between God and his people.[44] Wisdom is somehow distinct from God the Creator (24:8), but she nonetheless possesses divine attributes like immortality (v. 9), omnipresence (vv. 3–6), and unlimited intellect (vv. 27–29). She makes her dwelling in God's dwelling places: the pillar of cloud (v. 4), the tabernacle (vv. 8, 10), the temple (vv. 10–12). This already suggests multiple persons in the Godhead, and so Wisdom appears as a divine person presented as feminine, one eminently desirable as a

---

41. Villeneuve, *Divine Marriage*, 144.
42. Villeneuve, *Divine Marriage*, 144.
43. Villeneuve, *Divine Marriage*, 131–47.
44. Villeneuve, *Divine Marriage*, 147–49.

spouse, such that the devout person's relationship with God's Wisdom has a spousal character—total, indissoluble, mutual self-giving characterized by love, affection, and delight.

Sirach also contains much didactic material on natural human marriage, and its teaching can be summarized in the following five points. First, a happy marriage to a good spouse is the greatest good of a man's life, incomparable to any material blessing, and it is so valuable that it must be considered a direct blessing from God. The husband of a good wife is happy (26:1), since she brings him "joy" and "peace" (26:2), since she is a "generous gift" from "the Lord" (26:3), who brings contentment in all circumstances (26:4 NABRE). A wife's beauty "surpasses every man's desire" (36:27 AT), and she is her husband's "best possession, a helper fit for him and a pillar of support" (36:29 ESVCE), without which a man is "plundered" and will "wander about and sigh" (36:30 ESVCE). Like the Song of Songs, Sirach describes a wife using temple imagery (26:13–18): she is a priceless "gift from the Lord" and a "supreme blessing" (vv. 14–15), her beautiful face and figure are like the "light" of the "holy lampstand" (v. 17), and her legs and feet are like "golden columns on silver bases" (v. 18 NABRE). Thus, a godly wife is like the temple, mediating the divine presence and anticipating matrimony as a means of grace in Christian faith. The beautiful face, stately figure, shapely legs, and steady feet of the wife manifest God's beauty reflected in his temple (26:17–18); thus, physical beauty reflects the goodness of God.

Second, because marriage is so important for human happiness and flourishing, and because of the great power of a wife over the nature of the marriage relationship, Sirach is bluntly honest about the misery that results when one's spouse lacks virtue. Just as a happy marriage to a virtuous spouse is the greatest human good, so the opposite—an unhappy union to a vicious spouse—is the greatest human misery (Sir. 25:13, 16, 23).

Third, Sirach never endorses either physical force or divorce against one's spouse, even while commending physical punishment for sons and servants (30:1–13; 33:25–33).[45] As in Proverbs, the meek husband is powerless to find any remedy for an evil wife in Sirach: "[He] takes his meals among the neighbors, and he cannot help sighing bitterly" (25:18). Vice in a wife provokes not anger or retaliation but intense sadness and grief: "An evil wife means a

---

45. Sir. 25:25–26 seems to permit divorcing an evil wife ("separate her from yourself," v. 26), but the Greek is "cut her off from your flesh," which most likely refers to a cessation of conjugal relations (cf. Gen. 2:24).

dejected heart, a *gloomy face*, and a *wounded heart*" and "drooping hands and weak knees" (25:23 ESVCE).

Fourth, Sirach holds men and women equally to a high standard of chastity, permitting no sexual activity outside of marriage. Men are warned strongly against socializing with other women, lest they develop an attraction that would compromise their marital covenant.[46] Men should practice "custody of the eyes" and restrict their gaze from attractive women who are not their wives,[47] anticipating Matthew 5:28. Taking sexual advantage of women from a lower social class is shameful (Sir. 41:22). The reciprocity of sexual virtue between men and women is best exemplified in Sirach 23:16–27, which first condemns sexual immorality in husbands (vv. 16–21) and then in wives (vv. 22–27). The sexually immoral husband "wanders from his bed [Greek *klinē*], saying in his soul, 'Who can see me?'" (23:18 AT). "Bed" here means his sexual relationship with his wife (cf. NABRE, ESVCE). Notably, the marriage bond commits the husband to sexual *exclusivity* with his wife, and sexual contact with any other woman, married or unmarried (9:2–9), violates this commitment.

Fifth, Sirach maintains the companionate view of marriage typical in the other Scriptures of Israel: a "wife and a husband who accommodate one another" are "beautiful in the sight of the Lord and of people" (Sir. 25:1 ESVCE). "Accommodate" is a serviceable rendering of *symperipheromenos*, but the meaning may be even more positive, like "carried away" with each other, as the same verb translates Hebrew *šāgāh*, "be intoxicated," in the Septuagint (cf. Prov. 5:19b MT and LXX). The point is that the happy cohabitation of husband and wife is pleasing to God and the human community; it is how things should be, the paradigm or norm for human behavior.

Two other passages of Sirach drive home the same point. A "blameless wife" is better than children and establishing a city (Sir. 40:19); though children are the result of marriage, they are not a *greater* good than the person of the spouse herself. In other words, the unitive end of marriage is not subordinated to the procreative. Likewise, a "wife with her husband" is better than either "friend" or "companion" (40:23): the communion of spouses exceeds other forms of human communion, and marriage offers (at least potentially) the closest form of companionship.

Finally, when all that Sirach says about marriage is considered, it becomes apparent that human happiness all depends on virtuous women. For Sirach,

46. Sir. 9:1–9; 19:2; 23:16–21; 41:17, 21–22; 42:12–14.
47. Sir. 9:5, 7–8; 41:20; 42:12.

there is no happiness in life for a man without a wife (36:30), and yet happiness in marriage is not guaranteed (25:13–26; 26:5–12); it hinges on the virtue of the woman (26:1–4, 13–18). A husband is virtually helpless in changing a vicious wife (25:13–26), so happiness in life for men is effectively dependent on women of noble character, without whom there can be no human flourishing.

Summary of the Wisdom Literature on Marriage

As we have seen, the Wisdom literature of the Old Testament has a great deal to contribute to a biblical theology of matrimony. By personifying Wisdom as a quasi-divine female person who constitutes the ideal "spouse" whom every young man should be eager to "marry," the Wisdom literature confirms the general scriptural portrayal of the bond between God and his people as a marital covenant, while reversing the typical gender imagery. It also implies that marriage lived well, between virtuous spouses, is a mysterious participation in covenantal communion with God, and the virtuous wife, in particular, is a kind of sign or embodiment of divine wisdom.

The explicit teaching on human marriage in the Wisdom literature emphasizes exclusive emotional and physical fidelity to one's first and only spouse (the "wife of your youth"), and it never envisions nor commends the various offenses against this exclusive, monogamous bond—divorce, physical force, or polygamy. The Wisdom literature entertains great ideals for marriage: it should be a source of happiness, satisfaction, and companionship for both husband and wife. The physical pleasures and attractions of marriage are good in themselves—even signs of the beauty of communion with God himself in the temple and the liturgy—but are in themselves penultimate (Eccles. 2:8–11), subordinate in importance to interior beauty—that is, virtue (Prov. 31:30). It is not exaggerated to say that marital fidelity is *the* quintessential characteristic of the life lived according to wisdom (ḥokmāh) for the sages of Israel. The sages also acknowledge that women as spouses play an indispensable and even controlling role in the success of marriages and, thus, ultimately in the flourishing of the human community. For the sages, human happiness lies in the hands of women, which is perhaps why the first Wisdom book ends with an encomium to the virtuous wife (Prov. 31:10–31)—and why the last Wisdom book makes Wisdom as wife the centerpiece of its structure (Sir. 24).

9

"Rejoicing at the Bridegroom's Voice"

Christ as Bridegroom in the New Testament

Having surveyed the Old Testament witness to marriage, both as a model of the divine covenant and as a fundamental reality in the lives of God's people, we turn now to the witness of the New Testament. Here, we must begin by recognizing the nuptial characterization of Christ's ministry in several New Testament texts, which represents the fulfillment of Israel's prophetic expectation of the return of the divine bridegroom to woo his people (e.g., Hosea 2:14–23 ET; Isa. 62:4–5; Ezek. 16:60–62). This spousal relationship between God and people restored in Christ becomes, in turn, the basis of Christian morality and sacramental practice. Therefore, the nuptial-covenantal bond between God and his people, between Christ and the Church, must be explored before engaging New Testament teaching on the celebration and practice of marriage (i.e., sacraments and morality). Accordingly, this chapter describes the ways that Christ is portrayed as bridegroom of the people of God in the New Testament, focusing especially on those books where the theme is most pronounced: Matthew, John, Paul's epistles, and Revelation.

Matthew

For Matthew, Jesus's role as bridegroom fulfills not only the theme of the Lord as husband of Israel—so prominent in the prophets—but also the motif of the Davidic king as bridegroom, as seen in the Song of Songs, Psalm 45, and other key passages of Israel's Scriptures (2 Sam. 5:1–3; 17:3). Matthew's royal genealogy of Jesus (Matt. 1:1–17) portrays Jesus as the heir of the whole royal Davidic tradition, a kind of "new Solomon" (cf. 12:42). The Solomonic theme is reinforced when wise men from the East arrive to seek out the child (2:1–12), recalling Eastern sages seeking Solomon long ago (1 Kings 4:29–34). The three gifts of the magi (Matt. 2:11) likewise fit the theme: *gold* is associated with no one in the scriptural tradition more than Solomon, who makes Jerusalem awash with it (1 Kings 10:14–22), and *frankincense* and *myrrh* occur together in the Old Testament only in the Song of Songs (3:6; 4:6, 14), as nuptial perfumes for Solomon and his bride. In this way, the gifts of the magi subtly designate Jesus as the royal bridegroom from his very infancy.

Jesus himself embraces this bridegroom role later in his ministry, as when he responds to a Pharisaic challenge on fasting: "Can the wedding guests mourn as long as the bridegroom is with them? The days will come, when the bridegroom is taken away from them, and then they will fast."[1] Here Jesus is the bridegroom, his disciples the wedding guests, and his passion his departure. For Jesus to take on the role of "bridegroom" evokes the eschatological resumption of the nuptial relationship between the Lord and Israel in the Prophets (Hosea 2:14–23; Isa. 54:1–8; 62:5), as well as the Song of Songs read as an allegory of the coming of the messiah. The bridegroom being "taken away" may evoke the dreams of the Song (3:1–5; 5:2–6:10), where the bride searches for the missing bridegroom, and it may also evoke Jeremiah's judgment oracles in which the "voice of the bridegroom" will be silenced (Jer. 7:34; 16:9; 25:10; cf. Joel 2:16).

Later in the Gospel, we find an evocation of Jesus as the Davidic bridegroom-king in these famous lines:

> Come to me, all who labor and are heavy laden, and I will give you rest. Take my yoke upon you, and learn from me; for I am gentle and lowly in heart, and you will find rest for your souls. For my yoke is easy, and my burden is light. (Matt. 11:28–30)

1. Matt. 9:15; cf. Mark 2:18–20. For a discussion of Mark's form of this microparable, see Sebastian R. Smolarz, *Covenant and the Metaphor of Divine Marriage in Biblical Thought: A Study with Special Reference to the Book of Revelation* (Eugene, OR: Wipf & Stock, 2011), 143–52. On the Matthean form, see André Villeneuve, *Divine Marriage from Eden to the End of Days: Communion with God as Nuptial Mystery in the Story of Salvation* (Eugene, OR: Wipf & Stock, 2021), 160–62.

The language here clearly evokes the catastrophic event of the "divorce" of northern Israel from the Davidic dynasty under Rehoboam in 1 Kings 12:1–20, an event also alluded to as the "kingdom divided against itself" in Matthew 12:25. In 1 Kings 12:1–20, the Israelites are "heavy laden" with the forced labor and taxation that Solomon has imposed on them, so they come to his son Rehoboam to request a lighter yoke (12:4), but Rehoboam's foolish young colleagues urge him to act like an abusive husband and respond with a swaggering sexual boast: "My little thing [qoṭānnî] is thicker than my father's loins" (12:10 AT). Israel responds like an aggrieved wife abandoning the house of her husband: "What portion have we in David? . . . To your tents, O Israel! Look now to your own house, David" (12:16).

Thus, Rehoboam is the bridegroom-king who abuses Bride Israel and provokes her departure, but Jesus is the Son of David who comes offering the long-desired "light yoke" that will win Israel's adherence and reunite king and people, "groom" and "bride." But the current generation of Israel does not embrace their Davidic bridegroom; rather, they continue to be "an evil and adulterous[2] generation" (Matt. 12:39) that does not recognize that, in Jesus, one "greater than Solomon is here" (12:42).

Near the end of Jesus's ministry, his entrance to Jerusalem (Matt. 21:1–11) recalls the inaugural procession of Solomon (1 Kings 1:38–40), in which he rides into the city on David's mule to the exuberant acclaim of the people. Zechariah foresees a recapitulation of this event by a messianic son of David, calling on the "daughter of Zion" to rejoice as her king arrives on a humble steed (Zech. 9:9). This oracle is implicitly nuptial, because the "daughter of Zion," or "virgin daughter of Zion" (cf. 2 Kings 19:21; Isa. 37:22; Lam. 2:13), is the personification of the people of God as one of the royal princesses of marriageable age, and the "king" who comes to her is her intended bridegroom. So Jesus enters Jerusalem as Davidic bridegroom-king, ready to "wed" Israel through a new covenant.

Jesus's passion-week parables in the temple develop the royal bridegroom theme. For example, he teaches that "the kingdom of heaven may be compared to a king who gave a marriage feast for his son" (Matt. 22:2), comparing God the Father to a king, Jesus to a bridegroom prince, his Judean contemporaries to recalcitrant invitees, and the poor and Gentiles to strangers gathered in a

2. The adjective "adulterous" (moichalis) implies that they are bound by the nuptial covenant to which they are being unfaithful, as opposed to being merely "sexually immoral" (pornois).

wedding hall (22:2–14).[3] Likewise, the parable of the wise and foolish virgins (25:1–13) distinguishes, within the community of God, between those who persevere to the end and embrace the bridegroom Messiah (the "wise virgins") and the nonpersevering (the "foolish virgins"). The parable could be applied to historic Israel, distinguishing the covenant faithful who receive Jesus as Messiah from the unfaithful who reject him (cf. John 1:11–13), or it could be applied to Jesus's followers (i.e., the nascent Church), distinguishing the long-suffering disciples from the transient (cf. the "rocky" and the "good" soils in Matt. 13:20–23). The "virgins" in the parable may evoke in modern readers the image of "bridesmaids," but in the spiritual sense they are each "brides"—that is, individual disciples awaiting communion with Jesus as their spiritual bridegroom.[4]

Jesus's subsequent anointing at Bethany (Matt. 26:6–13) also has nuptial connotations. Mark's parallel (Mark 14:3–9) even mentions "an alabaster flask" of "pure nard" (14:3), and the only Old Testament occurrences of "alabaster" and "nard" are in the Song of Songs (1:12; 4:13–14; 5:15). Furthermore, Song 1:12 foreshadows the Bethany anointing: "While the king was on his couch, my nard gave forth its fragrance." Jesus is the royal bridegroom of the Song, reclining on the couch, receiving the nard from the woman, who symbolizes his bride, the community of the disciples. But Jesus connects this nuptial symbolism to his burial: "In pouring this ointment on my body she has done it to prepare me for burial" (Matt. 26:12). The nuptial theme in the Bethany anointing and the burial of the Lord is developed much further in John (12:1–8; 19:38–42), as we will see presently.

John

John develops to a much greater degree the nuptial characterization of Jesus and his ministry that is already clear, if sporadic, in Matthew and Mark, beginning with his first "sign" at Cana (John 2:1–11) and ending climactically with the crucifixion, burial, and resurrection (19:1–20:18).[5]

3. Smolarz, *Covenant and the Metaphor of Divine Marriage*, 152–62, esp. 155–56; Villeneuve, *Divine Marriage*, 163–65.
4. See the discussion in Smolarz, *Covenant and the Metaphor of Divine Marriage*, 162–73; Villeneuve, *Divine Marriage*, 165–67.
5. The literature on nuptiality in John is extensive. In the following, we draw on Adeline Fehribach, *The Women in the Life of the Bridegroom: A Feminist Historical-Literary Analysis of the Female Characters in the Fourth Gospel* (Collegeville, MN: Liturgical Press, 1998); Jocelyn

Jesus reveals himself as a divine bridegroom at the wedding at Cana (John 2:1–11). To understand the Cana scene, we must first observe the day structure of the opening of John's Gospel. John's opening line, "In beginning was the Word . . ." (John 1:1), evokes the creation account (Gen. 1:1), and subsequent discussion of "light" and "darkness" (John 1:4–9) recalls the first day (Gen. 1:3–4). Thus, John 1:1–28 is literarily the "first day" of the Gospel, because only at verse 29 do we get an indication of temporal movement: "The *next day* [John the Baptist] saw Jesus coming toward him." By use of the phrase "the next day," John delimits the second day (1:29–34), the third day (1:35–42), the fourth day (1:43–51), and the wedding three days later (2:1)—a total of seven days, a figurative and literary "new creation week." On the seventh day, the first woman appears in the Gospel, the "mother of Jesus" (2:1b), parallel to Eve, who appears in the creation narrative on the seventh day: Adam is created on the sixth (Gen. 1:26), falls into deep sleep (2:21), and awakens on the seventh to behold his bride (2:22–23).[6] To reinforce the parallel with Eve, Jesus calls her "woman" (John 2:4), as Adam does Eve (Gen. 2:23). Jesus and his mother stand in the foreground of the Cana wedding as the New Adam and New Eve of the New Covenant.

Now, by Jewish custom the bridegroom would provide wine for the typically week-long wedding celebration; thus, the steward rebukes the bridegroom for saving the best until last (John 2:10), under the assumption that he has provided the wine. Thus, at Cana *Jesus performs the bridegroom's duty*; furthermore, he does it *superlatively* and *supernaturally*, providing up to 180 gallons of the finest wine (2:6)—tens of thousands of dollars in modern-day values. Wine signifies joy in the Old Testament,[7] and a new bridegroom had to bring joy to his wife (Deut. 24:5 NABRE). So Jesus is the messianic bridegroom who fulfills the mitzvah of Moses for bridegrooms (Deut. 24:5)

McWhirter, *The Bridegroom Messiah and the People of God: Marriage in the Fourth Gospel*, SNTSMS 138 (Cambridge: Cambridge University Press, 2006); Brant Pitre, *Jesus the Bridegroom: The Greatest Love Story Ever Told* (New York: Image, 2014), 29–121; Sandra M. Schneiders, *Written That You May Believe: Encountering Jesus in the Fourth Gospel*, rev. ed. (New York: Herder & Herder, 2003); Ann Roberts Winsor, *A King Is Bound in the Tresses: Allusions to the Song of Songs in the Fourth Gospel*, StBibLit 6 (New York: Peter Lang, 1999); and Villeneuve, *Divine Marriage*, 169–226.

6. Others would count the three days before Cana ("on the third day," John 2:1) inclusively, ending up with six days, parallel to the creation of "male and female" on the sixth day (Gen. 1:27). Regardless, an appeal to the creation week is clear, as is the parallel between Adam and Eve and Jesus and the Blessed Mother.

7. Deut. 14:26; Judg. 9:13; 2 Sam. 13:28; Neh. 8:10; Esther 1:10; Pss. 4:7; 104:15; Prov. 31:6; Eccles. 2:3; 9:7; 10:19; Song 1:4; Isa. 16:10; 22:13; 24:7, 11; 25:6; Jer. 48:33; Zech. 10:7.

by restoring joy to this bridal party—symbolic of Israel, who has lost her joy due to her sins under the Old Covenant, represented by the "six stone jars" (John 2:6). This is the "first sign" of Jesus's ministry (2:11), and the immediately following pericope (2:13–22) identifies the seventh and last. Challenging Jesus's right to cleanse the temple, the Judeans say, "What *sign* have you to show us for doing this?" (2:18). Jesus responds, "Destroy this temple, and in three days I will raise it up" (v. 19). John explains: "He spoke of the temple of his body" (v. 21). Therefore, both the destruction of his temple-body *and* its raising up after three days—that is, the passion, death, and resurrection—will constitute the "sign" of Jesus's authority over the temple, an implicit claim to divinity.

John places Jesus's "first sign" (John 2:1–12) at Cana immediately before the forecast of his last "sign" (2:13–22) at Calvary, because Cana (2:1–12) and Calvary (19:17–20:18) stand like bookends—that is, an *inclusio*—around the central narrative of John. Several unique elements occur in John only in these two pericopes: the mother of Jesus (2:1–5//19:25–27), the presence of wine (2:3–10//19:28–30), and the provision of liquid from Jesus's person (2:7–10//19:34). Moreover, subtle nuptial motifs unite John 19:17–20:18 with the more obvious nuptial features of John 2:1–12 (see below). The wedding feast at Cana is a mystical prefigurement of the "wedding" at Calvary, where Jesus shows himself the bridegroom of all humanity by giving his body and the nuptial "wine" of his blood (19:34) to his bride.

John the Baptist confirms the bridegroom status of Jesus at Cana (John 2:1–12) in the following chapter by describing himself as the "friend of the bridegroom" who "rejoices greatly at the bridegroom's voice" (3:29–30). John's succinct parable characterizes Jesus as the bridegroom (cf. Mark 2:19–20//Matt. 9:15), himself as the "friend" or "best man," and the faithful remnant of Israel as the "bride."[8] The "bridegroom's voice" evokes multiple Scriptures: in Jeremiah, the cessation of the "voice of the bridegroom" portends divine judgment (Jer. 7:34; 16:9; 25:10), and its restoration signifies eschatological fulfillment (33:10–11). Likewise, the bride cries out in Song of Songs 2:8: "The voice of my beloved! Behold, he comes." Further, John's statement "this joy of mine is now full" (John 3:29) evokes the mitzvah of Deuteronomy 24:5, the duty of the bridegroom to bring joy, fulfilled by Jesus already at Cana.

8. See the discussion in Smolarz, *Covenant and the Metaphor of Divine Marriage*, 174–81; Villeneuve, *Divine Marriage*, 192–95.

The Baptist's identification of Jesus as "bridegroom" immediately precedes the most heavily nuptial pericope in John's Gospel, that of the woman at the well (4:1–42).[9] The evangelist says that Jesus "had to pass through Samaria" (4:4 ESV), when in fact Jesus could have done as other Jews did, crossing the Jordan to travel to Galilee through Perea. Thus, the "necessity" here (Greek *deō*, v. 4) is theological, not logistical. He must visit the descendants of northern Israel (i.e., the Samaritans), because Hosea has promised that the Lord would woo them back to himself in Hosea 2:14–23 (ET), the main prophetic subtext for the entire narrative of John 4:1–42, in which the Samaritan woman functions as an icon of the wayward northern Israelites, from whom she descends.

John sets the scene with images evoking northern Israelite traditions. The location Sychar is a city of "Samaria"—the ancient capital of the north (1 Kings 13:32; 16:24)—located "near the field that Jacob had given to his son *Joseph*" (John 4:5 ESV), the ancestor of the two largest northern tribes, Ephraim and Manasseh, from whom the Samaritans have descended and in whose tribal territories they still live.[10] Thus, Sychar is either near or a more recent name for ancient Shechem, the natural capital of the Josephite tribes and the onetime capital of Israel.[11] Furthermore, "Jacob's well was there" (v. 6), purposefully evoking Genesis 29:1–14, where Jacob encounters his future bride Rachel at a well and provides her water (29:10). Nor should we forget Genesis 24:1–67, where Abraham's steward encounters Rebekah at a well and courts her for Isaac, or Exodus 2:15–22, where Moses sits down by a well in Midian, provides water for the daughters of Reuel, and marries Zipporah.

Thus, as we expect, after Jesus sits down by the well (John 4:6), there comes a woman of Samaria (v. 7a). Jesus asks, "Give me a drink" (v. 7b), evoking the courtship of Rebekah, in which the request for a drink is the steward's sign for identifying the divinely ordained bride (Gen. 24:10–14). The Samaritan woman responds not with Rebekah's generosity (Gen. 24:18–19) but a rebuff: "How is it that you, a Jew, ask for a drink from me, a woman of Samaria?" (John 4:9 ESV). Jesus turns the tables, insisting that, if she knew him, she would have asked him for a drink (v. 10). That is, Jesus is a water provider,

9. Villeneuve, *Divine Marriage*, 195–203.
10. "Joseph" was a high-frequency Samaritan name. See Kristin Weingart, "What Makes an Israelite an Israelite? Judean Perspectives on the Samarians in the Persian Period," *JSOT* 42, no. 2 (2017): 155–75, here 173–74, esp. n. 54.
11. See Josh. 24:1, 25; Judg. 9:6; 1 Kings 12:1, 25.

as were Jacob (Gen. 29:10) and Moses (Exod. 2:17–19) before him, yet he surpasses them both.[12] Then Jesus and the woman discuss the true source of "living water" (John 4:10–15), a double entendre. In Hebrew and Aramaic, "living water" idiomatically means *running* water, necessary for certain ritual cleansings.[13] Yet Jesus speaks to the woman of life-giving water—in other words, the Holy Spirit: "The water that I shall give . . . will become . . . a spring of water welling up to eternal life" (v. 14; cf. John 7:38). This alludes to Solomon's description of his bride as a "well of living water" (Song 4:15). Thus, Jesus's "water" makes one a "well of living water"—that is, a bride of the New Solomon—just as Rachel and Zipporah become brides to the men who give them running water (cf. Gen. 29:10; Exod. 2:17).

The woman understands Jesus on a natural level: "Give me this water, that I may not thirst, nor come here to draw" (John 4:15). But the latent nuptiality of the whole encounter now becomes explicit: "Go, call your *husband*" (v. 16). The woman protests that she has no husband (v. 17). Jesus responds, "You have had five husbands, and he whom you now have is not your husband" (v. 18). The woman's personal history embodies the religious history of her people. The Samaritans were mixed-race descendants of both the poorest Israelites left behind in the Assyrian exile (2 Kings 17:6)[14] and the *five* Gentile nations that the Assyrians brought in (17:24), who introduced *five cults* of foreign gods (17:30–31) called *baʿālîm*, "lords" or "husbands."[15] In time, the Samaritans abandoned foreign cults and worshiped the Lord exclusively, yet they did so in defiance of the Davidic covenant, by which God chose Zion as the sole place of worship (Ps. 132:11–18), and they built an unauthorized temple on Gerizim instead.[16] The Samaritans had physically and religiously "intermarried" with five different nations and their cults, and they had returned to the Lord but not in proper covenant relationship, so Jesus says, "He whom you now have is not your husband" (John 4:18). Moreover, the phrase "he whom you now have" could mean the man in her immediate company—that is, *Jesus is*

---

12. For Jesus as similar but superior to Moses and Jacob, respectively, see John 1:17, 51.

13. Cf. Deut. 21:4; Temple Scroll (11Q19) 45:16.

14. Second Kings 17:6 is hyperbolic, as archaeology shows that the lowest classes—Israelite farm laborers—remained. See Gary N. Knoppers, *Jews and Samaritans: The Origins and History of Their Early Relations* (Oxford: Oxford University Press, 2013), 18–44.

15. Cf. Hosea 2:15, 19 MT and NABRE (= Hosea 2:13, 17 RSV, etc.).

16. On the date of the building of the sanctuary on Gerizim, see Sandra L. Richter, "The Archaeology of Mount Ebal and Mount Gerizim and Why It Matters," in *Sepher Torath Mosheh: Studies in the Composition and Interpretation of Deuteronomy*, ed. Daniel I. Block and Richard L. Schultz (Peabody, MA: Hendrickson, 2017), 304–37.

not her husband, Jesus the Lord God of Israel, with whom these Samaritan Israelites are not in right covenant relationship.

The woman's response—"Our fathers worshiped on this mountain; and you say that in Jerusalem is the place where men ought to worship" (John 4:20)—seems at first a distraction from the awkwardness of discussing her personal life, but it actually raises precisely the issue that keeps the Samaritans from a proper "marriage"[17] with the Lord: the illicit sanctuary on Gerizim. Jesus's response—"The hour is coming when neither on this mountain nor in Jerusalem will you worship the Father" (v. 21)—makes sense since his body has already been identified as the eschatological temple (2:21). The woman does not understand but suddenly makes a surprising confession of faith: "I know that Messiah is coming . . . ; when he comes, he will show us all things" (4:25). This provides Jesus an opportunity to reveal his identity: "I AM, who speaks to you" (v. 26 AT).[18] Jesus is the great "I AM" (cf. Exod. 3:14), the spiritual bridegroom who, at Sinai, wed himself to Israel, from whom the woman and her townsfolk have descended. Dazed by this revelation, the woman abandons her water jar and returns to town declaring, "Come, see a man who told me all that I ever did. Can this be the Christ?" (John 4:29). The townspeople do come and are convinced: "We have heard for ourselves, and we know that this is indeed the Savior of the world" (v. 42). The Lord has returned and wooed Israel in the persons of the Samaritan woman and the citizens of Sychar, thereby fulfilling Hosea, who predicted not only that the Lord would "allure" and "speak tenderly" to northern Israel but also that Israel would respond with youthful receptivity, calling God "my husband" and not "my Baal" (i.e., "lord," Hosea 2:14–16), who would "betroth" Israel to himself "for ever," in "righteousness," "justice," "steadfast love," and "mercy" (2:19–20).

The eucharistic discourse of John 6 is also relevant to the nuptial Christology of the Gospel. The statement "He who eats my flesh [*sarx*] and drinks my blood abides in me, and I in him" (John 6:56; cf. 6:53–58) implies a one-flesh (*sarx*) union between the believer and Jesus, comparable to marriage: "'The two shall become one flesh [*sarka mian*]' [cf. Gen. 2:24 LXX]. So they are no longer two but one flesh [*mia sarx*]" (Mark 10:8). Thus, despite an absence of explicit nuptial images in John 6, the bread of life discourse engages deeply with the bridegroom theme of the Gospel,[19] culminating in Jesus giving his

17. Cf. 2 Sam. 5:1–3, where northern Israel echoes the nuptial language of Gen. 2:23.
18. Greek *Egō eimi, ho lalōn soi.*
19. Villeneuve, *Divine Marriage*, 203–4.

St. Augustine on the Union of Christ and the Church

Augustine could be quite explicit in describing the nuptial dimension of Christ's passion:

> Like a bridegroom, Christ came forth from his chamber, and with a presage of his nuptials he went into the field of the world. . . . He reached the marriage couch of the Cross, mounting it, and there consummated his marriage . . . and thereby forever joined the woman to himself. "I have betrothed you to one spouse," the apostle says, "that I might present you to Christ a chaste virgin" (2 Cor. 11:2). . . . Therefore oh brethren, let us rejoice in this union of God and man, of Bridegroom and bride, of Christ and the Church, of the Savior and the Virgin.[a]

a. Augustine, *Sermo suppositus* 120.8 (PL 39:1987), trans. by Robert Baldwin in "Marriage as a Sacramental Reflection of the Passion: The Mirror in Jan van Eyck's *Amolfini Wedding*," *Oud Holland* 98, no. 2 (1984): 57–75, here 59.

flesh for his bride, the Church: "The bread which I shall give for the life of the world is my flesh [*sarx*]" (6:51; cf. Eph. 5:25b, 29–31).

The climax of Jesus's nuptial self-giving, his passion, begins in John with the anointing at Bethany (John 12:1–8; cf. Mark 14:3–9).[20] John mentions not only Mary's "pure nard" (cf. Mark 14:3) but also that "the house was filled with the fragrance [*osmē*] of the ointment" (John 12:3), more strongly evoking Song of Songs 1:12 (LXX): "While the king was on his couch, my nard gave forth its fragrance [*osmē*]." As in the other Gospels, Jesus connects the nuptial nard with his burial: "Let her alone, let her keep [the rest of] it for the day of my burial" (John 12:7). This anticipates John's nuptial portrayal of Jesus's death and interment, beginning in John 19, where the nuptial motifs become more intense.[21] Jesus, the royal Davidic bridegroom, approaches his death wearing a crown: "and the soldiers plaited a crown of thorns, and put it on his head" (19:2), possibly evoking (for the attentive reader) Song of Songs 3:11: "O daughters of Zion, . . . behold King Solomon, with the crown with which his mother crowned him on the day of his wedding."[22] Indeed, the

20. Winsor, *King Is Bound*, 17–33; Villeneuve, *Divine Marriage*, 206–10.
21. For nuptial motifs in John 19, see Villeneuve, *Divine Marriage*, 214–20.
22. Pitre, *Jesus the Bridegroom*, 102–4.

mother of the king does appear at the foot of the cross, where Jesus addresses her, "Woman, behold, your son!" and where he says to John, "Behold, your mother!" (John 19:26–27). The *Sitz im Leben* of these statements is, arguably, the birthing chamber, for in what other context does one announce to a mother that she has a son? And where else would one introduce a son to his mother? Jesus acts as midwife or husband, introducing a newborn son to his mother and vice versa. John may have in mind a kind of spiritual birth and motherhood here,[23] a mystical fulfillment of Isaiah 66:7: "Before [Zion] was in labor she gave birth; before her pain came upon her she delivered a son" (ESV). The Blessed Mother is Isaiah's "virgin daughter of Zion," who gives "birth" to a spiritual son, John, even before she enters the "labor" and the "pain" of witnessing her natural son's death.

Jesus's statement "I thirst" (John 19:28) alludes to his only other expression of thirst in the Gospel, to the Samaritan woman in John 4:7, which in turn evokes the famous request for a drink that reveals the divinely chosen bride in Genesis 24:12–21. The deeper meaning of "thirst," then, is a desire for humanity to reciprocate Jesus's spousal love for them. Note the contrast with Cana: there, the guests thirst and Jesus provides wine; at Calvary, Jesus thirsts and humanity provides the wine. At Cana, the divine bridegroom provides over a hundred gallons of the finest wine to satiate the thirst of the wedding guests. At Calvary, humanity provides a sponge full of "sour wine" (John 19:29 ESV; Greek *oxos*) for the thirst of the divine bridegroom. This is the disparity between God's spousal love for humanity and humanity's love for God.

Jesus then exclaims, "It is consummated!" (John 19:30 Douay). The Greek verb used here—*tetelestai*, from *teleō*, like Latin *consummatum*—could describe the performance of the rites of marriage, such that a bride who had completed those rites could be termed a "consummated" woman.[24] Thus, a marital sense for Jesus's final exclamation is possible, while not excluding other senses, as polyvalence is frequent in John.

The Roman soldiers pierce Jesus's side, and immediately there comes out "blood and water" (John 19:34). In this, many of the Fathers see birth imagery, since blood and water come forth from the womb.[25] The use of the Greek *pleura* for both Jesus's "side" (19:34) and Adam's (Gen. 2:21 LXX)

23. Villeneuve, *Divine Marriage*, 217.
24. See LSJ 1772a–b (definition 3.3).
25. Villeneuve, *Divine Marriage*, 218.

Tertullian on Adam as a Figure of Christ

Tertullian articulates a common patristic tradition by explicating the typological relationship of Adam's sleep and Christ's death on the cross: "As Adam was a figure of Christ, Adam's sleep shadowed out the death of Christ, who was to sleep a mortal slumber, that from the wound inflicted in his side might in like manner (as Eve was formed) be typified the Church, the true Mother of the living."[a]

a. Tertullian, *A Treatise on the Soul* 43 (*ANF* 3:222).

suggests that, like a New Eve from the New Adam, the Church is born from the side of Christ.[26] Thus, the intra-Johannine prophecy is fulfilled: "Out of his heart shall flow rivers of living water" (John 7:38), portraying Jesus's body as the New Temple (cf. 2:21) from which flows the Holy Spirit, borne by the sacramental river of baptismal water and eucharistic blood. Since the sheer number of animals being sacrificed during Passover produced torrents of bloody water flowing out of the drainage pipes of the Herodian temple, the connection of John 19:34 with the temple would have been obvious to first-century Jewish readers.[27] Probably all of these meanings of the flow from Christ's side—consummation, birth, temple-body—were intended by the evangelist.

Joseph of Arimathea and Nicodemus take custody of Jesus's body (John 19:38–39). For the embalming, Nicodemus brings a hundred pounds of "myrrh and aloes," ointments mentioned together in Israel's Scriptures only in nuptial contexts—for instance, the seduction scene of Proverbs 7:17 ("I have perfumed my bed with myrrh [and] aloes"), the royal wedding of Psalm 45:8 ("Your robes are all fragrant with myrrh and aloes"), and the description of the bride of the Song of Songs ("Your shoots are an orchard of pomegranates with . . . myrrh and aloes," 4:13–14). It is unlikely that John is unaware of this connotation. Moreover, Nicodemus brings a truly stupendous amount of these extremely costly ointments—a hundred pounds! Jesus receives a burial fit for

26. See Augustine, *Commentary on the Psalms*, Ps. 127:4 (*NPNF*[1] 8:607b).
27. *Letter of Aristeas* 88–91; *m. Middot* 3:2–3; *m. Yoma* 5:6; *b. Pesaḥim* 64a–b.

a bridegroom-king, complete with exotic, fragrant oils strongly associated with romance and marriage.

John tells us, "Now in the place where he was crucified there was a garden, and in the garden a new tomb where no one had ever been laid" (John 19:41). The garden calls to mind both Eden and the garden imagery of the Song of Songs, building on clear allusions to Eden and creation (John 1:1–2:11// Gen. 1:1–2:3) and the Song (John 12:3//Song 1:12) earlier in the Gospel. The tomb, likewise, is virginal, one in which "no one had ever been laid" (John 19:41). The holy sepulchre, then, symbolizes the bride of Christ, the Church, which receives the body of her royal bridegroom, calling to mind the virgin bride of the Song: "A garden locked is my sister, my bride, / a garden locked, a fountain sealed" (Song 4:12). As the virgin womb received the flesh of Christ's incarnation, the virgin tomb receives the flesh of his passion; for the womb and the tomb (i.e., the earth or grave) are strongly correlated in Israel's Scriptures.[28] Furthermore, Nicodemus, who places Jesus's body in the tomb, is the very one who earlier asks, "How can a man be born when he is old? Can he enter a second time into his mother's womb and be born?" (John 3:4). Death and burial did function in the Hebrew imagination as a return to the mother's womb (cf. Job 1:21; Eccles. 5:15; 2 Esd. 5:48; Sir. 40:1), but a second birth from that "womb" was never expected! Jesus's second birth from the womb of the earth serves as a model for all Christians, who share his death in baptism (Rom. 6:3–4) and, like him, are born "again" (John 3:3 ESV).[29]

The finale of the chain of nuptial symbolism that adorns John's passion account is the resurrection appearance to Mary Magdalene—John 20:1–2, 11–18—patterned on the first dream sequence of the Song of Songs (Song 3:1–5).[30] In both cases, the young woman goes out at night (John 20:1//Song 3:1) to search for her beloved, but she cannot find him (John 20:1b–2//Song 3:2). She then encounters the night watchmen (John 20:12//

---

28. For example, burial is a return to the mother's womb (Job 1:21; Eccles. 5:15); the womb is the "depths of the earth" (Ps. 139:15) or the "grave" (Jer. 20:17); and the grave is the "womb of the earth" (2 Esd. 5:48) or the "mother of all" (Sir. 40:1, cf. Wis. 7:1). See the discussion in Gregory Vall, "The Enigma of Job 1,21a," *Biblica* 76, no. 3 (1995): 325–42.

29. Given the established doctrine of the virginal conception and birth prior to the writing of John (Matt. 1:18–25; Luke 1:34–35), given the availability in earlier biblical literature of the womb-tomb correlation, and given the presence of Nicodemus, who earlier discusses the "return to the womb" and second-birth ideas with Jesus (John 3:1–15), this complex of correlations is probably intended by the evangelist.

30. Winsor, *King Is Bound*, 35–44; Villeneuve, *Divine Marriage*, 221–22.

St. Cyril of Jerusalem on Mary

The literary allusions to Song of Songs 3:1–5 in John 20:1, 11–18, have long been recognized. Here, St. Cyril of Jerusalem describes the relationship of the texts in detail:

> Mary came seeking Him, according to the Gospel, and found Him not: and presently she heard from the Angels, and afterwards saw the Christ. Are then these things also written? He says in the Song of Songs, "On my bed I sought Him whom my soul loved." At what season? "By night on my bed I sought Him Whom my soul loved": Mary, it says, came while it was yet dark. "On my bed I sought Him by night, I sought Him, and I found Him not." And in the Gospels Mary says, "They have taken away my Lord, and I know not where they have laid Him" (John 20:13). But the Angels being then present cure their want of knowledge; for they said, "Why do you seek the living among the dead" (Luke 24:5)? He not only rose, but had also the dead with Him when He rose (Matt. 27:52). But she knew not, and in her person the Song of Songs said to the Angels, "Saw ye Him Whom my soul loved? It was but a little that I passed from them (that is, from the two Angels), until I found Him Whom my soul loved. I held Him, and would not let Him go" (Song 3:3–4). For after the vision of the Angels, Jesus came as His own Herald; and the Gospel says, "And behold Jesus met them, saying, All hail! And they came and took hold of His feet" (Matt. 28:9). They took hold of Him, that it might be fulfilled, "I will hold Him, and will not let Him go." Though the woman was weak in body, her spirit was manful. "Many waters quench not love, neither do rivers drown it" (Song 8:7); He was dead whom they sought, yet was not the hope of the Resurrection quenched.[a]

a. Cyril of Jerusalem, *Catechetical Lecture* 14.12–13 (*NPNF²* 7:97).

Song 3:3a),[31] with whom she discusses her beloved (John 20:13//Song 3:3b). No sooner does she encounter the watchmen than she discovers her beloved (John 20:14–16//Song 3:4a) and grasps him tightly (John 20:17//Song 3:4b). Similar to the Samaritan woman at the well, Mary Magdalene functions in this scene as a figure symbolic of a group—in this case, the body of the

31. In Second Temple Judaism, angels were the "watchers" or "watchmen" of heaven (*Jub.* 4:15, 22; 7:21; 8:3; 10:5; *1 En.* 1:5; 10:7, 9, 15; 12:2–4; 13:10; 14:1, 3; 15:2, 9; 16:1–2; 20:1; 82:10).

disciples, the Church, who is the loving bride of Christ and who seeks him out for the nuptial embrace.

Paul

The paradigm of Christ as the bridegroom of the Church manifests itself several times in Paul's epistles. In Romans 7:1–6, Paul uses the analogy of marriage to describe the transition from the Old Covenant to the New Covenant for Jewish believers. They were once "married" to the law, but now they are dead to the law (7:4–6). And since death ends marriage and makes possible a new union (7:1–3), they now "belong to another, to him who has been raised from the dead" (7:4).[32] Thus, the Torah and Christ are two husbands to whom Jewish believers have been wed. Similarly, in 1 Corinthians 6:16–20, Paul grounds Christian sexual morality in the fact that the believer's union with Christ is even more intimate than conjugal union. One who sleeps with a prostitute becomes "one body with her," but the one united to the Lord is "one spirit with him" (1 Cor. 6:16–17).

There is both an individual and a corporate dimension to believers as the "bride" of Christ. In 2 Corinthians 11:2–3, Paul likens the Corinthian church to a "pure bride" that he "betrothed" "to Christ," but he fears they will be "deceived" like Eve and will go "astray from a sincere and pure devotion to Christ."[33] Most famously, Paul takes his paradigm for the practice of Christian marriage in Ephesians 5:22–33 from the covenantal relation of Christ and his body.[34] For Paul, the spousal relationship of Christ to the Church manifests a superlative devotion and affection:

> Husbands, love your wives, as Christ loved the church and gave himself up for her, that he might sanctify her, having cleansed her by the washing of water with the word, that he might present the church to himself in splendor, without spot or wrinkle or any such thing, that she might be holy and without blemish. (Eph. 5:25–27)

Christ is "head" and "Savior" of the Church, which is his body (v. 23). He "loves," "gives himself up for," "sanctifies," "cleanses," and "presents" the

---

32. Smolarz, *Covenant and the Metaphor of Divine Marriage*, 208–13.

33. Smolarz, *Covenant and the Metaphor of Divine Marriage*, 190–97; Villeneuve, *Divine Marriage*, 247–49.

34. For a masterful treatment of nuptiality in Ephesians, see Villeneuve, *Divine Marriage*, 250–76. Also cf. Smolarz, *Covenant and the Metaphor of Divine Marriage*, 219–26.

Church to himself in splendor (vv. 25–27). He does not hate but "nourishes" and "cherishes" the Church, who are "members of his body" (vv. 29–30). Paul concludes:

> "For this reason a man shall leave his father and mother and be joined to his wife, and the two shall become one flesh." This mystery is great, but I say [it is] about Christ and the Church. (Eph. 5:31–32 AT)[35]

Thus, for Paul, the foundational text about the origin and purpose of marriage in the Bible (Gen. 2:24) primarily describes Christ and the Church, and then secondary meanings applied to natural marriage follow.[36] We will revisit this important text when reviewing the practical teaching on marriage in the New Testament. For now, it suffices to see that St. Paul's spousal construal of the person and ministry of Jesus is equally as rich as John's.

Revelation

The Revelation to John, like the Gospel that bears his name, persistently portrays Jesus as bridegroom of God's people. In Revelation 3:20, for example, Jesus stands knocking at the door to gain entrance and dine with those within, probably an allusion to the bridegroom of Song of Songs 5:2, who knocks and calls on the bride, his "sister" and "love," to open for him. Jesus is the bridegroom for each human being, "knocking" to seek entrance into their lives. If one "opens the door," Jesus will share the messianic banquet—the Eucharist—with that person: "I will . . . eat with him, and he with me" (Rev. 3:20b).

The whole plot of Revelation revolves around spiritual marriage.[37] After the initial letters to the churches of Asia Minor (chaps. 1–3), the narrative consists of a series of plagues that fall from heaven onto the earth (chaps. 4–16), culminating in the overthrow and destruction of a great harlot woman

---

35. Greek *to mystērion touto mega estin. egō de legō eis Christon kai eis tēn ekklēsian.*

36. See the discussion in Clinton E. Arnold, *Ephesians*, ZECNT 10 (Grand Rapids: Zondervan, 2010), Kindle loc. 10665–734.

37. For an extensive treatment of nuptial themes in Revelation, see Smolarz, *Covenant and the Metaphor of Divine Marriage*, 228–365, 370–73. On p. 371, Smolarz asserts that "the main conflict of Revelation concerns two juxtaposed women: the bride of Christ and the harlot, representing the corrupted Jerusalem system." Similarly, Villeneuve, *Divine Marriage*, 277–94: "Nuptial imagery in Revelation runs through the entire book" (277). Cf. Pitre, *Jesus the Bridegroom*, 114–35.

(chaps. 17–18) who is replaced by the "bride" of the Lamb (19:7), who is also "new Jerusalem, . . . prepared as a bride adorned for her husband," and who comes "down out of heaven from God" (21:2) in the final chapters of the book (chaps. 19–22). Thus, the central action of the book is the removal of the harlot and her replacement with the bride.

The proper interpretation of the book hinges on the identification of the harlot in chapter 17. Who is she? Revelation 17:18 says, "The woman whom you saw represents *the great city* that has sovereignty over the kings of the earth" (NABRE). The reader might immediately think of Rome as "the great city." However, internal indications point to a different solution. Revelation 11:8 identifies "the great city" as symbolically "Sodom" and "Egypt," the place "where indeed their Lord was crucified" (NABRE). Thus, the "great city" unambiguously refers to Jerusalem. The city's "sovereignty over the kings of the earth" in Revelation 17:18 must be understood in terms of Old Testament imagery, in which Zion is the master city of the whole earth, the "hill" on which God has set his great suzerain who rules the nations decisively with an iron rod (Ps. 2:6, 8–9). The harlot woman of Revelation 17 can be understood as the earthly Jerusalem,[38] destroyed in AD 70 when the seven-headed "beast" of Rome turned on her and consumed her (cf. Rev. 17:16). Israel or Jerusalem as harlot is a common motif in the prophets,[39] as is Jerusalem as Sodom.[40] The great wealth of the city as portrayed in Revelation 18 is no impediment to this interpretation, as first-century Jerusalem was considered the richest city of the eastern Roman Empire "by far,"[41] according to the geographer Pliny the Elder. And according to the future Roman general Titus, as recorded by Josephus, the wealth of Jerusalem surpassed even that of Rome itself.[42]

Thus, the central "plot" of Revelation can be summarized as the destruction of the old Jerusalem and her replacement by the new. The old was adulterous toward her husband, the Lord, and devolved into harlotry. The new is the pure bride, wholly devoted to her bridegroom.

While there are subtle bridal and nuptial motifs scattered throughout Revelation, the imagery becomes explicit and intense at the beginning of the conclusion of the book, in chapter 19, after the destruction of the harlot. Then

38. Smolarz, *Covenant and the Metaphor of Divine Marriage*, 234–45, 256, 271, 282.
39. See Isa. 1:21; Jer. 2:20; 3:1, 6, 8; Ezek. 16; 23; Hosea 2:5.
40. Isa. 1:7–10; 3:9; Jer. 23:14; Lam. 4:6; Ezek. 16:46–56; Amos 4:11.
41. "Longe modo." Pliny, *Natural History* 5.66–73.
42. Josephus, *War* 6.335.

a "great multitude" explodes in jubilation, for the "marriage [*gamos*] of the Lamb has come, and his wife [*gynē*] has made herself ready," dressed in the "fine linen" that is the "righteous deeds of the saints," as the angel asserts, "Blessed are those who are invited to the marriage supper of the Lamb" (Rev. 19:6–9, modified). Only John and Revelation employ the image of the "Lamb of God," and there is no doubt that it designates Jesus Christ (John 1:29, 36). The image probably draws on Isaiah 53:7, which describes the servant of the Lord as "like a lamb that is led to the slaughter," and other passages of the Prophets that suggest that the messiah or God's servant will have a self-sacrificial mission. The "marriage supper of the Lamb" draws on the fusion, already evident in the Gospels, of the prophetic theme of a nuptial covenant between God and Israel with that of the eschatological banquet.

The nuptial theme recedes into the background in Revelation 19:11–20:15, as the author seems to introduce a kind of flashback retrospective on salvation history using a different set of symbolic images mostly taken from warfare and the military. But in Revelation 21, the narrative returns to the nuptial theme and develops it further. John exclaims, "I saw the holy city, new Jerusalem, coming down out of heaven from God, prepared [*kosmeō*] as a bride [*nymphē*] adorned for her husband" (21:2). A few verses later, an angel arrives to give John a tour: "Come, I will show you the Bride [*nymphē*], the wife [*gynē*] of the Lamb" (21:9).

The bride of the Lamb is shown to have the characteristics of the various sanctuaries of Israel throughout her history, all of which were viewed, in Jewish tradition, as trysting places between God and his people: Eden, Sinai, the tabernacle, the temple, the eschatological temple of Ezekiel.[43] So the bride has a gate system with gates on the east, west, north, and south that recall the description of Ezekiel's visionary temple (Ezek. 48:30–35). It has a radiance "like a jasper, as clear as crystal" (Rev. 21:11), resembling the pavement of the throne of God on Sinai (Exod. 24:10). The city is a perfect cube, like the Holy of Holies of Solomon's temple (1 Kings 6:19–20). The foundations are adorned with the twelve gemstones of the breastplate of the high priest in the Mosaic tabernacle (Exod. 39:8–14). The city is the source of light and water for the cosmos (Rev. 21:22–27; 22:5), as various prophets predicted for the eschatological Jerusalem (Ezek. 47:1–12; Joel 3:18; Zech. 14:6–8). It contains the river of life and the tree of life from the garden of Eden (Rev. 22:1–2; cf.

43. Villeneuve, *Divine Marriage*, 19–103.

Gen. 2:9–14). The city both *contains* and also simply *is* the faithful people of God of the Old and New Covenants, the one people of God of all time, who are bride to his bridegroom. So the end of the book of Revelation makes a fitting summary of the nuptial theme of God and his people that has run through the whole of Scripture, beginning with Genesis.

The Implications for Matrimony

Although the bridegroom imagery applied to Christ and the bridal imagery applied to the body of disciples or the Church throughout the New Testament do not directly address the practice of matrimony among believers, they do reveal the ideals for the institution of marriage held by the sacred authors and, if we believe in divine inspiration, ultimately God himself. In one sense, all morality is an *imitatio Dei*, an attempt by humanity to follow the pattern established by God, and if this is so, there is a certain normativity about *how*, for example, Jesus lives out his role as bridegroom of his people. So then, what qualities does Christ the bridegroom exhibit in the nuptial parables and images that describe him throughout the Gospels, the Epistles, and Revelation?

The first quality to be noted is *joyfulness*. Again and again, Jesus's role as bridegroom is associated with joy and rejoicing, as Jesus is the husband who fully lives out the mitzvah to "gladden" his wife (Deut. 24:5). Thus, already from the first bridegroom parable in the Gospels (Matt. 9:14–15; Mark 2:18–20), the presence of the bridegroom brings joy: "Can the wedding guests mourn as long as the bridegroom is with them?" (Matt. 9:15). The implied answer is no. His presence among them is a cause for celebration, and so the disciples do not fast. Likewise, when the royal bridegroom messiah processes into Jerusalem, the daughter of Zion is commanded: "Rejoice! . . . Your king comes to you" (Zech. 9:9). In the wedding parables of Matthew 22:2–12 and 25:1–13, it is taken for granted that the wedding banquet is an experience of joy and satiation in which any reasonable person would wish to participate.

This quality continues in John, where we have seen that Cana is a manifestation of Jesus as the joy-bringing bridegroom, since wine is an icon of rejoicing.[44] John the Baptist confirms this: "The friend of the bridegroom, who stands and hears him, rejoices greatly at the bridegroom's voice; therefore

---

44. Judg. 9:13; 2 Sam. 13:28; Neh. 8:10; Esther 1:10; Pss. 4:7; 104:15; Prov. 31:6; Eccles. 2:3; 9:7; 10:19; Isa. 22:13; 24:11; 25:6; Jer. 48:33; Zech. 10:7.

this joy of mine is now full" (John 3:29). The mission of Jesus as bridegroom is to bring a fullness or abundance of joy, an abundance represented by his abundant provision of wine in John 2 and of bread in John 6, pointing to the Eucharist through its two species. And certainly the vision of the wedding of the Lamb and his bride in Revelation 19–22 is not lacking an abundance of joy: "Let us rejoice and exult and give him the glory, for the marriage of the Lamb has come!" (Rev. 19:7). All sorrow is put away: "He will wipe away every tear from their eyes, and death shall be no more, neither shall there be mourning nor crying nor pain any more" (21:4).

A second quality of the divine bridegroom especially evident in John is *provision*. The bridegroom provides abundantly for the needs of the bride. We see this in the two particularly nuptial miracles: Cana (John 2:1–11) and the multiplication of the loaves (6:1–15), in both of which the assembly represents the bridal people of God, and Jesus provides for their needs to the point of satiation (cf. 6:11b). The theme of provision is also evident in John 4:1–42, where Jesus insists that, even though he is asking for a physical drink, nonetheless he is the one who can provide abundant living water for the woman (vv. 10, 13–14), thus identifying himself mystically with Jacob and Moses, who provide abundant water for their future brides. Paul's vision of Christ the bridegroom in his relationship to the Church in Ephesians 5:25–29 likewise emphasizes provision: Christ the husband "gives himself up," "sanctifies," "cleanses," "loves," "nourishes," and "cherishes" his bride. Similarly, in Revelation, Christ provides abundant water from the fountain of life (21:6; 22:1, 17), the crown of life (2:10), white garments (3:5, 18), gold (3:18), eye salve (3:18), supernatural light (21:23–25; 22:5), the hidden manna (2:17), and the tree of life and its fruit (2:7; 22:2, 14).

A third quality of the divine bridegroom is *self-gift* or self-sacrifice, the donation of his very self—his "body," "blood," or "flesh," which by metonymy refer to his whole person—to and for the bride. This is especially evident in the Gospel of John, where the two great provision miracles—Cana and the feeding of the five thousand—produce wine and bread, respectively, which are signs of his blood and flesh given for the life of the world (John 6:51) and, in particular, those of the world who are receptive to him—that is, the body of disciples or the Church. Obviously, too, the whole nuptial portrayal of the passion, death, burial, and resurrection of the Christ in John speaks of the bridegroom's gift of self. John's narrative imagery makes the same point that Paul articulates explicitly: "Christ loved the church and *gave himself up for her*" (Eph. 5:25). Revelation likewise portrays Jesus as a "Lamb who was slain" (Rev. 5:12; cf. 5:6; 13:8), the very point of the image being to stress Jesus's self-sacrifice on behalf of his bride, the Church. Tying this to the quality of provision, one can say that the greatest of the goods the bridegroom provides is his very self.

A fourth quality of the bridegroom is, of course, *love*, which undergirds all the rest. The point of all Jesus's spousal acts in the Gospel of John, whether providing wine (chap. 2), bread (chap. 6), or his very body and blood (chap. 19), is to demonstrate and manifest the truth of this assertion: "As the Father has loved me, so have I loved you" (15:9). In fact, Jesus has loved with the greatest of loves: "Greater love has no man than this, that a man lay down his life for his friends" (15:13). The Gospel of John is a narrative illustrating Paul's synopsis: "Christ loved the church and gave himself up for her" (Eph. 5:25). John echoes the same sentiment in Revelation, speaking of Christ as the one who "loves us and has freed us from our sins" (Rev. 1:5) and recording Christ himself as both saying to the Church, "I have loved you" (3:9), and referring to the faithful as "those whom I love" (3:19).

What qualities of the ideal bride do the imagistic texts of the New Testament portray? If the primary task of the bridegroom is to *love* the bride—that is, to take the initiative in extending love toward her, a love that is ultimately a gift of self—then the first task of the bride is to *receive* that love, which is ultimately the gift of the bridegroom himself. What distinguishes human beings who constitute the "bride" from those who do not is their *receptivity*—in other words, whether they *receive* the bridegroom:

> He came to his own home, and his own people received [*paralambanō*] him not. But to all who received [*lambanō*] him, who believed in his name, he gave power to become children of God. . . . And from his fulness have we all received [*lambanō*], grace upon grace. (John 1:11–12, 16)

In the Septuagint, *lambanō*, "take, receive," regularly renders Hebrew *lāqaḥ*, "take, receive," which is frequently used of "taking" or accepting a spouse.[45] Such acceptance is almost always from the masculine perspective of a husband "taking" a woman as a wife, but Ezekiel 16:32 illustrates that the verb can also be used of a woman receiving her husband. In light of the nuptial theme that runs throughout John, we can understand "all who

45. E.g., Gen. 4:19; 6:2; 11:29; 12:15, 19; 20:2, 3; 21:21.

received him" as the Church, the body of those who accept or receive the bridegroom's love.

Matthew's wedding parables of the kingdom contrast those who receive the bridegroom with those who do not. In the parable of the royal son's wedding (Matt. 22:2–14), the original invitees do not accept the invitation to the wedding and thus do not receive the bridegroom, but those who are gathered from the highways and byways do receive him. In the parable of the ten virgins (25:1–13), wise virgins are ready to "meet" (*hypantaō* or *apantaō*) the bridegroom and then enter in with him to the wedding, all actions that indicate acceptance and reception of the bridegroom, whereas the foolish are not present to receive him. In John 6:56, it is those who receive the body and blood of Jesus the bridegroom who will be saved: "He who eats my flesh and drinks my blood abides in me." This eucharistic imagery appears also in the invitation of Revelation 3:20: "Behold, I stand at the door and knock; if anyone hears my voice and opens the door, I will come in to him and eat with him, and he with me." The eschatological bridegroom offers himself, and the receptive person becomes the bride and enjoys the nuptial banquet with him.

Yet the ideal bride not only receives but also *reciprocates* the love of the bridegroom. In the anointing at Bethany pericopes (Matt. 26:6–13; Mark 14:3–9; John 12:1–8), Mary functions as an image of the ideal bride inasmuch as she reciprocates the generous expressions of the bridegroom's love. This is especially evident in John's Gospel, in which Jesus has already shown himself to be a lavishly generous bridegroom (chaps. 2 and 6); and then in John 12:1–8, Mary appears with what is—especially for her resources—an extremely lavish gift of ointment to mark out Jesus as the bridegroom Messiah. Jesus defends Mary's actions and implies that they are commendable (v. 7) and that he deserves the generosity of the expenditure (v. 8). Mary is a commendable image of the bride, because according to her means, she returns the generous expressions of love from the bridegroom.

The reciprocation theme can also be discerned in Jesus's two requests for a drink in John's Gospel: to the Samaritan woman (4:7) and from the cross (19:28). These requests, we have seen, are based on the paradigm of Genesis 24:10–21, where the request for a drink is the sign that Abraham's servant asks of God in order to find a generous bride for Isaac—one who would volunteer the abundant provision of water for ten camels. It is appropriate, then, to regard the request for a drink from the Samaritan woman, as well as the implied request for a drink from humanity from the cross (John 19:28), as a request from the divine bridegroom for a sign of the reciprocation of his love, for a corresponding return of his generosity. In these two instances, neither the Samaritan woman nor the bystanders at the cross make the generous response—in contrast to Mary of Bethany (12:1–8) and Nicodemus (19:39), who do.

A third virtue of the bride suggested by the nuptial motif throughout the New Testament is *exclusivity*: she gives herself only to her bridegroom and refuses all others. This is expressed above all by the idea of virginity: the virgin bride has not given and will not give herself to another but waits patiently for the bridegroom. This is expressed in the parable of the ten virgins, each of whom is really more an individual bride than a bridesmaid, as we have suggested above. Likewise, the donkey on which Christ the royal bridegroom enters Jerusalem is one "on which no one has ever sat" (Mark 11:2); the holy sepulchre that receives the body of Christ the bridegroom is a tomb "where no one had ever been laid" (John 19:41); and Paul tells the Corinthian church that he betrothed them "as a pure bride to her one husband," but he fears they may "receive" or "accept" a "different spirit" or a "different gospel" (2 Cor. 11:2, 4). Virginity is a reciprocation of love. Just as the bridegroom gives himself totally and without reservation to the bride, so the bride gives herself totally and without reservation to him—nothing of herself has been or will be given to any other.

The final virtue is closely related: *fidelity*. Exclusivity is the gift of self to only one other person; fidelity is the maintenance of exclusivity over time, in the face of challenges and temptations. The theme of fidelity is quite clear in Matthew's parable of the ten virgins: the wise virgins are those prepared to persevere through the long night of waiting for the bridegroom, and they are still ready to receive him when he comes. This virtue of fidelity is related also to the theme of "remaining" or "abiding" that runs throughout the Gospel of John: "He who eats my flesh and drinks my blood abides in me, and I in him" (6:56); "Abide in me, and I in you" (15:4). This mutual "remaining" or "abiding" (Greek *menō*) is implicitly nuptial, as in matrimony the bodies of spouses mingle in the conjugal embrace so that they remain "in" each other. The exclusive, mutual self-gift is perpetuated over time by "remaining." Paul essentially exhorts the Corinthian church to fidelity in the face of different spirits and different gospels that arise to tempt their exclusive devotion away from Christ (2 Cor. 11:3–4). And there are many signs of implicit fidelity in Revelation's nuptial motif, for the spotless bride of the Lamb who emerges in Revelation 19–21 turns out to be the same faithful people of God who suffer through the persecutions and tribulations portrayed in Revelation 6–18 (cf. 2:10,

23; 17:14). The bride of the Lamb is really the same as the heavenly queen of Revelation 12—who has to endure and persevere through the lethal onslaughts of the dragon—and the 144,000 virgins who have remained chaste through all the tribulations (14:1–5, 12).

Summary of Christ as Bridegroom in the New Testament

The images of Christ as bridegroom and Church as bride, which strategically recur throughout the New Testament, are primarily a theological model of the covenant relationship of the Second Person of the Trinity with his people, but the use of the imagery entails assumptions about the virtues or qualities desirable in spouses. These virtues show gendered differentiation and complementarity. For the bridegroom-husband, they include joyfulness, provision, sacrificial self-gift, and love; and for the bride-wife, they include receptivity, reciprocation, exclusivity, and fidelity.

10

"What God Has Joined Together"

Marriage in the Gospels

The purpose of this chapter is to survey and summarize the teaching of the Gospels on the practice of matrimony. The relevant texts are as follows: First, we look at the normative example set by the marriage par excellence of the New Testament, that of St. Joseph and the Blessed Mother, described in Matthew 1:18–25; 2:13–23; and Luke 1:26–38; 2:1–52. Second, we examine the teaching on marriage in the Gospels, which revolves around two major foci: indissolubility (Matt. 5:31–32; 19:1–15; Mark 10:11–12; Luke 16:18) and temporality (i.e., cessation in the eschaton; Matt. 22:23–33; Mark 12:18–27; Luke 20:27–40).

The Normative Example of the Holy Marriage

Matthew and Luke alone describe the marriage of Jesus's parents. Matthew provides some background for their betrothal in Matthew 1:18–19:

> When his mother Mary had been betrothed to Joseph, before they came together she was found to be with child of the Holy Spirit; and her husband Joseph, being a just man and unwilling to expose her, resolved to divorce her quietly. (RSV, modified)

Joseph and Mary have had a typical Jewish courtship, being betrothed some time before taking up residence together. The elapse between betrothal and wedding allowed the groom to prepare the home where the new couple would reside. But the legal bond began at betrothal; thus, Joseph is called *ho anēr autēs*, literally, "her man"—that is, "husband" (v. 19a)—and dissolution requires "divorce"—*apoluō*, "release, dismiss" (v. 19b).

Matthew describes Joseph as "just" or "righteous" (Greek *dikaios*, Hebrew *ṣaddîq*; cf. Gen. 6:9)—that is, one careful to observe the Mosaic law—high praise in Second Temple Judaism! Yet the law did not forbid divorce of an unfaithful bride; rather, it mandated death (cf. Deut. 22:21; John 8:3–5). Significantly, Joseph is *dikaios* precisely for *not* pressing the letter of the law, for true "righteousness" includes not merely justice but also mercy (Isa. 30:18; Hosea 2:19; Matt. 23:23). He is unwilling to "expose" her (*deigmatizō*, lit., "point [her] out") but intends to "dismiss" (*apoluō*) her "secretly" (*lathra*), preserving her so far as possible from public ridicule and other social or legal consequences. Doubtless this is painful for Joseph, since the apparently incontrovertible facts seem to contradict what he knows to be the character of his beloved.[1] Yet seemingly forced to acknowledge some wrongdoing on her part, he still adopts the gentlest course of action possible, which Matthew declares to be *dikaios*, "righteousness," an exemplary virtue for a husband: gentle and careful concerning his wife's reputation (cf. Ruth 3:14; Eph. 5:29), even in the most trying of situations.

Thankfully, the Lord does not let Joseph suffer long with the pain and confusion of the situation; rather, he soon sends the angel to inform him, "Do not fear to receive Mary your wife, for that which is conceived in her is of the Holy Spirit" (Matt. 1:20 RSV [modified]). Joseph obeys immediately

1. Most of the Fathers understand Matt. 1:19–20 to indicate that St. Joseph suspects the Blessed Mother of infidelity. Thus Augustine: "Joseph, 'being a just man,' with great mercy spared his wife, in this great crime of which he suspected her. The seeming certainty of her unchastity tormented him, and yet because he alone knew of it, he was willing not to publish it" (Aquinas, *Catena Aurea* 3119, on Matt. 1:19). Yet some Fathers, including Origen, Jerome, and Rabanus Maurus, hold that St. Joseph knows from the beginning that the conception is of the Holy Spirit, and he fears to take Mary as his wife (v. 20) because he feels unworthy to be the husband of the mother of the Christ: "He sought to put her away, because he saw in her a great mystery, to approach which he thought himself unworthy" (Origen, quoted in *Catena Aurea* 3119, on Matt. 1:19). This interpretation requires understanding the words of the angel in Matt. 1:20 ("Do not fear to take Mary . . . , for that which is conceived in her is of the Holy Spirit") in this sense: "Do not fear to take Mary . . . [simply because] that which is conceived in her is of the Holy Spirit." In other words, "Do not let her conception by the Holy Spirit make you afraid to receive her as your wife."

St. Jerome and St. John Chrysostom on Joseph

The Fathers grapple with the moral dilemma that Joseph, a devout man living under the old law, faces when discovering his wife appears to be guilty of an offense punishable by death. Referring to Matthew 1:19, St. Jerome raises the question, "But how is Joseph thus called, 'just,' when he is ready to hide his wife's sin? For the Law enacts, that not only the doers of evil, but they who are privy to any evil done, shall be held to be guilty." St. John Chrysostom offers an explanation: "But it should be known, that 'just' here is used to denote one who is in all things virtuous. . . . Therefore being 'just'—that is, kind, merciful—he 'was minded to put away privily' her who according to the Law was liable not only to dismissal, but to death [Deut. 22:20–24]. But Joseph remitted both, as though living above the Law." The *Glossa Ordinaria* on this verse sums up the patristic consensus about Joseph as "just": "For that is true virtue, when neither mercy is observed without justice, nor justice without mercy; both which vanish when severed one from the other."[a]

a. Thomas Aquinas, *Catena Aurea* on Matt. 1:19, in *Catena Aurea: Commentary on the Four Gospels, Collected out of the Works of the Fathers; St. Matthew,* trans. and ed. John Henry Newman (London: John Henry Parker, 1841), 45–46.

and receives[2] his wife—significantly, she is already considered his "wife" (*tēn gynaika autou*), but now he receives her into his house. But he "knew her not before she had borne a son" (v. 25, modified). As St. Jerome already explained in his own day, the grammatical construction here does not imply consummation thereafter,[3] and the unanimous tradition of the Fathers affirms that she remained perpetually virgin.[4]

A continent marriage may seem unreasonable to moderns, but in these particular circumstances, it would have made sense for a devout Jewish man

2. Greek *paralambanō*, lit., "take or receive alongside"—gentler than the usual Greek *lambanō*, "take," used for Hebrew *lāqaḥ*, "take [to wife]"—employed perhaps to avoid the sexual connotation.

3. Jerome, *Against Helvidius* 6–7.

4. For a review of the patristic sources and discussion of the relevant scriptural texts, see James B. Prothro, "Semper Virgo? A Biblical Review of a Debated Dogma," *Pro Ecclesia* 28, no. 1 (2019): 78–97.

like St. Joseph to adopt this lifestyle. Modern Westerners construe sexuality primarily as a form of recreation, but for ancient Jews, it fell under the category of ritual cleanliness. Intercourse rendered a man ritually unclean according to the Mosaic law (Lev. 15:16–18) and thus unable to enter the temple or engage in other acts of worship. Therefore, some very devout Jewish men—for example, the Essenes—abstained from intercourse altogether in order to follow a lifestyle described as "perfect holiness" (CD 7:5). Furthermore, since sexual activity led to uncleanness (Lev. 15:16–18), it was prohibited within the temple courts, and some like the Essenes even extended this prohibition to the entire holy city, Jerusalem: "No-one should sleep with a woman in the city of the temple, defiling the city of the temple with their impurity" (CD 12:1–2).[5] Thus, it is not difficult to see why Joseph, a devout Jewish man of the Second Temple period, having been informed that his wife's body would receive a child called "holy," "the Son of God," and "the Son of the Most High" (Luke 1:32, 35), would refuse to render the sanctuary of his wife's body unclean. Who would dare to enter the tabernacle God has sanctified for himself?[6]

Excluding relations, Joseph and Mary receive each other in every other way as husband (*anēr*, Matt. 1:19) and wife (*gynē*, 1:20, 24), and Joseph receives Jesus as his own son by bestowing on him the name Jesus (1:25), an exercise of paternal authority.

The next glimpse of the holy couple comes after the magi's departure, when an angel warns Joseph in a dream to "rise, take the child and his mother, and flee to Egypt" (Matt. 2:13) for fear of Herod, and Joseph rises and takes the child and his mother by night and departs to Egypt (2:14). The child is divine and the mother sinless, yet the angel gives instructions for the family to Joseph—humble yet still husband, father, and head of the family (cf. Eph. 5:23–24; 6:1–4). As so often, God's order of authority does not necessarily follow the order of holiness or even ontological status. Joseph's authority is oriented toward the protection of and provision for his wife and child, both of whom occupy the central stage of salvation. This illustrates the principle that authority is oriented toward service and servanthood, as Joseph's son will later clearly teach (Luke 22:24–27). Likewise, after the death of Herod,

5. Florentino García Martínez and Eibert J. C. Tigchelaar, *The Dead Sea Scrolls Study Edition*, 2 vols. (Leiden: Brill, 1997), 1:517.
6. So Jerome: "Helvidius, I say, would have us believe that Joseph . . . dared to touch the temple of God, the abode of the Holy Ghost, the mother of his Lord" (*Against Helvidius* 8 [*NPNF*² 6:338]).

Joseph is told, "Rise, take the child and his mother, and go to the land of Israel," and Joseph "rose and took the child and his mother, and went" (Matt. 2:20–21). Joseph's suspicions of Herod's son Archelaus and confirmatory guidance from his dreams lead Joseph to settle the holy family in Nazareth (2:22–23). This is the last we hear of Joseph in Matthew. The evangelist has portrayed Joseph as an ideal husband and father, a man whose righteousness includes observance of the law but also mercy (Hosea 6:6; Matt. 9:13; 12:7), a man docile and immediately responsive to God's word (Matt. 1:24; 2:14, 21), unconcerned with his own interests and pleasures, using his authority for the welfare of others, of "the child and his mother" (2:13–14, 20).

For his part, Luke portrays the holy couple as two partners united in will and action, who cooperate harmoniously in raising the Savior. For Luke, they are a unity: "the parents" (*hoi goneis*; 2:27, 41, 43).

Luke introduces Mary as "a virgin betrothed to a man whose name was Joseph" (Luke 1:27), so her bond with Joseph is always part of her identity in this Gospel. Thus, her response to Gabriel's annunciation of Jesus's conception requires some comment: "How will this be? For I do not know a man" (1:34 AT).[7] This has elicited speculation that she has taken a vow of virginity, a practice not well attested among Jewish women in antiquity.[8] It may be simpler to take the statement as indicating that, though betrothed, she is not yet cohabiting with her husband. But it is not a denial of her marital bond with Joseph.

In Luke 2, Joseph and Mary are portrayed as living together and acting harmoniously with each other in the upbringing of the holy child. Joseph travels to Nazareth for the census with his "betrothed"[9]—that is, she is his legal wife, but they have not consummated the marriage. While "they"—the holy couple—are in Bethlehem, the time comes for her to deliver, and she gives birth to her firstborn son (Luke 2:7). The shepherds come and find "Mary and Joseph, and the babe lying in a manger"—the whole family together (v. 16). In Jesus's upbringing, the holy parents are conscientiously law observant: "When the time came for their purification according to the law of Moses,

7. Greek *Pōs estai touto, epei andra ou ginōskō.*
8. Essene literature attests to celibacy among their men, but not their women. Philo does describe a Jewish Essene-like group in the region of Alexandria that practiced both male and female celibacy, whom he calls the "Therapeutae"—i.e., the "healers" or "healthy ones." See David Winston, *Philo of Alexandria: The Contemplative Life, The Giants, and Selections*, Classics of Western Spirituality (Mahwah, NJ: Paulist Press, 1981).
9. Greek *tē emnēsteumenē autō* (Luke 2:5).

they brought him up to Jerusalem to present him to the Lord" (2:22). They bring two turtledoves or pigeons (2:24) for the purification sacrifice, indicating poverty, an inability to afford a sheep (cf. Lev. 12:8), just as one would expect for a manual laborer (*tektōn*, "craftsman," Matt. 13:55) like Joseph. Simeon amazes both parents: "His father *and* his mother marveled at what was said about him" (Luke 2:33). Luke again emphasizes the piety of the parents: "When they had performed *everything according to the law of the Lord*, they returned into Galilee" (2:39). But they are never gone from Jerusalem for long, because, as Luke says, "his parents went to Jerusalem every year at the feast of the Passover" (2:41). The law only obliges Joseph (cf. Exod. 23:17), but the holy parents (*hoi goneis*) make the pilgrimage together, a supererogation for Mary. Mary and Joseph always act together to care for Jesus: "as *they* were returning"; "his *parents* did not know it"; "*they* sought him"; "*they* returned"; "*they* found him" (Luke 2:43–46). When they discover him in the temple, they are described neither as angry nor relieved but as "astonished" (*ekplēssō*). Mary speaks for the holy couple, revealing the closest thing to friction within the holy family recorded in Scripture: "Child, why have you treated us in this way? Behold, your father and I myself have been in pain [*odynōmenoi*] seeking you!" (v. 48 AT)—suggesting hurt and perplexity more than anger. Mentioning Joseph first ("your father") indicates that he has taken the lead in searching for the boy, as one might expect. Jesus responds, "Did you not know that I must be in my Father's house?" But the holy parents, Luke says, "did not understand the saying"; nonetheless, Jesus "went down with *them*" and was "obedient to *them*," while Mary in particular "kept all these things in her heart," probably indicating Luke's source for these stories (2:49–51). This is the last we hear of the holy couple in Luke.

In summary, Matthew and Luke both show Joseph and Mary as similarly virtuous: docile and immediately obedient to God's word as it is revealed to them; conscientious in observing the law; and truly married though never physically united, for mutual consent creates the covenant, not the physical act. Matthew portrays the holy marriage all from the perspective of Joseph, an ideal husband whose life is consumed by his God-given mission to care for "the child and his mother." Luke portrays the holy couple as two persons with one will, cooperating harmoniously to fulfill God's law and their common vocation to raise the Savior. There is no struggle for control in their marriage: Joseph is not overbearing, nor is Mary headstrong. Their freedom from sin mitigates this effect of the fall (Gen. 3:16).

Teaching on Marriage in the Gospels

Jesus directly addresses the practice of marriage three times in his ministry: in the Sermon on the Mount (Matt. 5:27–32); when the Pharisees confront him about divorce (Matt. 19:3–15; Mark 10:2–15; Luke 16:18; 18:15–17); and when the Sadducees raise the issue of marriage and the afterlife (Matt. 22:23–33; Mark 12:18–27; Luke 20:27–40).

The Sermon on the Mount (Matt. 5:27–32)

The topic of marriage arises in the context of the "six antitheses" (Matt. 5:21–48), where Jesus corrects the law of Moses or its received interpretation. The second and third antitheses pertain to matrimony: the violation of sexual exclusivity (i.e., adultery, 5:27–30) and the attempt to dissolve the bond (i.e., divorce, 5:31–32).

"You have heard that it was said, 'You shall not commit adultery'" (Matt. 5:27), Jesus says, alluding to the Mosaic law.[10] Jesus radicalizes this law: "But I say to you, everyone beholding a woman with the intent to desire her already has committed adultery with her in his heart" (5:28 AT). Jesus's reading of the commandment against adultery (Exod. 20:14) forbids even the seed of adultery in the heart, for "out of the heart come evil thoughts, murder, adultery, fornication" (Matt. 15:19). Job anticipates Jesus by refusing to "look upon a virgin" (Job 31:1), and Solomon does also by warning his "son" of gazing on a loose woman: "Do not desire her beauty in your heart, and do not let her capture you with her eyelashes" (Prov. 6:25). Jesus interprets the Mosaic law in light of the deeper meditation on the nature of lust and adultery in the Wisdom literature. The radical statements that follow, concerning plucking out one's eye or chopping off one's hand to avoid the fate of hell (Matt. 5:29–30), are less novel than they appear; rather, they follow in the tradition and spirit of the grave warnings against the adulteress as a path to Sheol in Proverbs (cf. Prov. 5:5; 7:27; 9:18).

The Lord's teaching allows no double standard of sexual ethics for men, and indeed, it prohibits all male sexual activity outside of marriage. Christ does not limit the circumstances under which lustful ogling constitutes adultery by the marital status of either the beholder or the beheld. Simply, any man (*pas ho blepōn*) who looks at any woman (*gynaika*) with the intention of desire (*pros to epithymēsai*) has committed interior adultery (Matt. 5:28).

---

10. E.g., Exod. 20:14; Lev. 20:10; Deut. 5:18.

A fortiori, any kind of actual *physical* contact with the intention of desire would be an even more serious form of sin, compounding interior adultery with at least partial external expression. Therefore, it is a grave sin endangering one to hell (5:29–30) for any man *even to desire* sexual contact with a woman other than his spouse—and even more so to act on that desire.

The following antithesis (Matt. 5:31–32) concerns divorce, but the Lord repeats the same teaching with much amplification in Matthew 19:3–20, to which we will now turn our attention.

Jesus Challenged by the Pharisees (Matt. 19:3–20)

In Matthew 19:3, the Pharisees question Jesus, "Is it lawful to divorce one's wife for any cause [*kata pasan aitian*]?" This question could mean: "Is there any cause at all that justifies divorce?" or "Can one divorce for any cause at all (i.e., even the most trivial)?" This was a disputed question in Jesus's day: the different schools of Pharisaism clashed over the interpretation of Deuteronomy 24:1, as the Mishnah relates:

> The School of Shammai[11] say: A man may not divorce his wife unless he has found unchastity in her, for it is written, *Because he hath found in her* <u>indecency</u> *in anything* (Dt 24:1). And the School of Hillel[12] say: [He may divorce her] even if she spoiled a dish for him, for it is written: *Because he hath found in her indecency* <u>in anything</u> (Dt 24:1). R. Akiba[13] says: Even if he found another fairer than she, for it is written, *And it shall be if she find no favour in his eyes. . .* (Dt 24:1). (*m. Giṭṭin* 9:10, emphasis mine)[14]

Rabbi Shammai was only recently deceased when the unnamed Pharisee would have questioned Jesus on this subject, so the debate within Pharisaism was still lively. On the other hand, the Essenes criticized the Pharisees for "fornication" (Hebrew *zǝnût*) by "taking two wives in their lifetimes" (CD 4:20–21)—that is, either simultaneous polygamy or serial polygamy by divorce and remarriage. In contrast, the Essenes argued for a strict lifelong monogamy on three exegetical grounds: first, the "principle of creation" (*yǝsôd habbǝrî'āh*) that

---

11. Rabbi Shammai the Elder, 50 BC–AD 30.
12. Rabbi Hillel the Elder, 110 BC–AD 10.
13. Rabbi Akiva, AD 50–135. "Akiba" is an alternate spelling.
14. Herbert Danby, *The Mishnah: Translated from the Hebrew with Introduction and Brief Explanatory Notes* (Oxford: Oxford University Press, 1933), 321.

"male and female he created them" (Gen. 1:27; CD 4:21). God, by creating only one man and one woman, has indicated his intention that each man and woman be paired strictly one to one for the course of their life. Second, all humans and animals went into the ark two by two (Gen. 7:9; CD 5:1). Those saved from the flood were strictly monogamous, in contrast to the polygamous "sons of God" (Gen. 6:2), who were drowned. Finally, the king of Israel was forbidden to "multiply wives for himself" (Deut. 17:17; CD 5:1–2). What is not permitted even to the king should be forbidden also to the people. Such was the Essene exegetical case against the laxity of Pharisaic marital law.

In his response to the Pharisees, Jesus takes a position close to that of the Essenes: "Have you not read that he who made them from the beginning made them male and female?" (Matt. 19:4; cf. Gen. 1:27). Jesus appeals here to what the Essenes called "the principle of creation"—the original creation best represents God's intentions for humanity. But Jesus adds:

> [Have you not read that] "for this reason a man shall leave his father and mother and be joined to his wife, and the two shall become one flesh"? So they are no longer two but one flesh. What therefore God has joined together, let not man put asunder. (Matt. 19:5–6)

The Greek text of Matthew seems to present Jesus as interpreting the passive voice of Genesis 2:24, "and be joined to his wife,"[15] as a "divine passive"[16]— that is, equivalent to the statement "and God joins him to his wife." Marriages, thus, are made in heaven and ought not to be destroyed on earth.

But if this is so, the Pharisees ask the next logical question: "Why, then, did Moses *command* one to give a certificate of separation [*biblion apostasion*] and to dismiss [*apoluō*] her [Deut. 24:1–4]?" (Matt. 19:7 AT). Jesus responds, "For your hardness of heart Moses *allowed* you to divorce your wives, but from the beginning it was not so" (19:8)—appealing once more to the "principle of creation" (cf. CD 4:21). "And I say to you: whoever dismisses [*apoluō*] his wife, except for immorality [*porneia*], and marries another, commits adultery" (Matt. 19:9, modified). Thus, Jesus corrects their misreading of the text of Deuteronomy 24:1–4: Moses *commands* nothing in these verses. Rather, he

15. The verb is passive both in Matthew's citation (*kollēthēsetai*, 19:5) and in the LXX (*proskollēthēsetai*, Gen. 2:24).
16. See E. M. Sidebottom, "The So-Called Divine Passive in the Gospel Tradition," *ExpT* 87, no. 7 (1976): 200–204.

St. Gregory Nazianzen on Marriage

Gregory Nazianzen is typical of the Fathers in taking Matthew 19:9 to permit separation for adultery but not remarriage:

> For I think that the Word here seems to deprecate second marriage. For, if there were two Christs, there may be two husbands or two wives; but if Christ is One, one Head of the Church, let there be also one flesh, and let a second be rejected; and if it hinder the second what is to be said for a third? The first is law, the second is indulgence, the third is transgression, and anything beyond this is swinish, such as has not even many examples of its wickedness. Now the Law grants divorce for every cause; but Christ not for every cause; but He allows only separation from the whore; and in all other things He commands patience. He allows to put away the fornicatress, because she corrupts the offspring; but in all other matters let us be patient and endure; or rather be ye enduring and patient, as many as have received the yoke of matrimony.[a]

a. Gregory Nazianzen, *Oration 37*, on Matt. 19:1–12 (*NPNF*[2] 7:340).

tacitly acknowledges that divorce takes place, and while he does not prohibit it, he says nothing to *mandate* it, either.

Parallels in Mark 10:11–12 and Luke 16:18 lack the exception for *porneia* here and in Matthew 5:32. There are three major interpretations of the *porneia* exception:[17] (1) The Church Fathers, with only one outlier (Ambrosiaster), understand *porneia* as adultery and hold that the Lord permits separation but not remarriage in such a case. (2) The Protestant-Orthodox view likewise understands *porneia* as adultery and permits remarriage at least to the innocent party. (3) Within Catholic scholarship in modern times, the position has gained ground that *porneia* renders the Hebrew *zᵊnût* and refers to ritually unclean (i.e., religiously forbidden) unions that—since they have been illicit and invalid from the beginning—may be dissolved.

In their pastoral application, the Fathers are on firm exegetical ground—if not primarily on the basis of Matthew 19:9, then certainly on the basis of

17. For a summary of these views, see Curtis Mitch and Edward Sri, *The Gospel of Matthew*, CCSS (Grand Rapids: Baker Academic, 2010), 240–41.

1 Corinthians 7:10–11, to be discussed below. However, a serious objection challenges all interpretations that take *porneia* as meaning "adultery": there is a specific Greek word for "adultery," *moicheia*, which Matthew distinguishes from *porneia* elsewhere (Matt. 15:19) but intentionally does *not* use here in 19:9. Second, a possibly fatal objection confronts the Protestant-Orthodox consensus: according to this consensus, Jesus simply agrees with Shammai, which would not have provoked the surprised protest of the Pharisees (19:7) or the dumbfounded response of the disciples (19:10). Rather, both reactions presume that Jesus is forbidding divorce per se.

Therefore, only the third position can offer a convincing explanation of the meaning of *porneia* in the first-century Palestinian Jewish context of Jesus's ministry and the Gospel of Matthew. Joseph Fitzmyer points out that Hebrew *zənût*, "sexual uncleanness," is always *porneia* in the Septuagint,[18] and in the Damascus Document (CD), "polygamy, divorce, and marriage within forbidden degrees of kinship could be referred to as *zənût*," such that "in CD 4:20 and 5:8–22 we have 'missing-link' evidence for a specific understanding of *zənût* as a term for marriage within forbidden degrees of kinship or for incestuous marriage; this is a specific understanding that is found among Palestinian Jews of the first century BC and AD."[19]

Fitzmyer argues that Matthew introduces the *porneia* exception in Matthew 19:9 in light of Acts 15:20, 29—in other words, to address the situation of Gentile converts entering Jewish-Christian congregations while in marriages prohibited by the Mosaic law. However, there was at least one high-profile marriage in the Palestinian Judaism of Jesus's own day that fell under the category of *zənût*/*porneia*—the marriage of Herod Antipas to his niece Herodias, which John the Baptist insisted should be dissolved.[20] John may have been formed in Essenism,[21] and from an Essene perspective this union was *zənût* for two reasons: both Herod Antipas and Herodias were divorced from spouses still living (cf. CD 4:20–21), and they were also uncle and niece, a union the Essenes deemed forbidden by their exegesis of Leviticus 20:19 (CD 5:7–9). The "historical Jesus," therefore, may have included the exception for *zənût*/*porneia* in his teaching on marriage to make clear he accepted

---

18. E.g., Num. 14:33; Jer. 3:2, 9; 13:27; Ezek. 23:27; 43:7, 9; Hosea 4:11; 6:10.

19. Joseph A. Fitzmyer, "The Matthean Divorce Texts and Some New Palestinian Evidence," *TS* 37, no. 2 (1976): 197–226, here 221.

20. Matt. 14:3–4; Mark 6:17–18; Luke 3:19.

21. John S. Bergsma, *Jesus and the Dead Sea Scrolls: Revealing the Jewish Roots of Christianity* (New York: Image, 2019), 31–43.

the dissolution of unlawful marriages, like the one the Baptist was executed for opposing. Therefore, we concur with the understanding reflected in the NABRE's translation: "I say to you, whoever divorces his wife (unless the marriage is unlawful) and marries another commits adultery" (Matt. 19:9). This makes the best sense of the logic of the passage, in light of intersectarian debates about marital law in first-century Judaism.

In response, the disciples demur: "If that is the case of a man with his wife, it is not expedient [*ou sympherō*] to marry" (Matt. 19:10 AT). Jesus responds, "Not all can receive this word [*logos*], but only those to whom it is given" (19:11 AT). The "word" [*logos*] or teaching that "not all can receive" is not the *indissolubility* of marriage (v. 9) but rather the *inexpediency* of marriage (v. 10). The ability to accept the celibate state is a gift, something literally "given" (Greek *dedotai*, from *didōmi*, v. 11). This is a "divine passive"—God is the unstated subject of the action. He gives the gift of celibacy. Jesus continues by referring to eunuchs so born, eunuchs so made, and "eunuchs for the sake of the kingdom of heaven" (v. 12). This last category refers to those among Jesus's contemporaries who voluntarily adopted celibacy for eschatological, religious motives, including (at least) John the Baptist and those Essenes who led a lifestyle of "perfect holiness" (*tammîm qōdeš*, CD 7:5) and perpetual continence. Jesus commends this lifestyle and enjoins it on all those to whom God has granted the ability to embrace it.

Lest the reader believe that Jesus objected in principle to procreation and the raising of children, Matthew places the blessing of the little children immediately following (Matt. 19:13–15): "Let the children come to me, and do not prevent them; for the kingdom of heaven belongs to such as these" (19:14 NABRE). This pericope indicates Jesus's special predilection for children. Luke's parallel (Luke 18:15–17) mentions "even infants" (*kai ta brephē*) being brought (v. 15). Jesus's affinity for children (and theirs for the kingdom of heaven) cannot be unrelated to the discussion of marriage and celibacy above. Jesus's praise for the celibate state should not be taken as a sign of the rejection of children and the marital unions that produce them. "Let the children come to me, and do not prevent them" articulates Jesus's "preferential option for the children." Contemporary ways of "preventing" the children from coming to Jesus include refusing them baptism, refusing them birth through abortion, and refusing them conception through prophylactics. All these prevent the little children from coming to Jesus. This is consistent with the predilection for new human life on God's part throughout the history of revelation: "Be fruitful and multiply" (Gen. 1:28); "Happy is the man who has his quiver full" (Ps. 127:5); "And what does he desire? Godly offspring" (Mal. 2:15); "Let the children come to me, and do not prevent them" (Matt. 19:14 NABRE). God is open to life, and by *imitatio Dei*, his people should be, too.

Marriage and the Resurrection (Luke 20:27–40)

The last teaching on marriage in the Gospels concerns the resurrection and the life to come, given by the Lord in response to a question from the Sadducees during Holy Week.[22] The Sadducees press Jesus about a hypothetical situation in which seven brothers have married the same woman in succession—whose then will she be in the life to come? (Luke 20:27–33). Jesus answers:

> The sons of this age marry and are given in marriage; but those who are accounted worthy to attain to that age and to the resurrection from the dead neither marry nor are given in marriage, for they cannot die any more, because they are equal to angels and are sons of God, being sons of the resurrection. (Luke 20:34–36)

Thus, we learn that the sacrament of matrimony, like the other sacraments, is not celebrated in heaven, because sacraments are efficacious signs received in faith in this life; and in the age to come, faith will be replaced by sight, and signs will be replaced by the realities signified. The sacraments are mediated encounters or acts of communion with Christ; in the life to come, there will be no need of mediation because communion with Christ will be direct. The role of spouses in this life is to act *in persona Christi* toward one another, mediating the love and grace of Christ to each other. In the future state, that role will no longer be necessary, nor will the procreative function of marriage be needed in a context in which the continuance of the race is assured, since no one dies ("they cannot die anymore," v. 36). They are "like angels in the heavens" (*hōs angeloi en tois ouranois*, Mark 12:25) or "equal to angels" (*isangeloi gar eisin*, Luke 20:36). They do not *become* angels—a common misconception—but are similar in this one specific: they do not marry. Jesus's remarks take on greater sociohistorical depth when we recall that the Qumran monks practiced celibacy and considered themselves a priestly people who were transformed into angel-like beings (an "angelomorphic priesthood") through their liturgical

22. Matt. 22:23–33; Mark 12:18–27; Luke 20:27–40.

St. Augustine on the Resurrected Body

Will being "equal to angels" (Luke 20:36) mean the erasure of sexual characteristics in the resurrected body? St. Augustine demurs:

> There are some who think that in the resurrection all will be men, and women will lose their sex. . . . I think that those others are more sensible who have no doubt that both sexes will remain in the resurrection. . . . In the resurrection, the blemishes of the body will be gone, but the nature of the body will remain. And certainly, a woman's body is her nature and no blemish. . . . Her members will remain as before with the former purpose sublimated to a newer beauty. . . . Therefore, woman is as much the creation of God as man is. There will be no concupiscence to arouse and none will be aroused, but her womanhood will be a hymn to the wisdom of God. . . . If she was made from the man, this was to show her oneness with him; and if she was made in the way she was, this was to prefigure the oneness of Christ and the Church.[a]

a. Augustine, *City of God* 22.17 (*NPNF*[2] 2:495–96).

practice.[23] There are strong similarities in the way the eschaton is being envisaged. A corollary to this conception of the eschatological state is that those who are given the gift of celibacy and embrace it (Matt. 19:11) have already begun to live eschatologically. Their celibate lifestyles are a sign of hope in the resurrection of the dead and life in the world to come. Celibacy is not a denial of nuptiality, but an embrace of eschatological nuptiality already in the present.

Summary of the Gospel Teaching on Marriage

The Gospels teach about matrimony both through the normative example of the holy marriage of Joseph and Mary and by recording the explicit teaching of their son. From the holy marriage, we learn that the consent of the spouses, not physical union, is constitutive of the matrimonial bond. Although

23. See Crispin H. T. Fletcher-Louis, "Heavenly Ascent or Incarnational Presence? A Revisionist Reading of the *Songs of the Sabbath Sacrifice*," SBLSP 37 (1998): 367–99; Fletcher-Louis, *All the Glory of Adam: Liturgical Anthropology in the Dead Sea Scrolls*, STDJ 42 (Leiden: Brill, 2002). For "angelomorphic priesthood," see Fletcher-Louis, "Heavenly Ascent," 389–90.

bodily union is the normal expression and culmination of the union of wills, nonetheless it is the union of wills, not bodies, that actually establishes the covenant bond. Matthew presents Joseph as a model for Christian husbands— a man whose justice is perfected by mercy, who is head of his household yet ever solicitous for the well-being of his wife and child, who is a self-effacing protector and provider. Luke presents the holy parents as an ideal couple, always operating as a harmonious unit, united in fulfilling the vocation given to them by God to raise their son, the Messiah.

Jesus's explicit teaching on matrimony in the Gospels is selective and strategic. In the Sermon on the Mount, he radically restricts sexual desire and a fortiori activity to the marital bond alone (Matt. 5:27–31). In response to the Pharisees (Matt. 19:3–20), he prohibits divorce for any cause save the presence of *porneia* (i.e., *zənût*), which invalidated the marriage in any case. Finally, in response to the Sadducees (Luke 20:27–40), he teaches that matrimony, like all the sacraments, is intended for and limited to this present temporal life, even if it anticipates and participates in the joy of communion with God in the life to come.

11

"This Is a Great Mystery"

Marriage in the Epistles

The key passages of the New Testament Epistles that address the theology and practice of marriage are found in 1 Corinthians 5–7 and Ephesians 5:21–33, with several brief but important statements elsewhere in the Pauline corpus and one passage from the Catholic Epistles.[1] Most epistolary instruction on marriage simply applies the main principles established by Jesus in the Gospels: (1) the indissolubility of a valid marriage;[2] (2) the possible dissolution of an invalid (*porneia*/*zənût*) marriage;[3] (3) a preferential option for the celibate vocation;[4] (4) an absolute prohibition of sexual activity outside marriage;[5] and (5) a restriction of matrimony to this present world.[6] The rest is either (a) the application to married couples of the Old Testament's spousal paradigm concerning the covenant between God and his people[7] or (b) the reapplication of marital principles from the Old Testament to the situation of the New Covenant.[8]

1. 2 Cor. 6:14; Col. 3:18; 1 Thess. 4:1–8; 1 Tim. 2:8–15; 5:9; Titus 2:1–5; 1 Pet. 3:1–7.
2. Rom. 7:2; 1 Cor. 7:10–13, 39//Matt. 5:31–32; 19:3–9; Mark 10:2–12; Luke 16:18.
3. 1 Cor. 5:1–13//Matt. 5:32; 19:9.
4. 1 Cor. 7:1–38//Matt. 19:10–12.
5. 1 Cor. 6:9–20; Heb. 13:4//Matt. 5:27–30; 15:19; Mark 7:21.
6. 1 Cor. 7:39–40//Matt. 22:30; Mark 12:25; Luke 20:34–36.
7. E.g., Ezek. 16:8–14//Eph. 5:21–33; Col. 3:18.
8. 2 Cor. 6:14–18//Ezra 10:11–14; 1 Pet. 3:1–7//Gen. 18:12; 24:18; 1 Thess. 4:1–8//Tob. 8:5–7.

In what follows, we will treat first the Corinthian texts, and then we will treat the Ephesian material, incorporating the smaller statements from other Pauline and Catholic Epistles when relevant.

The Corinthian Correspondence

The Corinthian church was large and occupied a good deal of Paul's attention. Corinth was the Las Vegas of the Roman Empire, a city notorious for the sex trade associated with its opulent temple of Aphrodite, which at one time employed about one thousand *hierodules* (sacred prostitutes) to service worshipers.[9] Thus, in his Corinthian letters Paul returns frequently to the themes of sexual purity and the Church as temple. Unsurprisingly, the young Corinthian Christians found it difficult to embrace Jesus's teachings on marriage, and their failures provided Paul an occasion to further develop the matrimonial guidelines laid down by the Lord.

In fact, a pressing issue of marital scandal in the Corinthian church dominates much of both letters: "Someone has the wife of his father!" (1 Cor. 5:1 AT). This relationship between the man and his father's wife constitutes a classic case of *porneia*/*zənût*, an unlawful union, which lacks indissolubility because it has not been a true marriage from the start. The Greek verb "have" (*echō*) could mean that either the man has formally married the woman[10] or he has simply been cohabiting with her,[11] but the point is merely a technicality, as Roman law recognized a cohabiting couple as legally married (marriage by *usus*).[12]

Nonetheless, such a union was forbidden by divine law (Lev. 18:8; Deut. 22:30), and the parties were to be expelled from the community (Lev. 18:29) or executed (Deut. 22:22). Jesus's permission for dismissal of one's spouse for *porneia* (Matt. 19:9), as well as the conciliar decree against *porneia* for Gentile converts in Acts 15:20, likely has just such a situation in mind, so Paul is applying dominical and conciliar teaching.

St. Paul is particularly incensed that the Christian community is not ashamed but "puffed up" (1 Cor. 5:2) and "boasting" (v. 6) about this immorality. So even at this earliest stage in the history of the Church, we witness the curious

9. Strabo, *Geography* 8.6.20; 12.3.36.
10. Matt. 14:4; 22:28; Mark 6:18; 12:23; Luke 20:33; John 4:16–18; Tob. 3:8.
11. Deut. 28:30 LXX; Isa. 13:16 LXX; John 4:18b.
12. Göran Lind, *Common Law Marriage: A Legal Institution for Cohabitation* (Oxford: Oxford University Press, 2008), 39–47.

phenomenon that persons and communities unwilling to live by the principles of marriage and sexuality laid down by Jesus invariably consider themselves more enlightened, superior, and "progressive" than the rest of the Church, as if they had attained some kind of moral, spiritual, or intellectual maturity that frees them from the simple morality clung to by the unenlightened, uneducated, immature, backward, regressive, conservative, "fundamentalist," and so forth. These "progressive" individuals and movements emphasize the freedom we have in Christ, but they actually foster or even promote addiction to various forms of sexual pleasure: "They promise them freedom, but they themselves are slaves of corruption; for whatever overcomes a man, to that he is enslaved" (2 Pet. 2:19). There is nothing new or progressive about this phenomenon—it is as old as the Church herself. In the life of discipleship, true progress is always toward holiness, not toward new ways to justify self-indulgence. To be sure, the Holy Spirit bestows freedom, but true freedom is directed toward truth and love: "For you were called to freedom, brethren; only do not use your freedom as an opportunity for the flesh, but through love be servants of one another" (Gal. 5:13). "Live as free men, yet without using your freedom as a pretext for evil" (1 Pet. 2:16).

St. Paul's reaction to the celebration of this scandalous sexual relationship by the Corinthian church (1 Cor. 5:2) provides an important counterpoint to the various Gospel injunctions against judging others (Matt. 7:1–2; Luke 6:37). Paul declares not only that he has already "judged" (*krinō*) the one who has done this but also that the Corinthian church should assemble and "deliver this man to Satan" (1 Cor. 5:3–5)—that is, remove him from the realm of Christ, which is the Church, and return him to the world, which is the realm of Satan (Eph. 2:2). This is an early form of excommunication.[13]

This man's sin poses a serious threat to the health of the church of Corinth. Paul compares his sexual immorality to yeast that begins small but eventually permeates the entire loaf. That is, if the church tolerates sexual immorality, such immorality will eventually become *pervasive* in the community, a dynamic empirically observed many times throughout history. Paul employs a eucharistic image for the need to eliminate this contagious sin: "Christ, our paschal lamb, has been sacrificed. Let us, therefore, celebrate the festival, not

---

13. George T. Montague, *First Corinthians*, CCSS (Grand Rapids: Baker Academic, 2011), 91–95. On p. 91, Montague asserts, "For the first time in Christian literature, we see a case of excommunication: Paul uses his full authority, along with that of the community, to expel the person."

with the old leaven, the leaven of malice and evil, but with the unleavened bread of sincerity and truth" (1 Cor. 5:7–8). Worthy celebration of the sacrament requires transformation of lifestyle.

Paul proceeds to expound on the principles underlying the practice of excommunication. "I wrote to you not to associate with any one who bears the name of brother if he is guilty of immorality or greed, or is an idolater, reviler, drunkard, or robber—not even to eat with such a one" (1 Cor. 5:11). The church as a community cannot show signs of approval and fellowship toward persons claiming to be Christians but whose known behavior contradicts the moral claims of the gospel. In cases such as these, the Christian community not only *may* judge but also *must* judge. "Is it not those inside the church whom you are to judge? God judges those outside," Paul insists, and then he paraphrases a refrain from Deuteronomy: "Purge the evil person from among you" (1 Cor. 5:12–13 ESV).[14]

After an interlude (1 Cor. 6:1–8), Paul returns to the topic of sexual morality and the norms of matrimony in 1 Corinthians 6:9–19. The problem is that the Corinthian Christians have interpreted Paul's teaching on "freedom from the law" to be an excuse for sexual license, as many Christians have done subsequently. So Paul first confronts this misconception directly: "Do you not know that the unrighteous will not inherit the kingdom of God? Do not be deceived; neither the immoral, nor idolaters, nor adulterers, nor sexual perverts . . . will inherit the kingdom of God" (1 Cor. 6:9–10).

Paul now quotes the rationalizations the Corinthians have used to justify carnal indulgence: "All things are lawful for me" (1 Cor. 6:12), and "Food is meant for the stomach and the stomach for food" (6:13). Certain Pauline and dominical teachings have given rise to these caricatures,[15] but such caricatures gravely misunderstand God's purposes in creation: "The body is not meant for immorality [*porneia*], but for the Lord, and the Lord for the body" (1 Cor. 6:13). This is nuptial language; Paul will proceed to develop the moral demands of matrimony starting from the fundamental reality of the believer's spousal union with Christ:

> Do you not know that your bodies are members of Christ? Shall I therefore take the members of Christ and make them members of a prostitute? Never!

14. Deut. 13:5; 17:7; 19:19–20; 21:21; 24:7; Judg. 20:13.
15. E.g., teachings reflected in Rom. 8:2, Gal. 5:1, and Mark 7:18–20, which surely circulated orally in the church from a very early period.

> Do you not know that he who joins himself to a prostitute becomes one body with her? For, as it is written, "The two shall become one flesh." (1 Cor. 6:15–16)

The body of a Christian is Christ's body, consistent with the strong one-flesh union of spouses in the Old Testament (e.g., Lev. 18:7). Therefore, the body of a Christian is holy, and to unite it with a person not one's spouse (e.g., a prostitute) profanes the body of Christ.

"But he who is united to the Lord becomes one spirit with him" (1 Cor. 6:17). Natural marital union constitutes the spouses as a *physical* union, one flesh; but union with Christ is even more profound, a *spiritual* union, through the gift of the Holy Spirit (Rom. 5:5). If copulation with a prostitute violates the one-flesh *marital* union, how much more so (a fortiori) does it violate the one-flesh, one-spirit union of the believer with Christ? The conclusion is inescapable: "Flee immorality! [*pheugete tēn porneian*]" (1 Cor. 6:18a AT). *Porneia* is unique among sinful acts in its potential to defile the holiness of the Christian's body, which is really Christ's body (6:18b). As Christ's body is the temple (John 2:21), so believers' bodies are the temple: "Do you not know that your body is a temple of the Holy Spirit within you, which you have from God?" (1 Cor. 6:19; cf. Eph. 2:19–22). The gift of the Holy Spirit has established a form of nuptial communion between the believer and Christ, such that the believer's body now belongs to God: "You are not your own; you were bought with a price. So glorify God in your body" (1 Cor. 6:19–20). Compare this to Paul's teaching that a wife rules her husband's body and vice versa (7:4). So the believer's spousal relationship with the Lord grants Christ the right of rulership over the believer's body (6:19–20).

Thus, from 1 Corinthians 6:9–20 emerges a spousal paradigm of the believer's relationship to Christ that guides the practice of matrimony within the Christian community. Every believer is espoused to Christ, one body and one spirit with him (1 Cor. 6:13–17; 2 Cor. 11:2–3). Marriage to another believer is licit, because the other believer is also Christ's body. Thus, one is free to marry "in the Lord" (1 Cor. 7:39), but one may not to be "mismated with unbelievers" (2 Cor. 6:14) or united to a prostitute (1 Cor. 6:15–17), for such persons are not part of Christ's body.

In 1 Corinthians 7, Paul expounds and develops the dominical teaching on marital indissolubility (Matt. 19:3–9). He also affirms the preferability of celibacy (Matt. 19:10–12)—"It is well for a man not to touch a woman" (1 Cor. 7:1b); "I wish that all were as I myself am" (7:7a); "To the unmarried and the widows I say that it is well for them to remain single as I do" (7:8)— while conceding that celibacy is a special grace from God: "But each has his own special gift from God, one of one kind and one of another" (7:7b; cf. Matt. 19:11–12).

Paul begins his discussion of marriage in 1 Corinthians 7 by stating a principle with which he concurs: "It is well for a man not to touch a woman" (7:1). Celibacy is a noble and desirable state for those to whom God gives the grace (Matt. 19:11–12). However, the married should not abstain: "But because of *porneia*, each husband should embrace [*echō*] his own wife, and each wife her very own [*ton idion*] husband" (1 Cor. 7:2 AT).

Paul's phrase "because of *porneia*" here means "because of [the temptation to] immorality" (so RSV, ESV). The Greek verb *echō*, "have," here means "embrace sexually," a well-attested sense,[16] as becomes clear in the subsequent verses. Because of the very real temptation to *porneia*, the married should embrace each other conjugally and not deny each other.

Unfortunately, many ancient and modern exegetes take *echō* here as "have [as spouse]," rendering 1 Corinthians 7:2 with this sense: "each man should be married to his own wife and each woman to her own husband." But this clearly contradicts Paul's teaching in verses 8–9 of the same chapter. First Corinthians 7:1–7 does not address the general advisability of marriage (as do vv. 8–9 and vv. 25–40); rather, it addresses the issue of *sexual abstinence* (v. 1),[17] which Paul strongly discourages for married couples. Unfortunately, as a result of misinterpreting verse 2 as a general exhortation to marriage, some streams of Christian tradition have overemphasized the "cure for concupiscence" as a motive for matrimony.

First Thessalonians 4:3–5 is also frequently misunderstood in the same way as 1 Corinthians 7:1–7 is:

For this is the will of God, your sanctification: that you abstain from unchastity [*porneia*]; that each one of you know how to take [*ktaomai*] a wife [*skeuos*,

16. See LXX Exod. 2:1–2; Deut. 28:30; Isa. 13:16; as well as Matt. 14:4; Mark 6:18; 12:23; John 4:18; and the discussion in David E. Garland, *1 Corinthians*, BECNT (Grand Rapids: Baker Academic, 2003), Kindle loc. 6134–41.
17. "What immediately follows in 7:2–5 reveals that he is not discussing whether Christians should get married or not but whether married partners should attempt to abstain from sexual intercourse." Garland, *1 Corinthians*, Kindle loc. 6111–12.

"vessel"] for himself in holiness and honor, not in the passion of lust like heathen who do not know God.

The RSV translates this passage as if it were a universal exhortation for Christian men to take a wife as an alternative to *porneia*. However, the best recent linguistic and literary study suggests that *ktaomai* in verse 4 means "control" and *skeuos* either "body" or "sexual organ" or both, giving the sense "let each of you control his own body [i.e., passions]" (cf. ESV).[18] Thus, 1 Thessalonians 4:4 is not a recommendation for universal marriage, but rather a recommendation for Christian men to grow in the virtues of temperance, self-control, and chastity.

Paul clarifies the meaning of 1 Corinthians 7:1–2 in the subsequent verse: "Let the husband pay the debt to his wife, and similarly the wife to the husband" (7:3 AT). Paul calls the marital embrace "the debt" (*tēn opheilēn*)—that is, an obligation of the state that the spouses have entered. His following statement is even more remarkable: "A wife does not hold authority over her own body, but the husband; similarly, the husband also does not hold authority over his own body, but the wife" (7:4 AT). The term for exercising authority here is a strong one—namely, the verb *exousiazō*, from the noun *exousia*, "authority," a very common term in the Gospels, especially related to Jesus's dominion in the spiritual realm to teach, exorcise, and forgive sin.[19] The perfectly balanced mutual authority of husband and wife in the area of physical union is striking. In a different context, Paul exhorts wives to subordinate themselves to their own husbands (Eph. 5:22), but in the case of this most intimate expression of their union, the wife "exercises authority" over the body of her husband (1 Cor. 7:4). Thus, matrimony is a sui generis relationship within the Christian community: in no other relationship (e.g., that between sisters and brothers, parents and children, or masters and servants) is there mutual authority over bodies.

Because of this principle of mutual authority, any abstention from relations must be agreed upon "harmoniously" (*symphōnos*): "Do not deprive one another, except perhaps by common consent [*ek symphōnou*] for a time, in order to have leisure to devote yourselves to prayer, and then be together again, lest Satan tempt you through your lack of self-control [*akrasia*]" (1 Cor. 7:5 AT). Paul immediately makes a qualification: "I say this by way of concession,

18. See Jeffrey A. D. Weima, *1–2 Thessalonians*, BECNT (Grand Rapids: Baker Academic, 2014), Kindle loc. 6736–854.
19. E.g., Matt. 7:29; 9:6; Mark 1:27.

not of command" (v. 6). The question is, what exactly has he said "by way of concession"? There are three possibilities:

(a) *The entire body of teaching in 1 Corinthians 7:2–5 is a concession.* This cannot be Paul's meaning, because very little in verses 2–5 can be understood as merely a concession. Paul is emphatic, and most verbs are imperative there: "Let each one embrace [*echetō*] his own wife" (v. 2); "Let the husband pay [*apodidotō*] the debt to his wife" (v. 3); "Do not deny [*mē apostereite*] each other" (v. 5, all AT).

(b) *The command not to refuse one another in verse 5 is a concession.* The same objection holds: this is expressed as a command and Paul indicates no hesitancy about it.

(c) *The permission to abstain periodically for prayer in verse 5 is a concession.* Only on this issue has Paul expressed any hesitancy: "except *perhaps* [*ei mēti*] by common consent for a season" (v. 5 AT). This is the one *concession* that Paul makes to his general *command* that husband and wife not refuse one another. It is not that he doesn't value continence: "I wish that all were as I myself am" (v. 7a). But like Christ, he recognizes that the gift of celibacy is not given to all: "But each has his own special gift from God, one of one kind and one of another" (v. 7b).

This same principle manifests in Paul's advice to the unmarried and widows (1 Cor. 7:8): "It is well for them to remain single as I do," he says, affirming the value of celibacy for the kingdom as in the Lord's teaching (Matt. 19:11–12). "But if they cannot exercise self-control [*enkrateuontai*]," he continues, "they should marry. For it is better to marry than to burn" (1 Cor. 7:9 AT). "Burn" can mean either "burn in hell" from sexual sin or "burn with passion." Several examples of burning and fire as metaphors for sexual desire in Greek literature (e.g., Sir. 9:8 LXX; cf. Prov. 6:27–28 LXX) make the latter option more likely.[20]

Paul now transmits the dominical teaching on the indissolubility of marriage (cf. Matt. 19:4–9): "To the married I exhort (not I but the Lord) that the wife should not depart from her husband—but if she does depart, let her remain unmarried or else be reconciled to her husband—and the husband should not abandon his wife" (1 Cor. 7:10–11 AT). "Depart" (*chōrizō*) and "abandon" (*aphiēmi*) could be synonyms for "divorce." Paul reiterates the

---

20. Montague, *First Corinthians*, 116–17.

St. Jerome and St. Augustine on the "Holiness" of Family Members

The Fathers struggled with 1 Corinthians 7:14, because it could be taken to mean that unbelieving family members did not need baptism. St. Jerome asserts:

> The children of believers are called holy because they are as it were candidates for the faith and have suffered no pollution from idolatry. Consider also that the vessels of which we read in the tabernacle are called holy and everything else required for the ceremonial worship: although in strictness of speech there can be nothing holy except creatures which know of and worship God. But it is a scriptural usage sometimes to give the name of holy to those who are clean, or who have been purified, or who have made expiation. For instance, it is written of Bathsheba that she was made holy from her uncleanness, and the temple itself is called the holy place.[a]

Augustine affirms that:

> Nevertheless, whatever be the sanctification meant, this must be steadily held: that there is no other valid means of making Christians and remitting sins, except by men becoming believers through the sacrament according to the institution of Christ and the Church. For neither are unbelieving husbands and wives, notwithstanding their intimate union with holy and righteous spouses, cleansed of the sin which separates men from the kingdom of God and drives them into condemnation, nor are the children who are born of parents, however just and holy, absolved from the guilt of original sin, unless they have been baptized into Christ; and in behalf of these our plea should be the more earnest, the less able they are to urge one themselves.[b]

a. Jerome, *Letter 85* (*NPNF*[2] 6:182).
b. Augustine, *On the Merits and Forgiveness of Sins, and the Baptism of Infants* 3.21 (*NPNF*[1] 5:78).

teaching of Jesus against divorce but acknowledges that in situations in which a wife has left her husband, she should remain unmarried in order to leave open the possibility of reconciliation. Paul phrases this teaching from the female perspective—the wife leaving her husband—but we may assume that the same principle holds for a husband who separates from his wife. Paul discourages but tolerates marital separation, yet he will not countenance a second marriage.

Now Paul confronts a situation Jesus never addressed, as it did not arise during his earthly ministry—namely, that of a Christian believer married to an unbeliever. Paul teaches that converts should not divorce unconverted spouses who are committed to the marriage (1 Cor. 7:12–13): "For the unbelieving husband is *consecrated* [*hagiazō*] through his wife, and the unbelieving wife is *consecrated* [*hagiazō*] through her husband"; therefore, "your children" are not "unclean [*akathartos*]" but "holy [*hagios*]" (7:14). "Consecration," "uncleanness," and "holiness" are cultic terms from the Mosaic covenant. Specifically, the consecration of persons in the Old Testament is frequently associated with ordination to the priesthood. Thus, the matrimonial bond configures spouses for a sacred role. This comports well with the Latin Rite understanding of spouses as ministers of the sacrament, which is neither contract nor convention but grace-conferring mystery, rendering spouses "consecrated" and children "holy." Yet what does Paul mean by "consecrated" and "holy"? The Church has never taken Paul to mean that children of Christian couples do not require baptism, for example. In the Mosaic covenant, "unclean" and "holy" distinguish those excluded from the worshiping community and those included in that community. Therefore, Paul apparently teaches that spouses and children of believers are members of the Church in some way.

Nonetheless, the grace-conferring nature of marriage requires the consent of both spouses: "If the unbelieving partner desires to separate, let it be so; in such a case the brother or sister is not bound" (1 Cor. 7:15). Based on this teaching, the Church permits "the Pauline privilege," the dissolution of a marriage formed when both parties were unbaptized. If the unbelieving partner departs, the believing partner may contract a new marriage in the Church.

Paul now returns to the topic of the unmarried (cf. 1 Cor. 7:8–9) and the prudence (or lack thereof) of contracting marriage as a Christian. Having "no command of the Lord," Paul gives his own "opinion" that "it is well for a person to remain as he is" (vv. 25–26), not seeking to change his marital state. "But if you marry, you do not sin," he clarifies, "yet those who marry will have worldly troubles, and I would spare you that" (v. 28). The time has grown short, and Christians should live detached from worldly things, for "the form of this world is passing away" (vv. 29–31).

In this passage (1 Cor. 7:8–31), Paul lowers the level of authority of this teaching: it is not a command of Christ but an "opinion" of someone "trustworthy." Eschatological urgency should mark the lifestyle of the Christian disciple, motivating him or her to avoid attachments to the present world, which marriage entails. This idea grows naturally from Jesus's teaching that marriage pertains only to this life and not the next (Matt. 22:30), as well as

St. Ambrose on Marriage and Celibacy

The Fathers strove to balance the goodness of marriage with the preferential option for celibacy. Typical is St. Ambrose, commenting on 1 Corinthians 7:25–28:

> Marriage, then, is honourable, but chastity is more honourable, for "he that giveth his virgin in marriage doeth well, but he that giveth her not in marriage doeth better." That, then, which is good need not be avoided, but that which is better should be chosen. And so it is not laid upon any, but set before him. And, therefore, the Apostle said well: "Concerning virgins I have no commandment of the Lord, yet I give my counsel." For a command is issued to those subject, counsel is given to friends. Where there is a commandment, there is a law; where counsel, there is grace. A commandment is given to enforce what is according to nature, a counsel to incite us to follow grace. And, therefore, the Law was given to the Jews, but grace was reserved for the elect. The Law was given that, through fear of punishment, it might recall those who were wandering beyond the limits of nature, to their observance, but grace to incite the elect both by the desire of good things, and also by the promised rewards.[a]

a. Ambrose, On Widows 12.72 (NPNF[2] 10:403).

from the prophetic tradition of celibacy going back to Elijah and Elisha. Just as an eschatological urgency lay on the "prophets who were before you" (Matt. 5:12), so it lays on those who share in Christ's prophetic role.

One of the goals of Paul's advice is that the Christian finds peace in the fulfillment of the call of discipleship on his or her life. "I want you to be free from anxieties" (1 Cor. 7:32), Paul insists, but the married are "anxious about worldly affairs" (v. 33), how to please their wives or husbands (vv. 33–34), whereas the unmarried are only "anxious about the affairs of the Lord" (vv. 32, 34). Significantly, Paul assumes Christian spouses, *both* husband *and* wife, will desire to please one another in their relationship. Marriage is no mere utilitarian institution but a personal union entailing mutual affection. Nonetheless, Paul acknowledges the danger that commitment to a spouse can conflict with commitment to the Lord. This reflects the dominical teaching that each disciple must be ready to place their commitment to the Lord above natural family ties: "If anyone comes to me and does not hate his own father and mother and wife and children and brothers and sisters, yes, and even his own life, he cannot be my disciple" (Luke 14:26). Paul does no more than draw out the implications of the Lord's teaching on discipleship: marriage can pose a challenge to the disciple by introducing a possible conflict of allegiance. However, there is a more attractive possible outcome, developed in Ephesians 5:21–33—that is, that spouses will learn to serve the Lord *by* serving each other, such that their mutual love will not be a competitor but an icon of their love for the Lord.

Paul continues in 1 Corinthians 7:36–38 by applying a fundamental principle—that marriage is good, but singleness for the Lord is better—to the situation of betrothed young men. They do no wrong by marrying their betrothed, but they do better to remain single. Likewise, widows are encouraged but not commanded to remain single:

> A wife is bound to her husband as long as he lives. If the husband dies, she is free to be married to whom she wishes, only in the Lord. But in my judgment she is happier if she remains as she is. And I think that I have the Spirit of God. (1 Cor. 7:39–40)

Significantly, the one restriction is that the widow's remarriage be "in the Lord"—that is, to another believer in Christ. Christian disciples are *not* free to marry those outside the household of faith (2 Cor. 6:14–16):

> Do not be mismated[21] with unbelievers. For what partnership have righteousness and iniquity? Or what fellowship has light with darkness? What accord has Christ with Belial? Or what has a believer in common with an unbeliever? What agreement has the temple of God with idols? For we are the temple of the living God.

Note the strong similarities with 1 Corinthians 6:12–19, where Paul argues against relations with prostitutes because the Christian is a temple of the Holy Spirit (6:19). The Christian believer is not free to marry one who does not share faith in Christ, nor is he or she free to marry one who claims to but does not practice (5:9–12). Those in the covenant must marry within the covenant—a biblical principle as old as Genesis 6:2. Exogamy quickly and effectively destroys the covenantal community, as Ezra and Nehemiah realized (Ezra 9:1–15; Neh. 13:23–27).

21. Greek *heterozygountes*, lit., "differently or unequally yoked."

We return to St. Paul's concluding advice to widows in 1 Corinthians 7:40: "In my judgment she is happier if she remains as she is." Paul later refines this advice in 1 Timothy 5:9–14:

> Let a widow be enrolled if she is not less than sixty years of age. . . . But refuse to enrol younger widows; for when they grow wanton against Christ they desire to marry, and so they incur condemnation for having violated their first pledge. . . . So I would have younger widows marry, bear children, rule their households, and give the enemy no occasion to revile us. (1 Tim. 5:9, 11–12, 14)

This reflects an early form of female religious life: widows were enrolled in an order and supported by the church while they devoted themselves to charitable works. But here an older Paul recognizes that young widows usually do not have the gift of celibacy—otherwise they would not have married initially—so making a permanent commitment to singleness after their husband's death is imprudent. This is harmonious with the principle of Matthew 19:11 and Paul's advice in 1 Corinthians 7:1–7—namely, that the celibate vocation is admirable but possible only for those "to whom it has been given" (Matt. 19:11b).

Ephesians

We turn now to Ephesians, widely and justly considered to contain St. Paul's most profound reflections on the nature of matrimony within the economy of the New Covenant.

The focal point of Ephesians' teaching on marriage is Ephesians 5:22–33, but its characteristic paradigm of a loving, one-body union between Christ and the Church emerges already much earlier in the epistle. In 1:6, Paul introduces the theme of Christ as bridegroom by calling him "the Beloved"—evoking the Song of Songs—and he identifies the "church" as Christ's "body" (1:22–23), because Christ has made Jews and Gentiles "both one," creating "one new man in place of the two" (2:14, 15)—evoking the "two shall become one" of Matthew 19:5–6 and Genesis 2:24. In Ephesians 2:19–22, Paul mixes architectural with physiological imagery: the Church as temple and the Church as body, respectively. He describes the Church as the "household of God, built upon the foundation of the apostles and prophets, . . . a holy temple . . . built . . . for a dwelling place"— all architectural images (vv. 19–22). But being "joined together," as if by joints and ligaments, and "growing" are bodily realities (v. 21; cf. 4:16). Similarly,

Paul describes church offices as directed toward the "building up [of] the body of Christ" (4:12), as the Church is to "grow up" into the "head" (4:15), from whom the "whole body, joined and knit together by every joint with which it is supplied, . . . upbuilds [*oikodomēn*] itself in love [*agapē*]" (4:16).

St. Paul's understanding of the Church as a body-temple may intentionally evoke Eve, the original bride, "built" (Hebrew *bānāh*) from the "rib, beam" (*ṣēlāʿ*) of Adam (Gen. 2:22), recognized as his own body (2:23) and as "one flesh" (*bāśār eḥād*) with him (2:24).

Thus, St. Paul's address to husbands and wives in Ephesians 5:21–33 is a culmination, extension, and application of an ecclesiology developed throughout the letter. This beautiful and strategic text challenges many modern readers who reject the idea that gendered role differentiation or even sexual complementarity is intrinsic to marriage. Too often the text is ignored or rejected before it is even understood—that is, before a patient process of exegesis has been completed. Such a process of exegesis not only needs to work carefully on the literal sense of the text, using the standard philological tools of analysis (lexicography, grammar, syntax, rhetoric), but it also needs to keep in mind the Church's three criteria for arriving at the spiritual sense of the text: the content and unity of Scripture, the living Tradition, and the analogy of faith (*Dei Verbum* 12; CCC 112–14). Only then does the text's meaning for the Church become clear.

Therefore, we will work through the successive sentences of Paul's teaching in Ephesians 5:21–33 with close attention, beginning with Paul's introductory statement in vv. 21–22, which also serves as a transition from the unit Ephesians 5:3–20 (on general Christian behavior) to the unit 5:21–33 (specifically on Christian marriage).

> *Hypotassomenoi allēlois en phobō Christou, hai gynaikes tois idiois andrasin hōs tō kyriō.*

> Placing yourselves under one another in fear of Christ, the women [placing themselves under] their very own men as to the Lord. (Eph. 5:21–22 AT)

A key verb for understanding this pericope is its very first word, *hypotassomenoi*—literally, "placing oneself under," from the prefix *hypo-*, "under," and the verb *tassō*, "set in place, arrange, order." It is a middle-passive participle with a reflexive sense, rendered variously in English translations as "submit" (ESV), "be subject" (RSV), "be subordinate" (NABRE). (Etymologically, the closest rendering is "subordinate oneself," since *subordinate* is virtually a calque of *hypotassō*.) Unfortunately, all these verbs tend to carry a negative connotation in English that *hypotassomai* probably did not carry in Greek; therefore, "defer to" or "show deference toward" may be a better dynamic equivalent.

Hypotassō is an important term in the New Testament, occurring thirty-one times. It is always a morally proper action, never a sin—but the failure to carry it out is described negatively (Rom. 8:7; 10:3).

Patterns of *Hypotassomai*, or "Placing Under," in the New Testament

These persons/things	are subordinate to these persons/things	in these texts
The boy Jesus to . . .	his parents	Luke 2:51
Demons to . . .	the disciples	Luke 10:17, 20
The mind set on flesh *not* to . . .	God's law	Rom. 8:7
Creation to . . .	futility	Rom. 8:20
Jews *not* to . . .	God's righteousness	Rom. 10:3
Every person to . . .	governing authorities	Rom. 13:1, 5
The spirits of prophets to . . .	prophets themselves	1 Cor. 14:32
Women to . . .	their husbands	1 Cor. 14:34–35
All things to . . .	Christ	1 Cor. 15:27 (3×)
The Son to . . .	God [the Father]	1 Cor. 15:28
The Corinthian Christians to . . .	every collaborator of the apostles	1 Cor. 16:15–16a
All things to . . .	Christ	Eph. 1:22
Believers to . . .	fellow believers	Eph. 5:21
The Church to . . .	Christ	Eph. 5:24
Wives to . . .	their husbands	Eph. 5:24
All things to . . .	Christ	Phil. 3:21
Wives to . . .	their husbands	Col. 3:18
Wives to . . .	their husbands	Titus 2:5
Slaves to . . .	masters	Titus 2:9
Christians to . . .	rulers and authorities	Titus 3:1
Everything to . . .	Christ	Heb. 2:8 (3×)
Christians to . . .	the Father of Spirits	Heb. 12:9
Christians to . . .	God	James 4:7
Christians to . . .	every human institution, whether emperor or governor	1 Pet. 2:13
Servants to . . .	masters	1 Pet. 2:18
Wives to . . .	husbands	1 Pet. 3:1
Holy women to . . .	their husbands	1 Pet. 3:5
Angels, authorities, and powers to . . .	Christ	1 Pet. 3:22
Younger Christians to . . .	the elders (presbyters)	1 Pet. 5:5

St. John Chrysostom on Ephesians 5:25

St. John Chrysostom comments as follows on Ephesians 5:25, which says, "Husbands, love your wives, as Christ loved the church":

> Thou hast seen the measure of obedience, hear also the measure of love. Wouldest thou have thy wife obedient unto thee, as the Church is to Christ? Take then thyself the same provident care for her, as Christ takes for the Church. Yea, even if it shall be needful for thee to give thy life for her, yea, and to be cut into pieces ten thousand times, yea, and to endure and undergo any suffering whatever—refuse it not. Though thou shouldest undergo all this, yet wilt thou not, no, not even then, have done anything like Christ. For thou indeed art doing it for one to whom thou art already knit; but He for one who turned her back on Him and hated Him. In the same way then as He laid at His feet her who turned her back on Him, who hated, and spurned, and disdained Him, not by menaces, nor by violence, nor by terror, nor by anything else of the kind, but by his unwearied affection; so also do thou behave thyself toward thy wife. Yea, though thou see her looking down upon thee, and disdaining, and scorning thee, yet by thy great thoughtfulness for her, by affection, by kindness, thou wilt be able to lay her at thy feet. For there is nothing more powerful to sway than these bonds, and especially for husband and wife. A servant, indeed, one will be able, perhaps, to bind down by fear; nay not even him, for he will soon start away and be gone. But the partner of one's life, the mother of one's children, the foundation of one's every joy, one ought never to chain down by fear and menaces, but with love and good temper. For what sort of union is that, where the wife trembles at her husband? And what sort of pleasure will the husband himself enjoy, if he dwells with his wife as with a slave, and not as with a free-woman? Yea, though thou shouldest suffer anything on her account, do not upbraid her; for neither did Christ do this.[a]

a. John Chrysostom, *Homily 20*, on Eph. 5:22–24 (*NPNF*[1] 13:144).

As a perusal of its usage in the New Testament shows, the action of *hypotassomai* is a virtue characteristic of the Christian life. It is a recognition and acceptance of legitimate authority. It does not indicate the ontologically lower status of the one placing him- or herself under the other, because even God himself practices *hypotagē*, "subordination," as when Jesus places himself under his earthly parents (Luke 2:51) or God the Father (1 Cor. 15:28).

Indeed, one of the radical aspects of the gospel is that it identifies subordination or *hypotagē* as a divine attribute: "[Jesus] went down with them and came to Nazareth, and deferred to them" (Luke 2:51 AT). The Creator submits himself to fallible human parents, respecting the authority structures of the natural order he himself created. This is an expression of Christ's humility, which was not merely accidental but *essential* to his redemptive mission, for "though he was in the form of God, [he] did not count equality with God a thing to be grasped, but emptied himself, taking the form of a servant. . . . He humbled himself and became obedient unto . . . death on a cross" (Phil. 2:6–8). In ancient paganism and moral philosophy, humility and its expression in subordination or obedience was not considered a virtue, but the gospel transforms it into a virtue and, indeed, the *imitatio Dei*.

Returning to Ephesians 5:22, we note that the voice of the implied verb is middle-passive with the force of a reflexive: "Let wives place themselves under their husbands" (AT). Here, as elsewhere (e.g., Col. 3:18), St. Paul addresses wives as moral agents and exhorts them to "place *themselves* under" or "subordinate *themselves* to" their husbands, and he *never once* exhorts husbands to "subordinate" their wives. This is significant and in keeping with the Old Testament tradition, which likewise *never once* authorizes husbands to compel the behavior of their wives. The act of submission must be the free act of a moral agent; in the context of marriage, it is the free and complete self-entrustment of the wife into the love of her husband, who is called to act *in persona Christi* toward her, as we will see below. The husband is not responsible for the behavior of his wife and not exhorted to "make" her behave in any way; rather, he is only responsible for his own behavior, and St. Paul limits the husband's behavior strictly to that which conforms to the sacrificial love of Christ toward his bride, the Church.

The last phrase of Ephesians 5:22 emphasizes that the *hypotagē* of wives toward their husbands is an expression ultimately of obedience to Jesus Christ: "Let wives subordinate themselves to their husbands *as to the Lord*" (AT). Wives should sanctify this act of self-giving by recognizing that its ultimate recipient is not their husbands but the Lord. It is true that Christians should sanctify all their labor by offering it to the Lord rather than men (Eph. 6:7; Col. 3:23), but in the context of the marital union of two believers (presumed in Eph. 5:22–33), the husband does act *in persona Christi* by receiving the act of *hypotagē* or self-entrustment from his wife. This is part of the sacramental nature of this bond. St. Paul expounds on the way that spouses act toward one another *in persona Christi*:

> For the husband is the head of the wife even as Christ is the head of the church, his body, and is himself its Savior. Now as the church submits to Christ, so also wives should submit in everything to their husbands. (Eph. 5:23–24 ESV)

The husband acts toward his wife in the person of Christ, the head of the Church—and this headship means being a "Savior" (*sōtēr*), one who acts to establish or restore the comprehensive well-being of another. Reciprocally, wives are called to act *in persona ecclesiae*—"in the person of the Church"— toward their husbands by submitting themselves as the Church does to Christ. But here we should recall the unity of Christ and the Church, his mystical body, so succinctly expressed by St. Joan of Arc: "About Jesus Christ and the Church, I simply know they're just one thing, and we shouldn't complicate the matter" (CCC 795). Thus, we may say wives are called to act *in the person of Christ the body* toward their husbands, and husbands are called to act *in the person of Christ the head* toward their wives, so both act *in persona Christi*.

By calling the husband the "head" of the wife, St. Paul indicates some kind of authority in the relationship. But in understanding how this is to be applied in practice, we must remember the "content and unity of the whole Scripture" (CCC 112)—in particular, the Lord's pointed words about how leadership in the Church is to be exercised. When the apostles dispute about greatness at the Last Supper, Jesus exhorts them not to "exercise lordship" like Gentile rulers, but rather to "let the greatest among you become as the youngest, and the leader as one who serves. For . . . I am among you as one who serves" (Luke 22:25–27). Jesus calls here for a radical reframing of what exercising authority means. The world's perspective is that leadership denotes ontological superiority and that service should flow from those led to the one leading. Jesus turns this model upside down, insisting not only that the one exercising authority should place him- or herself below the others, but also that service flows from the leader to those being led. Not only did Jesus teach this, but he practiced and modeled it, especially through his passion and death.

There are currents in contemporary theology that identify all structures of authority as either sinful or the result of sin, and hold that the gospel entails the establishment of an egalitarian society free of authority structures. This perspective is contrary to biblical revelation, which identifies a structure of authority even within the coequality of the Godhead (John 14:28; 1 Cor. 15:27–28) and describes authority structures written into creation even prior to the entrance of sin into human history (Gen. 1:26–30; Rom. 13:1, 5). The holding or exercising of authority is not sinful; rather, it is necessary for the good functioning of any society of human, angelic, or divine persons. What is sinful is the exercise of authority for one's own benefit—that is, selfishly. God is love, and the essence of love is the gift of self; therefore, the proper exercise of authority should always consist of the gift of self to others, not self-aggrandizement. This principle should guide the behavior of every authority figure in the Church or within Christian society: the pope, bishops, pastors, teachers, civil authorities, religious superiors, employers, chairpersons, or husbands and fathers of families. Properly exercised, leadership is a very great service, a profound expression of charity. The immature and adolescent seek positions of power to aggrandize themselves; the wise and mature avoid them because they know that the moral burden of being responsible for the welfare of others demands a degree of self-sacrifice far beyond that required of those who follow.

Returning to Ephesians 5:24, we observe that St. Paul exhorts wives to place themselves under their husbands "in everything" (*en panti*), meaning "without reserve" or "completely," a total act of self-abandonment. This corresponds to the husband's total act of self-abandonment through sacrifice in the following verse (5:25). Thus, we should not soften the exhortation by saying that "in everything" is merely an ideal. It is not just an ideal; the wife should intend an unreserved and total entrustment of herself to her husband, just as the Church's self-entrustment to Christ is total. However, this total self-gift can be impeded by sin, either her own or her husband's. Submission "in all things" presumes that the husband corresponds and loves like Christ "in all things." But we must remain cognizant of the "content and unity" of Scripture; accordingly, "in all things" does not abrogate the limitations on obedience clearly established elsewhere in the Bible. Thus, *en panti* cannot include cooperation in sin. Loyalty to God supersedes all other loyalties, even the strongest natural or sacramental bonds: "If anyone comes to me and does not hate his own father and mother and wife and children and brothers and sisters, yes, and even his own life, he cannot be my disciple" (Luke 14:26); "We must obey God rather than men" (Acts 5:29). Thus, the deference of the wife to her husband never obliges her to cooperate in sin, including sins against herself. In fact, like all Christians, she has a moral obligation to oppose sin, including the sin of those who hold positions of authority.

Furthermore, we should keep in mind that when it comes to a married couple's physical relationship, there is a complementary and mutual exercise of authority and deference: "For the wife does not exercise authority over [*exousiazō*] her own body, but the husband does; likewise, the husband does not exercise authority over his own body, but the wife does" (1 Cor. 7:4 AT).

St. Paul then turns to husbands, laying upon them an even more demanding role: "Husbands, love [*agapaō*] your wives, even as Christ loved the church and handed himself over [*heauton paredōken*] for her" (Eph. 5:25 NABRE). Here, St. Paul commands husbands to love their wives, using the verbal form of *agapē*, the strongest Greek word for love, typically used for God's love, in distinction from *erōs*, erotic or romantic love, or *philos*, the love of friendship. It is the love exercised by Christ toward the Church, which culminated in "giving himself up for her" or, more literally, "hand[ing] himself over for her" (*heauton paredōken hyper autēs*). The verb *paradidōmi* is the preferred term in the Gospels for describing Jesus's betrayal into the hands of the hostile authorities.[22] Paul and other New Testament authors appear to be drawing on the unique use of the term in Isaiah 53, where the servant of the Lord acts as both priest and victim, since "the Lord has handed him over [*paredōken auton*] for our sins," "his soul was handed over [*paredothē*] unto death," and "on account of their sins [he] was handed over [*paredothē*]" (Isa. 53:6, 12 LXX [AT]). Yet nowhere in the Septuagint do we find the reflexive expression Paul uses of Christ: "to hand oneself over."[23] Rather, Paul seems to be reading Isaiah 53:6–12 with the understanding that Jesus is both the Lord who hands the servant over (cf. Rom. 8:32) and also the servant himself (cf. John 10:18: "No one takes [my life] from me, but I lay it down of my own accord"). Paul understands Jesus as Isaiah's priestly servant, as earlier in Ephesians 5: "Christ loved us and gave himself up for us, an offering and sacrifice to God for a pleasing aroma" (v. 2 AT). "Pleasing aroma," *osmēn euōdias*, renders Hebrew *rêaḥ nîḥôaḥ*, a technical term in so-called priestly texts of the Pentateuch for an acceptable sacrifice to God.[24] Thus, in Ephesians 5:25 Paul calls husbands to imitate Christ in his love for the Church, which is a specifically *priestly* ministry. The following verses are dense with cultic terms:

22. Matt. 20:18–19; 26:15, 24–25, 45; Mark 9:31; 10:33; Luke 24:20; John 19:11, 16.
23. Cf. Gal. 2:20: "gave himself for me"; Eph. 5:2: "gave himself up for us."
24. E.g., Gen. 8:21; Exod. 29:18, 25, 41; Lev. 1:9.

that he might sanctify [*hagiazō*] her, having cleansed [*katharizō*] her by the washing of water [*hydōr*] with the word, that he might present [*paristēmi*] the church to himself in splendor, without spot or wrinkle or any such thing, that she might be holy [*hagia*] and without blemish [*amōmos*]. (Eph. 5:26–27)

Paul describes Christ's relationship with the Church as that of a priest toward a sacred offering or a sacred place (i.e., a sanctuary). "Sanctify" or "consecrate" (*hagiazō*) is applied to persons (priests, firstborn sons, Israel generally) or things (liturgical vessels and furniture, the altar, the sanctuary, dedicated objects) given over to sacred use (e.g., Num. 18:8–9). Greek *katharizō* describes the ritual cleansing of persons and vessels, often by washing (*louō*) with water (*hydōr*) (cf. Num. 14–15 LXX), to be brought into God's presence. Greek *paristēmi*, "present," may be Paul's rendering of the Hebrew *hiqrîb*, "bring near, present," a common term for bringing something into the divine presence (e.g., Lev. 1:2, 3, 5). Everything offered to God is "holy" (*hagia*), and all sacrificial offerings had to be "without blemish" (*amōmos*, e.g., Lev. 1:3, 10), a term also frequent in Psalms, conveying moral purity (e.g., Pss. 15:2; 18:23). Thus, Paul's language all comes from the context of cult and priesthood.

In addition, Paul's image of a husband washing his bride must surely allude to Ezekiel 16:8–14,[25] where the Lord bathes, washes, anoints, and clothes Bride Israel with luxurious garments until she is "exceedingly beautiful," of "regal estate," and "perfect through the splendor" the Lord has "bestowed" (vv. 13, 14). Although Bride Israel proceeds to defile herself (vv. 15–52; cf. 36:16–21), Ezekiel foresees a time when God will once more renew his covenant with her (vv. 59–63; cf. 34:25) and cleanse her from all her "uncleannesses" (36:25), granting her a "new heart" and a "new spirit" (36:26)—indeed, putting his own spirit within her (36:27). The nuptial and cleansing imagery of Isaiah 4:2–5 is similar.

In sum, St. Paul describes Christ as a priest preparing the Church as a holy offering to himself, and he simultaneously evokes prophetic passages portraying the Lord as a bridegroom washing Israel as bride in preparation for their covenantal union. This model of love is to be emulated by each Christian husband toward his own wife:

In the same way [*houtōs*], husbands are obliged to love their own wives as their own bodies. He who loves his wife loves himself. (Eph. 5:28 AT)

25. Peter S. Williamson, *Ephesians*, CCSS (Grand Rapids: Baker Academic, 2009), 167.

Greek *houtōs*, "thus, in this way," refers to what precedes as a model for the way spousal love is to be expressed. Then St. Paul uses an emphatic construction rarely translated literally—not merely an imperative ("husbands must") or subjunctive ("husbands should") but a form of *opheilō*, "to be obligated, to owe a debt," plus the infinitive of *agapaō*, thus: "Husbands are under obligation [or "owe a debt"] to love their wives as their own bodies." Paul has used a related term, *opheilē*, "debt, duty," to describe the moral obligation of spouses to embrace one another physically (1 Cor. 7:3). Thus, Paul stresses the gravity of the moral obligation for husbands to love their wives after the model of Christ himself. It is not optional counsel or supererogation for some; rather, it is a duty for all.

The phrase "love their own wives as their own bodies" may well draw on Old Testament texts from Leviticus and the Song of Songs. Leviticus 19:18b states, "You shall love your neighbor as yourself," which can be applied especially to one's spouse, since the word "neighbor" (Hebrew *rē'a*) also describes the spouses of the Song as "friends" (*rē'îm*, Song 5:1) and the bridegroom as "my friend" (*rē'î*, 5:16). Therefore, if the law commands love of neighbor as one's self, how much more so does it command love of one's wife, the most intimate of "neighbors" (Song 5:1)? Yet Paul does not say "love their own wives as their own *selves*" but "as their own *bodies*," substituting Greek *sōma* for Leviticus 19:18b's generic *seauton* ("self"), thus alluding to Eve's creation (Gen. 2:21–24) and the bodily identity of husband and wife—for example, "They shall become one flesh" (Gen. 2:24 ESV; cf. Eph. 5:31!). So "he who loves his wife loves himself" (Eph. 5:28b) unites Leviticus 19:18b with Genesis 2:24 to conclude that love of one's wife is the first moral obligation after love of God (cf. Mark 12:31).

St. Paul continues: "For no man ever hates his own flesh [*sarx*], but nourishes and cherishes it, as Christ does the church, because we are members of his body" (Eph. 5:29–30). Here, Paul preempts interpretations of his teaching in which a husband's Christlike authority could be used to benefit himself and harm his wife. Far from it! That would be against not only the gospel but the natural order: "no man ever hates his own flesh" (v. 29a). Paul has not used the term "flesh" above, but it emerges from his subtext, Genesis 2:24 (LXX), alluded to previously (Eph. 5:28b) and quoted subsequently (v. 31). Rather than "hate," a man naturally "nourishes" (*ektrephō*) and "cherishes" (*thalpō*) his flesh—two terms with a *maternal* (!) connotation: *ektrephō* combines the preposition *ek-*, here an intensifier, with *trephō*, "to nourish" or specifically "to nurse";[26] *thalpō* originally meant "to warm," but its association with mother birds brooding their eggs caused a generalization of its meaning to "care for, raise, cherish."[27] Observe Paul's use of identical or closely related terms elsewhere: "We were gentle among you, like a nursing mother [*trophos*] taking care [*thalpō*] of her own children" (1 Thess. 2:7 ESV).[28] Thus, Paul describes Christ's care for the Church and a husband's care for his wife using quasi-maternal imagery.

Finally, St. Paul quotes the Old Testament subtext that has underlain his previous exhortations: "For this reason a man shall leave his father and mother and be joined to his wife, and the two shall become one flesh" (Eph 5:31). Then he immediately comments:

> This is a great mystery [*mystērion mega*], but I speak in reference to Christ and the church. In any case, each one of you should love his wife as himself, and the wife should respect her husband. (Eph. 5:32–33 NABRE)

What does Paul mean by calling the union between man and wife a *mystērion mega*? We must note the immediate qualification: *egō de legō eis Christon kai eis tēn ekklēsian*, "But I am speaking about Christ and the Church" (AT). In other words, the "great mystery" is the application of the union of man and wife to Christ and the Church:[29] "Paul sees a typology present in the divine institution of marriage that finds its antitype in the relationship between Christ and the church."[30] In other words, the great mystery is that the real or deeper meaning of marriage is that it is a sign of the union of Christ and the Church, from the moment it was instituted in Eden and throughout human history subsequently. It is not simply that marriage is an "illustration, model, or analogy" but a "new reality"[31]—in other words, there is a kind of metaphysical resonance between the union of man and woman in marriage and the union of Christ and the Church, such that we can justifiably say matrimony is a sign that participates in the reality that it signifies—it is truly a *sacrament*.

---

26. See Deut. 32:18 LXX; Luke 23:29 ESV; 1 Thess. 2:7 ESV.
27. Clinton E. Arnold, *Ephesians*, ZECNT 10 (Grand Rapids: Zondervan, 2010), 666.
28. Arnold, *Ephesians*, 665.
29. Williamson, *Ephesians*, 172.
30. Arnold, *Ephesians*, 673.
31. Arnold, *Ephesians*, 674.

There is much more Paul could say about this great mystery, but he strongly resists the impulse to digress and returns to the practical point at hand—that is, the praxis of marriage within the Ephesian church:

> In any event, as for you all: each and every one of you must love his own wife as himself, and the wife should respect her husband. (Eph. 5:33 AT)

Addressing the men of the congregation, Paul uses redundant and therefore emphatic language: *hymeis hoi kath' hena, hekastos*, "You all, every one of you, each one [of you]." Paul is trying to make it unavoidably clear that the moral obligation to love one's wife as one's own self lies on every individual man of the congregation, not just the leaders or the spiritually mature or some other subset of the male congregants. No married man within the Church can escape this mandate!

The reciprocal responsibility of wives is stated more generically and less forcefully: "the wife should respect [*phobeō*] her husband" (Eph. 5:33 NABRE). *Phobeō* is literally "fear," but in this context it means "religious reverence" and forms an *inclusio* with verses 21–22:

> Be subordinate to one another *out of reverence for Christ*
> [*en phobō Christou*, lit., "in the fear of Christ"],
> wives to their own husbands *as to the Lord* [*hōs tō kyriō*]. (AT)

The phrases *en phobō Christou* and *hōs tō kyriō* qualify the kind of respect or fear that wives should have toward their husbands. It is a religious reverence, because the husband has a sacramental role of acting *in persona Christi* toward his wife. So just as Boaz is the representative of the Lord who expresses the Lord's compassion for Ruth by spreading his own "wing" (*kānāp*) over the young widow (cf. Ruth 2:12; 3:9), so the husband is Jesus's representative to express Jesus's self-sacrificial love toward his wife, and this sacred role deserves a religious reverence, not so much for the man himself but for the One he represents. It is a particularization of the general rule that Christians are to see Christ in others and serve him through others.

It is opportune at this point to bring in the teaching of St. Peter on the husband-wife relationship, although Peter is primarily concerned with addressing the situation of mixed marriages—a result of the conversion of one of the spouses (usually the wife) from a marriage originally contracted between unbelievers:

Likewise you wives, be submissive [*hypotassomenai*] to your husbands, so that some, though they do not obey the word, may be won without a word by the behavior of their wives, when they see your reverent and chaste behavior. Let not yours be the outward adorning with braiding of hair, decoration of gold, and wearing of fine clothing, but let it be the hidden person of the heart with the imperishable jewel of a gentle and quiet spirit, which in God's sight is very precious. So once the holy women who hoped in God used to adorn themselves and were submissive to their husbands, as Sarah obeyed Abraham, calling him lord. And you are now her children if you do right and let nothing terrify you. (1 Pet. 3:1–6)

Similar to Paul in Ephesians 5:21–22, the exhortation is for wives to *hypotassō* themselves under their husbands. Peter authorizes no one to compel this—it must be a free act of the will. Yet unlike Ephesians 5:21–33, here the primary goal is not the mystical imitation of Christ and the Church but the conversion of the unbelieving husband. Peter calls on wives to subordinate their short-term interests to the long-term goal of the conversion of their husbands to Christ. A man converted to Christ, then, would adopt a much different view of marriage than the pagan world and would be open to becoming the Christlike spouse Paul envisions in Ephesians 5:25–33: a self-sacrificial servant of his wife.

St. Peter goes on to discuss the nature of true beauty and how Christian wives might make themselves attractive. His comments may give evidence that the congregations to which he wrote were being effected by the Roman "new woman" phenomenon, a kind of ancient feminism in which women of means disregarded the authority of their husbands and indulged themselves in cosmetics, jewelry, sexually suggestive attire, and promiscuous affairs.[32] This kind of indulgence in "the lust of the flesh and the lust of the eyes and the pride of life" (1 John 2:16), characteristic of this lifestyle, made it antithetical to early Christianity. The gospel called for a lifestyle of simplicity,

---

32. "Wealthy women of high social standing had begun to enter public life in new ways. They were seeking education (including the fields of politics and law), obtaining jobs in the workplace, and even attaining important positions in city government. [Bruce] Winter has documented well how some of these women even discarded their veils (a traditional Roman symbol of the husband's authority over his wife) and began carrying on illicit relationships with both single and married men. These women often dressed immodestly, wore lavish jewelry, overused cosmetics, and used contraceptives (and, if not successful, aborted the unwanted child). This was by no means an isolated phenomenon in the empire" (Arnold, *Ephesians*, 374, citing Bruce W. Winter, *Roman Wives, Roman Widows: The Appearance of New Women and the Pauline Communities* [Grand Rapids: Eerdmans, 2003], 17–81).

not indulgence, and the prioritization of the interior life (the "hidden person of the heart," *ho kryptos tēs kardias anthrōpos*) over exterior ostentation. Peter then addresses those husbands who have already converted to Christ:

> Likewise you husbands, cohabit [with your wives] according to knowledge, bestowing honor on the weaker feminine vessel, since [they are] joint heirs [with you] of the grace of life, in order that your prayers may not be hindered. (1 Pet. 3:7 AT)

We note that, first of all, husbands are commanded to "live together" (*synoikeō*, "dwell in the same house") with their wives—a subtle point, but the sharing of a common life is integral to the marital relationship. This they are to do *kata gnōsin*, "according to knowledge"—that is, "intelligently, wisely." This "wise" manner of cohabitation means "bestowing honor on the weaker feminine vessel." Greek *skeuos*, "vessel," can refer to one's body and by extension one's person (cf. 1 Thess. 4:4 ESV). Here, it refers to the wife, who is physically weaker but nonetheless a "joint heir of the grace of life"—in other words, of eternal life. So there is both difference and equality within the spousal relationship. In this present world, there is a differential in physical strength between the spouses, but in the life to come, there is equal inheritance of the grace of God. Cognizant of the ultimate and eternal equality of their wives as children of God and recipients of eternal life, husbands should—far from taking personal advantage of the situation—heap honor on them to compensate for their present weaker state.[33] Peter applies here the gospel principle, so opposed to the perspective of the world, that weakness should elicit honor rather than contempt. As Paul teaches, the "weaker" parts of the body are "indispensable," and God gives "greater honor to the inferior part, that there may be no discord in the body, but that the members may have the same care for one another" (1 Cor. 12:22, 24–25). First Peter 3:7 is a particularization of the principle of 1 Corinthians 12:22–25 to Christian spouses.

Failure to be considerate toward one's spouse and to bestow honor on her will result in the hindrance of one's prayers (1 Pet. 3:7b)—namely, divine retribution expressed as the denial of the husband's prayers. God, ever the enforcer of covenants, is witness and guarantor of the spouses' proper behavior.

33. The Greek verb-object combination *aponemō timēn*, "bestow honor," is a stock phrase in ancient Greek; see Josephus, *Ant.* 1.156; 14.445; 20.60–61, 247; *Life* 422.

Summary of the Teaching on Matrimony in Ephesians

Ephesians 5:21–33 is the most comprehensive teaching on the nature and role of marriage within the New Covenant economy found in the Epistles. Marriage involves a total self-gift of each spouse to the other, without reservation, in imitation of Christ, yet in complementary modes. Acting in imitation of Christ the body, the wife entrusts herself entirely (*en panti*) to the loving care of her husband. The husband, in turn, acting in imitation of Christ the head, offers himself without reserve, to the point of death ("gave himself up for her"), to love his wife, which includes "sanctifying," "cleansing," "nourishing," and "cherishing" her (vv. 26–29). We see that Christ—and by extension, the husband—is described as a priest in his relationship with his spouse. The phrase "gave himself up for her" is an allusion to the priestly "servant of the Lord" of Isaiah 52:13–53:12, who is both priest and sacrifice, who "makes himself an offering for sin" (Isa. 53:10). Likewise, the actions of "cleansing" and "presenting" are drawn from the context of the sacrificial liturgy in the temple, in which the priest would wash and prepare the offerings to ensure they were "holy and without blemish." The Church—and by extension, the wife—is being described as the temple city Jerusalem, as Paul's imagery in Ephesians 5:26–27 primarily evokes Ezekiel 16:8–14, where the temple city Jerusalem is described as a spotless bride (cf. Rev. 21:2, 9–11, 16, 27).

While at first it might seem that the exhortation for wives to *hypotassomai* or submit themselves to their husbands "in everything" would leave them vulnerable to any whim of their spouses, in actuality we discover that the husband's authority as "head" of his wife is profoundly constrained. Indeed, Paul constrains a husband's authority by an internal criterion that admits of no exceptions: every action toward his wife must follow the example of Christ's self-sacrificial love for the Church. Thus, any self-centered, self-interested, or selfish exercise of Christlike headship is deauthorized and is, in fact, an oxymoron, a self-contradiction. So while respecting the created order and the traditional social expectations that the husband and father is the authority figure in the home and deserves deference because of his role, nonetheless Paul imposes a constraint on the exercise of that authority that, in effect, makes the husband a servant of his wife's good. The hermeneutically suspicious might say Paul "subverts" the traditional husband-wife relationship, but it would be better to say he "redeems" it. Authority structures, be they ever so mild, are nonetheless necessary for the cooperative action of any society, even one consisting of only two persons. Thus, authority structures are not evil in themselves. Evil arises from the use of authority for the self-interest of the one in authority.

Ephesians 5:21–33 gives strong scriptural support for understanding matrimony specifically as a sacrament, although ironically Paul's explicit statement that marriage is a "great mystery" (*mystērion mega*) in verse 31 is not itself the strongest evidence. More significant is the clear portrayal of both spouses as acting *in persona Christi* toward each other: the wife as Christ the body and the husband as Christ the head, the wife submitting herself as Christ does to the Father and the husband sacrificing himself as Christ did for the Church, the two so bound in a reciprocal sacrament of submission and sacrifice, two modes of expression of the one love that flows from Christ. This accords with the Church's understanding of the spouses as ministers of the sacrament, not just of the wedding rite (*sacramentum in fieri*) but throughout the marriage (*sacramentum in esse*). Moreover, the spouses are described as having a role in sanctifying one another, which entails that they are conduits of divine grace toward one another. In Ephesians 5:21–33, the sanctifying role of the husband with respect to the wife is very clear, as Paul calls husbands to imitate the sanctifying and cleansing activity of Christ (vv. 26–27). Conversely, in 1 Peter 3:1–6, the apostle emphasizes the sanctifying role of the wife, whose embrace of her role as Christ the body exercises a power of attraction over her spouse, leading to his obedience to "the word" (v. 1). Paradoxically, the wife's submission to her unbelieving husband in 1 Peter 3:1–6 is foreseen as leading to *his* submission to Christ, which eventuates in his adopting the husbandly role of sacrificial servant toward his spouse, as envisioned in Ephesians 5:23–30. Nonetheless, our point is that the Petrine and Pauline teachings on marriage complement one another and reveal the sanctifying effect of spouses on one another (cf. 1 Cor. 7:14).

Summary of the Epistolary Teaching on Matrimony

We have found that most of the epistolary material consists of an application and exposition of the dominical teaching. Thus, the rebuke of various forms of sexual immorality in 1 Corinthians 5:1–13; 6:9–20; 1 Thessalonians 4:1–8; and Hebrews 13:4 flows from the moral teaching of Matthew 5:27–30 and its implications. The indissolubility of valid marriage (Matt. 19:3–9 and parallels) is explicitly rearticulated in 1 Corinthians 7:10–11, 39. The superiority of apostolic celibacy and the necessity of a call to that state (Matt. 19:10–12) undergird the instructions concerning the prudence of contracting marriage in 1 Corinthians 7:8–9, 25–38, and 1 Timothy 5:9–16. The intrinsic goodness of procreation and children (Matt. 19:13–15) underlies the commendation of marital relations to husbands and wives in 1 Corinthians 7:1–5 and of childbearing in 1 Timothy 2:15; 5:14. The limitation of marriage to this temporal life (Matt. 22:23–33) is explicitly rearticulated in 1 Corinthians 7:39 and reflected in Paul's discussion of the temporal troubles associated with marriage in 1 Corinthians 7:25–35.

The two major ways that apostolic teaching extends beyond that of the Lord concern mixed marriages between believers and unbelievers (1 Cor. 7:12–16; 2 Cor. 6:14–18; 1 Pet. 3:1–6) and the application of Christ's relationship with the Church to the practice of Christian marriage (Eph. 5:21–33). The issue of mixed marriages did not arise during the earthly ministry of the Lord, since the New Covenant was not fully established until his passion. Regardless, these unions should never be contracted intentionally (2 Cor. 6:14–18) and can be dissolved if the unbelieving partner separates (1 Cor. 7:15), but otherwise the apostolic teaching urges spouses to be faithful to their role in the marriage as if married to a believer, in the hope and expectation that their spouse will be drawn to the Lord (7:12–14; 1 Pet. 3:1–6).

The richest reflection on marriage in the Epistles results from Paul's application of the spousal relationship of Christ and the Church—evident already in the synoptics but especially in John—to the practice of marriage between believing spouses (Eph. 5:21–33). Both spouses are called to act in the person of Christ toward each other, albeit in reciprocal modes, such that the marriage becomes a microcosm and an icon of the mystical body of Christ.

12

Conclusion

*The Symphonic Witness of Scripture
to the Dignity of Matrimony*

We have now completed a review and reflection on the witness of the entire canon on the subject of matrimony. It is appropriate to attempt a summary and synthesis of what we have learned from this testimony.

We have seen that, from the marriage of Adam and Eve in the garden to the wedding feast of the bride and the Lamb at the end of Revelation, matrimony has always been close to the center of the outworking of God's plan for the mission and salvation of the human race. Further, as one progresses through salvation history, one observes a constant, gentle dance between matrimony as practiced by the people of God and the matrimonial dimension of the covenant relationship between God and his people—that is, the covenant between man and wife reflects the covenant between God and humanity. This fundamental dynamic appears already in the first chapters of Genesis. In Genesis 1:1–2:3, God is revealed as both a singularity and a plurality, one who acts as "he" (1:27) but refers to himself as "us" (1:26). This mysterious oneness in a plurality of persons is reflected in God's image bearers on earth, *ʾādām*, who are both male and female, both "him" and "them" (1:27). This unity in plurality, which is essential to fully imaging God, is actualized in matrimony, the covenantal union of *ʾādām*-male and *ʾādām*-female, a union without which *ʾādām* cannot fulfill their mission to "be fruitful and multiply, and fill the earth" (1:28). In the higher-resolution account of marriage in Genesis 2:4–25, we find indications that the bodies of the two first spouses are sacred temples, residences of the Holy Spirit (Gen. 2:7; cf. Job 27:3; 32:8; 33:4), and the woman in particular is "built" as the complement (*kənegdô*) of the man in order to supply divine assistance (*'ēzer*). Thus, even in a state of nature, the union of man and wife has a supernatural dimension, the communion of two persons sanctified by the indwelling of the Spirit of God in order to supply grace—God's assistance (*'ēzer*) to one another.

The account of the fall into sin gives witness to the metaphysical resonance of the covenant between God and humankind with that between man and wife. Damage to one damages the other. Adam and Eve disrupt their covenantal relationship with God through an act of distrust and disobedience, and the same act introduces distrust (Gen. 3:7) and conflict (3:16) in their own spousal relationship. Nonetheless, since the hope of their eventual salvation and victory over the Evil One is tied to their descendants (3:15), the matrimonial bond remains central to the working out of salvation history. So, expelled from the garden, Adam and Eve unite in an act of communion described as "knowing" each other (4:1), and children are born to them. Cain and his line wander far from the will of God, and his wicked descendant Lamech is the first to offend against the true nature of matrimony by taking two wives (4:19). In time, this practice proliferates until polygamy is common (6:2) and brings social pathologies in its wake (6:5), provoking God to cleanse the earth by water, but not before gathering into the safety of the ark monogamous pairs of every bird and animal and representatives of the human race (7:15). From monogamous Noah and his monogamous sons, the earth is repopulated after the flood (9:1; 10:1), but the enigmatic encounter between Noah and Ham (9:20–27) recapitulates the fall in the garden, reintroduces sin into human history, and bears the aroma of a perverse offense against matrimony.

In the wake of the tower of Babel debacle, God chooses Abram as the instrument for restoration of the divine blessing to all humanity (Gen. 12:1–3), but God's promises of great nationhood and a royal dynasty can only be realized through marriage and the raising up of future generations. This is why the marriages of the patriarchs and their spouses, the matriarchs, garner such extensive attention throughout the patriarchal narratives. The matriarchs are women of faith who complement their husbands and at times intervene directly to guide the flow of salvation history (27:1–46). Admittedly, the patriarchs are imperfect in their practice of matrimony, notably by endangering their spouses (12:10–20; 20:1–18; 26:6–11) and taking additional wives (16:3; 29:28; 30:4, 9). Yet the patriarchs never desire multiple wives; the additional ones are pressed on them by others (16:1–3; 29:23; 30:3, 9), and the sacred author and the narrative pejorativize this behavior by showing the personal grief (16:4–9; 21:11, 15–16; 29:31; 30:1–2) and the disruption of familial peace (37:1–36) that result from having multiple wives and their rivalrous sons. Thus, it is only through God's merciful intervention on multiple occasions that the blessing and task of being fruitful and multiplying is fulfilled for the patriarchs (Exod. 1:7).

With the proliferation of Israel in Egypt and the coming of Moses, we enter into a new epoch of the divine economy. For the first time, the formal covenant is solemnized between God and the descendants of Abraham (Exod. 24:1–8), and the text describes this covenant in such a way as to facilitate a nuptial rereading of the narrative that understands that covenant to be a kind of marriage between God and his people (Deut. 6:5; 30:20; Jer. 2:1–3; Hosea 2:18–23). The fundamental "constitution" of this covenant relationship, the Ten Commandments, assumes the normativity of monogamy (Deut. 5:16) and contains multiple laws protecting the inviolability of the marital bond (5:18, 21). Furthermore, for the first time, positive laws are promulgated to regulate the practice of marriage within the people of God. In general, the marriage laws of Moses are concerned to protect the wife, as the more vulnerable spouse, from unjust treatment (Exod. 21:9–11) and to defend sexual fidelity within marriage (Deut. 22:22). They do contain accommodations for the Israelites' "hardness of heart" (Matt. 19:8), even while pointing implicitly to the institution's divine ideals (Deut. 24:5). So on the one hand, polygamy (Exod. 21:10) and divorce (Deut. 24:1–4) are acknowledged as realities, but on the other hand, divorce is described as "covenant breaking" or "treachery" (*bāgad*, Exod. 21:8) and remarriage as "being defiled" (*huṭṭammā'āh*, Deut. 24:4). Not everything legally permitted is encouraged.

Over the course of the Historical Books, the covenant between God and Israel continues to be described in quasi-marital terms, and strikingly the infidelity of Israel to her spouse-like commitment to God frequently expresses itself in literal marriage to pagan foreigners. Thus, exogamy with Gentile pagans constitutes a constant threat to the stability and prosperity of Israel throughout the Historical Books, whether it is Samson's dalliances with Philistine women (Judg. 14–16), Solomon's many foreign wives (1 Kings 11:1–4), or the economically motivated marriages of Judean repatriates to the women of the land (Ezra 9–10; Neh. 10:28–31; 13:1–3, 23–37). The blessing on Israel rises and falls with their practice of marriage. Thus, the Historical Books include two lovely romances (Ruth, Tobit) that embody and transmit the ideals, norms, and praxis of matrimony within the community of God's covenant: endogamy between virtuous and covenant-keeping partners; exclusive and indissoluble monogamy; affectionate companionship between spouses; desire for and openness to children; and concern for the interests of parents, extended family, and the national/religious community.

The prophetic books, on the other hand, deal with marriage almost exclusively as an icon of the covenant between God and Israel. The prophets recognize the nuptial dimension of the Sinai covenant already latent in some of the terms and expressions of the Pentateuch, and they develop it in lavish and explicit ways. So we find extended allegories of the marriage of God and Israel in Hosea (chaps. 1–3), Isaiah (chaps. 1–3, 54, 62), Jeremiah (chaps. 1–3), and Ezekiel (chaps. 16, 23). In the course of these descriptions, certain Israelite ideals for matrimony—such as indissolubility, generosity, attraction, affection, freedom, mutuality, exclusivity, and safety—can be recognized. The canonical collection of prophets then concludes with Malachi, who strikingly inveighs against the infidelity of postexilic Judean men to their Judean wives as a breach of divine covenant, fulminating the decree "I hate divorce, says the LORD the God of Israel" (Mal. 2:16). The message is similar to that of the Historical Books: the fidelity of God's people to their spousal relation with God is often epitomized by their fidelity to their natural spouses.

The same theme is developed in the Wisdom literature. Proverbs sets the tone by emphasizing the virtues of love, affection, and faithfulness toward the "wife of one's youth," so much so that marital fidelity becomes the quintessential expression and metaphor for the lifestyle of wisdom—and conversely, adultery becomes the quintessential expression and metaphor for the lifestyle of folly. Wisdom is personified as a wife (Prov. 31:10–31), and folly is personified as an adulteress (9:13–18). The Song of Songs continues the exploration of marital love in its many dimensions: as a literal spousal relationship between man and wife within the covenant community, as an idealized union between the messianic king and the people of Israel represented as or by his royal bride, and ultimately as a sign and sacrament of the covenantal union of the Lord and his people. The Wisdom of Solomon explores the marital metaphor for one's relationship with divine wisdom (Wis. 7–9), and all the matrimonial themes and motifs of the Wisdom literature are gathered into a synthesis in Sirach, which concludes that human flourishing ultimately depends on a virtuous wife (Sir. 36:29–30; 40:19, 23), who constitutes a blessing so great it can only be attributed to God himself (26:1–4, 14–18). Indeed, God's gift of wisdom to his people is also presented, ultimately, in nuptial terms as well (Sir. 24).

When we approach the New Testament, we find matrimony functioning in the Gospels and Epistles in two distinct but interrelated ways: first, as the model of Jesus's mission to the human race and covenantal relationship with the Church and, second, as a central institution within the society of God's people, which should be practiced in imitation of Christ's bond with the Church. Among the synoptic Gospels, the motif of Christ's mission as bridegroom is best developed in Matthew, but it is especially in the Fourth Gospel that this perspective is brought to the forefront of the text. John narrates his account of the Lord's ministry by setting up Cana (2:1–11) and Calvary (19:1–41) as literary bookends, two units that mirror one another. Only here in this Gospel do we find the presence of the Blessed Mother, the imagery of wine, and Jesus producing drink. Both narratives are heavily nuptial and eucharistic, conveying the message that, from beginning to end, Jesus is the divine bridegroom who has come to give his body to his bride, an act perpetuated in the sacraments. Between Cana and Calvary, John develops the bridegroom theme especially through the comments of John the Baptist (3:29–30), the conversation with the Samaritan woman (4:1–42), and the anointing at Bethany (12:1–8). The climax of the nuptial theme is the appearance to Mary Magdalene (20:1, 11–18), a model disciple, in an encounter patterned after Song of Songs 3:1–5. This motif of Christ as bridegroom is scattered sporadically throughout Paul's epistles, but it is best developed in Ephesians 5:22–33, where Paul employs it to establish a model for Christian marriage. It is pervasive in Revelation, the whole plot of which can be summarized as the putting away of an adulterous woman, the old Jerusalem/Israel (Rev. 17–18), and her replacement by a spotless bride of the Lamb, the Church (Rev. 19–22). The Christ-as-bridegroom motif and the complementary Church-as-bride theme do not speak directly to the practice of marriage; rather, they project ideals for the matrimonial relationship that include joyfulness, provision, sacrificial self-gift, and love on the part of the bridegroom or husband, as well as receptivity, reciprocation, exclusivity, and fidelity on the part of the bride or wife.

Jesus's teaching on marriage is not extensive but establishes five fundamental principles: (1) the indissolubility of a valid marriage;[1] (2) the possible dissolution of an invalid (*porneia*/*zənût*) marriage;[2] (3) a preferential option for the celibate vocation;[3] (4) an absolute prohibition of sexual activity outside marriage;[4] and (5) the restriction of matrimony to this present world.[5] It is primarily the apostle Paul who builds on the dominical teaching while working out the implications of the gospel for the way Christians conduct themselves with respect to courtship, sexuality, and marriage. Much of Paul's teaching is the reaffirmation, with variation or expansion, of the principles taught by the Lord,[6] but in 1 Corinthians 5–7 and Ephesians 5:22–33, he goes beyond the explicit teaching of Christ to address novel issues arising in the early Christian community. St. Paul insists that the Church cannot tolerate the public flouting of divine teaching on marriage among her members (1 Cor. 5:11), and he further asserts that those who boldly violate the principles of marital and sexual purity will not be saved (6:9–10, 15–16). The holiness of the Christian's body through the indwelling of the Holy Spirit makes sexual immorality impossible (6:19–20). While Paul affirms Jesus's preferential option for celibacy (7:1, 25–38), he recognizes that not all have the gift of continence (7:7b, 36), and further, he prohibits abstinence within marriage apart from exceptional circumstances (7:2–5). Remarkably, within the physical relationship of husband and wife, there is perfectly mutual authority and submission (7:4). Believers should remain with their unbelieving spouses, but they are free if such a spouse departs (7:12–16). But marriages between two believing spouses are elevated to a sacrament of the union of Christ and his Church (Eph. 5:22–33), in which spouses act *in persona Christi* toward one another in a sexually complementary way—husbands to their wives as Christ the head (v. 23) and wives to their husbands as Christ the body (v. 24), each called to total self-gift through sacrifice (v. 25) and submission (v. 22), respectively (v. 33). In this way, the conflict between spouses introduced by sin (Gen. 3:16) is overcome, and Christ, the New Adam, restores Christian couples to the peace of Eden and the unashamed one-flesh union (Gen. 2:24–25).

1. Matt. 5:31–32; 19:3–9; Mark 10:2–12; Luke 16:18.
2. Matt. 5:32; 19:9.
3. Matt. 19:10–12.
4. 1 Cor. 6:9–20; Heb. 13:4//Matt. 5:27–30; 15:19; Mark 7:21.
5. 1 Cor. 7:39–40//Matt. 22:30; Mark 12:25; Luke 20:34–36.
6. Cf. 1 Cor. 7:10–11//Matt. 19:3–9; 1 Cor. 5:1–13//Matt. 19:9; 1 Cor. 7:1–38//Matt. 19:10–12; 1 Cor. 6:9–20//Matt. 5:27–30; 1 Cor. 7:39–40//Matt. 22:30.

We began this work noting the rejection of matrimony as a sacrament by those ecclesial groups that had their origin in the Reformation, citing as an example John Calvin's remark:

> The last of all is marriage, which, while all admit it to be an institution of God, no man ever saw to be a sacrament, until the time of Gregory. And would it ever have occurred to the mind of any sober man? It is a good and holy ordinance of God. And agriculture, architecture, shoemaking, and shaving, are lawful ordinances of God; but they are not sacraments.[7]

In charity to Calvin, we might observe that this passage does not represent his thought and his exegesis at its best. But we hope to have shown, at this point, how wholly misleading and reductionistic it is to place matrimony as just one of several domains of human experience, like agriculture and architecture, when Sacred Scripture displays a sustained interest in the institution and reality of marriage from the beginning of creation in Genesis to the culmination of all things in Revelation. There are few, if any, comparable realities that can serve as a unifying theme of salvation history and the divine economy. We fear that the loss of the sense of the sacredness of marriage and its centrality to the plan of salvation reflected in the Reformers' writings has progressively developed into the total confusion concerning the definition, purpose, and structure of matrimony that we are witnessing within Western culture, a confusion that makes its influence felt even within the Church. It is hoped that the present study will contribute to a recovery of a reverence for matrimony as an icon of God's nature and as a foretaste of the eternal, personal communion with God for which all human beings have been created.

7. John Calvin, *Institutes of the Christian Religion*, trans. Henry Beveridge, 2 vols. (Grand Rapids: Eerdmans, 1989), 2:647.

Suggested Resources

Atkinson, Joseph C. *Biblical and Theological Foundations of the Family: The Domestic Church*. Washington, DC: Catholic University of America Press, 2014.

Elliott, Peter J. *What God Has Joined: The Sacramentality of Marriage*. New York: Alba House, 1990.

Hugo, John. *St. Augustine on Nature, Sex, and Marriage*. Princeton: Scepter, 1969.

Hunter, David G., ed. *Marriage and Sexuality in Early Christianity*. Minneapolis: Fortress, 2018.

John Paul II. *Man and Woman He Created Them: A Theology of the Body*. Translated by Michael Waldstein. Boston: Pauline Books & Media, 2006.

Pitre, Brant. *Jesus the Bridegroom: The Greatest Love Story Ever Told*. New York: Image, 2014.

Scola, Angelo Cardinal. *The Nuptial Mystery*. Translated by Michael K. Borras. Ressourcement: Retrieval and Renewal in Catholic Thought. Grand Rapids: Eerdmans, 2005.

Villeneuve, André. *Divine Marriage from Eden to the End of Days: Communion with God as Nuptial Mystery in the Story of Salvation*. Eugene, OR: Wipf & Stock, 2021.

Selected Bibliography

Arnold, Clinton E. *Ephesians*. ZECNT 10. Grand Rapids: Zondervan, 2010.

Augustine. *St. Augustine on Genesis*. Translated by Roland J. Teske. FC 84. Washington, DC: Catholic University of America Press, 1991.

Batzig, Nicholas T. "John's Use of the Song of Songs in the Book of Revelation." *Feeding on Christ* (blog), July 1, 2013. https://feedingonchrist.org/johns-use-of-the-song-of-songs-in-the-book-of-revelation/.

Beale, G. K. *The Temple and the Church's Mission: A Biblical Theology of the Dwelling Place of God*. NSBT 17. Downers Grove, IL: IVP Academic, 2004.

Belonick, Deborah. "Father, Son, and Spirit—So What's in a Name?" In *The Politics of Prayer: Feminist Language and the Worship of God*, edited by Helen Hull Hitchcock, 297–306. San Francisco: Ignatius, 1992.

Bergsma, John S. "The Creation Narratives and the Original Unity of Work and Worship in the Human Vocation." In *Work: Theological Foundations and Practical Implications*, edited by R. Keith Loftin and Trey Dimsdale, 11–29. London: SCM, 2018.

———. *Jesus and the Dead Sea Scrolls: Revealing the Jewish Roots of Christianity*. New York: Image, 2019.

———. *The Jubilee from Leviticus to Qumran: A History of Interpretation*. VTSup 115. Leiden: Brill, 2007.

———. "A 'Samaritan' Pentateuch? The Implications of the Pro-Northern Tendency of the Common Pentateuch." In *Paradigm Change in Pentateuchal Research*, edited by Matthias Armgardt, Benjamin Kilchör, and Markus Zehnder, 287–300. BZABR 22. Wiesbaden: Harrassowitz, 2019.

Bergsma, John S., and Scott W. Hahn. "Covenant." In *The Oxford Encyclopedia of the Bible and Theology*, edited by Samuel Balentine, 1:151–66. 2 vols. Oxford: Oxford University Press, 2015.

———. "Noah's Nakedness and the Curse on Canaan (Genesis 9:20–27)." *JBL* 124, no. 1 (2005): 25–40.

Bergsma, John S., and Brant Pitre. *The Old Testament*. Vol. 1 of *A Catholic Introduction to the Bible*. San Francisco: Ignatius, 2018.

Block, Daniel I. *The Gospel according to Moses: Theological and Ethical Reflections on the Book of Deuteronomy*. Eugene, OR: Cascade Books, 2012.

Brueggemann, Walter. "Of the Same Flesh and Bone (Gn 2,23a)." *CBQ* 32, no. 4 (1970): 532–42.

Brum Teixeira, José Lucas. *Poetics and Narrative Function of Tobit 6*. Deuterocanonical and Cognate Literature Studies 41. Berlin: De Gruyter, 2019.

Calvin, John. *Institutes of the Christian Religion*. Translated by Henry Beveridge. 2 vols. Grand Rapids: Eerdmans, 1989.

Catena Aurea: Commentary on the Four Gospels, Collected out of the Works of the Fathers; St. Matthew. Translated and edited by John Henry Newman. London: John Henry Parker, 1841.

Danby, Herbert. *The Mishnah: Translated from the Hebrew with Introduction and Brief Explanatory Notes*. Oxford: Oxford University Press, 1933.

Davidson, Richard M. "Proverbs 8 and the Place of Christ in the Trinity." *JATS* 17, no. 1 (2006): 33–54.

Dumbrell, William J. "The Covenant with Noah." *RTR* 38, no. 1 (1979): 1–9.

Elliott, Peter J. *What God Has Joined: The Sacramentality of Marriage*. New York: Alba House, 1990.

Fastiggi, Robert. "The Ends of Marriage according to the 1917 and the 1983 Codes of Canon Law in Light of Vatican II." *Antiphon* 18, no. 1 (2014): 32–47.

Fehribach, Adeline. *The Women in the Life of the Bridegroom: A Feminist Historical-Literary Analysis of the Female Characters in the Fourth Gospel*. Collegeville, MN: Liturgical Press, 1998.

Fitzmyer, Joseph A. "The Matthean Divorce Texts and Some New Palestinian Evidence." *TS* 37, no. 2 (1976): 197–226.

———. *Tobit*. Commentaries on Early Jewish Literature. Berlin: De Gruyter, 2003.

Fletcher-Louis, Crispin H. T. *All the Glory of Adam: Liturgical Anthropology in the Dead Sea Scrolls*. STDJ 42. Leiden: Brill, 2002.

———. "Heavenly Ascent or Incarnational Presence? A Revisionist Reading of the *Songs of the Sabbath Sacrifice*." SBLSP 37 (1998): 367–99.

Foh, Susan T. "What Is the Woman's Desire?" *WTJ* 37, no. 3 (1975): 376–83.

Garland, David E. *1 Corinthians*. BECNT. Grand Rapids: Baker Academic, 2003.

Garrett, Duane, and Paul R. House. *Song of Songs/Lamentations*. WBC 23B. Grand Rapids: Zondervan Academic, 2004.

Girgis, Sherif, Ryan T. Anderson, and Robert P. George. *What Is Marriage? Man and Woman: A Defense*. New York: Encounter Books, 2012.

Grube, G. M. A. "The Marriage Laws in Plato's *Republic*." *ClQ* 21, no. 2 (1927): 95–99.

Hahn, Scott. *First Comes Love: Finding Your Family in the Church and the Trinity*. New York: Image, 2002.

———. *Kinship by Covenant: A Canonical Approach to the Fulfillment of God's Saving Promises*. New Haven: Yale University Press, 2009.

Harris, Murray J. "The Translation of *Elohim* in Psalm 45:7–8." *TynBul* 35 (1984): 65–89.

Heereman, Nina. "Behold King Solomon on the Day of His Wedding: A Symbolic-Diachronic Reading of Song 3:6–11 and 4:12–5:1." PhD diss., École Biblique et Archéologique Française de Jérusalem / Université de Fribourg, 2017.

Hieke, Thomas. "Endogamy in the Book of Tobit, Genesis, and Ezra-Nehemiah." In *The Book of Tobit: Text, Tradition, Theology*, edited by Géza G. Xeravitz and József Zsengellér, 103–20. JSJSup 98. Leiden: Brill, 2005.

Holmstedt, Robert D. "The Relative Clause in Biblical Hebrew: A Linguistic Analysis." PhD diss., University of Wisconsin–Madison, 2002.

Horowitz, Maryanne Cline. "Aristotle and Woman." *Journal of the History of Biology* 9, no. 2 (1976): 183–213.

Hubbard, Robert L., Jr. *The Book of Ruth*. NICOT. Grand Rapids: Eerdmans, 1988.

Hugenberger, Gordon P. *Marriage as a Covenant: Biblical Law and Ethics as Developed from Malachi*. Grand Rapids: Baker, 1998.

Hugo, John. *St. Augustine on Nature, Sex, and Marriage*. Princeton: Scepter, 1969.

Hunter, David G., ed. *Marriage and Sexuality in Early Christianity*. Minneapolis: Fortress, 2018.

John Paul II. *Man and Woman He Created Them: A Theology of the Body*. Translated by Michael Waldstein. Boston: Pauline Books & Media, 2006.

Knoppers, Gary N. *Jews and Samaritans: The Origins and History of Their Early Relations*. Oxford: Oxford University Press, 2013.

Köhler, Ludwig, and W. Baumgartner. *Lexicon in Veteris Testamenti libros*. Leiden: Brill, 1958.

Krause, Martin. "II Sam 11:4 und das Konzeptionsoptimum." *ZAW* 95 (1983): 434–37.

Leithart, Peter. "Temple Man." *Patheos*, February 16, 2010. https://www.patheos.com/blogs/leithart/2010/02/temple-man/.

LeMon, J. M., and B. A. Strawn. "Parallelism." In *Dictionary of the Old Testament: Wisdom, Poetry and Writings*, edited by Tremper Longman III and Peter Enns, 502–15. Downers Grove, IL: IVP Academic, 2008.

Lewis, C. S. "Priestesses in the Church?" In *God in the Dock: Essays in Theology and Ethics*, 255–63. Grand Rapids: Eerdmans, 2014.

Lind, Göran. *Common Law Marriage: A Legal Institution for Cohabitation*. Oxford: Oxford University Press, 2008.

Loader, William. *The Pseudepigrapha on Sexuality: Attitudes towards Sexuality in Apocalypses, Testaments, Legends, Wisdom, and Related Literature*. Grand Rapids: Eerdmans, 2011.

Macintosh, A. A. *A Critical and Exegetical Commentary on Hosea*. ICC. Edinburgh: T&T Clark, 1997.

Malone, Andrew S. "God the Illeist: Third-Person Self-References and Trinitarian Hints in the Old Testament." *JETS* 52, no. 3 (2009): 499–518.

Manteau-Bonamy, H. M. *Immaculate Conception and the Holy Spirit: The Marian Teachings of St. Maximilian Kolbe*. San Francisco: Ignatius, 1998.

McDowell, Catherine L. *The Image of God in the Garden of Eden: The Creation of Humankind in Genesis 2:5–3:24 in Light of* mīs pî pīt pî *and* wpt-r *Rituals of Mesopotamia and Ancient Egypt*. Siphrut 15. Winona Lake, IN: Eisenbrauns, 2015.

McWhirter, Jocelyn. *The Bridegroom Messiah and the People of God: Marriage in the Fourth Gospel*. SNTSMS 138. Cambridge: Cambridge University Press, 2006.

Milgrom, Jacob. *Numbers*. JPS Torah Commentary. Philadelphia: Jewish Publication Society, 1990.

Miller, Geoffrey David. *Marriage in the Book of Tobit*. Berlin: De Gruyter, 2011.

Milligan, Susan. "The Value of Women: Large Portions of the American Public Value Women Most for Physical Attractiveness." *U.S. News and World Report*, December 5, 2017. https://bit.ly/Value_of_Women.

Mitch, Curtis, and Edward Sri. *The Gospel of Matthew*. CCSS. Grand Rapids: Baker Academic, 2010.

Montague, George T. *First Corinthians*. CCSS. Grand Rapids: Baker Academic, 2011.

Moore, Carey A. *Tobit: A New Translation with Introduction and Commentary*. AB 40. New York: Doubleday, 1996.

Moran, W. L. "The Scandal of the 'Great Sin' at Ugarit." *JNES* 18, no. 4 (1959): 280–81.

Morrow, Jeff. "Creation as Temple-Building and Work as Liturgy in Genesis 1–3." *Journal of the Orthodox Center for the Advancement of Biblical Studies* 2 (2009): 1–13.

Murphy, Roland E. "The Unity of the Song of Songs." *VT* 29 (1979): 436–43.

Oswalt, John N. *The Book of Isaiah: Chapters 40–66*. NICOT. Grand Rapids: Eerdmans, 1998.

Pitre, Brant. *Jesus the Bridegroom: The Greatest Love Story Ever Told*. New York: Image, 2014.

Plato. *The Republic, and Other Works*. Translated by B. Jowett. New York: Anchor Books, 1973.

Pontifical Council for the Family. "The Truth and Meaning of Human Sexuality: Guidelines for Education within the Family." Holy See. December 8, 1995. https://www.vatican.va/roman_curia/pontifical_councils/family/documents/rc_pc_family_doc_08121995_human-sexuality_en.html#.

Prothro, James B. "Semper Virgo? A Biblical Review of a Debated Dogma." *Pro Ecclesia* 28, no. 1 (2019): 78–97.

Rabinowitz, J. J. "The 'Great Sin' in Ancient Egyptian Marriage Contracts." *JNES* 18, no. 1 (1959): 73.

Ratzinger, Joseph Cardinal (Benedict XVI). *"In the Beginning . . .": A Catholic Understanding of the Story of Creation and the Fall*. Translated by Boniface Ramsey. Ressourcement: Retrieval and Renewal in Catholic Thought. Grand Rapids: Eerdmans, 1995.

Reyburn, William D., and Euan McG. Fry. *A Handbook on Genesis*. UBS Helps for Translators. New York: United Bible Societies, 1998.

Richter, Sandra L. "The Archaeology of Mount Ebal and Mount Gerizim and Why It Matters." In *Sepher Torath Mosheh: Studies in the Composition and Interpretation of Deuteronomy*, edited by Daniel I. Block and Richard L. Schultz, 304–37. Peabody, MA: Hendrickson, 2017.

Rom-Shiloni, Dalit. "'How Can You Say, "I Am Not Defiled . . ."?' (Jeremiah 2:20–25): Allusions to Priestly Legal Traditions in the Poetry of Jeremiah." *JBL* 133, no. 4 (2014): 757–75.

Sarna, Nahum M. *Exodus*. JPS Torah Commentary. Philadelphia: Jewish Publication Society, 1991.

———. *Genesis*. JPS Torah Commentary. Philadelphia: Jewish Publication Society, 1989.

Sasson, Jack M. "Bovine Symbolism in the Exodus Narrative." *VT* 18, no. 3 (1968): 380–87.

Schillebeeckx, Edward. *Marriage: Human Reality and Saving Mystery*. Translated by N. D. Smith. London: Sheed & Ward, 1965.

Schneiders, Sandra M. *Written That You May Believe: Encountering Jesus in the Fourth Gospel*. Rev. ed. New York: Herder & Herder, 2003.

Scola, Angelo Cardinal. *The Nuptial Mystery*. Translated by Michael K. Borras. Ressourcement: Retrieval and Renewal in Catholic Thought. Grand Rapids: Eerdmans, 2005.

Shamah, Moshe. *Recalling the Covenant: A Contemporary Commentary on the Five Books of the Torah*. 2nd ed. New York: Ktav, 2015.

Sidebottom, E. M. "The So-Called Divine Passive in the Gospel Tradition." *ExpT* 87, no. 7 (1976): 200–204.

Smit, Laura A., and Stephen E. Fowl. *Judges and Ruth*. BTCB. Grand Rapids: Brazos, 2018.

Smith-Christopher, Daniel. "The Mixed Marriage Crisis in Ezra 9–10 and Nehemiah 13: A Study of the Sociology of Post-Exilic Judaean Community." In *Second Temple Studies*, vol. 2, *Temple Community in the Persian Period*, edited by Tamara C. Eskenazi and Kent H. Richards, 243–65. JSOTSup 175. Sheffield: JSOT Press, 1994.

Smolarz, Sebastian R. *Covenant and the Metaphor of Divine Marriage in Biblical Thought: A Study with Special Reference to the Book of Revelation*. Eugene, OR: Wipf & Stock, 2011.

Thompson, J. A. *The Ancient Near Eastern Treaties and the Old Testament*. London: Tyndale, 1963.

Tigay, Jeffrey H. *Deuteronomy*. JPS Torah Commentary. Philadelphia: Jewish Publication Society, 1996.

Vall, Gregory. "The Enigma of Job 1,21a." *Biblica* 76, no. 3 (1995): 325–42.

Villeneuve, André. *Divine Marriage from Eden to the End of Days: Communion with God as Nuptial Mystery in the Story of Salvation*. Eugene, OR: Wipf & Stock, 2021.

Weima, Jeffrey A. D. *1–2 Thessalonians*. BECNT. Grand Rapids: Baker Academic, 2014.

Weingart, Kristin. "What Makes an Israelite an Israelite? Judean Perspectives on the Samarians in the Persian Period." *JSOT* 42, no. 2 (2017): 155–75.

Wenham, Gordon J. *Genesis 1–15*. WBC 1. Nashville: Nelson, 1987.

Westbrook, Raymond. "Adultery in Ancient Near Eastern Law." *RB* 97, no. 4 (1990): 542–80.

———. "The Prohibition on Restoration of Marriage in Deuteronomy 24:1–4." In *Studies in Bible 1986*, edited by Sara Japhet, 387–405. Scripta Hierosolymitana 31. Jerusalem: Magnes, 1986.

Wilcox, Charles T., et al., trans. *St. Augustine: Treatises on Marriage and Other Subjects*. FC 27. Washington, DC: Catholic University of America Press, 1955.

Williamson, Peter S. *Ephesians*. CCSS. Grand Rapids: Baker Academic, 2009.

Winsor, Ann Roberts. *A King Is Bound in the Tresses: Allusions to the Song of Songs in the Fourth Gospel*. StBibLit 6. New York: Peter Lang, 1999.

Winston, David. *Philo of Alexandria: The Contemplative Life, The Giants, and Selections*. Classics of Western Spirituality. Mahwah, NJ: Paulist Press, 1981.

Wold, Donald J. "The Meaning of the Biblical Penalty *Kareth*." PhD diss., University of California, Berkeley, 1978.

Wolters, Al. *The Song of the Valiant Woman: Studies in the Interpretation of Proverbs 31:10–31*. Carlisle, UK: Paternoster, 2001.

Yamauchi, Edwin M., and Marvin R. Wilson, eds. *Dictionary of Daily Life in Biblical and Post-Biblical Antiquity: Complete in One Volume*. Peabody, MA: Hendrickson, 2017.

Youngblood, Ronald F. "1, 2 Samuel." In *The Expositor's Bible Commentary*, edited by Frank E. Gaebelein, 3:551–1104. 12 vols. Grand Rapids: Eerdmans, 1992.

Subject Index

Abraham, 9, 42–54, 56, 62–67, 180, 244
  blessed by God, 9, 43–45, 50
  breaks his covenant with God, 40, 46–47
  call of, 44–45, 52
  childlessness of, 45, 48
  death of, 44, 50, 52
  descendants of, 43–44, 47, 49–51, 64, 67, 95, 244
  first covenant ceremony of, 18, 44–45
  marriage of, 9, 48–49, 52–53, 66, 119, 237
  practices bigamy, 45–46
  second covenant ceremony of, 44, 46–47
  testing of, 44, 49–50
  See also covenant: Abrahamic; seed: of Abraham
Absalom, 103–6
abstinence. *See* celibacy
ʾādām (humanity), 13–16, 24–25, 31–32, 37, 47, 242–43
Adam, 1–3, 17–26, 30–37, 40, 46, 178n6, 242–43
  descendants of, 15, 34, 36–37
  expelled from the garden, 33–34, 243
  God's creation of, 15, 113, 178
  marriage of, 1–2, 18–24, 26, 32–36, 41, 106, 113, 163, 242
  naming creation, 18, 22, 32–33
  New, 19–20, 145, 178, 185, 247
  as a priest in the garden, 17, 21, 28, 32
  reconciled with Eve, 32–33, 243

  rib of, 20, 24, 166, 184, 226
  temptation of, 28–34, 39–41, 46, 145, 243
  See also ʾādām (humanity); covenant: with Adam; creation; Eve
adultery, 45, 64, 69, 90n35, 104–5, 110, 176, 190, 208, 216, 246
  death penalty for, 82, 86, 93
  as folly, 147, 151, 153, 245
  Jesus's teaching on, 6, 204–9
  as a metaphor for idolatry, 70, 123–24, 136
  ritual for a woman suspected of, 83, 132–33
  as a sin, 66, 73–75, 81–82, 86, 104, 106, 135, 146–47, 151, 204
  See also harlotry (zānāh); Mosaic law: regarding adultery; sin: sexual
affection, 53, 57–58, 60, 66, 86, 100, 171
  of Christ to the Church, 188, 228
  of God toward Israel, 127
  as an ideal of matrimony, 126, 144, 149, 245
  mutual, 119, 223
  in the Song of Songs, 160, 165
ʾāhēb (love), 54, 71–72, 95, 104, 139–40, 150, 159, 167
allegory, 107, 123, 132, 134, 136–37, 144, 154, 158, 161, 175, 245
altar, 69, 166, 233
Ammon, 48, 63–64, 81, 108, 110

angels, 38, 47–48, 51, 112–13, 187n31, 191, 199, 201–2, 227, 231
  bodies of, 210–11
  resurrection and, 187, 211
  See also Raphael
Aquinas, Thomas, xi, 8n15, 91, 199n1
ark, the, 39, 48, 66, 134, 166, 206, 243
Assyrians, 123, 136, 181
Augustine, 7, 20, 37–38, 56, 63, 89, 93n37, 183, 199n1, 211, 221

Baal, 70–71, 84, 124–25, 182
Babel, tower of, 40–41, 43, 243
baptism, xiii, 1, 4–6, 185–86, 209, 221–22
barrenness, 45–46, 53, 55–56, 80, 100–101, 103, 132
Bathsheba. *See* David: Bathsheba and
Benjamin, 59–61
bestiality, 81, 83
betrothal, 50–52, 69, 125n15, 128, 161, 163
  gifts of, 51, 77–78, 82, 86, 167
  ritual of, 99–100, 199
  See also Mary: marriage of
bigamy, 36, 41, 46, 53, 55, 66, 86, 133
birthright, 53–54, 59
blessing, 34, 41, 47, 49, 99, 111, 123, 125n14, 126, 147, 209, 245
  between spouses, 112–13, 119
  curses and, 72, 79, 83–84

Scripture and Other Ancient Sources Index